FUZZY-SET
SOCIAL SCIENCE

CHARLES C. RAGIN

FUZZY-SET
SOCIAL SCIENCE

THE UNIVERSITY OF CHICAGO PRESS

CHICAGO AND LONDON

CHARLES C. RAGIN holds a joint appointment as professor of sociology and political science at Northwestern University. He also holds an appointment in the Department of Sociology and Human Geography at the University of Oslo, Norway. He has published over fifty journal articles and book chapters. His books include *The Comparative Method: Moving beyond Qualitative and Quantitative Strategies, Issues and Alternatives in Comparative Social Research,* and *Constructing Social Research: The Unity and Diversity of Method.*

The University of Chicago Press, Chicago 60637
The University of Chicago Press, Ltd., London
© 2000 by Charles C. Ragin
All rights reserved. Published 2000
Printed in the United States of America
09 08 07 06 05 04 03 02 01 00 1 2 3 4 5
ISBN: 0-226-70276-6 (cloth)
ISBN: 0-226-70277-4 (paper)

Library of Congress Cataloging-in-Publication Data

Ragin, Charles C.
    Fuzzy-set social science / Charles C. Ragin.
        p. cm.
    Includes bibliographical references and index.
    ISBN 0-226-70276-6 (alk. paper) — ISBN 0-226-70277-4
    (pbk. : alk. paper)
    1. Social sciences—Research. 2. Fuzzy sets. I. Title.
H62.R233 2000
300′.1′511322—dc21

                                            99-086553

♾ The paper used in this publication meets the minimum requirements of the American National Standard for Information Sciences—Permanence of Paper for Printed Library Materials, ANSI Z39.48–1992.

CONTENTS

PART ONE

DIVERSITY-ORIENTED RESEARCH

ILLUSTRATIONS

TABLES

PREFACE

When I was in graduate school I spent countless hours at the computer center studying bivariate scatterplots. (There were no personal computers in the dark ages of the 1970s.) I was impressed by how often these plots had a triangular shape, with all the points plotting either above or below one of the two diagonals of the square box framing the plot. I thought this pattern should have a straightforward interpretation. After all, if the variable Y can have low or high values when X is low but can have only high values when X is high, then we have learned something important about the relationship between X and Y, namely, that the value of X seems to place a floor on the value of Y. I showed the plot to one of my advisers and asked his opinion. He offered the textbook reply: The plot showed serious heteroscedasticity; the estimate of the standard error of the slope of the line describing the linear relationship between X and Y provided by ordinary least squares (OLS) could not be trusted. Use generalized least squares (GLS) to fix this problem, I was told. So what I thought was an interesting relationship turned out to be a data problem, at least from a textbook perspective.

In fact, triangular plots can be interpreted, and usually the interpretations are very interesting. There is a *very strong* link between triangular plots and most forms of social science theorizing. For example, while in graduate school I produced a triangular plot, using data on electoral districts in Great Britain, showing that when the percentage employed in manufacturing is low, the degree to which people vote along class lines can be high or low. However, when the percentage employed in manufacturing is high, the level of class-based voting is always high. In this triangular plot, the points were all above the main diagonal of the box framing the points. From a linear regression point of view, this pattern is a mess. However, from the perspective of theory, it is not. The typical theoretical argument has the form: "In manufacturing areas class-based voting is high." This argument does *not* claim that having a high level of manufacturing is the *only way* to generate a high level of class-based voting. Thus, points that fall in the upper left-hand corner of the plot (low percentage of manufacturing combined with a high level of class-based voting) do *not* contradict the theoretical argument. Thus, triangular plots can be perfectly consistent with theory, even though they are full of error from a linear regression viewpoint.

As I show in this book, it is very difficult to interpret triangular plots and put them in the service of social science without seeing them as set-theoretic relationships. In the plot just described, for example, it is possible to view "electoral districts with high levels of employment in manufacturing" as a subset of "electoral districts with high levels of class-based voting." Not only are set-theoretic relationships central to the analysis of social data, they are also central to almost all forms of social science theorizing. Most theoretical arguments, as in the example just offered, concern set-theoretic relationships, not linear relationships between variables. Thus, there is a fundamental *mismatch* between the analysis of linear relationships—the central concern of the most popular and most used quantitative methods—and theoretical discourse. A triangular plot is simply a problem to be corrected unless you have the tools to analyze it as a set-theoretic relationship, which is one of the things that the fuzzy-set approach offers. Thus, fuzzy-set analysis provides the opportunity to bring theory and data analysis into much better alignment and to correct the current mismatch.

This book is about much more, however, than triangular plots, set-theoretic relationships, or even fuzzy sets. I address broad topics in social science methodology, focusing especially on the logic of "discovery"—research that involves a dynamic interplay between theory and data, with the primary goal of generating new insights. There is a long tradition of distinguishing between discovery and justification in many disciplines, a contrast that emphasizes the disjunction between the logic of "learning about the world" and the logic of "testing hypotheses." In the social sciences today, we have relatively well-developed tools for testing theories. However, many of these tools and procedures interfere with the logic of discovery, often posing serious obstacles. The approach I present in this book strengthens discovery in social research, enriching the dialogue between ideas and evidence and freeing researchers from what I call the "homogenizing assumptions" of variable-oriented methods.

Some who are more mathematically oriented than I am will see many opportunities for streamlining and automating the new techniques of data analysis I present in this book, perhaps making them more inference-friendly as well. "Regression through the origin," for example, solves some analytic problems; the use of a "neural net" approach solves others. I welcome efforts to add greater technical sophistication to the ideas I present. My approach, however, has been to keep researchers close to their data and thus minimize the number of analytic layers separating them from their evidence. Besides, I want the book to be accessible. After all, it presents an entirely new approach to the analysis of social data.

It is important to point out as well that my goal in this book is *not* to supplant conventional forms of quantitative analysis with fuzzy-set methods. Conventional quantitative analysis has an important place in social science, offering researchers very powerful tools for both description and theory testing. Rather, my intention is to offer new tools for discovery. These new tools can be applied to many forms of quantitative and qualitative evidence, and the results of their application may well alter how researchers use conventional techniques. Thus, while fuzzy-set analysis is an end in itself—yielding new insights about social life, uncovering its many facets, and simplifying its complexity—the approach also can be used in combination with existing methods.

ACKNOWLEDGMENTS

It is difficult even to imagine listing all the people who have contributed over the past several years to the thinking that I present in this book. I am sure I will miss many, including some who have been very helpful or influential.

I have presented lectures on this material for three years now, and often an anonymous questioner will cause me to rethink an entire pillar of my argument. I have been confronted with difficult questions at every lecture on the themes of this book, including colloquia and workshops at University of Washington, University of North Carolina, University of Wisconsin, Johns Hopkins University, University of Pennsylvania, Columbia University, University of Chicago, University of New Mexico, Harvard University, and Massachusetts Institute of Technology (a chronological listing). I am sure I have not made the best possible use of all the good advice I was offered on these occasions, but I am confident that my argument is much better for the wear and tear it has received.

I thank my colleagues, local and long-distance, who have commented on various versions of the ideas presented in this manuscript. Their valiant efforts, along with my notes from conversations, now cover my desk. I thank Howard S. Becker, Michael Burawoy, Bruce Carruthers, David Collier, Kriss Drass, Roger Gould, Brian Gran, John R. Hall, Bruce Kogut, Jon Kvist, David Laitin, John W. Meyer, Lars Mjøset, Paul Nieuwbeerta, Martin Rein, John Richters, John D. Stephens, Arthur Stinchcombe, John Walton, Bruce Western, and Christopher Winship. Special, added thanks go to Jon Kvist and to Bruce Kogut, who not only gave me detailed comments but also tried out some of my ideas with their data. Special thanks also go to Kriss Drass, a long-term long-distance colleague who not only offered useful comments but also worked on implementing these ideas in computer algorithms— swatting logic bugs that almost got away.

I also thank the two cohorts of students who attended my course in comparative methodology at the University of Oslo's International Summer School in Comparative Social Science Studies (1996 and 1998). These postgraduate students, from all over Europe, were my guinea pigs. In intensive weeklong courses, these students endured the first detailed presentations of my ideas about fuzzy-set analysis. Their supportive reactions spurred me on, and I subjected an early draft of my manuscript to students enrolled in a graduate methods class at Northwestern University in the winter of 1999. The response was again very good and very helpful. My students helped me identify important sections of the manuscript in need of major surgery.

A variety of institutions and organizations also have supported this work. Direct or indirect support came from the National Science Foundation (Sociology Program, research grant no. 9108716), various units at Northwestern University (the Institute for Policy Research, the Center for International and Comparative Studies, the Department of Sociology, and the Department of Political Science) and the University of Oslo (the International Summer School in Comparative Social Science Studies and the Department of Sociology and Human Geography). I also thank Doug Mitchell of the University of Chicago Press for his steadfast support and encouragement.

My greatest thanks and biggest debt belong to my wife, Mary Driscoll. Not only did she make room for this book in our life together, she also helped me struggle with the ideas and the writing, from the day it was launched to the very end. She listened to me labor over the initial ideas for the book in long walks along Lake Michigan's shore and in the mountains of northern New Mexico, and her thinking is reflected in the "big picture" that holds the book together. She also wrote detailed comments on what I thought were "final versions" of each chapter, including several completely different versions of chapter 1. It no longer shocks me to hear her state emphatically, "This is not chapter 1!" I tricked her, though, by giving her the version that appears here as the introductory chapter only a short time before the Press's deadline. In the weeks before this deadline she carried me over the finish line, as she did when I finished writing *Constructing Social Research,* helping me finish the book while taking care of all the details of our domestic economy.

FUZZY-SET
SOCIAL SCIENCE

Social scientists generally stay away from anything labeled "fuzzy" because their work is so often described this way by others, especially by scholars in the "hard" sciences. My initial title for this book, *Fuzzy Social Science,* made so many of my colleagues cringe that I felt compelled to change it so that the adjective "fuzzy" applied to sets, not to social science. Today, however, "fuzzy" has a new usage that is unrelated to its original meaning of "unclear" or "muddled" (Kosko 1993; Grint 1997). When applied to a set, it signals that relevant objects can have varying degrees of membership in the set (Zadeh 1965).[1] For example, people can have varying degrees of membership in the set "tall"; investments can vary in their degree of membership in the set "low-risk." Fuzzy sets are especially useful for categories that are imprecise, like "tall" or complex in construction, like "low risk."

Today, fuzzy sets are used in many different fields and technical arenas to address a variety of questions and problems, both mundane and abstract (Ross 1995). The range of applications is ever-expanding, reaching from artificial intelligence to washing machines and the stock market. Much of the literature on fuzzy sets is concerned with the problem of control—how to develop machines that "act smart" in the face of ambiguity or complexity (Dubois, Prade, and Yager 1993). Often these applications involve programming machines with expert human knowledge. Consider, for example, the problem of automating a tractor-trailer so that it can back up to a loading dock under a variety of different conditions. Much of the human knowledge that would

1. Kaplan and Schott (1951) presented many of the basic ideas of the approach well in advance of its unveiling as fuzzy logic in the mid-1960s.

go into this task comes in the form of fuzzy sets describing the various conditions an automated tractor-trailer might encounter (e.g., "slippery" pavement). Applications of this type have received a great deal of attention, and for most of the reading public "fuzzy sets" means "smart machines."

Like others, I am fascinated by these applications. However, these uses of fuzzy sets do not strike close to home for social scientists, and their impact on the social sciences has been slight (Smithson 1988). The terminology of fuzzy sets does crop up occasionally, and a few scholars have attempted to apply some of the ideas (e.g., Smithson 1989; Zetenyi 1988), but for the most part scholars have not recognized the potential of fuzzy sets for transforming social science methodology. Part of the problem is that scholars have attempted to integrate fuzzy sets into their existing repertoires of methods without altering their usual practices in any way. In fact, however, to appreciate the power of fuzzy sets it is necessary to adopt a broader understanding of data analysis and its place in the process of social research.

Fuzzy sets offer researchers an interpretive algebra, a language that is half-verbal-conceptual and half-mathematical-analytical. Thus, the greatest value of fuzzy sets for social scientists is their potential for enlivening, intensifying, and extending the "dialogue" between ideas and evidence in social research. This dialogue is the systematic interplay between theory and data analysis that occurs in most studies— the back-and-forth between the use of data to improve theory and the use of theory to guide the exploration of data. Most theoretical arguments, as verbal formulations, deal with set-theoretic relationships. Because fuzzy sets also address set-theoretic relationships, they offer the opportunity for creating a very close correspondence between theory and data analysis. In short, with fuzzy sets researchers can analyze evidence in ways that directly reflect their theoretical arguments. Thus, as I note in the preface, fuzzy sets have the potential to transform research that is oriented toward "discovery," toward gaining new insights about the world (Diesing 1971). My primary goal in this book is to show how to use fuzzy sets to strengthen discovery in the social sciences.

While most social science research involves discovery in some way, this type of inquiry is faltering in many areas of social science. I believe that the main problem is the dominance of "conventional" forms of quantitative analysis.[2] While there is nothing wrong with quantification

2. I use the qualifier "conventional" in a sociological manner. A particular way of analyzing social data based on core notions about cases and variables has become

and the social sciences certainly need analytic rigor, quantitative analysis—especially as it is usually practiced—often constrains the dialogue between ideas and evidence in unproductive ways (Richters 1997). For example, these methods often assume that cases are homogeneous (e.g., in how causal conditions operate), when researchers should be trying to pinpoint and understand their heterogeneity. For the most part, these limitations are overlooked or seen as strengths because they are core elements of the theory-testing template that structures much social science discourse. As I show in this book, however, it is possible to conduct a far richer dialogue between ideas and evidence using fuzzy sets.

My argument has three main pillars:

First, I argue that social scientists interested in discovery must relinquish many of the "homogenizing assumptions" that undergird conventional quantitative analysis. These homogenizing assumptions structure how social scientists view populations, cases, and causes and thus constrain the dialogue between ideas and evidence in ways that limit discovery. I argue that researchers should instead focus on "diversity" using analytic strategies that are more common in qualitative inquiry. These strategies are easy to implement when the number of cases is small—the usual situation in qualitative inquiry. However, they are rarely used when Ns are large because of analytic difficulties (Ragin 1997). This book, especially part 1, formalizes and extends these "diversity-oriented" techniques to investigations involving large Ns.

Second, I argue that it is possible to use fuzzy sets to extend and deepen diversity-oriented research strategies. In a nutshell, diversity-oriented research attends to heterogeneity and difference, especially to differences in kind, using a "configurational approach" to social phenomena—viewing cases as specific configurations of aspects and features (i.e., configurations of set memberships). This approach searches for heterogeneity within "given" or preconstituted populations and conceives of "difference" in terms of kinds and types of cases, replacing the conventional view of difference as variation (i.e., as deviation from the mean). Fuzzy sets augment the configurational approach by allowing degrees of membership in types and kinds. Thus, the incorporation of fuzzy sets allows for "variation" without forsaking the core emphasis on types and kinds of cases.

Third, and most important of all, I argue that the link between theory and data analysis in the social sciences can be greatly improved using

---

dominant in sociology, political science, and related disciplines over the past several decades. The dominance of this way of analyzing data has conventionalized it.

fuzzy sets for the simple reason that fuzzy sets can be carefully tailored to fit theoretical concepts. Before explaining this position, I briefly describe, for those new to the topic, exactly what a fuzzy set is.

Fuzzy Sets

A conventional (or "crisp") set is dichotomous: An object (e.g., a survey respondent) is either "in" or "out" of a set, for example, the set of Protestants. Thus, a conventional set is comparable to a binary variable with two values, 1 ("in," i.e., Protestant) and 0 ("out," i.e., non-Protestant). A fuzzy set, by contrast, permits membership in the interval between 0 and 1 while retaining the two qualitative states of full membership and full nonmembership. Thus, the fuzzy set of Protestants could include individuals who are "fully in" the set (fuzzy membership = 1.0), some who are "almost fully in" the set (membership = .90), some who are neither "more in" nor "more out" of the set (membership = .5, also known as the "crossover point"), some who are "barely more out than in" the set (membership = .45), and so on down to those who are "fully out" of the set (membership = 0). It is up to the researcher to specify procedures for assigning fuzzy membership scores to cases, and these procedures must be both open and explicit so that they can be evaluated by other scholars.

While it might appear to most social scientists that a fuzzy set is merely the transformation of a binary variable into a continuous variable, this understanding is not correct. Indeed, this common misperception of fuzzy sets may explain why social scientists have been so slow to grasp their analytic power and significance. A fuzzy set is much more than a "continuous" variable because it is much more heavily infused with theoretical and substantive knowledge. Despite the adjective "fuzzy," compared with the conventional variable, a fuzzy set is more empirically grounded and more precise.[3]

To grasp the critical difference between fuzzy sets and continuous variables, consider the contrast between a conventional measure of degree of Protestantism, applied to individuals, and the fuzzy set of Protestants. Imagine that the conventional measure is based on a variety of

---

3. Please note that there is an important distinction between fuzzy concepts and fuzzy membership (Lakoff 1973, 1987). A concept may be fuzzy in the more conventional sense of unclear, and membership in the set implied by the concept may be fuzzy because the concept is fuzzy. In this work, however, I am concerned with concepts that are relatively clear in meaning, at least to the researchers who use them, and the degree of membership of relevant objects in the sets implied by such concepts.

indicators of Protestant behaviors, attitudes, and beliefs and that these different indicators strongly correlate with each other, justifying their combination into a single index of degree of Protestantism. Assume further that this scale is both valid and reliable. But where on this scale is a full-fledged Protestant? Where on this scale is a full-fledged non-Protestant? Where on this scale is the cut-off value (or values) separating those who are more in the set of Protestants from those who are more in the set of non-Protestants?

To answer these questions, the researcher needs not only an index of Protestantism, the fine-grained measure just described, but also a good base of substantive knowledge about Protestantism and a solid grasp of its theoretical relevance—why degree of membership in the set of Protestants matters and how it should be assessed. Without this infusion of theoretical and substantive knowledge, the fine-grained measure of Protestantism remains vague and imprecise—*uncalibrated*. From a fuzzy-set perspective, the conventional variable's great capacity for making fine-grained distinctions with respect to relative levels must be grounded in knowledge; otherwise, its precision is wasted.

In the hands of a social scientist, therefore, a fuzzy set can be seen as a fine-grained, continuous measure that has been carefully calibrated using substantive and theoretical knowledge relevant to set membership. This infusion of knowledge transforms rankings that are almost entirely relative in nature (e.g., degree of Protestantism) to ones that show degree of membership in a well-defined set (e.g., degree of membership in the set of Protestants). As I show subsequently, this infusion of knowledge often redefines portions of the range of a conventional continuous variable as irrelevant. For example, the range of variation in the Protestantism index above a certain value may be irrelevant to the fuzzy set of Protestants because these scores may all signal full membership in the set—scores of 1.0. Likewise, the range of variation in this index below a certain value also may be irrelevant to the fuzzy set of Protestants because these scores may all signal full nonmembership in the set—scores of 0 (for a detailed discussion of these principles, see chapter 6).

Fuzzy Sets in the Dialogue Between Ideas and Evidence

Fuzzy sets are especially valuable in the back-and-forth between theory and data analysis precisely because they are heavily infused with theoretical and substantive knowledge. This infusion of knowledge makes it possible to tailor fuzzy sets to theoretical concepts. This book elaborates various uses of fuzzy sets as interpretive tools, showing how they transform and enrich the dialogue between ideas and evidence. For illustration consider the following features of fuzzy sets:

Fuzzy sets combine qualitative and quantitative assessment in a single instrument. All fuzzy sets consist of two qualitative states, full membership and full nonmembership, and all the quantitative variation that exists between these two qualitative states. Further, fuzzy sets distinguish between objects that are "more in" versus "more out" using the crossover point (.5). For example, the fuzzy set of "religious fundamentalists" has four main parts: those who are fully out of the set (fuzzy membership = 0), those who are not fully out of the set but still more out than in (fuzzy membership > 0 but < .5), those who are more in than out of the set but still not fully in (fuzzy membership > .5 but < 1.0), and those who are fully in the set (fuzzy membership = 1.0).[4]

This integration of qualitative and quantitative assessment in a single instrument gives fuzzy sets an important advantage over conventional variables in the dialogue between ideas and evidence. Consider the proposition that religious fundamentalists are politically conservative. In conventional social science, this statement has two main interpretations with respect to the meaning of religious fundamentalists. The first is that being a religious fundamentalist (a qualitative state) increases either the probability of being politically conservative or the level of political conservativism. The second is that the level of religious fundamentalism (a continuous variable) correlates either with the probability of being a political conservative or with the level of political conservativism.[5] In the first formulation there are two qualitative conditions: one embracing all religious fundamentalists, the other embracing everyone else. In the second formulation, there are many different levels of religious fundamentalism defined primarily in relation to each other (i.e., above versus below the average level). Both ways of interpreting social science concepts are considered valid. Typically, researchers simply choose the formulation that seems most sensible given the question at hand.

With fuzzy sets, however, researchers are not forced to choose be-

4. Cases also may reside at the crossover point (fuzzy membership = .5), the point of maximum ambiguity in whether a case is more in or more out of a set. Thus, this location could be considered an important "fifth" main part of a fuzzy set. (See my discussion of "five-value" fuzzy sets in chapter 6.)

5. Social scientists usually prefer measures with fine-grained distinctions. Thus, the favored formulation would be to treat both religious fundamentalism and political conservativism as variables with many different levels and to correlate them as interval-scale measures.

tween strictly binary and completely relative formulations because fuzzy sets embody both qualitative states (i.e., full membership and full nonmembership) and variation by level (i.e., degrees of membership between 0 and 1) in a single instrument. Thus, using fuzzy sets it is possible to operationalize multiple interpretations of a concept. For example, the proposition about religious fundamentalists (that they are politically conservative) could apply to all individuals displaying some degree of religious fundamentalism, even very minimal levels (i.e., fuzzy membership > 0). The expectation would be that there should be some pattern of correspondence between degree of membership in the set of fundamentalists and the outcome (political conservativism) observable even for those with weak membership in the set of religious fundamentalists. Alternatively, the statement could apply only to individuals who are more "in" the set of religious fundamentalists than "out" (i.e., those with fuzzy membership > .5). The expectation here would be that some pattern of correspondence between fundamentalism and conservativism should be visible for those individuals with membership scores exceeding .5. Or, the statement might apply only to individuals who are full-fledged religious fundamentalists, with a pattern of corre spondence observable only for individuals with fundamentalism scores of 1.0. Fuzzy sets permit the investigation of all three interpretations simultaneously.

Take another example: Some political scientists have argued in various ways that "democratic countries don't make war with other democratic countries" (see Russett 1993). But countries vary in the degree to which they are democratic (Bollen 1993)—in the degree to which they belong in the set of democratic countries. Does the statement apply, in varying degrees, to all countries with at least some presence or level of democracy (for example, a dictatorship that permits political parties)? Or does it apply only to countries that are more democratic than not? Or does it apply only to full-fledged democracies? With fuzzy sets it is possible to address these varied interpretations of the proposition with a single instrument and to draw conclusions that are more nuanced than is possible with conventional variables.

Thus, by combining qualitative and quantitative assessment in a single instrument, fuzzy sets make it possible for researchers to address varied interpretations of social scientific concepts in an explicit manner. Almost all concepts refer simultaneously to qualitative and quantitative differences. Concepts are typically expressed qualitatively in theoretical discourse (e.g., the statement about democratic countries above) but also allow for varying degrees (e.g., variation in degree of democracy).

These two aspects of social scientific concepts often spawn great controversies, with social researchers talking past each other. For example, a quantitative analyst might document a cross-national relationship, using data on many countries, between degree of "democracy" and some other variable, and feel confident about its breadth. A qualitative analysts might scoff at this analysis because it includes a vast majority of undemocratic countries. Fuzzy sets remedy this type of analytic chaos by joining qualitative and quantitative assessment, forcing researchers to distinguish between qualitative and quantitative aspects when they operationalize their concepts. Thus, researchers who use fuzzy sets can establish a very close correspondence between the content of the concepts appearing in theoretical statements and propositions, on the one hand, and the analysis of empirical evidence, on the other.

Fuzzy sets provide tools for the assessment of set-theoretic relationships. Set-theoretic relationships are implicit in most social science discourse. To state, for example, that "religious fundamentalists are politically conservative," is not to say that the only path to political conservativism is through religious fundamentalism. Rather, religious fundamentalism is viewed as one of several possible routes to political conservativism, which certainly allows for the possibility that most political conservatives are not religious fundamentalists. While this set-theoretic relationship might not be perfect, it would not be unreasonable to expect religious fundamentalists to be a rough subset of political conservatives. Essentially, the expectation here is that most who are religious fundamentalists are also politically conservative, even though most who are politically conservative may not be religious fundamentalists. Thus, in this example, the variable treated as causal (religious fundamentalism) could be seen as an imperfect subset of the variable portrayed as the outcome (political conservatism).

Consider another rough subset relationship. Most professionals have advanced degrees, even though not all those with advanced degrees are professionals (many with advanced degrees drive taxis; others own their own businesses; some are full-time parents, and so on). Thus, professionals are a rough subset of people with advanced degrees. In this example, the variable that is treated as the outcome, having a career as a professional, is a rough subset of the variable that is seen as causal, holding an advanced degree. In other words, the set-theoretic relationship in this example is the reverse of what it is in the previous example, at least from a causal point of view.

At the level of discourse, the two statements are parallel in structure.

We state the subset first. (1) "Religious fundamentalists are politically conservative." (2) "Professionals have advanced degrees." However, in causal terms the two statements are the reverse of each other. The causal condition comes first in the first statement and second in the second statement. In conventional forms of quantitative analysis, there is no simple way to take account of these different set-theoretic relationships. Most social scientists would assess both statements by correlating the variables in question. If religious fundamentalism and political conservativism correlate, this evidence would be cited as support for the causal argument implicit in the first statement. If possessing an advanced degree and having a professional career correlate, this evidence would be cited as support for the causal argument implicit in the second statement. In short, the fact that rough set-theoretic relationships are clearly embedded in the two statements, along with the fact that these two set-theoretic relationships are the opposite of each other, at least from a causal point of view, would be ignored by practitioners of conventional methods.

The issue of set-theoretic relationships is central to the link between theoretical argumentation and empirical analysis and therefore is not something that social scientists should ignore. Note that the two statements presented above involve very different kinds of causal reasoning (see Mackie 1974, 1985). In the first statement, the causal condition (religious fundamentalism) is one of several possible routes or paths to the outcome (political conservativism). It may not be one of the more important routes; it is simply a route. In the second statement, having an advanced degree is a prerequisite for most professional careers, a virtual necessary condition. Having an advanced degree is not one of many possible paths to a career as a professional; it is the major hurdle on the (almost) only route. These different causal structures account for the opposite set-theoretic relationships embedded in the two statements, with the causal condition the subset in one statement and the outcome the subset in the other.

Conventional methods (e.g., correlation) and conventional measures (e.g., interval- and ratio-scale variables) cannot be used to address set-theoretic relationships. Indeed, such relationships are completely outside their scope. Yet, set-theoretic relationships are the bread and butter of theoretical argumentation and discourse; they are embedded or implied in most theoretical statements. As I show in this book, it is possible to address set-theoretic relationships with fuzzy sets. For example, it is possible to assess whether the set of religious fundamentalists is a rough subset of the set of political conservatives, using measures that attend to fine-grained differences in both religious fundamentalism and political conservatism.

The features of fuzzy sets just discussed are only two of their many aspects that make them especially powerful for linking ideas and evidence in social research. I explore these features in part 2 of this book, after first laying the proper foundation in the diversity-oriented approach.

Fuzzy Sets and Diversity-Oriented Research

Fuzzy sets have much to offer all of social science. However, their value is greatly enhanced when used in tandem with the diversity-oriented approach. This approach brings many of the special features of qualitative analysis, including an interest in set-theoretic relationships, to research involving large Ns. Indeed, the pairing of these two—fuzzy sets and the diversity-oriented approach—is central to this book. Without the frame of the diversity-oriented approach, the value of fuzzy sets to social science is limited. Most conventional data-analytic techniques use linear algebra and thus do not address set-theoretic relationships. Likewise, without fuzzy sets, the scope of social phenomena that is amenable to the diversity-oriented approach, with its emphasis on configurations of set memberships, is restricted to categorical social data. In short, the key link between fuzzy sets and the diversity-oriented approach is that they both deal with sets and set-theoretic relationships.

Imagine the response of a conventional quantitative researcher to the two features of fuzzy sets just discussed. The embedding of qualitative states (i.e., full membership and full nonmembership) on continua looks like a bad idea. Why compress the two ends of a continuous variable, converting values at one end to scores of 1 (full membership) and values at the other end to scores of 0 (full nonmembership)? From the conventional viewpoint it is almost always a mistake to throw away variation. Linear models work best when the extremes of the distribution of a continuous variable are well populated with cases (Chatterjee and Price 1991). Likewise, the conventional quantitative researcher has little use for set-theoretic relations. In the conventional view, the proximate goal of quantitative analysis is to explain variation in one or more dependent variables. It does not matter whether an independent variable is a rough subset of the outcome (e.g., religious fundamentalism and political conservatism) or the reverse (e.g., holding an advanced degree and having a career as a professional). If either of these relationships exists, then the causal condition should correlate with the outcome.

The diversity-oriented approach, by contrast, focuses directly on set-theoretic relationships. Full elaboration of this approach is the goal of part 1 of this book; here I mention a few of its main features. At its core, this approach is concerned with exploring and constructing types and kinds of cases, with a special concern for causal heterogeneity—the different paths to an outcome. Thus, this approach builds on and extends the techniques I developed in *The Comparative Method* (1987). In the diversity-oriented view, what may appear to be a single population may be packed with many different types, subtypes, and mixed types of cases. Types are most visible when cases are viewed not as collections of analytically distinct variables but as configurations of set memberships. Once cases are understood in terms of their configurations of set memberships, it is possible to examine their heterogeneity, especially with respect to the different combinations of causal conditions linked to an outcome. For example, a researcher might study the different configurations of background characteristics linked to political conservatism without assuming that the same causal conditions operate in the same way in all cases. For some types of cases "rural background," for instance, might contribute to political conservatism; for others, it might work against it. In the diversity-oriented view, the important point is not that causal conditions may have opposite effects in different contexts, but that the researcher must view cases as configurations—as combinations of aspects and conditions.

With categorical data, it is relatively easy to see cases as configurations of set memberships because of the straightforward correspondence between categories and sets (Ragin 1987). Using ordinal, interval, and ratio-scale data, however, this one-to-one correspondence evaporates, and it becomes more difficult to view cases as belonging to types, that is, to view them as instances of configurations. Without the aid of fuzzy sets, the diversity-oriented approach is limited to social data that are wholly categorical in nature. Using fuzzy sets, however, it is possible to address all kinds of data and all aspects of cases, even those involving fine-grained differences in degree or level. Thus, fuzzy sets provide a way to extend the view of cases as configurations of set memberships, first presented in *The Comparative Method*, using many different kinds of evidence.

While the use of fuzzy sets is "detachable" from diversity-oriented research and vice versa, the two work best hand in hand. The bond that joins them is their common focus on sets and the analysis of set-theoretic relationships. This book shows how the diversity-oriented approach amplifies the social scientific relevance of fuzzy sets and how fuzzy sets amplify the range of the diversity-oriented approach.

Plan of the Book

Part 1 of *Fuzzy-Set Social Science* describes the central features of diversity-oriented research and culminates with an example of the approach. As I present this approach, I also discuss aspects of conventional quantitative analysis that interfere with its use as a discovery tool: (1) its dependence on populations that are constituted prior to data collection and analysis; (2) its heavily variable-oriented discourse, a framework that is antithetical to the analysis of cases as interpretable configurations of aspects, and (3) its additive-linear view of causation, an understanding that depends upon strong homogenizing assumptions about cases, which, in turn, make this approach insensitive to causal complexity.

The foundation for my critique of conventional quantitative analysis is provided by qualitative, case-oriented social science. In this approach, researchers conceive populations as meaningful sets of cases that often must be formed and conceptualized in the course of an investigation. They view cases as configurations of aspects and seek to understand them at the level of the specific instance. They see causation as conjunctural and plural—causes may combine in different and sometimes contradictory ways to generate the same outcome. I present diversity-oriented research as a middle path between qualitative, case-oriented research and quantitative, variable-oriented research. In some respects, part 1 of *Fuzzy-Set Social Science* can be seen as a rebuttal of King, Keohane, and Verba's treatise on methodology, *Designing Social Inquiry* (1994). They argue, in essence, that the way to improve qualitative research is to make it as much like quantitative research as possible. I argue the opposite, namely, that many of the special features of qualitative research should be integrated into quantitative research.

Chapter 1 situates diversity-oriented research between the quantitative analysis of patterns observable across many cases (i.e., conventional variable-oriented research) and the qualitative, in-depth study of small Ns (i.e., case-oriented research). I offer a general discussion of these two strategies and of the gulf that separates them, arguing that diversity-oriented research bridges this gulf. Instead of giving priority to either cases or variables, diversity-oriented research emphasizes "types" and "kinds," a formulation that views cases configurationally, as combinations of aspects.

Chapters 2 through 4 address the three main pillars of quantitative social science—populations, variables, and causation. I focus on the contrasts between conventional quantitative methods and the diversity-oriented approach. For populations, the contrast is between the conventional understanding of populations as given or "preconstituted" and the diversity-oriented view of populations as categories that must be constituted and refined in the course of an investigation. For variables, the main contrast is between the conventional understanding of variables as analytically distinct aspects of cases and the diversity-oriented view of cases as configurations of aspects. This discussion builds on Paul Lazarsfeld's (1937) concept of "property spaces" and their use in the construction of types. For causation, the main contrast is between the conventional view of causation as a contest between independent variables to explain variation in an outcome and the diversity-oriented view that causation is often both conjunctural and multiple. In the conventional view, each single causal condition, conceived as an analytically distinct variable, has an independent impact on the outcome. In the diversity-oriented view, causes combine in different and sometimes contradictory ways to produce the same outcome, revealing different paths.

Chapter 5 formalizes the diversity-oriented approach with an application. The key focus of the application is the problem of studying causal complexity—how to use information on configurations of set memberships to assess causation that is both conjunctural and multiple. Causation this complex is difficult to assess. I show that by testing the sufficiency of all possible combinations of conditions drawn from the researcher's property space it is possible to address causal complexity in a way that shows the different paths to a single outcome.

While part 1 synthesizes much of my recent work on methodology, it is important to note that this presentation incorporates a number of important advances. First, it offers a clear exposition of the concept of property space and shows the links between property spaces and "truth tables," the centerpiece of the techniques I present in *The Comparative Method* (1987; see also Becker 1998). Second, it establishes the centrality of the analysis of both set-theoretic relationships and necessary and sufficient causation to social scientific inquiry. Third, it demonstrates that the assessment of necessity and sufficiency need not be "all or nothing," but instead may be probabilistic and partial in nature. Last, it shows that even when there is great causal complexity (defined as situations in which no single cause is either necessary or sufficient), the investigation of combinations of causal conditions is still possible.

While dramatic in scope, the methodology presented in part 1 is limited in the way it views and represents diversity. In conventional set theory, a case is either in or out of a set (e.g., the set of males, the set of democratic countries, the set of not-for-profit organizations, and so on); a case cannot be partially in or partially out. Everyday experience indicates that this "in-or-out" conception of set membership is too restrictive; membership in sets is often partial. Thus, while a great deal of diversity is revealed when researchers examine configurations of set memberships, a lot is hidden when membership in sets is constrained to be crisp—either in or out. In fact, the membership of most social phenomena in the sets social scientists use to characterize them is usually fuzzy, not crisp. That is, cases (e.g., countries) exhibit varying degrees of membership in categories (e.g., the set of democracies).

Part 2 shows how to use fuzzy sets to enrich social research, building on the foundation of the diversity-oriented approach presented in part 1. A central argument of part 2 is that diversity has two main aspects. The first aspect of diversity is that which is based on "differences in kind" arising from categorical distinctions. The second aspect of diversity involves the varying degrees of membership that instances may exhibit in the categories and types used to characterize them. Conventionally, social scientists think of the first kind of diversity as nominal-scale and the second kind as ordinal, interval, or ratio-scale. I demonstrate in part 2 that fuzzy sets capture both kinds of difference simultaneously—in the same analytic breath—and that for this reason they offer especially powerful analytic tools for social scientists. Most social scientific concepts invoke qualitative and quantitative distinctions at the same time. This fact can be seen in everyday sociological concepts like "rich," which invoke a categorical distinction but also permit degree of membership, and in sophisticated ideal-typic notions such as "bureaucratic." The key to understanding the power of fuzzy sets is to see that it is possible to specify qualitative breakpoints on continua and to incorporate these qualitative breakpoints directly into the analysis of evidence that varies by level. With fuzzy sets, researchers can analyze set-theoretic relationships while still attending to phenomena that vary by level or degree. They do not have to forfeit the study of variation by level in order to study cases as configurations or to explore causal complexity.

My presentation of fuzzy-set methods follows the template of part 1. After offering a detailed presentation of the nature of fuzzy sets in social research (chapter 6), I address the fuzzy-set approach to the problem of viewing cases as configurations of set memberships and the associated problem of constituting populations. Because of their deep complementarity, these two topics are joined in chapter 7. I demonstrate several advantages of fuzzy-set methods over the crisp-set configurational approach presented in part 1. For example, using fuzzy sets, cases vary in the degree to which they are instances of a location in a property space, and this information can be used to aid the evaluation of the usefulness of the property space.

Chapters 8 and 9 discuss, in turn, the analysis of necessary and sufficient conditions. I demonstrate that the core of the analysis of necessity is an evaluation of the argument that an outcome is a subset of a cause. Likewise, the core of the analysis of sufficiency is an evaluation of the argument that a cause or causal combination is a subset of an outcome. Thus, the study of causal complexity is, in essence, the study of set-theoretic relationships. These chapters demonstrate that the fuzzy subset relationship is central to the analysis of causal complexity when using data that vary by level or degree.

Chapter 10 provides two applications of these arguments, both involving country-level data. The first application is an analysis of causal conditions relevant to "severe IMF protest" (mass demonstrations and riots in response to austerity programs mandated by the International Monetary Fund). The second is an analysis of causal conditions relevant to "generous welfare states" in advanced industrial democratic countries. Chapter 11 summarizes part 2 by addressing the use of fuzzy sets as interpretive tools.

PART I

Diversity-Oriented Research

ONE

DIVERSITY-ORIENTED RESEARCH

BETWEEN COMPLEXITY AND GENERALITY

Two main traditions can be distinguished in the history of ideas, differing as to the conditions an explanation has to satisfy in order to be scientifically respectable. The one tradition is sometimes called *aristotelian*, the other *galilean*. [. . .] As to their views of scientific explanation, the contrast between the two is usually characterized as causal *versus* teleological explanation. The first type of explanation is also called mechanistic, the second finalistic. The galilean tradition in science runs parallel with the advance of the causal-mechanistic point of view in man's effort to explain and predict phenomena, the aristotelian tradition with his effort to make facts teleologically or finalistically understandable.

—von Wright, *Explanation and Understanding*

INTRODUCTION

Social scientists often face a fundamental dilemma when they conduct social research. On the one hand, they can emphasize the *complexity* of social phenomena—a common strategy in ethnographic, historical, and macrolevel research—and offer sensitive, in-depth case studies of specific instances. On the other hand, they can make broad, homogenizing assumptions about cases and document *generalities*—patterns that hold across many instances. Research strategies that focus on complexity are often characterized as "qualitative," "case-oriented," "small-N," or "intensive." Examples of this include in-depth case studies of the social cohesion of large immigrant communities in Manchester, the origins of the Korean War, and the construction of gender in sports bars in Peoria, Illinois. Strategies that focus on generality are often characterized as "quantitative," "variable-oriented," "large-N," or "extensive." Some examples of this are broad-based studies of the connection between diversification and profitability across large multinational corporations, the link between technology and scale of destruction in armed conflicts, and the correlates of alternative gender identities.

This methodological divide is somewhat artificial and overly simplistic. Still, it has provided ample fodder for conflicts and controversies in many academic fields and arenas, from the pages of introductory textbooks to hiring and firing decisions at top social science departments (Shea 1997). While the contrasts between these two styles of social research are substantial, it is easy to exaggerate their differences and to caricature the two approaches, for example, by portraying quantitative work on general patterns as scientific but sterile and oppressive and qualitative research on small Ns as rich and emancipatory but soft and subjective. It is important to avoid these caricatures because the contrasts between these two general approaches provide important leads both for finding a middle path between them and for resolving basic methodological issues in social science.

In this chapter, I am mostly interested in these two approaches as different ways of connecting ideas and evidence, especially evidence that comes in the form of *multiple cases* or *instances*. How do we learn from multiple instances? How should we conduct *cross-case analysis*? The case-oriented strategy addresses a relatively small number of cases in an in-depth manner, paying attention to each case as an interpretable whole. In essence, this strategy is an extension of the single-case study to multiple cases with an eye toward configurations of similarities and differences. In this approach, in-depth knowledge of cases provides the basis for constructing limited generalizations that hold for the cases studied. These generalizations may or may not have wider relevance. The variable-oriented strategy, by contrast, is to look for broad patterns across many cases, usually by correlating aspects, and to draw inferences based on these broad patterns. In the variable-oriented strategy, small Ns are seen as untrustworthy because they are more likely than large Ns to provide distorted representations of broad, population-wide patterns. For the case-oriented researcher, confidence comes from depth; for the variable-oriented researcher, it comes from breadth.

As I show in this chapter and in part 1 of this book, there is a middle ground between the two strategies of depth and breadth. This middle ground emphasizes the study of diversity, an approach that emphasizes seeing cases as configurations of aspects and disaggregating populations into types. The main purpose of this chapter is to situate diversity-oriented research between two methodological traditions, case-oriented and variable-oriented. Prominent in this examination is a discussion of practical differences separating case-oriented and variable-oriented research—basic contrasts in how researchers go about the seemingly mundane task of drawing conclusions from data (see also Myles and Huberman 1994). By focusing on the practical level, it is possible not only to understand why practitioners of these two methodological styles often talk past each other, it is also possible to see how basic ideas about cases, causes, populations, and variables constrain and shape the dialogue between ideas and evidence. I argue that the homogenizing assumptions of the variable-oriented approach pose obstacles to discovery in social research and that these obstacles are addressed in the diversity-oriented approach. While this chapter sketches many of the key features of diversity-oriented research, full presentation of the approach is the purpose of part 1.

Variable-Oriented versus Case-Oriented Research

Two empirical observations serve as a useful starting point in the analysis of these two methodological styles. First, in most social science subdisciplines there is an inverse relation between the number of cases and the number of aspects of cases (or "variables") that researchers study. Second, researchers tend to gravitate toward the study of either many cases and relatively few variables or many variables and relatively few cases. These two research styles offer alternate ways of constructing representations of social life from multiple instances. Of course, there are other ways to construct representations from multiple instances, but these two are the most common in social science.

The inverse relation between the number of cases and the number of variables in a study can be seen clearly in an extreme contrast: the in-depth study of the lives of a small number of individuals and a survey study with thousands of respondents. The case-study researcher examines many aspects of each case and attempts to construct a representation of each individual from the interconnections among the aspects of each case. In effect, the case-study researcher's goal is to show how the different aspects mutually constitute the whole case and then to compare and contrast the different wholes. A survey researcher, by contrast, studies one or a small number of dependent variables across a very large number of cases and attempts to identify a parsimonious set of causal variables that explains as much variation as possible in the dependent variables. This researcher constructs a generic representation based on patterns observed across many cases (e.g., using correlations among variables). In contrast to comparative case-study research, which is deep but not very wide (i.e., "intensive"), survey research is wide but not very deep (i.e., "extensive").[1]

Social scientists who study cases in an in-depth manner often see empirical generalizations simply as a means to another end—the interpretive understanding of cases.[2] In this view, a fundamental goal of social science is to interpret significant features of the social world and thereby advance understanding of how existing social arrangements came about and why we live the way we do. The rough general patterns that social scientists identify simply aid the understanding of specific cases; they usually are not viewed as predictive. Besides, the task of interpreting and then representing socially significant phenomena (or the task of making selected social phenomena significant by representing them) is a much more immediate and tangible goal. Empirical generalizations and social science theory are important, but their importance derives primarily from their service to the goal of interpretive understanding. By contrast, those who study patterns across many cases with an eye toward formulating generalizations believe that the fundamental goal of social science is to advance general, explanatory theories addressing wide expanses of the social terrain. In this view, social scientists should uncover general patterns, refine their theories, and use this abstract, theoretical knowledge to advance the common good. Thus, systematic theory is seen as the centerpiece of good social science as an end in itself.

1. This division within the social sciences reproduces the gulf between the humanities, where the key issue is the possibility and adequacy of representation, and the physical sciences, where the problem of scientific inference is paramount. While representation and inference are both important in social science, social scientists differ in how they weight these two goals. At its core, this broad division among social scientists reflects their disagreement regarding the limits of social scientific generalization. Those who study the complexity and specificity of social phenomena tend to be skeptical of empirical generalizations; those who study patterns across many cases do so with an explicit eye toward constructing such generalizations.

2. Theoretically decisive case studies, of course, seek theoretical generality as opposed to empirical generality. For example, researchers often choose specific cases because they are extreme in some way and thus present social phenomena is a "pure" way (e.g., Dumont 1970). Other researchers choose specific cases because they seem completely ordinary and thus should not skew findings or results in any particular way (e.g., Becker at al. 1961). Overall, the relationship between case studies and theoretical generalization is difficult and tortuous, and researchers must make a special (and strong) case to support the connection.

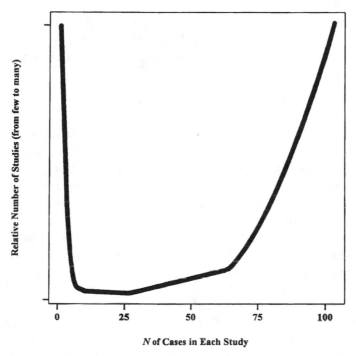

Figure 1.1 Plot of relative number of studies against N of cases in each study.

This bifurcation of social scientists with respect to the issue of generalization is evident in their published work. The examination of almost any research area in the social sciences reveals that there is a sharp divide separating those who do small-N qualitative studies from those who do large-N quantitative studies. In comparative sociology and comparative politics, for example, a frequency distribution showing the number of studies with different size Ns reveals a clear U-shaped pattern, illustrated in figure 1.1 (see also Bollen, Entwistle, and Alderson 1993; Ragin 1989; Sigelman and Gadbois 1983). At the small-N end of the horizontal axis there are many studies, just as there are at the large-N end of this axis. But in the middle the relative number of studies is very low. There are few comparativists who conduct studies of ten or twenty countries, but many who study one or two (case study research) or more than fifty (i.e., enough to permit the use of conventional quantitative methods). This U-shaped distribution is replicated in many other research areas.

AN EVER-WIDENING GULF

A number of factors reinforce both this division and, more generally, the tendency for social scientists to gravitate toward one or the other styles of cross-case analysis:

1. It is very difficult to conduct an in-depth study of a large number of cases. Imagine trying to keep up with the day-to-day politics of eighty countries to know each country's politics well. Imagine a survey researcher trying to keep track of the life histories of hundreds of individuals. After a dozen or so cases, the interviewees would start to blur together. To treat each case as a singular entity and understand it on its own terms is very difficult and time-consuming. Empirical intimacy with cases comes at a very high price. Thus, social scientists who do in-depth research tend to restrict themselves to relatively small Ns. Those who conduct quantitative analyses of large Ns usually must forfeit the opportunity to gain in-depth knowledge of the cases they study.

2. Social scientists tend to identify themselves and each other as qualitative or quantitative and they tend to sort themselves according to their familiarity with and tolerance for quantitative methods of data analysis. Graduate training is organized along this divide, reproducing these difference among students. Finally, "invisible colleges" (Crane 1972) have formed based on these two methodological orientations. Thus, the social organization of disciplines tends to reinforce the U-shaped distribution illustrated in figure 1.1.

3. Social scientists have a limited repertoire of methods. Case-study methods are geared toward the acquisition of in-depth knowledge of a small number of cases, with an eye toward understanding how all the different pieces fit together *within* each case. Generally, the "how" of each case is something that researchers construct in their heads, and it is very difficult to keep track of configurations of similarities and differences across more than a handful of cases.[3] Quantitative methods, by contrast, work well only when there are many cases—the more the better. The success of a research project often hinges on having a large *N*, which, in turn, makes statistical signifi-

---

3. Consider for example, the fact that a study of only 10 cases has 45 paired comparisons contained within it (Ragin 1987; Griffin and Ragin 1994). A study addressing the logically possible combinations of only 8 presence/absence attributes involves the consideration of 256 different configurations, most of which must be addressed as "thought experiments" (Weber 1949).

cance more probable. It is very difficult to achieve statistical significance with $N = 20$; it is much easier with $N = 200$. There are few
techniques explicitly designed for intermediate-sized Ns (however,
see Ragin 1987; Ragin, Berg-Schlosser, and De Meur 1996). These
methodological limitations push researchers toward the two ends of
the N-of-cases dimension.

4. Most social scientists value both kinds of knowledge—broad, theoretically relevant knowledge (e.g., the general conditions that favor
"rational" decision making) *and* culturally or historically specific
knowledge (e.g., the origins of affirmative action as a national policy
in the United States). Case-oriented methods are best suited for
questions that are about culturally or historically specific phenomena. Variable-oriented methods are typically used to identify broad,
theoretically relevant patterns. From this perspective, the U-shaped
distribution illustrated in figure 1.1 appears to some to represent a
justifiable and convenient division of labor, with case-study researchers seeking in-depth knowledge and quantitative researchers seeking
knowledge of general patterns (Eckstein 1975).

5. Social scientists hold conflicting views regarding how connections
within cases should be studied. In small-N research, aspects of cases
are understood in the context of the separate wholes they form. This
configurational view sees parts as mutually constitutive and interconnected within a given case. In large-N research, by contrast, aspects
of cases are connected primarily in cross-case analysis: A strong pattern of covariation across cases (e.g., a strong correlation between
"human capital" variables and income) is the main evidence used to
support an argument that aspects of cases are empirically connected
in some way (e.g., people with more human capital use it to "get
ahead").

6. When researchers attempt in-depth analysis of an intermediate-sized
N (say, $N = 20$), they often are confronted with what seems like
unmanageable diversity. Because they can achieve some in-depth
knowledge of cases when they study intermediate-sized Ns, they are
able to identify intricate patterns and other subtleties that would be
invisible in a quantitative, variable-oriented analysis. But it is difficult to represent this complexity with conventional techniques. At
the two ends of the N-of-cases dimension (see figure 1.1), by contrast, the answers to the questions social scientists ask tend to be
more straightforward, often univocal. A single case, in the end, typically gives a single answer. The commonalities across a small number of cases (say, three to five) likewise may provide the basis for

a single answer. At the other end of the N-of-cases dimension, researchers base their answers on patterns observed across many cases—evident, for example, in correlations—which average out the idiosyncrasies of individual cases, which in turn yield representations of generic processes—another form of univocality.

Given the prevalence of the U-shaped distribution of number of studies by number of cases and the many reinforcing factors just described, it is not surprising that the gulf between these two worlds of social research is one of the most enduring features of social science. Those who do case-oriented work can offer answers that are intensively correct, embracing a small number of cases in a detailed and integrative way. Those who do variable-oriented studies can provide answers that are extensively correct, embracing many observations. The case-oriented researcher justifies findings by showing their compatibility with other aspects of the case or cases in question. The variable-oriented researcher justifies findings by showing their generality.

The Problem of Bridging These Two Worlds

While easy to explain, there is no simple way to justify this U-shaped pattern. It is true that social scientists value both kinds of knowledge— in-depth knowledge of cases and broad statements about patterns that hold across many cases. It is also true that these two forms of knowledge are different, as von Wright (1971) indicates in the passage quoted at the beginning of this chapter. But in-depth knowledge of cases is often dependent on knowledge of patterns that hold across many cases, and vice versa. Case-oriented researchers, for example, often cite general patterns that they themselves have not documented to explain case-specific phenomena (e.g., citing the "well-known" tendency for peasants to be highly risk-averse to explain the failure of an agricultural diversification program). If these general patterns turn out to be without empirical support, then the case-specific argument is suspect (e.g., political corruption, ignored by the researcher, may have felled the diversification project). Likewise, it is very difficult to explain broad patterns across many cases without reference to case-level phenomena (Abbott 1991). Variable-oriented researchers regularly cite unobserved case-level mechanisms to explain the cross-case patterns they document. If these mechanisms cannot be confirmed at the case level, then the variable-oriented conclusions are suspect (Collier 1993, 1998).

Consider also the fact that a deep complementary relationship between case-oriented and variable-oriented research augments their mutual dependence. With variable-oriented techniques, for example, it is very difficult to address questions about actors' motives and subjectivities or to observe event sequences and causal connections (Rueschemeyer 1991; Rueschemeyer and Stephens 1997). Case-oriented methods, by contrast, excel in these areas. With case-oriented techniques, however, it is difficult to gain confidence that findings are general in any way. This is one of the central strengths of the variable-oriented approach (Goldthorpe 1991, 1997; King et al. 1994; Lieberson 1992, 1998; Lijphart 1971, 1975).[4]

The complementarity and mutual dependence of these two worlds of social research undermines the idea that there can be a convenient division of labor between the two camps. As much as they might want to, the two camps cannot ignore each other. Perhaps this mutual dependence, combined with an unhealthy measure of mutual suspicion, explains the periodic eruption of conflicts over method in academic journals, departments, and other arenas.[5] While it seems unlikely that these two worlds will ever merge, it is clear that their tendency toward mutual suspicion is unhealthy (Shea 1997).

One way to link the two worlds is to build general knowledge of cross-case patterns from many, many case studies. This general knowledge can be gleaned from accumulated case-based knowledge or from strategically conducted studies of specific cases and situations (Lieberson 1985).[6] Rarely, however, is general knowledge constructed in this manner. Indeed, the two forms of knowledge usually are constructed

4. Because the two approaches are complementary, there are many ways to construct useful hybrid strategies (Janoski 1991). For example, a case-study researcher might apply a variable-oriented, quantitative method to strengthen some of his or her inferences and at the same time extend his or her knowledge of the case (King et al. 1994). This tactic is common among social historians and historical sociologists who use quantitative methods (e.g., Tilly 1986). Another hybrid strategy is to use a small number of case studies to flesh out and document patterns observed across many cases (Paige 1975).

5. Consider, for example, the report of deep divisions in political science reported in the *Chronicle of Higher Education* (Shea 1997). There is a deep division between the proponents of the rational choice perspective and those who favor in-depth knowledge of countries. This rift is especially pronounced in comparative politics, the branch of political science most concerned with area studies, the specificity of political systems, and their embeddedness in culture.

6. More generally, Lieberson (1985) sees small-N studies as strategic only and doubts their usefulness for inference. One could imagine, however, an entire case-oriented methodology organized around the idea of strategic selection of sites that could be used to buttress inferences.

independently, and few scholars have tried to distill and systematize the knowledge generated from many case studies.[7]

As an alternative, accumulated case-based knowledge could be used to evaluate the results of large-N, variable-oriented studies of cross-case patterns. If a deep chasm separates knowledge generated from accumulated case studies, on the one hand, and knowledge generated from the study of patterns across many cases, on the other, then one or both are suspect or at least need to be qualified or revised in some way. This comparison of results happens only occasionally, however, because the two ways of generating knowledge produce findings that are often incompatible and sometimes contradictory.

An excellent example of the problem of case-based knowledge contradicting variable-oriented knowledge is detailed in Dietrich Rueschemeyer, Eveleyne Huber Stephens, and John Stephens's work *Capitalist Development and Democracy* (1992). Variable-oriented research has demonstrated a consistent link between economic development and democracy, documented via the strong correlation between these two variables (level of economic development and strength of democracy) in quantitative cross-national research. Typically this research has cited causal mechanisms directly linked to economic development (e.g., social mobilization) to explain the correlation. Case-study research, by contrast, has shown no such link. Rueschemeyer et al. argue that while it is true that economic development and democracy are strongly correlated across cases, the mechanisms producing this correlation are not directly tied to economic development per se. They study many countries in moderate depth, focusing on configurations of similarities and differences, and show that various combinations of class-based and institutional factors have shaped democratic institutions in different regions of the world. Contradictions of the type documented by Rueschemeyer et al. make it very difficult to bridge the two worlds of social research.

The Impact of Analytic Procedures on the Disjuncture

Despite the many interdependencies and complementarities of case-oriented and variable-oriented research and the dependence of both sets of researchers on the same body of social theory, there are very good reasons to expect disjunctures in the knowledge they produce. Primary among these reasons is the simple fact that the two approaches

---

7. Exceptions to this statement include such scholars as Barrington Moore, Jr. (1966), Reinhard Bendix (1978), and Immanuel Wallerstein (1974).

use very different analytic procedures to construct representations of social phenomena (Ragin 1994a). Consider, for example, the contrast between computing a correlation between a causal and an outcome variable, a popular analytic step in variable-oriented work, and identifying the causally relevant conditions linked to a specific outcome across a small number of cases, a well-worn analytic path in case-oriented research (e.g., Brinton 1965; Chirot 1994; Hobsbawm 1981; Wolf 1969). While both procedures seem deceptively simple and straightforward, these two ways of constructing representations of social phenomena from evidence involve sharply contrasting orientations toward cases, outcomes, and causes. That is, they differ fundamentally at a *practical* level. It is not necessary to invoke the contrasting emphases of the two worlds of social research—inference versus interpretive understanding—to account for the disjunctures in the knowledge they produce (as in Truzzi 1974).

Cases

When variable-oriented researchers compute a correlation between two variables, the cases become more or less invisible, and variables take center stage. Furthermore, the set of cases included in the computation must be fixed before the researcher can compute the correlation. Once this set is fixed, usually at the outset of an investigation, it is rarely altered. What matters most is that the cases (which are understood as "observations") belong to the same general "population" and that they be drawn from this population with an eye toward randomness or representativeness or some combination of such criteria. If the relevant population is moderate in size (e.g., counties in North Carolina, members of the U.N., and so on), then all observations may be included in the analysis.

In a comparative case study of commonalities, by contrast, cases have clear identities and are usually chosen specifically because of their significance or their theoretical relevance (George 1979). Furthermore, the set of relevant cases may shift during the investigation because the researcher may decide that one or more cases do not seem like the others. For example, a researcher studying social revolutions might decide that the Mexican case does not fit well with the Russian, Chinese, and other cases and then drop it from the investigation. This flexibility is maintained throughout the investigation because the core concepts (e.g., "social revolution") may be revised as the researcher learns more about relevant instances. In the end, the delineation of an empirical category and the clarification of core theoretical concepts relevant to this category may be the primary achievements of the research effort—that is, beyond the new interpretive insights into cases offered by the researcher.

Outcomes

In correlational studies researchers usually identify a "dependent variable"—an outcome that varies across cases. Typically, such outcomes are aspects of cases that vary by level, for example, level of bureaucratization, level of democracy, and so on. Sometimes the outcome variable is categorical, indicating, for example, whether or not some event has occurred (e.g., debt renegotiation), and sometimes it is a frequency or a rate (e.g., the murder rate). The important consideration, in this procedure, is that the outcome must vary across relevant "observations." The goal of the research typically is to explain, if possible, why each case has the value or level on the dependent variable that it does. Typically, cases are assessed relative to the average of all cases, using some measure of central tendency such as the mean as a statistical benchmark for evaluating each case. Such research is centrally concerned with the question of "why." For example, a researcher might seek to explain why some countries are more democratic than average and others less so, why some organizations are more bureaucratic than average and others less so, or why some people have more education than average and others less so.

In a comparative case study of commonalities, by contrast, the outcome is often something that does not vary substantially across cases. In a study of peasant revolts, for example, cases are chosen precisely because they all display the same outcome—peasant revolts. Recall that the goal of this type of research is to identify common causal conditions linked to a specific outcome across a relatively small number of cases.[8] Thus, the focus is on cases with a specific outcome, not cases that vary widely in how much they have this outcome. While the outcomes in a study of this type will not be exactly identical (for example, not all peasant revolts are exactly alike), the researcher must demonstrate that the outcomes in the cases selected are in fact enough alike to be treated as instances of the same thing. Finally, unlike correlational studies, which are centrally concerned with the question of "why" (as in: Why

---

8. The study of the causal conditions shared by instances of an outcome is primarily directed toward the identification and evaluation of necessary conditions (see especially chapter 4).

some more than others?), comparative case studies are centrally concerned with the question of "how" (as in: How does it happen?). How
do couples break up (Vaughan 1986)? How do community organizations get started? How do peasant revolts come about?

Causes

In a correlational study, causation typically is inferred from a pattern
of covariation. If a variable thought to represent a cause or to be an
indicator of a key causal condition is strongly correlated with the outcome variable, then the researcher may make a causal inference. Usually, the researcher will assess the relative strength of several causal
variables at the same time. The typical goal is either to find out which
one explains the most variation in the outcome variable or simply to
assess the relative importance of the different variables. In effect, the
independent variables compete with each other to explain variation.
The causal variable that is least correlated with the other causal variables and most strongly correlated with the outcome variable usually
wins the competition. In most investigations, each causal variable is
considered sufficient, by itself, for the outcome or some increment in
the outcome. That is, each one is considered an "independent" variable
capable of affecting the outcome variable, regardless of the values of
other causal variables.

In a comparative case study of commonalities, by contrast, causation
is typically understood conjuncturally, in terms of combinations of conditions. The goal of this type of analysis is to identify the causal conditions shared by the cases. Causal conditions do not compete with each
other, as they do in correlational research; they combine. How they
combine is something that the researcher tries to piece together using
his or her in-depth knowledge of cases. Because all the cases have more
or less the same outcome, the usual reasoning is that the causal conditions shared by cases provide important clues regarding which factors
must be combined to produce the outcome in question. Further, the
researcher may argue that these common causal conditions are necessary for the outcome (see chapter 4). The search for such conditions
is not a simple mechanical process of listing potential causal conditions
and then seeing which ones are constant across relevant cases. Often
the researcher tries to construct a composite portrait, often linked to
a general narrative, from his or her in-depth knowledge of the cases
included in the study. When constructing this argument, the researcher
is especially sensitive to the possibility that a given causal requirement

(i.e., one of the necessary conditions) can be met in several different ways (see, e.g., Moore 1966).[9]

These and other practical differences in how case-oriented and variable-oriented researchers work with evidence to construct representations of social phenomena provide many opportunities for disjunctures in their findings. These practical differences also create a great deal of mutual suspicion. For example, from the perspective of variable-oriented work, the study of commonalities across a small number of instances is fraught with analytic sins and errors, among which are the following: (1) The number of cases is too small to warrant any kind of inference. (2) The procedure selects on the dependent variable (i.e., focuses on extreme or noteworthy cases, all with more or less the same value on the outcome variable). This practice deflates otherwise robust correlations (Geddes 1990; King et al. 1994; Collier 1995; Collier and Mahoney 1996). (3) The most important causal factors do not vary and thus are impossible to assess. Likewise, from the perspective of case-oriented work, the examination of the correlation between a causal and outcome variable across many cases is fundamentally flawed. For one, there are typically so many cases that there is no way for the researcher to know if they are all really comparable and thus belong together in the same analysis. Also, it is difficult to determine how something "comes about" by comparing cases with different levels of the outcome. The partial instances (i.e., those with lower scores on the outcome variable) are likely to provide many false leads. It is also pointless to try to isolate the "independent" effect of any causal condition when several factors usually must be combined for a particular outcome to occur (Ragin 1987, 1997).

While the practical differences between the two approaches reinforce the gulf between them, they also provide important clues for how to build a bridge. The best way to build this bridge is to find a middle ground where the concerns of both worlds can be met. This middle ground obviously involves compromises on both sides, but it should provide a way to address their practical differences, especially their different approaches to the construction of representations of social phenomena from empirical evidence.

9. This approach is not limited to the search for a single combination of causal conditions linked to an outcome. The researcher may identify several combinations, which in turn might prompt a reformulation of the outcome into types. I focus on the search for common causal conditions in this discussion to simplify the presentation and sharpen the contrasts in analytic procedures.

In the remainder of this chapter, I sketch this middle ground. I emphasize the study of *diversity,* a concept that bridges complexity and generality and provides the basis for a third world of cross-case analysis. The development of the diversity-oriented approach is the first of the three pillars of this book's central argument. The diversity-oriented approach drops many of the restrictive, homogenizing assumptions of conventional variable-oriented analysis without forsaking its emphasis on breadth—on studying many cases. By freeing researchers from these homogenizing assumptions, the diversity-oriented approach opens up the dialogue between ideas and evidence in social research, enlarging the potential for discovery.

Diversity: Between Complexity and Generality

The concept of *diversity* provides a way to balance the representational concerns of social scientists who lean toward the humanities—case-oriented researchers—and the inferential concerns of those who favor the hard sciences—variable-oriented researchers. Diversity is best understood as a synthesis that transcends these two opposing principles of generality and complexity. To study diversity is to take a broad view of social phenomena, as in much variable-oriented work, without imposing homogenizing assumptions at the outset of the research, the usual variable-oriented strategy (for example, the assumption that all cases are drawn from the same "population"). In short, the goal of diversity-oriented research is to find a middle path between treating analytic objects as members of fixed, homogeneous populations, on the one hand, and focusing exclusively on the specificity of individual cases, on the other.

When social scientists attend to the diversity of social phenomena, they make special allowance for kinds and types. Studying social phenomena in terms of their different kinds or types lies midway, conceptually speaking, between studying general patterns across "all" cases, on the one hand, and attending to the complexity of specific cases, on the other. Consider, for example, a researcher interested in military coups. The researcher could see coups as members of a single, all-inclusive population and investigate how they vary—in scale, intensity, duration, consequences, and so on. This study would focus on generality—on broad patterns observed across "all" cases. Alternatively, the researcher might select a relatively small number of coups for in-depth analysis and try to elucidate the specific character of these coups. The coups selected might be chosen because of their historical significance for a particular region of the world, or they might be especially well suited for answering a specific theoretical question, or they might be selected for some other reason. This study would focus on complexity, the specific character of the selected coups, and culminate in an in-depth representation of a relatively small, carefully delineated subset of coups.[10]

The study of the diversity of military coups would bridge the concerns manifested in these two common types of investigations. Rather than assuming that all coups are members of a single population or focusing on a carefully delimited subset of coups (or even on a single coup), a study of the diversity of coups would focus on their varied forms. After all, the broad category *military coups* may lack empirical integrity. Phenomena that superficially seem to be members of the same population and that are all conventionally labeled *military coups* in fact may belong in several different empirical categories. A study of the diversity of coups might culminate in a conceptual map showing types of coups and their varied causes and consequences, including mixed types. One conclusion of a study of the diversity of coups, for example, might be that under certain conditions (e.g., specific geopolitical contexts), some types of coups contribute to the long-term advance of democracy and social justice.[11]

It is clear that studying diversity is different from studying complexity, the usual focus of case-oriented research. In research that emphasizes complexity every case may seem unique, and researchers may spend considerable time and energy simply trying to find a handful of cases that are similar enough to permit comparisons. Often, case-oriented researchers resort to "contrast-oriented" (Skocpol and Sommers 1980; Skocpol 1984) and "particularizing" (Tilly 1984) comparisons precisely because the differences among their cases seem to greatly

---

10. Those who do small-N case-oriented studies sometimes go to great lengths to argue that the few cases examined in an investigation are the best cases to study for a given question, that these cases are the most representative of the general process in question, or that they are the most decisive relative to the theoretical issues at hand (see, e.g., Bendix 1978; Lipset 1950, 1963; Moore 1966; Skocpol 1979).

11. It is important to point out that allowing for multiple forms and types does not dictate that they *must* be found. Nor is it necessary in a diversity-oriented study to produce a conceptual map showing *all* types of a particular phenomenon (e.g., all types of military coups). The key consideration in studies that attend to diversity is that researchers constantly question key empirical categorizations and refrain from accepting any category boundary as fixed, at least not until the research is more or less complete.

outweigh their similarities. Diversity-oriented research, by contrast, tends to see social phenomena in terms of types and kinds and thus allows for middle-range generalizations—statements that refer to categories of social phenomena (e.g., types of military coups). In essence, diversity-oriented research emphasizes similarities among cases in the formulation of types and sees the specification of types, subtypes, and mixed types as an important means for understanding and explaining differences. Thus, like variable-oriented research, diversity-oriented research seeks to comprehend many cases at once.

Studying the diversity of social phenomena, however, is distinctly different from the variable-oriented study of covariation. For example, suppose a variable-oriented study of wars revealed that the greater the cultural differences between the opposing sides, the greater the loss of life (net of the independent effects of other causal conditions). While breathtaking in scope, this type of analysis might encompass strikingly heterogeneous cases. In order to examine the link between cultural differences and loss of life in wars, it would be necessary first to constitute and delimit the set of relevant wars as comparable cases—as members of a single population. But what is war? Should civil wars be included? Anticolonial uprisings? Armed rebellions? Wars that last three days? A week? Wars that involve less than one hundred fatalities? Should wars between preindustrial countries be included? Wars between preliterate peoples? How should the phenomenon, once defined, be delimited historically or geographically? Should it be?

Before the variable-oriented researcher can compute a single correlation assessing any possible connection between cultural differences and loss of life, the set of relevant cases must be well defined and delineated—it must be fixed. Once the set of relevant cases is established, conventional statistical techniques treat these cases as equivalent observations, like independent coin tosses. Thus, using these techniques presupposes a substantial degree of homogeneity among cases. Furthermore, once this population boundary is set, the question of homogeneity is typically not reopened. Any change in the boundary of the set of relevant observations would change the correlations among the variables used to characterize the cases included in the set. Fixing a population boundary in variable-oriented research tends to fix the assumption of case homogeneity as well. Thus, these procedures, which are central to this approach, mask the diversity of social phenomena, cloaking them in fixed "populations."

In diversity-oriented research, by contrast, population boundaries are not taken for granted, nor are they fixed. Instead, they are fluid.

They can be revised up until the very end of a research project, as the investigator's knowledge of cases grows and deepens. Furthermore, in the diversity-oriented approach researchers are ever-cognizant of the possibility that the sets they study may need to be disaggregated into types or kinds and studied separately. Thus, in this third type of cross-case analysis, investigators may disaggregate and differentiate, as in case-oriented research, but not to the point that every case seems unique.

The concept of diversity advanced here seeks both generality and complexity in the emphasis on the delineation and systematization of types, forms, trajectories, and paths. It avoids the homogenizing bias of the variable-oriented approach, evident in its dependence on fixed populations, and the particularizing bias of the case-oriented approach, evident in its tendency to focus almost exclusively on differences and thus highlight the specificity of each case.

Studying Diversity: Practical Considerations

In the remainder of this chapter, I offer a brief sketch of several of the core features of diversity-oriented methods. This discussion also serves as an overview of the balance of part 1 of *Fuzzy-Set Social Science,* culminating in chapter 5 with an application of the diversity-oriented approach to configurational data on set memberships, using Boolean algebra (i.e., crisp sets). In part 2 of this work, I use insights from fuzzy-set theory to broaden and deepen this approach. The end product is a methodology appropriate for studying social diversity in its varied forms and manifestations.

At first glance, the problem of studying diversity seems simply to recreate one of the basic dilemmas sketched at the beginning of this chapter—the difficulty of knowing a large number of cases in an in-depth manner. However, there are practical procedures useful for studying the diversity of cases that avoid the many homogenizing assumptions of the variable-oriented approach. To study the diversity of social phenomena it is necessary to formalize and extend several aspects of the case-oriented approach. Here, as before, I focus on practical aspects of constructing social scientific representations from empirical evidence on multiple cases. My goal in integrating these features into diversity-oriented research is to bring some of the logic and intensity of case-oriented research to investigations involving large numbers of cases. The basic problem is to examine similarities and differences across many cases while preserving the integrity of cases as complex configurations.

Diversity-oriented research borrows from case-oriented research the following features:

1. *Its understanding of cases as configurations:* In case-oriented research the different parts of a case are defined in relation to each other—in terms of the whole they form. For example, one aspect of a country's political system (e.g., its multiparty character) is understood in the context of other features of the country (e.g., its ethnic diversity). This way of approaching cases is not the same as using one aspect to "account for" another (e.g., as in using degree of ethnic diversity to explain why a multiparty system exists in some countries but not in others). It is a matter of interpretation: Having a multiparty system conveys different things about a political system depending on whether significant ethnic diversity exists. Similarly, at the individual level, the meaning of regular church attendance could be very different for those who are political activists versus those who are politically inert. In the configurational view, to change one important aspect of a case potentially alters the character of the case as a whole.

2. *Its view of populations as flexible, manipulable constructions:* Often in case-oriented work, a key research issue involves the conceptual identification of cases—what are they cases of? Rather then starting with a delineated population of observations or a sample drawn from a seemingly "known" population, the case-oriented researcher typically starts with orienting concepts and a handful of cases that, at first glance, seem relevant to the concepts. In the course of the research, there is often a reciprocal clarification of these concepts and of the boundaries of the empirical category of cases relevant to the concepts (Ragin 1994a; 1997). The set of relevant cases may shift substantially in the course of the research; it may subdivide into types; it may broaden; it may contract to a single case or even to a theoretical case. How the boundaries of this set change depends on the nature and direction of the dialogue between the researcher's ideas and his or her empirical evidence. The end product of such research is usually both empirically and theoretically relevant because empirical cases help researchers elaborate their theoretical ideas, which, in turn, deepen their understanding of their cases.

3. *Its emphasis on outcome-oriented investigation:* Case-oriented studies typically address specific qualitative changes in specific contexts. In some studies the qualitative changes are dramatic (e.g., countries with social revolutions, as in Skocpol 1979); in others the changes

emerge very slowly through time (e.g., countries experiencing similar historical transformations of certain institutional arrangements; see Bendix 1978). Very often the boundaries of an investigation are set initially by the universe of relevant qualitative changes (e.g., a study of instances of the emergence of strong national identities in postcolonial countries). Thus, case-oriented investigations are often outcome-oriented in the sense that the starting point of such studies is very often the identification of some qualitative change or aspect common to a set of cases. When case-oriented researchers confront diverse outcomes, a common practice is to grasp such diversity as divergent paths.[12]

4. *Its view of causation as conjunctural and heterogeneous:* In case-oriented investigations, explanations of outcomes typically cite combinations or "conjunctures" of causal conditions. The classic example of this kind of explanation is Weber's (1978) explanation of the conditions that combined to give rise to rational capitalism in the West, a causal conjuncture that Weber argued was unique. John Stuart Mill ([1843] 1967) called this type of causation *chemical* because the outcome, a qualitative change, results from a combination of causal conditions. In case-oriented social science, attention typically is directed toward understanding how the different causal conditions combine in each case to produce the outcome in question. A common finding is that different conditions combine in different and sometimes contradictory ways to produce the same outcome. Thus, an interest in causal heterogeneity often accompanies a conjunctural view of causation. There is no presumption that the same causal factors operate in the same way in all contexts and all cases. The effect of any particular causal condition may depend on the presence or absence of other conditions, and several different conditions may satisfy a general causal requirement—that is, they may be causally equivalent at a more abstract level.

These practical features of case-oriented research, which are also central to diversity-oriented research, pose serious obstacles to the conduct of conventional variable-oriented social research:

The first feature—the idea that aspects of cases should not be viewed in isolation from each other—challenges conventional conceptions

12. When cases follow diverging paths from common origins, the researcher can use different paths to define types of cases and then examine similarities among cases following a given path and differences between sets of cases following alternate paths.

of the variable. In variable-oriented research, variables are typically viewed as analytically distinct and separable aspects of cases, and most statistical analyses assume that the meaning of a category or a value on a variable is more or less the same across all cases. The variable *years of education*, for example, should indicate the same thing for all cases. It should not indicate intellectual imprisonment for some and enlightenment for others—depending on these individuals' other characteristics. The idea that each aspect should be examined in the context of other aspects of the same case wreaks havoc on most variable-oriented analytic procedures because this principle suggests that apparent similarities (e.g., having twelve years of education) may be illusory.

The second feature challenges conventional notions about populations. In variable-oriented research, populations typically are seen as empirically given—for example, the population of a country as shown in a census—and are rarely contested. Furthermore, as previously noted, most variable-oriented techniques (such as correlation and regression analysis) are predicated on population and sample boundaries that are more or less fixed at the outset of data analysis. To vary the population boundary throughout an investigation, in effect allowing it to be flexible and to shift, poses a practical impossibility.

The third feature—the emphasis on outcome-oriented analysis— argues that researchers should begin their research by focusing on the best and clearest examples of whatever outcome they are interested in. (This practice dovetails with the emphasis on keeping population boundaries fluid and establishing them in the course of the research.) From the perspective of variable-oriented analysis, however, this strategy is equivalent to studying a dependent variable that has little or no variation—another practical impossibility. In case-oriented research relevant negative instances are difficult to identify until the positive instances are well known and understood (Ragin 1997). Thus, in this approach it is common first to study causal similarities and differences among only positive instances. In statistical parlance this amounts to selecting on the dependent variable—a sin to be avoided (Geddes 1990; King et al. 1994).

The fourth feature—the focus on causal conjunctures and causal heterogeneity—poses major obstacles to the use of additive-linear models, the metatheoretical foundation of most forms of variable-oriented analysis. The guiding principle of such models is that it is possible and useful to assess the independent effect of each causal variable, net of the effects of all other causal variables. The assessment of the relative importance of different causal variables is the primary basis for "theory testing" in the variable-oriented approach. However, if causation is complex and each outcome may result from various conjunctures of conditions, then it is impossible to estimate each cause's "independent" effect. In variable-oriented work, causal conjunctures are assessed through analysis of statistical interaction. But interaction models present intractable estimation and specification issues, especially when higher-order interactions are present, when the number of cases is modest, or when their diversity is limited (Ragin 1987).

The many obstacles to variable-oriented analysis posed by these practical features of case-oriented work exist for one simple reason: *Conventional variable-oriented analysis is predicated on very powerful and consequential homogenizing assumptions.* These homogenizing assumptions are clearly visible in the understandings of cases, variables, populations, and causes that form the core of the variable-oriented approach, at least as it is conventionally practiced. As I show in the remainder of part 1, diversity-oriented research incorporates key features of the case-oriented approach precisely to avoid these homogenizing assumptions. To make such assumptions in social research seriously undermines the study of the diversity.

TWO

CONSTITUTING POPULATIONS

The social scientist finds himself in continuous effort to combine two ideals: vision and precision. Clearly, he needs precise instruments if he wants to develop testable propositions. But the social world is very complex and doesn't provide us with the well delineated objects from which the natural sciences start. Thus, he also needs a great deal of creative imagination—of vision—to decide on the objects about which such propositions should be developed.
—Lazarsfeld, foreword to *Constructive Typology and Social Theory*

THE CENTRALITY OF POPULATIONS TO
CONVENTIONAL SOCIAL SCIENCE

The most common form of social science involves the examination of patterns across multiple cases, "cross case analysis." A researcher studying wars might investigate hundreds of wars; a demographer studying divorce might survey thousands of couples; an ethnographer interested in professional athletics might interview and observe dozens of athletes in a variety of sports. In variable-oriented work multiple instances of "the same thing" are highly valued because they create the possibility of quantitative analysis and statistical inference—if cases are plentiful and sampling is adequate. A quantitative analysis of wars, for example, might show that the greater the cultural differences between the opposing sides, the greater the loss of life, controlling for the effects of other relevant causal conditions. If observed, this pattern would have an important impact on social scientists' view of war, and it could become a key element in their representations of the phenomenon. Cross-case analysis is also central to many types of case-oriented work. An ethnographic researcher, for example, might observe a variety of street vendors in order to construct a composite portrait of street vending and its place in the urban economy. He would construct his portrait from similarities and differences observed among many street vendors.

The investigation of cross-case patterns presupposes two interconnected research acts: (1) formulating a clear definition of what is a "case" or "instance" and (2) specifying the empirical boundaries of the set of cases relevant to an investigation—the population. Consider an analogy from medicine. A researcher wants to assess the effectiveness of a drug in alleviating the symptoms of a particular disease. To conduct this test, the researcher must be confident that the drug is administered to patients with the disease in question and therefore must know which patients have the disease.[1] How can this be accomplished? First, the disease itself must be clearly defined and identified as a singular phenomenon. Second, the patients included in the study must be diagnosed correctly, as equivalent, comparable instances of the disease. Correct diagnosis is often a problem in medicine, especially given the considerable overlap in the symptomatology of diseases. If there are several diseases with roughly the same symptoms and patients with different diseases are unwittingly included in the same study, then the test of the effectiveness of the drug will be greatly compromised. Very often, the invalidity of tests in such situations is unknown to researchers.[2]

Any science based on the examination of patterns observed across multiple instances faces these problems. The systematic analysis of cross-case patterns presupposes the delineation of a set of relevant observations. There is a clear tension, however, between defining and delimiting (i.e., "constituting") populations and studying diversity. As explained in chapter 1, to study diversity is to attend to heterogeneity and difference, especially to differences in kind. Studies that attend to diversity usually start with the assumption that cases that seem to

---

1. Actually, the drug and a placebo would be administered in a double-blind manner to patients with the disease. This aspect of the research design is irrelevant to the present discussion.

2. Even when diagnosis is more or less straightforward, there may be additional problems due to unrecognized heterogeneity, which may compromise or invalidate findings. For example, for many years research on heart attacks was conducted almost exclusively on men, and it was generally assumed that the findings from these studies were relevant to women as well. But men and women differ in severity of heart attacks. Men have more attacks, but women have a much higher rate of mortality from heart attacks. Today it is recognized that researchers should take these important gender differences into account.

be similar, comparable instances of the same thing—at least at first glance—actually may be quite different. In fact, to attend to diversity, researchers often must problematize the populations, the zones of homogeneity, that others have constructed. The tension between constructing populations and studying diversity revolves around this simple contradiction: To constitute a population, researchers focus on similarities; to attend to diversity, they focus on differences, with an eye toward deconstructing previously constituted populations.

This chapter explores the tensions between constructing populations and studying diversity. I focus especially on the contrasts between the use of populations in variable-oriented and case-oriented research. I first examine conventional understandings and practices in variable-oriented research, where populations are often treated as "given." I argue that because populations tend to be fixed at the outset of this type of research and are rarely revised in the course of an investigation, a great deal of diversity may go undetected. Consequently, differences in kind may be relegated to the error vector of probabilistic models. Next, I examine two types of case-oriented social science—case-study research (i.e., single case studies) and comparative case-study research. In case-study research, investigators are often centrally concerned simply with identifying their case—specifying what "it" is a "case" of (Platt 1988, 1992). When a case is examined in-depth, it often presents a rich array of possible substantive conclusions, depending on which larger population of relevant cases the researcher invokes. In comparative case-study research, researchers move back and forth between their ideas and their evidence. They form populations by progressively refining the empirical boundary of the set of relevant observations while at the same time clarifying the concepts guiding the investigation. In comparative case-study research, the population relevant to an investigation may not be fully formed and delimited until the research is virtually complete.

Diversity-oriented research follows the lead of case-oriented research in problematizing populations and emphasizing their constructed nature. Populations are viewed as no more than working hypotheses and are open to revision in the course of an investigation.

POPULATIONS IN VARIABLE-ORIENTED RESEARCH

Most types of variable-oriented social science are acutely dependent on fully formed populations. The quintessential variable-oriented research act is to compute the strength of the correlation between two variables across a set of cases. Before any calculations can take place, however, it is necessary first to determine which data points should be included—to define and delimit the set of relevant cases. This set is typically conceived as a population, a subpopulation, or a sample drawn from a population or subpopulation. Thus, having a reasonably well-delimited population is a precondition for the quantitative analysis of cross-case patterns.[3] Once constituted by the researcher, a population is treated as an analytic space containing "like objects"—comparable, substitutable, independent instances of "the same thing." Cross-case analysis of such instances culminates in a representation of patterns that holds for the members of the population.

The concept of population is rarely problematized in variable-oriented research. In this approach, most populations are seen simply as empirically given. The resident human population of a country or some other territorially defined unit is the typical starting point of an investigation. Social scientists sample from such populations or from relevant subpopulations (e.g., persons gainfully employed, voters, households, small businesses, welfare recipients), and data sets are constructed from such samples. If the concept of population is addressed at all in research of this type, it is usually only in relation to the sample: whether the sample drawn by the researcher is adequate for generalizing about the population the researcher wishes to invoke—the "target" population. For example, is a sample drawn from Chicago households with telephones adequate for generalizing on all Chicago households? And if so, is this sample adequate for generalizing beyond Chicago—to the households that populate other large cities in the United States, "like" Chicago?

Given populations are especially favored in conventional variable-oriented research because such populations are already empirically and socially delimited. That is, they are preconstituted: adults in the United States, member nations of the U.N., small businesses in Peoria, and so on. The substantive significance of given populations typically justifies their use. This practice dovetails with the needs of governments, large corporations, and other large organizations (e.g., foundations and international agencies). It is no accident that the most advanced techniques for sampling from and generalizing to given populations have been

3. When social researchers constitute populations, differentiating relevant from irrelevant phenomena, they make important qualitative distinctions. Thus, the constitution of populations is one of the *qualitative* foundations of quantitative research.

developed by government census bureaus and related offices, marketing research firms and agencies, and those involved in the game of winning elections. Census bureaus and other statistical offices serve the practical needs of government agencies; marketing firms serve those who are in the business of making profits in large markets; political polls serve the needs of those who wish to win elected office; and so on.

It is both fortuitous and unfortunate that there are so many substantively significant, empirically delimited, given populations. On the one hand, because there are many populations of this type, there is a lot for empirically oriented social scientists to study, especially those who work for large organizations interested in controlling or simply knowing about their clients or constituencies. There is also a lot of work for those who oppose these powerful organizations. Opposition groups pursue their objectives in many of the same arenas as their foes, and when they do, they often must use the same tools. On the other hand, however, the ready availability of preconstituted populations obscures important aspects of the concept.

While many populations are preconstituted (e.g., a census of the U.S. population), many more must be theoretically defined and constituted by the researcher because they are not given in any simple or straightforward way. In fact, it is often very difficult to define and delimit the set of cases relevant to a question. Consider, for example, a study of "IMF riots"—violent protest against austerity measures mandated by the International Monetary Fund (Walton and Ragin 1990). Suppose a researcher is interested in the relationship between the class composition of those engaged in these riots, on the one hand, and the amount of looting and property damage that resulted, on the other. To investigate this question, the researcher would first constitute a set of relevant IMF riots as comparable cases—he would construct a population of such riots. But what is an IMF riot? Should orderly demonstrations that briefly got out of hand be included? What about labor strikes that became violent? What about ongoing armed struggles that were made more intense once austerity measures were announced? What if a massive outbreak was just starting, but quick and decisive action by the police and army neutralized it—was it a riot? What if there was a small riot, involving only fifteen or twenty people and only minor property damage occurred—was it a riot? How should IMF riot, once defined, be delimited temporally and geographically—and should it be? Before the researcher can compute a single correlation assessing any possible connection between aspects of IMF riots, the set of relevant cases must be established. Different ways of defining and delimiting IMF riots would lead to different population boundaries and ultimately to different findings.

Consider another example, a "partially given" population: Suppose the United States experienced a wave of race riots in many of its major cities following some precipitating event of national significance. As part of an effort to explain the riots, a researcher will try to identify what distinguishing features the cities with race riots shared and whether they differed systematically from the cities without riots.[4] One of the very first analytic issues that the researcher would have to address in this investigation would be the definition and specification of the set of cities relevant to the analysis. Because the goal is to explain why some cities had riots and some did not, it would be necessary to have both kinds of cities in the analysis. It is a relatively straightforward matter to identify "positive cases" (the cities with riots). After all, they were all "major" cities, and newspaper accounts would provide an easy list. But which cities without riots should be included for comparison, and how many?

Assume there were many "major" cities without riots. Should the population for this analysis be defined as "major cities in the United States," and, if so, how should the researcher define and operationalize *major*? Number of residents? Political or economic importance? Should all state capitals be included? And what about medium-sized cities with major manufacturing centers in them? The operationalization of *major* is neither obvious nor straightforward, and different ways of operationalizing it would yield different sets of "negative cases" (major cities without riots) to compare statistically with the positive cases.

Researchers familiar with this issue know all too well that shifting the boundary of the set of negative cases often alters the results of the statistical analysis, sometimes in profound ways. For example, assume race riots occurred in a substantial subset of large cities but not in medium-sized or small cities (defined in terms of number of residents). If the investigator were to define the relevant population of observations as "all cities in the U.S." (which would include large, medium-sized, and small cities), then one of the best predictors, and perhaps the only strong predictor, of riots would be city size, as indicated by

---

4. Of course, this researcher might be interested not only in the differences between cities with riots and cities without riots, but also in the varying intensity of riots across cities that experienced them. In Tobit analyses (Phelps 1976), these two kinds of questions can be joined.

the number of residents. But is city size a predictor of riots or should it be used to delimit a smaller, more uniform population of observations?[5] Is it reasonable for the definition of the population to determine the major finding?

Of course, there are various solutions to this problem, some practical and some technical. The point is simply that it is not always a straightforward or simple matter to delimit a population empirically, even when the population in question seems to be clearly anchored in substantive concerns (e.g., a wave of race riots). It is important to recognize further that the way in which populations are defined and delimited has a substantial impact on findings.

More generally, populations that are shaped by the theoretical interests that social scientists bring to their research (e.g., an interest in elites or bureaucracies) are often the most difficult to define and delimit. These populations are less "given" than the populations delimited by governmental and other corporate actors (e.g., the population of "registered voters"), and thus their boundaries are more open to debate. The point here is *not* that some populations are preconstituted for social scientists by large organizations and corporate actors and some are constituted by social scientists. To a very large degree all populations are socially constituted. Consider the population of adult males. What is an adult? What is a male? Consider the population of families. What is a family (Gubrium and Holstein 1990)? Rather, the point is that the populations that are most decisive from the perspective of social theory may be the most difficult to constitute.

ANALYTIC CONSEQUENCES

Not only is it important to recognize that populations must be defined and delimited before variable-oriented research can proceed, it is also important to understand the analytic consequences of this dependence on prior constitution. Two consequences are especially pertinent to the

5. In other words, is city size an explanatory variable or a "scope condition" (Walker and Cohen 1985)? In conventional social science the distinction between explanatory variables and scope conditions is crucially important, but it is rarely treated as problematic. As noted, in this approach, most populations are seen as *empirically* given or as merely convenient. They are only occasionally contested. Explanatory variables, by contrast, are thought to be based in the researchers' theoretical ideas about the phenomena they seek to explain and are more open to contestation.

issue of diversity and how to study it: the problem of unrecognized heterogeneity and the related problem of inflexibility.

Unrecognized heterogeneity. The first consequence of the dependence on prior constitution follows directly from the fact that the analysis of differences (i.e., cross-case patterns) must come after the delimiting of populations in variable-oriented work. Sometimes populations contain subgroups that are so distinct that they should be treated as analytically separate populations, not as members of the same population. Often, this mixing of different kinds of cases in the same population is missed by the investigator because this heterogeneity is mistaken for the play of random forces that are always present in social phenomena. Cases may be treated simply as "deviant" if they display low probability outcomes, when in fact they belong to qualitatively distinct populations that, in turn, warrant separate analysis. Thus, the researcher may relegate unrecognized heterogeneity to the error vector of probabilistic models when it should be conceived, if properly recognized, as multiple populations (i.e., as diversity).[6]

Inflexibility. The second consequence of prior constitution compounds the problems posed by the first. Recall that a population is typically conceptualized as a zone of homogeneity, an analytic space thought to contain like objects. Once delimited, the boundaries of a population tend to remain more or less fixed throughout a variable-oriented investigation. Any substantial change in the boundary of the set of relevant observations could alter the relations among key variables. For example, the decision to drop "wars lasting less than two years" from a study of the relationship between cultural distance and casualty rates in wars would almost certainly alter all relevant correlations. Thus, researchers tend to avoid changing their population's definition or boundaries in the middle of a research project. To do so would be to risk voiding all accumulated findings. Fixing a population boundary in variable-oriented research, therefore, tends to fix the assumption of homogeneity as well. The question of homogeneity is rarely reopened, and diversity may be hidden as a result.

The problems of unrecognized heterogeneity and inflexibility are important because of the close interplay between the constitution of populations and the analysis of the relationships among variables. In variable-oriented work researchers' understandings of constituted pop-

---

6. Researchers who study residuals in regression analysis are sometimes able to uncover heterogeneity, but this route is not fail-safe. Cases can reside very close to a regression line even in the face of severe specification errors.

ulations usually entail the assumption of *causal homogeneity*—the idea that causal factors operate in the same way for all cases. After all, the members of a population are understood as substitutable instances. It is reasonable, in this light, to assume that causal conditions operate in more or less the same manner in each case. When there is causal homogeneity within a population, the effect of a causal factor (e.g., presence/absence of college degree) on an outcome (e.g., income) is roughly the same for most cases (e.g., a positive increment, within a certain range). True, there will be cases that deviate from the general pattern visible across all cases, but this deviance is thought to exist because causal factors operate in a probabilistic manner, not because the population in question contains different "kinds" of cases (i.e., cases that rightly belong to separate populations).

For illustration of the interplay between the constitution of populations and causal analysis, consider again the researcher studying race riots in major U.S. cities. This time, assume that the problem of defining "major" cities has been resolved to everyone's satisfaction. Suppose further that riots in cities in the northern half of the United States were linked to economic conditions—the gap between Whites and Blacks, while riots in cities in the southern half were linked to political conditions—insufficient representation of African Americans in political institutions. Thus, the most important variable distinguishing major northern cities with riots from major northern cities without riots is the economic gap between Whites and Blacks. For major southern cities, however, the most important variable is the political representation of African Americans. Suppose also that this regional difference is unknown to the researcher and that he or she has no special reason to look for it.

More than likely, the analysis of major cities as a single population would show weak effects of economic gap and political representation on riots. In short, the strong impact of economic gap in the north would be diluted by its lack of impact in the south, while the strong impact of political representation in the South would be diluted by its lack of impact in the North. Thus, instead of producing strong, region-specific findings, the researcher would generate equivocal results—findings compromised by the heterogeneity of the population when constituted as a single data set. This researcher would conclude that economic gap and political representation have only modest effects on riots in major U.S. cities.

In this example, the effects of political versus economic conditions depends on context (South versus North). A contextual variable, like region in this example, mediates the relationship between other variables, altering the impact of explanatory variables on the outcome variable. Thus, the impact of political representation is not the same for all cases, nor is the impact of economic gap. When context plays an important part, as it does here, there is causal heterogeneity. When there is causal heterogeneity, the members of the researcher's population are not "substitutable instances of the same thing," at least when it comes to the causal conditions and outcome in question. The differences among cases may be strong enough to warrant conceiving them as distinct kinds of cases belonging to separate populations.

The pattern just described, where cities in the southern half of the United States differ from cities in the northern half of the United States with respect to the causes of riots, is simple and straightforward. A sharp researcher might catch it. Maybe a less sharp researcher who just happened to read the right newspaper accounts would look for the pattern and find it. But what if the pattern of contextual effects is very subtle or complex? What if there is a strong contextual variable that is unanticipated? Of course, it is impossible to examine the impact of contextual factors that cannot be anticipated or even imagined. Still, the point remains: Every population may contain, potentially at least, enough causal heterogeneity to undermine its constitution as a unitary entity.

The finding that a single population contains several different kinds of cases, as indicated by causal heterogeneity, poses difficult but not insurmountable obstacles to variable-oriented research. There are various technical procedures for dealing with this problem. The most common is to construct a variable that differentiates subpopulations and then to use this variable to condition or contextualize the effects of other variables. If the researcher in the example just elaborated, for example, had checked for regional differences using an interaction model of this type, he would have found these effects. The point of the example, however, is not to argue in favor of interaction models but rather to illustrate the interplay between the constitution of populations and causal analysis. More generally, the example shows that any examination of cross-case patterns is powerfully conditioned by the definition and constitution of the relevant population.

The assumption of causal homogeneity is the rule, not the exception, in variable-oriented work today.[7] It is firmly embedded in the linear,

---

7. In the not too distant past, researchers paid more attention to causal heterogeneity. Typically, these researchers used tabular method of data analysis, using techniques developed by Paul Lazarsfeld (see Merton, Coleman, and Rossi 1979).

additive models that provide the basis for most quantitative analyses. If the constitution of a population is undermined by evidence of causal heterogeneity, researchers must either reconstitute the population—thus voiding much of the progress in their investigation—or else abandon the assumption of causal homogeneity and the additive, linear models that depend on it. Thus, it is no surprise that once populations are constituted, researchers tend to avoid looking for causal heterogeneity. In the absence of a strong theory to guide the search for causal heterogeneity or at least prior evidence that it exists, the path of least resistance is to guard the boundaries of the population as originally constituted and remain faithful to the assumption of causal homogeneity. This path is especially attractive when researchers use populations that appear to be given.

POPULATIONS IN CASE-ORIENTED RESEARCH

The strongest challenge to the idea that populations are given comes from case-oriented social research. This amorphous category embraces a variety of research styles, ranging from ethnographers studying the on-going construction of meaning in everyday life to historically oriented scholars investigating large-scale phenomena such as wars and revolutions. In case-oriented research, populations are seen as working hypotheses that may be revised at any point in the research process. Thus, case-oriented work problematizes populations and emphasizes their constituted nature. This understanding of populations is clearly evident in case-study research, the most elemental form of case-oriented research, but it is also central to qualitative investigations of cross-case patterns, which I label comparative case-study research in the discussion that follows.

Case-Study Research

Case-study researchers base their conclusions not on the analysis of cross-case patterns but on in-depth investigation of a single case. A common concern in case-study research is to assess the larger sets or populations that the case under investigation belongs to: What is *this* case a case of (see Ragin and Becker 1992)? Thus, a major objective in most case studies is to consider the many potentially relevant populations a case might belong to and to evaluate its memberships. This assessment provides the basis for judging the general relevance of the case and for formulating statements about its empirical significance (Walton 1984, 1991, 1992; Wieviorka 1988, 1992).

The problem of identifying relevant populations is closely linked to the theoretical issues inspiring the research project. For example, the lifestyles of those in a particular religious community might call into question conventional sociological conceptions of the family; a series of political demonstrations might challenge the usual distinction between institutionalized and noninstitutional channels of political expression; and so on. Thus, in much case-study work, the question of populations is not simply an issue of classification (e.g., is this case an instance of social *or* political revolution?) but often one of theoretical advancement as well. Thus, studying a case in an in-depth manner not only clarifies the case and its theoretical relevance but also may provide a basis for refining or reconstructing theoretical categories (Amenta 1991; Bradshaw and Wallace 1991; Stake 1995; Yin 1994).[8]

For illustration of the nature of populations in case-study research, consider the following: A researcher studying an elementary school in St. Louis concludes that racial consciousness is highly developed among its students because of the strong link between race and class boundaries in this school. The African American children mostly come from lower- and working-class homes. The European American children mostly come from middle- and upper-middle-class homes. The researcher's implied causal argument is that the greater the correlation between race and class, the stronger the racial consciousness. Note that the researcher in this hypothetical study did not actually observe variation in the degree of race/class correlation or in the strength of racial consciousness. Rather, he observed that both were strong in a single case. Thus, the researcher's selection of the race/class correlation as the primary causal condition rests on the strength of corroborating ethnographic evidence, not on an observed pattern of covariation.

If asked, What is this case a case of? most case-oriented researchers would say that it is a case of strong racial consciousness among children. That is, they would emphasize the outcome. This understanding of the population locates this case in the set of instances of strong racial consciousness, which in turn might include not only schools, but also public settings, neighborhoods, and other places where people from different racial groups interact on a routine basis. Looking at the case study from this point of view, the implicit argument is that wherever

---

8. The fact that a case may belong to several different theoretically relevant populations may constitute its primary value as a case. Because of its multiple memberships, it may be uniquely well suited for addressing specific theoretical questions.

children display a high degree of racial consciousness, a careful observer is likely to find that it is fueled and perhaps engendered by the strong link between race and class in the setting. If an accumulation of case studies of instances of strong racial consciousness among children confirmed this link, then one could argue that a strong correlation between race and class is a condition for strong racial consciousness, perhaps even one of several *necessary* conditions (see chapter 4).

Relevant populations also can be constituted from causal conditions. Before addressing this issue, it is important to examine the hypothetical case study more closely, especially with respect to its causally relevant features. While it would be seductive to frame the study's argument monocausally (the greater the race/class coincidence, the stronger the racial consciousness), it would be simplistic to do so. In fact, there are several features of this case that could be considered causally relevant to its high level of racial consciousness, including aspects of its setting:

1. It is an elementary school (a prime location for acquiring racial consciousness in the United States).
2. It located in a racially heterogeneous urban area.
3. It has a substantial proportion of both African American and European American students.
4. There is a substantial link between race and class among the students in this school.

At the most basic level, the case-study researcher in this example would argue simply that settings that are *similar* to the one studied—with respect to relevant causal conditions—should exhibit strong racial consciousness. In essence, the argument would be that the conditions identified by the researcher are sufficient for racial consciousness. Notice, though, that in the extreme, the definition of *similarity* could be very strict, so much so that very few instances would qualify. For example, it could be argued that a strong correlation between race and class yields a high level of racial consciousness only when an elementary school in a racially heterogeneous urban area has 60% European American students and 40% African American students—the same as the racial composition of the school studied.

More typically, however, case-study researchers do not define similarity so narrowly. A common tack is to conceive causally relevant conditions as a set of concentric circles, with the broadest, most inclusive condition constituting the largest potential population, and the least inclusive combination of causal condition constituting the smallest potential population. For example, using the causally relevant conditions just listed, the implied argument, "the greater the race/class coincidence, the stronger the racial consciousness" could be true for the following:

1. elementary schools;
2. elementary schools in racially heterogeneous urban areas; or
3. elementary schools in racially heterogeneous urban area that also enroll a substantial proportion of both European American and African American students.

The first set is the broadest and most inclusive; the third is the least inclusive. Of course, this set of concentric circles could be extended in both a more inclusive or a less inclusive direction. For example, a set that is more inclusive than the first contains all settings where children of different races interact with each other on a routine basis (e.g., middle schools, church groups, summer camps, community centers—in addition to elementary schools). A set less inclusive than the third would be a set that incorporates more causally relevant conditions, increasing the similarity with the case studied. For example, suppose the faculty of the school studied is composed mostly of European Americans. A more narrowly circumscribed population would add "predominantly European American faculty" to the conditions specified in the third case.

Note that there is an interplay between population definition and causal analysis in case-study research. Any causally relevant feature of a case can be interpreted either as a condition for the operation of a cause or as a cause. If the feature is treated as a condition, it may become part of the definition of the population—the larger set of cases thought to be comparable to the case under investigation. If it is treated as a cause, then it becomes a central part of the investigator's argument and a key component of any hypothesis the researcher might draw from his or her case study. For example, it might be reasonable to see racial consciousness as a function of not only the correlation between race and class, but also as a function of racial composition. Perhaps the closer a school approximates a racial balance, the greater the racial consciousness. In this formulation there are two features treated as causal factors (race/class correlation and racial composition) and two that can be used to define the relevant population (elementary schools in racially heterogeneous urban areas).

Of course, there is no way to know from a single case which features are key causal factors and which should be used to define relevant populations. The investigator's theory and substantive knowledge must provide the necessary guidance. The central point is that case-study researchers may construct a variety of different populations as they decide how to frame the results of their research. Further, there is an array of possible populations, ranging from less inclusive ones, those that resemble the case under investigation in many respects, to very broad, inclusive populations, resembling the studied case in perhaps only one way. The entire process of case-study research—learning more about a case to see what lessons it has to offer—can be seen, in part, as an effort to specify the population or populations that are relevant to the case. When a case-study researcher completes a study and draws conclusions, these populations may be invoked explicitly or they may be implicated in various summary statements about the case. In short, there is a close link in case-study research between the constitution of populations and statements about the generality of its findings. Statements about generality, in turn, may be based on the outcome (and thus implicitly invoke arguments about necessary conditions) or about causes (and thus implicitly invoke arguments about sufficient conditions).

Comparative Case-Study Research

While the role of populations in case-study research offers a dramatic and powerful contrast with their place in variable-oriented research, a closer contrast is provided by the role of populations in case-oriented research concerned with multiple cases. This type of research shares with variable-oriented research the idea that knowledge can be derived directly from the study of cross-case patterns. In contrast with variable-oriented researchers, however, comparative case oriented researchers see cases as complex configurations of events and structures. They treat them as singular, whole entities purposefully selected, not as homogeneous observations drawn at random from a fixed population of equally plausible selections.

Most comparative case-study research starts with the deceptively simple idea that social phenomena in like settings (such as organizations, neighborhoods, cities, countries, regions, cultures) may parallel each other sufficiently to permit comparing and contrasting them. The clause "may parallel each other sufficiently" is a very important part of this formulation (Lijphart 1975; McMichael 1990). The researcher's specification of relevant cases at the start of an investigation is often nothing more than a working hypothesis that the cases initially selected are in fact alike enough to permit comparative analysis. In the course of the research, the investigator may decide otherwise and drop some cases, or even whole categories of cases, because they do not appear to belong with what seem to be the core cases. Sometimes, this process of sifting through cases leads to an enlargement of the set of relevant cases and a commensurate broadening of the scope of the guiding concepts. For example, a researcher might surmise in the course of studying "military coups" that the relevant category should be enlarged to include "irregular transfers of executive power."

This sifting of cases is usually carried on in conjunction with concept formation and elaboration (Bonnell 1980). Concepts are revised and refined as the boundary of the set of relevant cases is shifted and clarified. Important theoretical distinctions often emerge from this dialogue of ideas and evidence. Imagine, for example, that Theda Skocpol (1979) had originally included Mexico along with France, Russia, and China at the outset of her study of social revolutions. The search for commonalities across these four cases might prove too daunting. By eliminating Mexico as a case of *social* revolution in the course of the research, however, it would be possible to increase the homogeneity within the empirical category and, at the same time, to sharpen the definition of the concept of social revolution.

Thus, in much comparative case-study research, cases usually are not predetermined, nor are they "given" at the outset of an investigation. Instead, they often coalesce in the course of the research through a systematic dialogue between ideas and evidence (see also McMichael 1990, especially his discussion of Polanyi).[9] In many such studies, the conclusion of this process of "casing" (Ragin 1992) may be the primary and most important finding of the investigation (e.g., Wieviorka 1992). In comparative case-study research the boundary around the "sample of observations" must be relatively malleable throughout the investigation,

9. It should be emphasized that this process of refining categories and clarifying concepts is different from reformulating disproved theories to make them fit the evidence. King et al. (1994:21), for example, argue that it is not appropriate to "add a restrictive condition and then proceed as if our theory, with that qualification, has been shown to be correct." They offer as an example of their concern the researcher who starts with a theory that democracies do not go to war with each other, but then after inspection of the evidence alters the theory to fit the data and "hypothesizes" that only democracies with welfare states avoid going to war with each other. It is indeed questionable to modify a proposition in light of evidence and pretend that a theory has been proven. However, if this modification is instead part of an attempt to learn more about the world (e.g., an effort to clarify the set of countries that do not fight each other) and not a part of an explicit program of theory testing, it is completely reasonable.

and this boundary may not be fully fixed until the research is virtually complete. Thus, any cross-case pattern (say, the correlation between two variables across cases) is open to revision up until the conclusion of the research because the cases that comprise the sample may be revised continually before that point.

Because the constitution and selection of cases is central to comparative case-study inquiry, researchers may intentionally select cases that differ relatively little from each other with respect to the outcome under investigation. In other words, the initial population may be defined as all cases displaying some phenomenon of interest to the investigator. For example, a researcher might attempt to constitute the population of "anti-neocolonial revolutions," both empirically and conceptually (e.g., Wickham-Crowley 1991), through the process of reciprocal clarification just described. At the end of this process his or her set of cases might exclude both lesser uprisings (e.g., mere anti-neocolonial "rebellions") and mass insurrections of varying severity that were successfully repressed.

After constituting the category and selecting the relevant cases, the next step in comparative case-study research is to identify the causal conditions that the cases share. For example, assume the researcher studying anti-neocolonial revolutions observed that all countries experiencing such revolutions also had "high levels of foreign capital penetration" and "widespread abuse of human rights" before the revolution. These causal conditions might play a key part in his or her explanation of anti-neocolonial revolutions. More generally, the search for causal commonalities shared by positive cases (instances of anti-neocolonial revolutions in this example) provides important clues regarding *necessary* conditions for the phenomenon under investigation. (I discuss these ideas in detail in chapter 4.) It is important to emphasize that in this part of the investigation, the population boundary remains flexible. If the process of identifying causal factors proves too daunting, the researcher may shift the boundaries of the population or perhaps differentiate types of the phenomenon (e.g., types of anti-neocolonial revolutions) and search for causal commonalities within each type. More generally, there is a flexible interplay between the constitution of populations and causal analysis in comparative case-study research.

Once theoretically relevant causal commonalities have been identified, the investigator constructs a composite portrait of the phenomenon under investigation. While this portrait is a common endpoint in comparative case-study work, researchers also may constitute a population of negative cases to compare with the positive cases (as in

Wickham-Crowley 1991). Case-oriented researchers identify negative cases so that they can evaluate the *sufficiency* of the causal conditions identified in the study of positive cases. For example, suppose the study of positive instances of anti-neocolonial revolution revealed that foreign-capital penetration and widespread abuse of human rights are both necessary conditions. That is, they were found to be causal conditions in all relevant positive cases and were key elements in the investigator's composite portrait. Is this combination of conditions sufficient for anti-neocolonial revolutions? Sufficiency can be assessed by examining negative cases to see if there are instances of the causal factor (foreign-capital penetration coupled with widespread abuse of human rights). If so, then the causal factor or combination causal conditions in question, while arguably necessary for the outcome, is not sufficient. (See my discussion of necessary and sufficient conditions in chapter 4.)

The constitution of negative cases is usually much more difficult than the constitution of positive cases. Instead of clarifying and identifying instances of an empirical outcome, the researcher must identify relevant instances of its absence. Potentially, this category is infinite. For example, the United States in the late twentieth century is an instance of the absence of anti-neocolonial revolution, but it is a truly trivial instance of its absence. The constitution of positive cases provides the best clues for the constitution of negative cases. Essentially, the set of negative cases should include "countries with a strong possibility of anti-neocolonial revolutions." The best guide for defining this set is provided by analysis of the positive instances. Negative cases should resemble positive cases in as many ways as possible, especially with respect to the commonalities exhibited by the positive cases. Thus, the specification of negative cases rests on the prior constitution of positive cases (Ragin 1997).

The examination of negative cases may prompt the investigator to rethink the constitution of his or her population. For example, if there are many negative cases that strongly resemble the positive cases with respect to causal conditions, the researcher might ask, Is there some alternate outcome that is equivalent in some way to an anti-neocolonial revolution? Perhaps the original set of positive cases should be enlarged to include this other outcome. Alternatively, the examination of negative cases might motivate the researcher to define the outcome of interest more narrowly, perhaps restricting the primary research focus to only the most extreme cases (e.g., the most violent and protracted anti-neocolonial revolutions). These changes in the boundaries of the positive and negative cases interact at each step of the analysis with the study of causal conditions.

The constitution of populations in comparative case-study research is a theory-laden, concept-intensive process that often involves an elaborate dialogue between ideas and evidence. Populations may be reconstituted at any phase of the research process: when positive cases are selected, when positive cases are compared with each other, when negative cases are selected, and when negative and positive cases are compared. In the end, populations and causal arguments coevolve, so much so that they could be described as mutually reinforcing.

POPULATIONS AS SCOPE CONDITIONS

Despite the many differences in how populations are conceived and constructed in variable- and case-oriented research, there are two commonalities that should not be overlooked. The first is the simple fact that in both approaches populations establish important *qualitative* distinctions. It does not matter at what point in the research process they are constituted—prior to cross-case analysis, as in most variable-oriented research, or near the end, as in much case-oriented research—population boundaries provide qualitative foundations for social scientific statements. They demarcate part of the empirical world as "relevant" and bracket out the rest. Second, in all forms of social research, including case-study research, there is an interplay between the constitution of populations and causal analysis. In variable-oriented research this interplay can be seen in the problem of constituting "quasi-given" populations (e.g., the population of "major cities," as discussed previously). In case-study research this interplay is apparent in the analytic flexibility surrounding the process of drawing general lessons from a single case. In comparative case-study research this interplay pervades the analysis of causal conditions shared by positive cases as well as the comparison of positive and negative cases.

These two similarities exist because populations function as "scope conditions" in many forms of social research (Walker and Cohen 1985). Scope conditions state the circumstances under which a pattern or relationship holds. They can be formulated as simple logical statements with the general form

$$\text{If } A, \text{ then } X \rightarrow Y,$$

where A is a condition or set of conditions that must be met for some relationship between X and Y to hold. In the study of the link between

X and Y, A does not vary because all cases included in the study must meet condition A. A establishes not only the scope of the relationship between X and Y, it also provides the basis for the claim that the cases included in the analysis are comparable and that it is therefore reasonable to use them to construct statements about cross-case patterns. In a variable-oriented study of the link between years of education (X) and wages (Y), for example, A might be "full-time employed adults in the United States in 1990." In a case-oriented study of the link between "widespread human rights abuses coupled with high levels of foreign investment" (X) and "anti-neocolonial revolution" (Y), A might be "less-developed countries that are plausible candidates for anti-neocolonial revolution, displaying at least one of its hypothesized causal conditions."

By viewing populations as scope conditions, it is possible to see why it is sometimes the case that one researcher's scope condition is another's causal condition. For example, in the cross-national study of welfare states, several scholars (e.g., Cameron 1978; Stephens 1979; Esping-Andersen 1990) have argued that among the advanced industrial societies (scope condition), where left-leaning political parties are strong (causal condition), governments tend to establish more generous welfare programs (the outcome). However, other researchers (e.g., Cutright 1965; Wilensky 1975) have not limited their scope to the advanced industrial societies and instead studied "all countries" (a broader scope condition). They find that where economic development is most advanced (causal condition), governments tend to establish more generous welfare programs (the outcome). Is economic development a causal condition or a basis for delimiting scope? The answer to this question is that it depends. The determining factors are the theoretical and substantive interests of researchers.

POPULATIONS IN DIVERSITY-ORIENTED RESEARCH

From the perspective of diversity-oriented research, conventional population boundaries pose three major problems. The first problem is the fact that when researchers delimit populations, they may assume more homogeneity than is usually warranted. Most populations contain unknown amounts of unrecognized heterogeneity. The broader and more inclusive a population, the greater the likelihood that it contains forms of heterogeneity that undermine its constitution. The second problem is related to the first: Once established, population boundaries may become reified and may even ossify over time. For example, while the population of "advanced industrial, democratic countries" seems like a reasonable starting point for an investigation, to reify this category would impose great analytic distance between rich and poor countries, making them seem more and more like separate species. The third problem is the simple fact that membership in a population, or in any social category for that matter, may be partial. For example, in a survey of "married couples" researchers might have a difficult time identifying which couples are "really" married—living as together as partners—that is, if they took the time to problematize the constitution of this population.[10]

For these and other reasons, diversity-oriented research shares with case-oriented research the view that populations are working hypotheses that may be revised at any point in the research process. Populations should remain as flexible as possible because they often mask heterogeneity. Furthermore, because populations are, in effect, assertions of sameness, they should be invoked only after the researcher has amassed evidence that such assertions are in fact justified. Diversity-oriented researchers problematize the constitution of populations throughout the research process. The next chapter shows that this is accomplished in part by viewing cases as configurations and allowing for the possibility that a single difference between two cases may be grounds for establishing a qualitative distinction—a difference in kind.

10. Typically, problems in the constitution of such populations get entangled with the models researchers use to examine cross-case patterns. For example, a researcher working with a given population of married couples might want to control for "strength of marital bond" (additively) in an analysis of the relationship between proportional contribution to total family income and the gendering of household tasks. However, this strategy does not solve the problem of varying degrees of membership in the relevant population; it simply gives the appearance of having addressed the problem.

THREE

STUDYING CASES AS CONFIGURATIONS

. . . the meaning of a low export ratio for Bohemia, a small country surrounded by the rest of the European world-economy, and a similar low ratio for Russia, a large empire on the edge of the European world-economy, must have been quite different. Bohemia's freedom of political action was ultimately far smaller and hence her economic dependence ultimately far greater.

—Wallerstein, *The Modern World-System*

INTRODUCTION

Social scientists who use conventional variable-oriented methods are not especially fond of arguments like the one just quoted. Essentially, Wallerstein is arguing that even though two cases (Bohemia and Russia in the sixteenth century) had roughly the same scores on a key variable (value of exports relative to the value of total domestic production— a key indicator of trade dependence), the interpretation of the data is different. The meaning of these scores is shaped by context—by other features of the cases in which these two, more or less identical scores are embedded. From the perspective of variable-oriented social science, the idea that a score must be interpreted *in context* essentially argues against the common view that aspects of cases can be evaluated separately from each other, especially with respect to their "independent" causal effects on some outcome. Indeed, the logic of conventional variable-oriented social science is explicitly organized around isolating the effect of each causal variable—estimating its effect on some outcome, net of the effects of competing variables.

Imagine a survey researcher arguing that an age of "65 or older" means very different things for different people, depending on other relevant features, among them gender, race, religion, and social class. This position would put an end to the common practice of treating age as an "independent" variable and estimating its separate or "unique" impact on relevant outcomes—for example, its net impact on voting preferences, net of the effects of other relevant causal variables. Following the line of reasoning indicated in the epigram at the beginning of this chapter, we would expect to find that the impact of age on voting preferences depends on context—on other relevant aspects of each voter. For some individuals being "65 or older" might make them more conservative; it might make others more liberal; it might make others more apathetic; it might have no impact on others; and so on.

Conventional variable-oriented research usually does not pay close attention to the context of a score on a variable. Consider the usual approach to measurement: First, the researcher identifies important features of cases—key dimensions of cross-case variation. A researcher studying the world economy, for example, might identify as one such aspect the degree to which different countries participate in international trade. Next, the researcher develops a measure or indicator of this feature and then proceeds to derive a score for each case. In this example, the researcher might use a common indicator such as the ratio of the value of exports to the value of gross domestic product (GDP) for each country. After obtaining scores for all relevant countries, the investigator then computes an average score and uses this measure of central tendency to define which countries have "low" scores and which countries have "high" scores. In this approach, countries well above the mean have "high" scores; countries well below the mean have "low" scores.

The notion of assessing scores *in context,* indicated in the epigram, challenges the conventional practice of equating cases with similar scores on a given variable. According to this alternate reasoning, two cases can have identically "high" or identically "low" scores, but without looking at each score's context, it would be very hazardous to equate them.[1] At its core, this alternate view questions an implicit assumption

1. Actually, most conventional variable-oriented methods are even less anchored in context than my discussion indicates. These methods not only equate similar scores, they also equate similar differences between scores. For example, a $1,000 difference in GNP per capita is treated as the same regardless of where it occurs in the range of GNP per capita values. Thus, the differences between $500 and $1500 in GNP per capita is equated, in causal impact, to the difference between $14,000 and $15,000. Anyone who has toured both less developed and more developed countries knows that the first difference is dramatic; the second is trivial.

of the variable-oriented approach: that the cases included in a sample are homogeneous enough to permit equating similar scores. Looking at each score's context provides a way to evaluate the assumption of homogeneity that is often entailed in the constitution of conventional populations and samples (e.g., the common practice of treating a set of "countries" as a sample). Returning to the epigram, it is clear that Wallerstein is arguing that it is hazardous to equate these two countries' low scores precisely because the two cases belong to different populations of countries. That is, considering their contrasting size and geographic location, they can be seen as different kinds of cases.

The principle that "context matters" is central to the configurational approach to cases. As noted in chapter 1, one of the key features of case-oriented research is its attention to cases as configurations of aspects, conceived as set memberships. As I show in this chapter, a configurational understanding of cases is central to diversity-oriented research. To view each case as a configuration, it is necessary to examine relevant aspects of a case all at once, as an interpretable combination of elements.

I develop this idea of cases as configurations first by presenting an overview of the understanding of cases that is integral to the single-case study. This research strategy typically refrains from explicit cross-case comparisons and instead emphasizes how aspects of a single case interconnect. I then extend the idea of configurational analysis to the study of multiple cases and show the link between looking at cases as configurations and studying their diversity. The key to understanding cases as configurations is to view them in terms of the different *combinations* of relevant attributes they exhibit. By grouping cases into a relatively small number of configurations of attributes, the researcher establishes a basis for specifying different "kinds" of cases. In this way, the researcher can understand types of cases as different configurations of attributes.

In the second half of this chapter I show how the idea of cases as configurations resonates with the "property space" approach to typology construction first advocated by Paul Lazarsfeld in the 1930s. In essence, Lazarsfeld (1937), and later Allen Barton (1955), advocated a configurational approach to the problem of reducing the complexity of social phenomena (see also Lazarsfeld and Rosenberg 1955; Lazarsfeld et al. 1972). Their approach, in effect, allows a researcher to translate a multidimensional attribute space into a handful of types. I extend their approach by showing that it is possible to formalize their technique of "functional reduction." This formalization, in turn, provides important tools for interrogating property spaces, revealing the ways in which the diversity within a given property space may be "limited."

This chapter also provides a demonstration of the use of configurations as analytic units, an approach that is integral to diversity-oriented research. While I limit my focus to the use of presence/absence dichotomies in this chapter (and in all of part 1), in part 2 I demonstrate how to extend these principles to phenomena that also vary by level or degree, using fuzzy sets.

THE LOGIC OF CASE-STUDY RESEARCH

Many social scientists conduct case studies. This research strategy, in fact, may be the most common form of social scientific inquiry. It is by far the most popular research strategy in anthropology and history, and it is much more common in political science and sociology than most scholars realize (Feagin, Orum, and Sjoberg 1991). Many researchers, however, are reluctant to see their work as case-study research. After all, one of the central goals of social science is to generalize, and social scientists are trained to be wary of drawing general conclusions from a single case. What's one case? The empirical world displays a great deal of randomness and unpredictability, according to this reasoning. General lessons drawn from a single case, therefore, must be inherently suspect (Sjoberg et al. 1991).

Many studies of cross-case patterns appear to be based exclusively on the analysis of large Ns when in fact they are also case studies. A study of the changing relationship between income and single parenthood in the United States over the post–World War II period, for example, can be seen as a case study, even though it might involve quantitative analysis of census and survey data on thousands of households, each conceived as a separate "case" in the quantitative analysis. In the end, the study is also about the United States in the second half of the twentieth century, not just the many individuals and families included in the analysis.[2] More than likely, the explanation of the changing relation between income and single parenthood would focus on interrelated aspects of the United States over this period. For example, to explain the weakening link between low income and single parenthood the researcher might cite the changing status of women, the decline

2. Michael Burawoy (in Burawoy et al. 1991) has developed this expansive notion of case-study research in his concept of the "extended" case method. His own work (e.g., Burawoy 1979) exemplifies this strategy.

in the social significance of conventional family forms, the increase in divorce, the decrease in men's job security, and other changes occurring in the United States over this period.

The logic of the case study is fundamentally configurational. Different parts of the whole are understood in relation to one another and in terms of the total picture or package that they form. The central goal is usually to show how different "parts" of a case interconnect, for example, how a weakening of the link between low income and single parenthood connects with other changes in the United States over the second half of the twentieth century. The "parts" that case-study researchers examine can be quite varied: institutions, path dependencies, social structures, historical patterns and trends, routine practices, singular events, event sequences, connections to other cases, the case's larger environment, and so on. While case-study researchers are sometimes tempted to take this approach an additional step and argue that the case in question involves a unique configuration of parts and that it could be constituted in one and only one way, this additional step is usually unwarranted. What matters most is that the investigator makes sense of multiple aspects of the case in an encompassing manner, using his or her theory as a guide.

Donald Campbell (1975) offers a rough formalization of this approach in his ruminations on the logic of case-study research. At first glance, Campbell argues, the case study appears to be totally lacking in scientific merit because there is only one case to explain and many possible explanations to choose from. He notes, however, that case-study researchers often reject theories because they do not explain the facts of their case. Further, despite having only one case, they often must struggle to find theories that work (see also Walton 1992). Why is it so difficult? The key to this puzzle is the simple fact that every theory has many implications, relevant both to features of the case in question and to causal processes and sequences operating within the case. Thus, the case-study researcher evaluates many theoretical implications relevant to his or her case to see if the case conforms to expectations (King et al. 1994). Not all features of the case are compatible with the initial theory, and the case-study researcher must either find an alternate theory that works better, revise an existing theory, or propose an entirely new one (Walton 1992).

Campbell (1975) suggests that each separate theoretical implication can be seen as a separate "observation" for "testing" a theory. Thus, a single case becomes many observations—some contradicting and some supporting competing theories. Collectively, competing theories and their different implications define all theoretically relevant aspects of the case in question. The researcher's task is to see which theory does the best job of explaining aspects of the case relevant not only to its own implications but also to the implications of competing theories. Thus, after defining and selecting relevant aspects of the case, the case-study researcher assesses the explanatory power of each theory. The theory (or combination of compatible theories) that best covers both its own implications and those of competing theories prevails and provides the basis for the investigator's representation of the case.

In the end, the researcher crafts an explanation, embedded in his or her representation of the case, that satisfies as many theoretical implications as possible in a coherent manner. The success of a case study hinges on (1) the number of relevant aspects of the case the researcher can encompass with his or her explanation, (2) the success of the researcher in showing that his or her portrait of the case actually makes sense of all the aspects that he or she has deemed theoretically relevant, and (3) the agreement of other scholars that all relevant aspects of the case in question have, in fact, been addressed by the researcher in a convincing manner. Of course, the most successful case studies accomplish much more than theoretical and substantive coherence. They also may advance theory (Burawoy et al. 1991) or establish important lessons for policymakers. Still, theoretical and substantive coherence should be considered preconditions for these more ambitious goals (Yin 1994).

COHERENCE AND CONFIGURATIONS IN CASE-STUDY RESEARCH

Whenever a researcher investigates a case with an eye toward how the different parts or aspects of a case interconnect, the inquiry has a configurational character. The organizing idea in such research is that the parts of a case constitute a coherent whole—that they have an integrity and coherence considered together. For example, researchers who study family systems often find that patterns of interpersonal accommodation are so enmeshed that a "dysfunction" cannot be remedied without addressing many different aspects of the family all at once. Likewise, researchers who study cultures often observe that cultural traits come in packages that seem to defy disassembly. Such configurations do not defy analysis, per se, because they can be viewed in terms of interrelated parts or aspects.

Campbell's (1975) argument that case-study researchers test multiple theoretical implications underscores the configurational character of this type of research. Because theoretical implications direct the case-study researcher's attention to "observations" (i.e., different aspects of a single case) that cannot be independent of one another, the researcher must make sense of them all at once, as a package. Furthermore, because different theories typically have implications about different aspects of the case, the researcher's attention is directed to a broad range of aspects, all of which may be connected in some way. Thus, case-study researchers examine overlapping configurations of aspects as they weigh the relative explanatory power of competing theoretical perspectives.

Because of their configurational nature, case studies often have a house-of-cards quality. A configurational understanding of a case can fall apart all at once if contradictory evidence is introduced. A central principle of configurational thinking that is relevant to social scientific inquiry is the idea that the character of the "whole case" may change qualitatively if a single key part is altered or changed in some way. For example, the conventional portrait of the Holocaust during World War II as the obsession of Hitler and his inner circle crumbled for many scholars with the publication of Daniel Goldhagen's *Hitler's Willing Executioners: Ordinary Germans and the Holocaust* (1996). The conventional account could not assimilate Goldhagen's new evidence, and the whole portrait changed.

It follows from these observations on case-study research that this research strategy is extraordinarily theory-dependent. Theory is used to make sense of the case as a configuration of theoretically relevant aspects, which cohere as a package. This package, in turn, can be remarkably fragile: the strands of theory that bind it together can easily unravel. Because case studies are configurational, a change in the evidence on a single key aspect of a case can change the character of the whole qualitatively. In this light, the common charge that case-study research is merely descriptive appears ludicrous. While many case-study researchers keep their theories hidden or implicit, the entire enterprise is sheer chaos without some form of theoretical guidance.[3]

———

3. It is also possible to view the proposition that "the case is a coherent configuration" as a hypothesis that can be evaluated and refuted.

MULTIPLE CASES, MULTIPLE CONFIGURATIONS

The principles of configurational thinking just described are relevant to the study of social phenomena in general, not just to the study of single cases. However, most social scientists who conduct cross-case analyses adhere to the variable-oriented approach, which in turn tends to treat cases not as configurations of aspects but as collections of distinct, analytically separable attributes. In the conventional variable-oriented view, to change one aspect of a case results in a case that differs only slightly from the original, not one that may differ qualitatively. In short, the conventional variable-oriented approach eschews configurational thinking.

Consider, for example, the study of individual-level differences. In conventional variable-oriented research, cases are viewed as "different" when they differ on many aspects and "similar" when they differ on only a few. For example, two cases with mostly the same values on predictor variables receive roughly the same predicted values on the outcome variable in multiple regression analysis.[4] In this framework, similarity and difference can be assessed in a straightforward accounting manner. For example, a White, suburban, middle-class, male professional with three children and a mortgage who votes for the Republican Party differs by only a single trait from a person with all these same characteristics but who votes for the Socialist Labor Party. Thus, from a variable-oriented viewpoint, they are very similar. Still, it might be very different to be trapped in an elevator with one versus the other. This qualitative difference captures the essence of viewing cases as configurations: Two cases may be similar in most ways but because they differ on one or more key aspects, their difference may be one of kind, not simply one of degree.[5] Furthermore, if two cases do differ qualitatively, it is hazardous to equate their similarities. These configurational notions are foreign to variable-oriented social science, at least as it is conventionally practiced.

The de facto repudiation of configurational thinking is integral to variable-oriented research strategy. It is clearly evident in this strategy's

4. The multiple regression framework also allows "compensation," which makes it possible for cases that differ in counterbalancing ways to have the similar predicted values on the outcome variable.

5. It is important to emphasize that in the configurational approach a single difference has the potential to warrant a qualitative distinction. It is not the case, however, that every difference justifies a qualitative distinction.

approach to the analysis of cross-case patterns. When confronted with more than a handful of cases, most researchers simply abandon the idea of cases as interpretable configurations and instead search for cross-case patterns. The search for cross-case patterns is usually correlational: researchers try to see if aspects of cases, conceived as variables, correlate. For example, a researcher might ask, ignoring Wallerstein's warnings, whether countries that are less trade-dependent have more political autonomy (i.e., from the countries that dominate the world economy) than countries that are more trade-dependent. This researcher would devise measures of both variables (trade dependence and political autonomy) and then assess their correlation across a range of countries to see if a strong inverse relation exists. Following Wallerstein's argument, however, one might object to this analysis because it ignores the different contexts of countries' scores on these variables and thus may equate scores that should not be equated.

The problem just sketched is *not* that the analysis, as described, is merely bivariate. In other words, the ignorance of context could not be remedied by controlling for the effects of country size and location on autonomy in a multivariate analysis of the impact of trade dependence on autonomy. To control for the effects of country size and location on autonomy does not address the core issue because the basic idea behind configurational thinking is that aspects of cases should be examined together, as packages.[6] By viewing aspects of cases configurationally, it is possible to assess whether the impact of similar scores (e.g., degree of trade dependence) on some outcome (e.g., political autonomy) differs by context.

It is important to detail, at this juncture, how a configurational approach differs from a conventional variable-oriented approach in its conception of cases and variables. In its most basic form, the idea of viewing cases as configurations can be captured by examining different combinations of values on relevant variables and treating each combination of values as a potentially different type of case. Consider the following illustration, which builds on the discussion of export dependence, country size, and country location. To keep the illustration sim-

6. For readers familiar with the language of statistical analysis, my argument here is that to study cases as configurations, it is necessary to start with a model of saturated interaction, using all relevant variables, and then to simplify this model in a top-down manner. In most social research, such models are very difficult to estimate, and when they can be estimated, they are very difficult to interpret. Typically, the interaction terms are highly collinear with each other and many different interaction models may fit a given data set equally well.

Table 3.1
From Variables to Types

Country Type	Variable		
	EXPORT RATIO	SIZE	LOCATION
A	Low	Small	Close
B	Low	Small	Far
C	Low	Large	Close
D	Low	Large	Far
E	High	Small	Close
F	High	Small	Far
G	High	Large	Close
H	High	Large	Far

ple, assume that the main causally relevant aspects of interest (export ratio, country size, and location) are all dichotomies. Thus, export ratio is either "high" or "low;" size is either "small" or "large"; and location is either "close to" or "far from" the core of the world economy. With three dichotomies, there are 2^3 (i.e., 8) logically possible combinations of values. The key to configurational thinking is to see these eight combinations of values as providing the basis for differentiating eight different kinds of cases, which, in turn, may constitute eight different "populations." In other words, from a configurational perspective the analysis of country characteristics just described involves not three independent variables, but eight configurations conceived as types of cases. The transformation of these three variables into eight types of cases is shown in table 3.1.

In this alternate conception of the relevant analytic space, Wallerstein's Bohemia is type A and his Russia is type D. That is, these two countries are treated as distinct kinds of countries, not as two countries that have similarly low export ratios, while differing in size and location. In this scheme a type-A country (low export ratio, small size, close to core) may be as different from a type-B country (low export ratio, small size, far from core) as it is from a type-H country (high export ratio, large size, far from core), even though a type-A country differs by only one attribute from a type-B country, while it differs by three attributes from a type-H country.

This view of cases as configurations implements the key principle of configurational thinking previously sketched—the idea that a single difference between two cases may constitute a difference in kind. Table 3.1 shows that by delineating all possible combinations of values of the relevant variables it is possible to specify different configurations, which in turn establishes a framework for delineating types of cases.[7] Thus to study cases as configurations it is not necessary to abandon variables altogether. Rather, it is necessary simply to abandon the idea that variables should be seen as independent, separable aspects of cases. Instead, variables should be seen as the components of configurations.

THE LINK BETWEEN STUDYING CONFIGURATIONS AND STUDYING DIVERSITY

While the configurational understanding of cases has its roots in case-oriented research and the study of small Ns, it is integral as well to diversity-oriented research. As explained in chapter 1, diversity-oriented research lies midway between studying general patterns across "all" relevant cases (conceived as homogeneous members of a single population), on the one hand, and attending to the complexity of a specific case or a narrowly circumscribed set of cases, on the other. To study diversity is to allow for the possibility that the cases included in a study differ by type or kind. As just demonstrated, the study of cases as configurations provides a useful framework for the specification of types. In this approach, conventional variables are conceived as raw material for delineating types, not as analytically distinct, independent attributes.

In diversity-oriented research, investigators are ever-conscious of the possibility that similarities among cases may be illusory. At first glance, the cases included in a study may seem similar, as different instances of the same general phenomenon. In the course of the research, however, focusing on configurational differences among cases may challenge the initial perception that the cases are all of the same kind. Instead, the researcher may differentiate types of cases. Attending to diversity thus involves careful consideration of the possibility that cases differ by type or kind, not merely by level or degree.

For example, consider a researcher studying gender and work in twenty microelectronic assembly plants in southeast Asia.[8] The initial impression might be that women are exploited everywhere, with modest variation in the degree or intensity of their exploitation. Close examination of these twenty cases with an eye toward their diversity,

---

7. As I show in part 2, this approach is not limited to dichotomies. Using fuzzy sets, it is possible to assess the degree to which each case conforms to each configuration and to use this information to evaluate causal conditions.

8. This example draws inspiration from the work of Leslie Salzinger (1997).

however, might challenge this simplistic conclusion. For example, the twenty plants might differ in how gender is intertwined with the labor process. In some factories, anarchy on the shop floor may permit men to dominate women and keep them in subordinate work roles. In others, management may hire women for production tasks and men for supervisory roles and then consciously manipulate traditional gender roles to motivate women to work harder. Examination of the remaining plants might reveal other distinct ways of manipulating gender in the workplace. All twenty might still be seen as instances of gender exploitation, and one could arguably rank them according to degree of gender exploitation. But the key finding in a study emphasizing diversity would be the different ways of gendering work exhibited by these cases. The conclusion would be that different ways of organizing work—conceived as configurations of hiring, shop floor, and other practices—give rise to different forms of gender exploitation.

In practical terms, this study would proceed simultaneously as a set of case studies and as a search for clusters of commonalities across subsets of cases. The researcher would use available theories to identify theoretically important aspects of assembly plants, especially those features relevant to the gendering of work. Examination of specific cases would help the researcher pinpoint the most important features of cases and prod him or her to consider how they might constitute coherent packages (i.e., as interconnected practices and structures). If two or more plants seemed similar in how they gender work, the researcher would try to identify the core elements that structure work in similar plants and establish preliminary types. Close examination of cases would also permit an assessment of the adequacy of current theories, which in turn would lead the researcher either to press on with his or her initial theoretical formulation or adopt a new one. After achieving some confidence that the important features of cases had been identified, the researcher could then specify different configurations of these aspects, looking at their combinations (as in table 3.1), and thus establish and refine the conceptual basis for delineating types of cases.

The important point here is that in the initial stage of a project, the researcher focuses on key aspects of cases relevant to some outcome, such as gender exploitation. Once identified, the researcher examines these aspects in various combinations to see which aspects form coherent packages and bring together cases that seem the same, while distinguishing cases that seem different. Thus, the researcher focuses on specific features of cases, identifying the most relevant, while at the same time considering how these features cohere with each other as distinct packages, especially across cases. The end result is a delineation of types, based on specific empirical configurations. Thus, examining cases as combinations of aspects provides the primary means for mapping their diversity. Indeed, looking at cases as configurations and allowing for the possibility that a single difference may constitute a difference in kind highlights their diversity.

It also should be noted that in the process of identifying the different configurations of attributes that make up types, the researcher also specifies, implicitly and by default, the combinations of features that do not exist, based on the evidence examined in the study. Some of these combinations may be infrequent or unlikely; others may involve combinations of characteristics that are impossible, incompatible, or simply unwieldy. In diversity-oriented research it is important to consider which combinations are not found and to explore the possible reasons for their absence. For example, if the researcher in the example just described found that there were no microelectronic assembly plants that combined internal labor markets and the conscious manipulation of traditional gender roles, it would be worthwhile to consider the reasons for the apparent incompatibility of these two features.

CONFIGURATIONS, TYPES, AND LAZARSFELD'S CONCEPT OF PROPERTY SPACE

One reason that the study of diversity, as outlined in this work, has not received appropriate attention over the past several decades is the simple fact that social scientists have conceived the problem of typology construction almost exclusively from the perspective of variable-oriented analysis. When variable-oriented researchers discuss types, they usually focus on statistical procedures such as cluster analysis and Q-factor analysis (Bailey 1994). These techniques typically use as input a data matrix of cases by variables and apply various computer algorithms to sort cases into a small number of groups. These procedures focus on similarities and differences among cases across a range of variables specified by the investigator. The usual goal is to inductively derive a small number of groupings such that within-group differences are minimized while between-group differences are maximized.

Typically, the number of groups that "emerge" from the application of these procedure is arbitrary, and it can vary widely from one analysis to the next, depending on the specific variables included, how they are measured, the nature of the clustering algorithm used, the way in which similarity is calculated, the researcher's tolerance for complexity, and

so on. Unfortunately, the procedures embedded in the computer algorithms that induce types are invisible to most researchers, and few
researchers have the experience or expertise to differentiate between
findings and methodological artifacts. Because the results of these procedures can vary so greatly from one analysis to the next, researchers
often become frustrated and simply abandon the effort to formulate
types altogether. Besides, researchers are not always sure what to do
with a typology once it is derived. Should it be conceived as a categorical variable in a multivariate analysis, or should it instead provide a
basis for differentiating qualitatively distinct populations or subpopulations? And how should researchers treat cases that vary in how well
they conform to types?

Modern methods of typology construction such as cluster analysis
result in classification schemes that are almost always "polythetic" and
usually "fully polythetic" (Bailey 1994). In a polythetic classification,
the cases that are grouped into a single category are allowed to differ
substantially from each other on one or more attributes as long as they
are similar on many of the attributes selected by the investigator for
inclusion in the analysis. In a fully polythetic classification, the cases
grouped into a category may fail to exhibit a single commonality. Thus,
for example, a fully polythetic grouping might include individuals who
are mostly but not all Republican, mostly but not all middle class,
mostly but not all White, mostly but not all suburban, and so on.

Clearly, polythetic schemes, and especially fully polythetic schemes,
violate the core principle of configurational thinking previously
sketched, namely, the idea that a single difference may constitute a
qualitative distinction or a difference in kind. Recall the stuck elevator
example: Two individuals are similar in all respects save one. Despite
their many similarities, it might be very different to be stuck on an
elevator with one versus the other. Using modern methods of cluster
analysis, however, these two individuals would almost certainly be assigned to the same cluster. From a configurational perspective, by contrast, they might be seen as qualitatively different and thus assigned to
different types.

The configurational principles advanced in this chapter hark back to
a much earlier tradition of typology construction, the "property-space"
approach developed by Lazarsfeld (1937) and elaborated by Barton
(1955). Lazarsfeld argued that most "type concepts" involve sets of attributes that make sense together as a unitary construct, for example, Weber's (1978) specification of the ideal-typic bureaucracy. He
noted further that too often social scientists use type concepts with-

out analyzing them—that is, without examining their component attributes. He argued that it is important to identify the component attributes because they provide the basis for elaborating a full typology, based on the different logically possible combinations of attributes that make up a type concept. In this approach, the attributes of a type concept constitute a "property space" with as many dimensions as attributes. Each combination of attributes is a specific location in the property space. Each of these locations, in turn, may constitute a different type.

Suppose, for example, a researcher determines that the "authoritarian personality," a type concept, has four component attributes. A full typology can be constructed using these four components as presence/absence dichotomies to produce a four-dimensional property space, which, in this example, could be represented as a two-by-two-by-two-by-two table. Each cell of this four-way table is one of the logically possible combinations of the four dichotomies. In this property space, Lazarsfeld would argue, the authoritarian personality can be seen as one of 16 personality types formed from the four attributes. (With four presence/absence dichotomies there are 2^4 or 16 logically possible combinations.) In Lazarsfeld and Barton's approach, the four dichotomies and the sixteen combinations they yield constitute the "property space" that is implicit in the conception of the authoritarian personality, a single type concept. Their combinatorial approach to property spaces dovetails with the understanding of types depicted in table 3.1 and with the configurational principle that a single difference between two cases may constitute a difference in kind.

"REDUCING" PROPERTY SPACES

As Lazarsfeld and Barton both note, it is quite likely that the researcher will have difficulty finding empirical instances of all logically possible combinations of attributes. In the authoritarian personality example, for instance, it might prove impossible to find individuals lacking all four attributes. Likewise, in the example elaborated in table 3.1, it might prove impossible to find one or more of the eight types of countries. Lazarsfeld and Barton argue that the fact that many of the combinations in a property space lack empirical instances is a great boon to social research, especially when the number of component attributes, and thus the number of combinations, is great. The basic idea here is that a simple and useful empirical typology can be formed from the combinations that exist. If a relatively small number of combinations exists empirically, then the researcher will be able to reduce a multidimensional property space to a handful of categories. Lazarsfeld (1937: 127–8) calls this simplification a *functional reduction*. The idea of functional reduction is echoed in Arthur Stinchcombe's remarks on typologies. He states that "a typology is a statement that a large number of variables have only a small number of combinations of values which actually occur, with all other combinations being rare or nonexistent. This results in a radical improvement in social scientific theory" (1968:47).

Consider as an example of this type of simplification (functional reduction of a property space) the hypothetical evidence on countries presented in table 3.2. This table borrows the three dichotomies used in table 3.1 (high versus low export ratio, large versus small size, close to versus far from the core of the world economy) and adds a fourth (exporter of raw materials versus exporter of finished goods). Imagine that the researcher in this example started with a type concept, "core country," and determined that this construct embraced four key attributes—large size, close proximity to the core of the world economy, high export ratio, and participation in the world economy as an ex-

Table 3.2
Example of Lazarsfeld's "Functional Reduction"

Combination No.	Variable				Substantial Empirical Instances?	Type
	NATURE OF EXPORTS	EXPORT RATIO	SIZE	LOCATION		
1	Raw	Low	Small	Close	No	
2	Raw	Low	Small	Far	Yes	4
3	Raw	Low	Large	Close	No	
4	Raw	Low	Large	Far	No	
5	Raw	High	Small	Close	No	
6	Raw	High	Small	Far	No	
7	Raw	High	Large	Close	No	
8	Raw	High	Large	Far	Yes	3
9	Finished	Low	Small	Close	No	
10	Finished	Low	Small	Far	No	
11	Finished	Low	Large	Close	No	
12	Finished	Low	Large	Far	No	
13	Finished	High	Small	Close	Yes	2
14	Finished	High	Small	Far	No	
15	Finished	High	Large	Close	Yes	1
16	Finished	High	Large	Far	No	

porter of finished goods. The elaboration of these four attributes as dichotomies yields the property space depicted in table 3.2. Suppose that the search for instances of the sixteen combinations, however, yielded substantial instances of only four of the logically possible combinations:

1. "core countries" (export finished goods, high export ratios, large in size, close to the core of the world economy);
2. "core-associated countries" (export finished goods, high export ratios, small in size, close to the core of the world economy);
3. "semiperipheral countries" (export raw materials, high export ratios, large in size, far from the core of the world economy); and
4. "peripheral countries" (export raw materials, low export ratios, small in size, far from the core of the world economy).

The researcher would conclude from this evidence that there are four types of countries, reflected in the four empirical combinations. The remaining twelve combinations, those lacking substantial empirical instances, are thus excluded from the typology. In the discussion that follows, combinations that lack empirical instances are called *hypothetical combinations*. They are hypothetical in the limited sense that they do not exist or are rare, not in the more abstract or theoretical sense that they all constitute "thought experiments."

Of course, the data that social scientists use are only rarely as tidy as that represented in table 3.2. Typically, when researchers construct property spaces, they find more empirical combinations than they could possibly anticipate. While not a central concern of this chapter, it should be noted that researchers can use various criteria to evaluate the frequency of combinations when deciding which are "empirically substantial" and which are "hypothetical." These criteria may be substantive, theoretical, probabilistic, or some combination of criteria. Substantive criteria, for example, might be used to define frequencies that constitute a critical mass. Theoretical criteria might be used to specify frequencies with properties of interest to a given theoretical principle or idea. Probabilistic criteria could be used to identify frequencies that exceed expected values given some model of randomness.

For example, a researcher might consider as empirically substantial only those combinations that reach a certain frequency threshold, defined using probabilistic criteria. With 16 logically possible combinations, the researcher might decide that the number of cases attached to a given combination must be significantly greater than 1/16 of the total number of cases for the combination to qualify as empirically substantial (von Eye 1990). A standard one-tailed z test for the difference between proportions (Hayes 1973:213–4) or a binomial probability test could be used to evaluate any positive gap between the observed proportion of cases displaying a given combination and the benchmark proportion (1/16 or .0625 in this example). Combinations that meet this threshold would be considered empirically substantial; those that fall short would be considered hypothetical. Alternatively, the researcher might control for one or more of the marginal distributions of the attributes that make up the typology when making this assessment (von Eye 1990:59–142). The point here is simply that researchers may use a variety of formal criteria to evaluate the frequency of combinations, not that any specific technique for making these assessments is best.

Most property spaces contain many hypothetical combinations—configurations that either lack empirical instances altogether or have a substantively or statistically insignificant number of instances. In general, the larger the number of dimensions that comprise a property space, the greater the number of hypothetical combinations. Hypothetical combinations may exist for a variety of reasons. Sometimes they exist simply because the property space has more locations than there are relevant cases. After all, it takes only thirty-three dichotomies to generate more logical combinations than there are people on Earth. Alternatively, combinations may lack instances because they involve impossibilities—for example, pregnant males. Many other combinations lack instances because of the confounded nature of social phenomena. For example, if two attributes are strongly correlated, say race and neighborhood, then some combinations will be relatively rare (e.g., African Americans living in wealthy suburban communities). Because social phenomena tend to be highly confounded, researchers generally find an abundance of hypothetical combinations in multidimensional property spaces.

The observation that property spaces often have an abundance of hypothetical combinations underscores the simple fact that social phenomena typically exhibit "limited diversity" (Ragin 1987:104–13). Researchers confront limited diversity whenever they are unable to locate instances of all the types contained within their property spaces. Limited diversity stems from the confounded nature of social phenomena (e.g., overlapping inequalities, as just noted) and is exacerbated by the tendency for social characteristics to occur in syndrome-like clumps—to "harmonize." Almost all combinations of social attributes that occur with substantial frequency (e.g., families that are middle class, White, gun-owning, and politically conservative, with children enrolled in fundamentalist Christian private schools) are suggestive of syndrome-like patterns extending well beyond the listed attributes. For example, this clump of characteristics might extend to NRA membership, rural background, and so on—to complete a common stereotype. Because harmonizing diversity is common in social life, it contributes to the abundance of hypothetical combinations in property spaces.

USING SET THEORY TO DESCRIBE LIMITED DIVERSITY

It is important when examining the distribution of cases within a property space to consider the ways in which diversity is limited, to see if the voids in the property space are patterned and if so, how. An understanding of the limits on diversity provides insights into the nature of the phenomenon under investigation and useful leads for constructing types. When there is a strong pattern to the combinations lacking empirical instances, the investigator should consider the possible social bases for these voids and incompatibilities. For example, it is certainly not coincidental that there are no African American females in charge of any of the largest U.S. corporations. The fact that there are no instances of this combination says something about the United States and the culture of its major corporations.

Set theory can be used to describe, in a very concise manner, the limitations on the diversity of cases within a property space. This approach offers simple procedures for summarizing in a single statement the nature of the hypothetical combinations (i.e., those lacking empirical instances) found in a property space. For illustration consider table 3.3, which shows a property space for the attributes of the members of a social science department at a large state university. How can the limited diversity of characteristics within this property space be described in a concise manner?

The table lays out a four-dimensional property space using four dichotomies relevant to the diversity within the department in question: gender (male versus female), race/ethnic background (European American versus minority), rank (tenured versus not tenured), and pay (above versus below average, compared with faculty members with the same number of years in seniority). At first glance, it appears that the members of this department are quite diverse with respect to the four dichotomies: There are male and female members; members from dif-

Table 3.3

Using Set Theory to Describe Hypothetical Combinations

Combination No.	Aspect				Empirical Instances
	GENDER	ETHNICITY	RANK	PAY	
1	Male	Minority	Untenured	Below	Yes
2	Male	Minority	Untenured	Above	Yes
3	Male	Minority	Tenured	Below	No
4	Male	Minority	Tenured	Above	No
5	Male	European	Untenured	Below	Yes
6	Male	European	Untenured	Above	Yes
7	Male	European	Tenured	Below	Yes
8	Male	European	Tenured	Above	Yes
9	Female	Minority	Untenured	Below	Yes
10	Female	Minority	Untenured	Above	No
11	Female	Minority	Tenured	Below	No
12	Female	Minority	Tenured	Above	No
13	Female	European	Untenured	Below	Yes
14	Female	European	Untenured	Above	No
15	Female	European	Tenured	Below	Yes
16	Female	European	Tenured	Above	No

ferent race/ethnic backgrounds; members at different ranks; and members who are paid above average and below average, relative to their years in seniority. However, as close inspection of table 3.3 reveals, not all sixteen logically possible combinations of these four dichotomies exist in the department; only nine do. Thus, there are seven hypothetical combinations of characteristics. How are these hypothetical combinations patterned?

The principles of set theory that provide the basis for translating these seven combinations lacking empirical instances into a single statement about limited diversity are simple and straightforward. In essence, set theory is used to group hypothetical combinations together, forming larger sets. When deriving these larger sets, the basic goal is to specify a small number of broad groupings that embrace as many hypothetical combinations as possible. For example, the two hypothetical combinations "male-minority-tenured-above" and "male-minority-tenured-below" (nos. 3 and 4 of table 3.3) can be joined to form the more inclusive combination, "male-minority-tenured." The greatest shorthand is achieved by deriving the smallest possible number of larger groupings with the smallest possible number of commonalities shared within each larger grouping. The end result is a reduction of the hypothetical combinations in a property space to a concise statement describing the limits on diversity that exist within it.

The details of these analytic procedures are presented in *The Comparative Method* (Ragin 1987:85–124), where I describe what is known as the "Quine-McCluskey algorithm" for the reduction of *truth tables,* the set-theoretic terms for what social scientists call property spaces (McCluskey 1956; McDermott 1985; Mendelson 1970; Quine 1952; Roth 1975). These procedures are also implemented in the computer program *Qualitative Comparative Analysis* (Drass and Ragin 1992).[9] Applying these procedures to the hypothetical combinations in table 3.3 results in a simple logical statement with two large groupings:

hypothetical combinations = female·above + minority·tenured.

In this statement multiplication (denoted with midlevel dots) indicates combinations of characteristics (logical *and*); addition indicates alternate combinations (logical *or*). Translated to prose, the equation states simply that this social science department lacks two kinds of faculty members: (1) those who combine being female with being paid above average, and (2) those who combine being minority with being tenured. Inspection of table 3.3 reveals that the first grouping covers rows 10, 12, 14, and 16; the second covers rows 3, 4, 11, and 12. Thus, all seven hypothetical combinations are embraced by these two groupings.

The evidence on limited diversity indicates that neither minority and tenured nor female and better paid are compatible with this department. For whatever reason, individuals who display these two combinations are not found. Of course, more research on the department in question would have to be conducted in order for the researcher to attach substantive significance to these two voids. Perhaps the minority members are all relatively recent hires, with freshly minted Ph.D.'s. Perhaps the various contributions of the female faculty members to the department's teaching, service, and research missions are undervalued by those who set salaries. More than likely, the researcher studying this department would be offered many different and contradictory explanations for the two voids identified in the table.

Logical statements such as the one just derived that describe limitations on the diversity in a property space are useful because they provide a basis for interrogating and learning about property spaces. For example, it is possible to use the statement describing the hypothetical

9. QCA 3.0 (Drass and Ragin 1992) can be downloaded from the archive at <http://www.nwu.edu/sociology>. Fuzzy-Set/Qualitative Comparative Analysis [FS/QCA] 1.0 (Drass and Ragin 1999) offers all the procedures available in QCA along with procedures for analyzing fuzzy-set memberships.

combinations, just presented, to construct statements about the diversity of *empirically substantial* combinations. For example, because the statement shows that there are no minority members who are tenured, it is possible to deduce that (1) if a member is minority, he or she is also not tenured, and (2) if a member is tenured, he or she is not a member of a minority. These two deductions can be made because minority members are a subset of untenured faculty, and tenured faculty are a subset of nonminority members. Inspection of empirical combinations in table 3.3 confirms these two simple deductions. Similarly, because the statement shows that there are no female members with above-average pay, it is possible to deduce that (1) if a member is female, her pay is below average, and (2) if a member's pay is above average, the member is not female. In other words, females are a subset of members with below-average pay, and members with above-average pay are a subset of male members. Again, inspection of the empirical combinations listed in table 3.3 confirms these simple deductions. The patterns just identified also can be viewed in terms of overlapping divisions that are likely to fuel conflicts within the department, specifically, the intersection of being female and receiving below-average pay and the intersection of minority status and being untenured.

The analysis of the limitations on diversity in table 3.3 shows that even though the academic department appears to embrace considerable diversity, at least at first glance, its diversity is in fact strongly patterned. It is important to emphasize that the patterning of diversity demonstrated here is both revealed and highlighted by the configurational understanding of social phenomena. This view of cases provides the foundation for the construction of evidence as property spaces and the associated view of each row of a property space as a potentially different kind of case. As I have just demonstrated, the use of set theory extends the property space framework and allows the deduction of formal statements describing diversity, especially the limited diversity that exists within a property space.

LIMITED DIVERSITY AND THE CONSTRUCTION
OF EMPIRICAL GENERALIZATIONS

There is another important reason to be concerned about limited diversity, beyond its resonance with viewing cases as configurations and the associated problem of constructing types. When diversity is limited, as it is in almost any study of naturally occurring social phenomena, researchers should always check to see if any of their conclusions mask

"simplifying assumptions" about the evidence. When researchers construct generalizations using evidence that is limited in its diversity, they
embed simplifying assumptions in their generalizations. This important
principle is best understood by example.

Suppose, for instance, that a researcher decides to study the morale
of the members of department depicted in table 3.3 and that, further,
this researcher believes that the aspects listed in the table are the main
causal conditions linked to morale differences. Based on several weeks
of observation, the researcher concludes that the department's minority
members are more demoralized than its nonminority members. In fact,
there is a perfect pattern—the minority members are all demoralized,
the nonminority members are not. This researcher draws the conclusion that minority status explains low morale.

In this hypothetical study, the investigator found a perfect relationship between minority status and morale and a weak relation between
rank and morale (after all, minority members are only a subset of the
nontenured). From this viewpoint, it seems quite reasonable to conclude that minority status is all that matters as far as morale is concerned. But the investigator's conclusion is actually about members
who are both minority and untenured, not simply about minority
members, because there are no minority members who are tenured.
To draw a conclusion about "the impact of minority status" without
acknowledging the other relevant characteristic that minority faculty
share is to assume implicitly that if there were any *tenured* minority
members, then they would resemble the existing minority members in
displaying the outcome in question (i.e., low morale).

This concern for simplifying assumptions inherent in the configurational view of cases contrasts sharply with conventional variable-oriented research where different aspects of cases tend to be examined as
"independent variables" engaged in a contest to explain variation in the
outcome. When aspects are examined as independent variables, which
is the norm in conventional multivariate analysis, the impact of limited
diversity is masked and obscured, as it would be in the present example. Variable-oriented researchers are typically unaware that their conclusions incorporate assumptions about cases for which they have no
evidence (e.g., minority members who are tenured). This issue pervades empirical social science because limited diversity is the rule, not
the exception, in the study of naturally occurring social phenomena.

I return to this topic—the impact of limited diversity on empirical
generalizations—in subsequent chapters. As I show in part 2, the examination of the impact of limited diversity is not limited to property

spaces constructed from categorical variables and conventional, crisp sets. These same concerns surface in the examination of aspects of cases that exhibit fine-grained variation by level or degree.

CONCLUSION

Seeing cases as configurations is a middle path between assuming that cases are "homogeneous enough" to equate their similarities, on the one hand, and attending to the specificity of each case, on the other. At the variable-oriented extreme, cases are studied primarily in terms of their component variables that, in turn, are treated as independent, analytically separable aspects. This transformation of cases disaggregates wholes and masks limited diversity. Referring back to table 3.3, it is clear that if the researcher were to study these variables as analytically separable and ignore their different combinations, then the department would appear to be much more diverse than it actually is. Further, as I have shown with a simple example, when researchers ignore limited diversity, assumptions about combinations of conditions that have not been examined can easily become embedded in empirical generalizations.

At the case-oriented extreme, by contrast, cases are selected and studied because of their special significance, so much so that researchers may lose sight of the larger context. For example, a researcher might conduct an in-depth study of the female untenured faculty in the department with the goal of documenting their efforts to thrive in a large and diverse academic department. However, this researcher might fail to consider the impact of several basic features of this department: (1) all women, whether tenured or not, receive below-average pay, and (2) untenured faculty who are both minority and female work in a department that lacks tenured minority faculty members. In short, the general character of the department might be obscured in the attempt to document the experiences of a relatively narrow category of faculty.

Viewing cases as configurations is a not a panacea. There is no substitute for insight or for in-depth knowledge of research subjects. Still, by viewing cases as configurations it is possible to avoid many of the homogenizing assumptions of the variable-oriented approach without adopting the laser beam–like focus of the case-oriented approach. As I have shown, it is possible to study cases as configurations by extending Lazarsfeld and Barton's property space approach, which in turn, provides a strong analytic foundation for constructing types and analyzing diversity.

FOUR

CAUSAL COMPLEXITY

CAUSAL COMPLEXITY AND THE STUDY OF DIVERSITY

Social diversity is manifested in many different ways. One of its clearest manifestations is in the variety of ways things happen. Choose almost any outcome that a social scientist might study and consider all the different ways it could come about. As an example, take democracy: In some countries, democracy developed through local institutions and matured gradually. In others, democratic institutions were borrowed wholesale from other countries, and political leaders established democracy more quickly. In still others, democracy was imposed from the outside all at once, sometimes by a colonial power, sometimes by the victor in a war. Causal heterogeneity of this type is not limited to large-scale, historically emergent outcomes like democracy. At a more mundane level, consider how many different ways there are for an individual to get ahead (or to fall behind) or how many different ways there are to strike up a conversation (or to avoid interacting with others). It follows that one important way to address social diversity is to pay close attention to the variety of ways a common outcome is reached— that is, to attend to causal complexity.

Of course, social scientists like to generalize about causes. If they can, they try to identify powerful, generic causes that are relevant to broad populations. At the individual level, the concept of self-interest is one such cause; so is the idea that it is important for individuals to accumulate human capital. At the macrosocial level, economic development is a popular general cause. Social scientists often argue that economic development fosters democracy, political stability, civic culture, tolerance, and so on. The urge among social scientists to find general causes and identify broad patterns is pervasive, and it is usually healthy.

After all, the opposite of focusing on broad patterns and general causes is to see each instance as irreducibly unique—different in almost every way from all other instances. But there can be too much of a good thing. Social scientists' preference for broad generalizations often leads them down the path of excessive abstraction and away from understanding diversity. For example, the finding that democratic stability is very often linked to economic development is important. However, our understanding of democracy is greatly deepened when we uncover the different ways democratic stability can be forged, even in poor countries (Rueschemeyer, Stephens, and Stephens 1992), and the different ways it may break down, even in advanced countries (Berg-Schlosser and De Meur 1994).

In this chapter I explore the link between social diversity and causal complexity. Along the way, I address various aspects of causation and the problem of establishing causal generalizations that strike a balance between complexity and generality. My goal is not to criticize conventional views of causation in the social sciences. Some scholars, for example, reject the use of causal imagery to describe cross-case patterns (e.g., the argument that "more education leads to higher income" based in part on a cross-case correlation between these two variables). Rather, I am concerned with assumptions about how causes operate—for example, the idea that causes are additive in their effects—that typically undergird quantitative analyses of cross-case patterns.

My starting point is the case study and the problem of generalizing from a single case. I proceed from a brief examination of the case study to basic ideas about causation, especially the concepts of causal necessity and sufficiency. I address the necessity and sufficiency of single causes and then augment the framework to address combinations of causes, multiple combinations of causes, and finally the issue of probability and inference in the study of necessity and sufficiency. I conclude by contrasting the understanding of causation advocated here—emphasizing causal complexity as an important key to understanding social diversity—with the understanding of causation that is implicit in conventional quantitative analysis.

My main argument is that researchers interested in diversity, especially as it is manifested in causal complexity, should avoid, as much as possible, making simplifying assumptions about the nature of causation. Specifically, I argue that researchers should avoid *assuming* that the individual causes they examine are either necessary or sufficient for the outcomes they study. I focus on techniques appropriate for studying causes that are sufficient only in combinations.

NECESSITY, SUFFICIENCY, AND CAUSAL GENERALIZATION

While the case study almost by definition offers little basis for causal generalization, it has the advantage of providing the investigator intensive knowledge of a case and its history and thus a more in-depth view of causation. Case-study researchers are able to triangulate different kinds of evidence from a variety of different sources in their attempts to construct full and compelling representations of causation in the cases they study. In short, case studies maximize validity in the investigation of causal processes.

Maximizing validity carries costs, however. While the case study is an excellent research strategy for studying "how" something comes about, it does not provide a good basis for assessing the generality or the nature of the causation the researcher identifies. For example, there is no way to tell from a single case if the causes identified by the researcher are either necessary or sufficient for the outcome in question. In the typical case study all causes identified as important by the researcher appear to be necessary conditions, for they are all present in the case in question and are typically understood as combinatorially decisive for the outcome under investigation. But are they truly necessary conditions? This question can be answered only by examining other, comparable instances of the outcome. There are other important issues that cannot be addressed in a case study. Examples of these issues include the size of the set of cases that is relevant to the causal pattern or process observed in the case study, the relevant boundary or scope conditions for the causal process observed by the case-study researcher, and whether the researcher identified all relevant causal factors.

A researcher studying a specific labor strike, for example, might conclude that the strike occurred as a result of worker opposition to the introduction of new machinery designed to increase worker productivity. In the report of the case study of this strike, the researcher might present a very compelling array of evidence supporting this conclusion, based on observations, interviews, experience working on the production line, the study of relevant documents, an analysis of the history of the plant in question, references to the existing literature on strikes, and so on. However, even with this compelling evidence in hand, it is impossible to know if it is reasonable to extend the researcher's argument to other cases. Claims about *generalizability*—that is, the portability of findings to other, comparable cases and settings—in social science usually rest on some form of *cross-case* analysis or evidence. That is, such statements usually are based on the examination of many cases, judged to be similar enough to warrant pooling the evidence they provide.

There are several different ways to address the generalizability of empirical findings.[1] I address two aspects of generalizability here because these two are of special importance to the study of social diversity as reflected in causal complexity. The first involves the *necessity* of the cause identified by the researcher. In the example just presented, one could ask: Are *all* strikes preceded by the introduction of new technology that is opposed by workers? Or, are strikes also prompted by other causes? The second aspect of generalizability of interest here involves the *sufficiency* of the cause in question. Is the cause identified by the researcher by *itself* capable of producing the outcome? In other words, whenever this cause occurs in like settings, regardless of what other causally relevant factors are present, will there be a strike? Or are there other essential ingredients—which may have escaped the researcher's grasp—that must be combined with the cause in question in order for a strike to occur?

To assess necessity, the researcher must work backward from instances of the outcome to the identification of relevant causes. As noted, a necessary cause must be present for the outcome in question to occur. Thus, all instances of the outcome should be preceded by the cause or exhibit the cause in some way. If another researcher were to identify strikes not preceded by the introduction of new technology, then this would challenge the claim that the cause identified by the first researcher is a necessary cause. Assessing necessity thus involves searching for instances of the outcome (in this example, strikes), and then assessing whether all instances of the outcome agree in displaying the same cause. If it can be shown that, in fact, all instances of the outcome share the same antecedent condition, then the researcher has established that the antecedent condition may be necessary for the outcome.[2]

1. Here I depart from conventional approaches, where generalizability would be conceptualized in terms of probabilities. For example, in conventional approaches a researcher might ask, What impact does the introduction of new technology opposed by the workers have on the *probability* of a strike? Does it increase the probability, and if so, by how much? It is not conventional to address causal necessity or sufficiency within a probabilistic framework. I return to this issue after establishing important analytic consequences of considering causal necessity and sufficiency in social research.

2. In the course of making this assessment, the researcher may discover that there are preconditions that were hidden from view in the first case. For example, the researcher might "discover" that his or her argument about strikes really only applies in industries that have been unionized for a long period of time.

Of course, the researcher addresses only those causes that are theoretically or substantively relevant in some way. Most researchers know, for example, that it is trivial to point out that "air for workers to breathe" is a necessary condition for strikes.

Necessary causes are not always sufficient causes. Even if it can be shown that all known and relevant strikes were preceded by the cause identified by the case-study researcher, it would be erroneous to conclude on the basis of such evidence that whenever this cause occurs, a strike results. It may be the case, for example, that another, unidentified cause also must be present and that there are actually two (or more) causes that, when combined, provide sufficient conditions for a strike.

To assess the sufficiency of a cause, the researcher must determine whether the cause in question always produces the outcome in question. Evidence that there are instances of the cause not followed by the outcome challenges the researcher's claim that the cause in question is sufficient. The assessment of sufficiency, therefore, involves searching for cases that are similar to the present case with respect to the cause in question (in this example, the introduction of technology opposed by workers) and then assessing whether they agree in displaying the same outcome (strikes). If all instances of the cause result in strikes, then the researcher may argue that the cause is sufficient for the occurrence of a strike. Combined with the evidence in support of necessity described previously, the researcher could claim that the cause identified in the case study is a necessary and sufficient condition for strikes.[3]

The sequence of analytic steps just presented roughly reproduces the "indirect method of difference" outlined by John Stuart Mill ([1843] 1967) in *A System of Logic*. The indirect method of difference is a double application of his "method of agreement." First, the researcher searches for and examines instances of the effect to see if they all agree in displaying the same antecedent condition (i.e., the researcher assesses the *necessity* of a cause). Second, the researcher searches for and examines instances of the cause to see if they all agree in displaying the effect

---

3. These two very different assessments are often conflated or confused in social research. Qualitative researchers often proceed from a set of cases defined by the outcome, attempt to identify causes that are uniform across all such cases, and then present these uniform causes as necessary and sufficient conditions. As is evident from the preceding discussion, however, researchers who use this strategy succeed only in establishing necessary conditions for an outcome, and in most instances they establish only a subset of the necessary conditions. It is also clear that such work rests on an assumption of causal homogeneity—the expectation that the same causes operate in the same way in all instances of an outcome.

(i.e., the researcher assesses whether the necessary cause identified in the first step is also *sufficient*). While the indirect method of difference does not provide the causal clarity of a laboratory experiment, it is an important way to assess causation when working with naturally occurring data—the usual situation for social scientists.

While Mill's indirect method of difference offers a relatively simple and straightforward research design, it is easy to be fooled about the complexity of causation by the sequential nature of the design just described. The design leaves the impression that the first task is to certify that a cause is necessary, while the second is to show that not only is the cause necessary but that it is also sufficient. This research plan thus assumes causal uniformity at the outset of the investigation because the search for common causes is predicated on the idea that instances of the outcome share basic similarities in how they came about. However, it is often the case that there are no necessary causes for an outcome— beyond those that simply establish the boundaries of the investigation (e.g., the presence of workers might be seen as a necessary but trivial condition for the occurrence of a labor strike).

In fact, causation is often complex in character because social phenomena are remarkable in their diversity, even phenomena that merit the same label, like *strikes*. Causes may be sufficient but not necessary, and they may be necessary but not sufficient. Furthermore, in many arenas of social scientific research causes may be neither necessary nor sufficient. In fact, this type of causation may be the most common form of social causation. While it is tempting to reject causes that are neither necessary nor sufficient as "not general" and therefore of only marginal interest to social science, to do so would be to deny the complexity and diversity of social phenomena, especially with respect to causation. Research strategies appropriate for uncovering and assessing social diversity must permit maximum causal complexity, and the most complex form of causation involves conditions that are neither necessary nor sufficient.

For elaboration of these ideas, examine table 4.1. It shows four types of causes. In cell 1 are causes that are both necessary and sufficient.

Table 4.1
Types of Causes

Cause	Sufficient	Not Sufficient
Necessary	cell 1	cell 2
Not necessary	cell 3	cell 4

Causes of this type have the greatest empirical scope (because they apply to all relevant instances) and the greatest empirical power (because the cause by itself produces the outcome). However, such causes are very rare in the study of social phenomena. In cell 2 are causes that are necessary but not sufficient. These causes also have great empirical scope, but they lack the empirical power of cell 1 causes because they work only in conjunction with other causes. Sometimes, such conditions merely establish the scope of an investigation without specifying central causal mechanisms. Causes in cell 3 are powerful because they can act alone to bring about an outcome, but their empirical scope is limited because there are other causes that also produce the same outcome. Finally, causes in cell 4 are limited both in empirical scope and power, because they do not produce the outcome on their own nor are they always present as antecedent conditions.

It is possible to use simple logical statements to express the causal concepts elaborated in table 4.1. Suppose the investigator considers four possible causes of strikes: (1) the introduction of new technology opposed by workers ("technology"), (2) stagnant wages in times of high inflation ("wages"), (3) reduction in overtime hours ("overtime"), and (4) worker resistance to outsourcing portions of an existing production process ("sourcing"). Suppose also that a researcher has evidence on all relevant production sites. Consider the following logical statements expressing different possible findings from these cases, with respect to the impact of new technology:

$$\text{technology} \rightarrow \text{strikes}, \tag{1}$$

$$\text{technology} \cdot \text{wages} \rightarrow \text{strikes}, \tag{2}$$

$$\text{technology} + \text{wages} \rightarrow \text{strikes}, \tag{3}$$

$$\text{technology} \cdot \text{wages} + \text{overtime} \cdot \text{sourcing} \rightarrow \text{strikes}, \tag{4}$$

where midlevel dots indicates logical *and* and plus signs indicates logical *or*. The first equation indicates that the researcher found that all strikes were preceded by a single cause (the introduction of new technology) and that this single cause invariably provoked strikes. In this equation new technology is a necessary and sufficient condition for strikes. The second equation indicates that the researcher found that two causes combined to produce strikes: new technology and stagnant wages. In this equation technology is a necessary but not sufficient condition for strikes (as is stagnant wages). The third equation indicates that the researcher found that either of two causes, new technology or stagnant wages, cause strikes. In some instances strikes occurred because new technology was introduced; in others, strikes occurred because wages were stagnant. In this equation new technology is a sufficient but not necessary condition for strikes (again, as is stagnant wages). Finally, the fourth equation shows that the researcher found that two different combinations of conditions caused strikes: workers struck when new technology was introduced while wages were stagnant, and they struck when overtime hours were reduced in concert with an attempt to outsource portions of the production process. In this equation, new technology is neither necessary nor sufficient for strikes.

The fourth type of causation (shown in equation [4]) is the most complex of the four presented in table 4.1. In this equation, none of the four single causes (new technology, stagnant wages, reduced overtime hours, or outsourcing) is either necessary or sufficient. Consequently, none of the single causes acts as a cause in all instances of the outcome (i.e., is a general cause), and none is capable of producing the outcome on its own (i.e., is singularly sufficient).

From the perspective of variable-oriented research the ideal cause should be relevant to as many cases as possible (i.e., it should be general) and also capable of acting independently to effect or influence the outcome. When causes operate the same way in all cases, the investigator can say that the cases included in a study are uniform with respect to the cause in question—that they display "causal homogeneity." When a cause is capable of acting by itself on an outcome, the investigator can say that its effect is independent of the presence or absence (or degree of presence) of other conditions. When there are several different causes and each one has an independent effect on the outcome (i.e., the strength of its effect is not altered by the presence or absence or level of other causes), then the effect of each cause can be described as "additive."

The single causes represented in equation (4) possess none of these attributes. Yet, the type of causation indicated in equation (4) may be the most common form of social causation. Even if it is not the most common form, a social science that attends to social diversity should assume at the outset of any empirical study that the causal processes under investigation may in fact be this complex—they may involve causes that are neither necessary nor sufficient. Of course, empirical investigation may reveal otherwise. The research may show that single causes under investigation are necessary or sufficient. But these simpler forms of causation should not be assumed at the outset, as is commonly done in conventional quantitative social science (especially via the assumption of additivity). Necessity and/or sufficiency must be established through empirical analysis.

ANALYTIC STRATEGIES RELEVANT TO DIFFERENT TYPES OF CAUSES

Social scientists have been slow to recognize that different analytic strategies are relevant to the assessment of different kinds of causes. At the most basic level, it is important to recognize that the study of necessity works backward from instances of an outcome and is a search for common antecedent conditions. The study of sufficiency, by contrast, works forward from instances of a causal condition (or, as I show subsequently, instances of a combination of causal conditions) to see if these instances agree in displaying the outcome. I elaborate on these different emphases and their implications in the discussion that follows, using dichotomous, presence/absence conditions and a simple two-by-two table.

In conventional variable-oriented research, all four cells of the crosstabulation of the presence/absence of an effect against the presence/absence of a cause are considered relevant to the investigator's argument. Basically, cases in the cells where the cause and the effect are present or where the cause and the effect are absent count in favor of the inference of a causal relationship, while cases in the two other cells count against it. This simple principle is the foundation of almost all quantitative analysis in the social sciences today, including Pearson's correlation coefficient, the computational foundation of conventional multiple regression analysis. As I show subsequently, however, the reasoning behind these calculations conflates the analysis of necessity and the analysis of sufficiency. Some errors of prediction violate sufficiency; others violate necessity. Furthermore, cases where both the cause and the effect are absent are not directly relevant to the assessment of either necessity or sufficiency. Most measures of association count cases in this cell as evidence in favor of a causal argument: the greater the number, the better. From the perspective of necessity and sufficiency, however, this common practice is misleading.

For illustration, first consider the pattern of empirical results that should accompany the finding that a cause is both necessary and sufficient (as detailed in cell 1 of table 4.1 and equation [1]). Recall that to assess necessity, the researcher must locate all relevant instances of an outcome and then assess whether they agree in displaying one or more antecedent conditions. Essentially, this assessment involves an examination of only those cases where the outcome is present. The key question is, Are there any cases where the outcome is present but the cause is absent? If there are such cases, then the test of necessity fails. The assessment of sufficiency, by contrast, involves only cases where the cause is present. The researcher examines instances of the cause and hopes to show that in all instances of the cause, the outcome is present. If there are instances of the cause without the outcome, then the test of sufficiency fails.

Table 4.2 shows a simple cross-tabulation of the presence/absence of a cause against the presence/absence of an outcome, consistent with a finding of *both* necessity and sufficiency. Essentially, the test of necessity involves only the first row of the table (cells 1 and 2). The test of sufficiency involves only the second column (cells 2 and 4). Note that cell 3 is not directly relevant to the assessment of either sufficiency or necessity; therefore, it does not matter how many cases are in this cell. More than likely, there would be many cases in this cell in the hypothetical study of strikes just described because the investigator has information on "all relevant production sites" and there would certainly be many that lacked both the cause and the outcome. Still, tests of sufficiency and necessity are not directly affected by cases in cell 3.

Next consider the situation where the researcher is interested only in assessing whether the cause in question is necessary (as detailed in cell 2 of table 4.1 and equation [2]). This situation often arises when the boundaries of the set of negative cases (i.e., cases not displaying the outcome) is unclear, arbitrary, difficult to pin down, or potentially infinite (e.g., the set of nonrevolutions in a study of revolutions). Thus, the investigation is restricted to positive cases and thus to the assessment of necessity. The relevant empirical pattern is shown in table 4.3. In this analysis, only the first row of the cross-tabulation is relevant. The researcher's objective is to show that there are no instances of the outcome lacking the cause (i.e., no cases in cell 1).

Next, consider the situation where the researcher is interested only in assessing whether a cause is sufficient (as detailed in table 4.1, cell

Table 4.2
Cause Is Necessary and Sufficient

Outcome	Cause Absent	Cause Present
Present	[cell 1] no cases	[cell 2] cases
Absent	[cell 3] not directly relevant	[cell 4] no cases

Table 4.3
Cause Is Necessary but Not Sufficient

Outcome	Cause Absent	Cause Present
Present	[cell 1] no cases	[cell 2] cases
Absent	[cell 3] not relevant	[cell 4] not relevant

Table 4.4
Cause Is Sufficient but Not Necessary

Outcome	Cause Absent	Cause Present
Present	[cell 1] not relevant	[cell 2] cases
Absent	[cell 3] not relevant	[cell 4] no cases

3 and equation [3]) and has no particular concern for necessity. This situation might arise in research where investigators believe that there are no necessary causes (of a nontrivial nature) for the outcome in question and that there is more than one way to generate the outcome.[4] The relevant empirical pattern is shown in table 4.4. In this analysis, only the second column of the cross-tabulation is examined. The key concern is to show that there are no cases in cell 4 (cause present, outcome absent). The researcher can effectively ignore information on cases where the cause is absent because they are irrelevant to the assessment of sufficiency. After all, the researcher is convinced that there are other causes that produce the outcome, so there probably should be cases in cell 1. Again, the number of cases in cell 3 is not directly relevant.

Finally, consider the situation in which the researcher believes that the cause in question is neither necessary nor sufficient. The analyst can anticipate finding cases in all four cells:

- where the cause in question is present and the outcome is absent (cell 4—because the cause by itself is not sufficient);
- where the outcome in question is present but the cause is absent (cell 1—because the cause is not necessary);
- where both the cause and outcome are present (cell 2—because there will be some instances of the single cause in which it is part of a sufficient combination of causes; see equation [4]); and
- where both the cause and the outcome are absent (cell 3).

4. "Trivial" necessary causes sometimes define the set of relevant cases (the population of observations).

In short, if the researcher believes that a cause is neither necessary nor sufficient but instead is part of one of several sufficient combinations of conditions (as in equation [4]), then the assessment of the relationship between a *single* cause and the outcome in question is of relatively little analytic value.

If, indeed, the most common form of social causation involves causes that are neither necessary nor sufficient, then the assessment of the cross-tabulation of a single cause with the outcome in question pro-vides little useful information. Instead, as I show in the next section, the investigator should cross-tabulate the outcome against *combinations* of causes. This shift in analytic strategy is the first step on the road to the analysis of causal complexity, defined here as a situation where no single cause is either necessary or sufficient.

NECESSITY AND SUFFICIENCY APPLIED TO CAUSAL COMBINATIONS

Social phenomena rarely result from single causes. Think about the outcomes that usually interest social scientists. They study social phe-nomena such as racial and ethnic conflicts, marriages, strikes, elections, revolutions, social movements, divorces, corporate mergers, street gangs, and so on—the many things that people do together. In virtually every phenomenon just mentioned, the causation involved is typically conjunctural—the relevant causes must be combined in the same time and place to produce the social phenomenon or outcome in question. There is no "one cause" of racial conflict or "one cause" of divorce. Social phenomena typically result from a combination of conditions, and very often the same outcome will result from several different com-binations.

Consider again the case-study researcher studying a specific labor strike. When case-study researchers focus on the causes that account for an outcome, they almost invariably cite a combination of causes, an intersection or conjuncture of causal forces in time and space. For example, instead of concluding that the strike resulted from a single cause (the introduction of new technology opposed by workers), more than likely the conclusion would be that several important causal con-ditions (low unemployment, a strong union, and poor communication between workers and management) accompanied the introduction of new technology, and it was this combination of conditions, this causal conjuncture, that provoked the strike. In essence, the researcher might argue that four causes (three describing important features of the setting and the fourth naming a precipitating event) combined to produce a qualitative outcome, the labor strike.

Just as it is possible to assess the necessity and sufficiency of a single cause, it is also possible to assess the necessity and sufficiency of a combination of causes. The procedures described in the previous section can be duplicated, except that the focus is on combinations of causes rather than on single causes. Again, imagine that the researcher has information on "all relevant production sites"—without worrying, for now, about how this set of cases might be constructed.

When a causal combination is *necessary* for an outcome, all instances of the outcome should exhibit the same combination of causal conditions. By examining instances of the outcome, it is possible to see if they share a specific combination of conditions (e.g., the four conditions identified in the hypothetical case study of the labor strike described in the preceding paragraphs). If they share a specific combination of conditions, then the combination can be treated as a necessary combination. Of course, it should be noted that if a combination of conditions is necessary for an outcome, then each single condition within the combination is also necessary for the outcome. This result follows logically because instances of an outcome that agree in displaying a combination of conditions also will agree in displaying each single condition in the combination.

When a causal combination is *sufficient* for an outcome, all instances of the causal combination should be followed by the outcome in question. By examining all relevant instances of the causal combination, it is possible to see if they agree in producing the outcome. If there are instances of the causal combination not followed by the outcome, then the test of the sufficiency of the causal combination fails.

For illustration, consider table 4.5. Once again, the assessment of necessity essentially involves the first row of the table (cells 1 and 2), while the assessment of sufficiency involves the second column of the

Table 4.5
Assessing a Causal Combination

Outcome	Causal Combination Absent	Causal Combination Present
Present	[cell 1] key cell for assessing necessity	[cell 2] cases
Absent	[cell 3] not directly relevant	[cell 4] key cell for assessing sufficiency

table (cells 2 and 4). In the assessment of necessity, cell 2 is expected to contain all the positive cases; cell 1 should be void of cases. Cells 3 and 4 are not directly relevant to the assessment of necessity. In the assessment of sufficiency, again cell 2 is expected to hold relevant positive cases; cell 4 should be void of cases. Cells 1 and 3 are not directly relevant to the assessment of sufficiency. While there are likely to be cases in cell 3, the number of cases in this cell is not directly relevant to the assessment of either the necessity or the sufficiency of a causal combination.

Imagine the application of these procedures to "all relevant production sites" using the results of the more elaborate case study, described previously, for guidance. Recall that in this hypothetical case study the investigator identified four causes that combine to provoke a strike (the introduction of new technology opposed by workers, low unemployment, a strong union, and poor communication between workers and management). Suppose the analysis of the cross-case evidence on many production sites revealed that all cells have cases except cell 4. The researcher could argue, based on this evidence, that the causal combination in question is sufficient but not necessary for strikes. By contrast, the finding that all cells have cases except cell 1 would support the argument that the causal combination in question is necessary but not sufficient for strikes. If both cells 1 and 4 prove to be void of cases, the investigator could argue that the causal combination is necessary and sufficient for strikes.

As noted previously, if a specific combination of causes is necessary for an outcome, then each single cause within the combination is also necessary for the outcome. It follows that if researchers were to test the necessity of the component conditions one at a time, they would find that each single condition passes the test of necessity (i.e., a showing of no "cell 1" cases). Thus, one simple way to identify a necessary combination of conditions is to test the necessity of each causal condition one at a time and then combine all conditions that pass this test into a single expression. A necessary combination of conditions is nothing more than the intersection of all the individually necessary conditions. This same procedure does not work, however, for combinations of conditions that are sufficient but not necessary. The component conditions of a sufficient combination of conditions generally fail the sufficiency test when examined one at a time. As I explain in chapter 5, it is important to examine all possible combinations of relevant conditions when assessing sufficiency.

MULTIPLE COMBINATIONS OF CAUSES

One situation not yet addressed is the possibility that *different* combinations of conditions may produce the same outcome. Suppose that there are two combinations of conditions that produce strikes. The first is the one just described (low unemployment, a strong union, poor communication with management, and the introduction of new technology opposed by workers). The second involves a different combination of four causes: a weak union, low wages, a concerted effort by the union to boost membership, and a speedup in the pace of production following a sharp increase in the demand for the product manufactured by the workers. (This second combination of causes does not involve the introduction of new machinery or production technology, only a speedup of production using existing techniques.)

Because there are two combinations, the analysis of cross-case evidence would show that neither combination is necessary. In both analyses there would be cases in cell 1 because there is plural causation and thus instances of the outcome caused by the other combination. In fact, because the two causal combinations display no common causal conditions, no single cause would pass the test of necessity. However, both combinations would pass the test of sufficiency. In both cross-case analyses, cell 4 would be void of cases, while cell 2 would contain the instances explained by the causal combination in question. This pattern of results is shown in table 4.6.

Table 4.6 demonstrates that the assessment of sufficiency is not undermined by the existence of multiple combinations of causes. Because the researcher focuses only on the results for the combination of causes in question (i.e., only cells 2 and 4) when assessing sufficiency, the impact of other causal combinations is excluded from the assessment. Thus, as table 4.6 shows, it is possible to assess the sufficiency of combinations of causal conditions one at a time—in isolation from one another.

This conclusion is important because of its implications for the study

Table 4.6
Assessing Multiple Causal Combinations

Outcome	First Causal Combination Absent	First Causal Combination Present
Present	[cell 1] cases explained by other causal combination	[cell 2] cases explained by first causal combination
Absent	[cell 3] not directly relevant	[cell 4] no cases

of social diversity as manifested in causal complexity. If, as I have argued, we live in a world of great causal complexity, then a common pattern will be for outcomes to result from different combinations of causal conditions. When there are different combinations of causes with no overlap in the single causes included in each combination (as in the present example), then no single cause is either necessary or sufficient. While it might seem that causation this complex should befuddle analytic social science, it is clear from the example just presented that the analysis of the sufficiency of causal combinations can proceed in a straightforward manner, with the key question being the distribution of cases in the second column of the cross-tabulation.

This analytic strategy—the examination of the sufficiency of combinations of causal conditions—is the preferred tactic for the study of causal complexity. This strategy makes no assumptions about the empirical scope or power of the causes examined in social research. It assumes neither causal uniformity (the same causes are involved in each instance of the outcome) nor causal additivity (causes act independently on the outcome) in the analysis of cross-case empirical evidence. The analysis of relevant empirical evidence may reveal these patterns (i.e., causal homogeneity or additivity), but they are not assumed to exist at the outset of the investigation, as in most quantitative social research today.

Finally, suppose a researcher assessed the two causal combinations just described and found them both sufficient. It would be reasonable as a next step to assess whether these two sufficient causal combinations account for all instances of strikes found in this particular set of cases. The relevant results are shown in table 4.7. If all instances of the outcome are covered by the two causal combinations, then there will be no cases in cell 1. In this table the two combinations are understood as alternate causal conjunctures or paths. The causal conditions specified in the last column of table 4.7 (i.e., "first or second causal combination present") can be interpreted as a logical statement, and the satisfac-

Table 4.7
Joining Multiple Causal Combinations

Outcome	Neither Causal Combination Present	First *or* Second Causal Combination Present
Present	[cell 1] no cases	[cell 2] cases explained by the causal combinations
Absent	[cell 3] not directly relevant	[cell 4] no cases

tion of this formula can be viewed as a necessary and sufficient condition for the outcome. The statement is

technology·employment·strong·communication
  + speedup·wages·weak·membership → strikes,

where "technology" equals introduction of new technology opposed by workers, "employment" equals low unemployment, "strong" equals strong union, "communication" equals poor communication between workers and management, "speedup" equals production speedup, "wages" equals low wages, "weak" equals weak union, "membership" equals union membership drive, midlevel dots equal logical *and,* and plus sign equals logical *or.* Essentially, this equation describes a pattern of "multiple conjunctural causation" (Ragin 1987). Different combinations of conditions are linked to the same outcome. As presented, the two causal combinations listed in the formula are mutually exclusive because the first specifies the presence of a strong union as a condition, while the second specifies the presence of a weak union as a condition.

THE IMPACT OF LIMITED DIVERSITY ON CAUSAL COMPLEXITY

The main focus of this chapter is on causal complexity, especially the possibility that no single cause may be either necessary or sufficient for an outcome. The main recommendation for dealing with causal complexity is to focus on the sufficiency of combinations of causal conditions. However, it is important to recognize that there are some situations in which the existence of necessary conditions will be obscured if scholars focus exclusively on the analysis of sufficiency. Generally, when the diversity of combinations of causal conditions is limited empirically (see chapter 3), researchers may overlook necessary conditions. Thus, it is always important to examine the impact of limited diversity on any conclusion that is drawn from analyses of necessity and sufficiency. Researchers must beware that their conclusions may incorporate assumptions about hypothetical combinations of causal conditions (see also chapter 3).

For a very simple illustration of the general problem, consider a researcher interested in the emergence of "generous" welfare systems in advanced industrial democracies. Suppose this researcher examines only two causal conditions: the presence/absence of strong "left parties" (e.g., social democratic parties in Scandinavia) and the presence/ab-

Table 4.8
Limited Diversity and the Analysis of Necessity and Sufficiency

Row No.	Strong Left Party	Strong Unions	Generous Welfare State	Number of Countries
1	Yes	Yes	Yes	6
2	Yes	No	No	7
3	No	No	No	5
4	No	Yes	?	0

sence of strong centralized unions. Suppose further that the empirical evidence follows the pattern presented in table 4.8. Using these two causal conditions as the main dimensions of the relevant property space, the table shows that only three of the four cells in this property space have cases. Thus, the diversity of cases, with respect to the relevant causal conditions, is clearly limited. There are no countries, in this hypothetical study, that combine strong unions and weak left parties.

Viewed from the perspective of causal sufficiency (where researchers work forward from causal conditions to outcomes), two causal arguments pass the sufficiency test for generous welfare systems: strong unions and the combination of strong unions and strong left parties. Logic and parsimony dictate that having strong unions, by itself, is sufficient for generous welfare systems; the combination of strong unions and strong left parties thus can be dropped (see chapter 5 for further explication of this elimination). Thus, viewing the evidence exclusively in terms of sufficiency leads to the conclusion that having strong unions is sufficient by itself for having a generous welfare system. Furthermore, the cross-tabulation of the presence/absence of this condition against the presence/absence of the outcome reveals a perfect relationship, demonstrating that it is also a necessary condition.

But what if necessity had been examined first? From the perspective of necessity, all instances of the outcome agree in displaying both strong unions and strong left parties. Thus, these two conditions are both necessary, using the procedures outlined previously for assessing necessity. Furthermore, when these two necessary conditions are tested for sufficiency, as a combination of conditions, it is apparent they pass this test as well. Viewed from the perspective of necessity first, therefore, the proper conclusion is that strong left parties and strong unions are jointly necessary and sufficient for generous welfare systems. Thus, it is clear from this simple example that the sufficiency test, described previously, obscures a necessary condition—having strong left parties.

Which conclusion is correct? In general, if a causal condition central to a researcher's argument can be shown to be a necessary condition (i.e., present in all instances of the outcome), then it should be evaluated as such. That is, once researchers have identified causal conditions that are uniform across instances of the outcome, then they should evaluate whether these conditions indeed make sense as necessary conditions, using theory, substantive knowledge, and whatever auxiliary evidence is at their disposal (e.g., in-depth knowledge of cases). If, in the end, this evaluation confirms the understanding of these causes as necessary, then they should be retained as necessary conditions. That is, such causes should not be subsequently eliminated simply because they appear to be logically redundant from the perspective of causal sufficiency. Thus, as a general rule, researchers should check for necessary conditions *before* they conduct sufficiency tests. Any causal condition that passes the test of necessity and that also passes the investigator's "plausibility" test should be retained as a necessary condition (see also chapter 5).

Observe that the two tests, necessity and sufficiency, give seemingly inconsistent answers in this example precisely because of the limited diversity of cases with respect to the combination of causes they display (see table 4.8). There are no cases that combine strong unions and weak left parties. If such cases existed and they all had generous welfare systems, then the researcher could more safely conclude that having strong unions, by itself, is necessary and sufficient for generous welfare systems. If, however, such cases existed and they lacked generous welfare systems, then the researcher could more safely conclude that strong unions must be combined with strong left parties for generous welfare systems to occur. Another way to say the same thing is to observe that, given limited diversity, no matter which conclusion the researcher presents, it involves statements (and thus assumptions) about combinations of conditions that have *not* been observed. The conclusion that strong unions and strong left parties must be combined for generous welfare systems to emerge assumes that if there were cases with strong unions and weak left parties, then these cases would not have generous welfare systems. Likewise, the conclusion that having strong unions, by itself, is enough assumes that if countries with strong unions and weak left parties existed, they would have generous welfare systems.

Conventional quantitative social science, for the most part, does not recognize the impact of limited diversity. In this approach, existing combinations of conditions are typically seen as the relevant universe of conditions (i.e., values are usually seen as "fixed"). Furthermore, these techniques usually privilege parsimony: the most parsimonious model is treated as the best. Thus, a quantitative analysis of the evidence in table 4.8 would lead quickly to the conclusion that having strong unions is the single cause of generous welfare systems. After all, the correlation between strong unions and generous welfare systems is perfect, while the correlation between strong left parties and generous welfare systems is weak. Why go any further? In fact, however, as I have just shown, the more parsimonious conclusion (i.e., where there are strong unions, generous welfare systems emerge) involves assumptions about the outcomes that hypothetical combinations would display, if in fact they did exist. Many implicit assumptions are hidden in the typical quantitative analysis, not only from investigators, but also from their audiences.

What is the most prudent course? In general, as I have argued, researchers should test for necessity before they examine sufficiency. That is, they should examine instances of the outcome to see if they agree on any of the causal conditions specified by the researcher. Of course, it is important for the researcher to further evaluate any conclusions from such assessments with auxiliary evidence. It is also important to recognize that if diversity is limited, any conclusion that investigators reach regarding causation involves assumptions about combinations of conditions for which researchers lack evidence.

Finally, it is worth emphasizing that limited diversity is the rule, not the exception, in the study of naturally occurring social phenomena. It poses analytic problems regardless of which technique investigators apply to their data.

USING PROBABILISTIC CRITERIA TO ASSESS NECESSITY AND SUFFICIENCY

For readers familiar with empirical social research, the discussion of necessity and sufficiency presented so far may seem fanciful. How often do social researchers, especially those working with large numbers of cases, find clear evidence of necessity or sufficiency in their cross-tabulations? All too often, cells 1 and 4 have plenty of cases in them. The idea that social scientists might find one or both of these cells empty seems preposterous, especially given how things usually turn out. Even when the analysis is limited to the examination of the sufficiency of combinations of conditions—the preferred tactic in the study of social diversity—the probability of finding cell 4 completely void of cases seems quite low.

There are many good reasons researchers should expect to find cases in cells 1 or 4—cases that challenge claims of necessity or sufficiency. The foremost reason is the fact that there is a lot of randomness in human affairs, as well as nonrandom factors that simply escape the purview of our theories. Consider again the example of strikes that occur in response to the introduction of technology opposed by workers. Suppose a charismatic worker makes a stirring speech on the behalf of the new technology and convinces workers not to go on strike, but instead to give the new production techniques a try. Suppose a flood closes the plant for a month, and then workers flock back to work, eager for overtime bonuses, when the waters recede. Suppose anarchists have infiltrated the union leadership, and the rank-and-file members refuse to follow any of their recommendations, no matter how sensible they may seem. There are many such minor, obscure, or random factors that might interfere with the expected connection between a cause and an effect. It is virtually impossible to construct social scientific models that take account of every possible factor that might influence some action or outcome. It comes as no great surprise, then, that many cases that "should" be in cell 2, at least from the perspective of the researcher, often end up in cells 1 or 4.

Consider also the fact that the data social scientists use are often imperfect and full of errors. Researchers studying strikes at "all relevant production sites" might make many mistakes in their observations, and the events themselves may be ambiguous. Also, as shown in chapter 2, it is all too easy to "misconstruct" a population. Consider as well the problem of deciding when new technology has been introduced. How new is "new"? What constitutes minor versus major changes in technology? Is the social scientist conducting this research qualified to judge production technologies? Consider the problem of coding strikes. What if a vote is taken in favor of a strike, but the action gradually crumbles on the very first day? Was it a strike? What if there is no strike vote, but a majority of workers call in sick when the new technology is introduced and production is shut down until employers reinstitute the old production techniques. Was it a strike?

Beyond these common problems of interpretation are simple human errors. What if the research is sloppy and coding forms are misread, misplaced, or misinterpreted? What if uncorrected data forms are accidentally mixed in with the corrected data forms? What if the assistant in charge of entering the data into the computer just had a fight with his or her lover? Cases can very easily find their way into the "wrong" cells. It is a wonder that social scientists ever produce "findings."

The procedures outlined in the previous sections for assessing necessity and sufficiency, therefore, must be modified to take these troubling aspects of social data—error, chance, randomness, and other factors—into account. In short, these common data and evidence problems provide a very strong motivation to employ analytic techniques that make some use of probability theory, especially techniques that address the problem of drawing inferences from imperfect evidence.

To make the discussion of these techniques more manageable, I limit it to the problem of using probabilistic criteria to make inferences about the sufficiency of combinations of conditions. However, the procedures I present for incorporating probabilistic criteria into the assessment of sufficiency also can be incorporated into the assessment of necessity. The only difference is that when studying necessity the investigator selects cases with the same outcome and examines whether they display the same causal condition, instead of selecting cases with the same cause or combination of causes and evaluating whether they display the same outcome.

THE QUASI-SUFFICIENCY OF CAUSAL COMBINATIONS

Rather than impose absolute standards in all investigations (i.e., the rule that cell 4 of table 4.6 should be completely void of cases in the assessment of sufficiency), researchers also can make inferences about sufficiency using probabilistic methods.[5] For example, a researcher might be interested in whether the evidence supports the claim that a particular combination of causes is "usually sufficient." He or she would evaluate cases with the causal combination in question to see what proportion display the outcome. If this proportion is significantly greater than, say, .65, then the causal combination in question might be labeled "usually sufficient" for the outcome. Or, a researcher might be interested in assessing whether the evidence supports the claim that a causal combination is "almost always" sufficient. If significantly greater than .80 of the cases displaying the combination of causes also manifest the outcome, then the researcher might claim that the causal combination is "almost always" sufficient. In short, it is possible to assess the *quasi-sufficiency* of causal combinations using linguistic qualifiers such as "more often than not" (.5), "usually" (.65), and "almost always" (.80)

5. Dion (1998) shows how to use Bayesian probability theory to assess necessity. The argument I present in this section extends his approach, applying it to the sufficiency of combinations of conditions, using conventional probability theory.

and applying formal statistical tests using these benchmark proportions.

Of course, the translation of linguistic qualifiers to proportions is not exact but approximate. The selection of the precise benchmark is to some extent arbitrary, but it must be made explicit by the researcher and thus be open to debate. The benchmark proportion can be varied, and results using different benchmarks can be compared. For example, the researcher might want to compare results using a .65 benchmark proportion ("usually sufficient") with results using a .50 benchmark ("sufficient more often than not") or a .80 benchmark ("almost always sufficient").[6]

Not only does the researcher specify a particular benchmark proportion of successes that the observed proportion of successes must exceed, he or she also must assess whether the observed success rate is *significantly* greater than the benchmark, using probabilistic criteria. That is, the researcher must conduct a formal test of the hypothesis that the observed proportion is greater than the benchmark proportion, using the null hypothesis that the observed proportion is either the same as (i.e., statistically indistinguishable) or less than the benchmark proportion. Essentially, this test involves estimating the standard error of the benchmark proportion (based on the number of cases involved in the assessment) and then using this standard error to evaluate the size of the positive gap separating the observed proportion from the benchmark proportion.

How does this assessment proceed? Again, consider the researcher studying strikes. The researcher believes that one of the sufficient combinations of conditions for the occurrence of strikes involves a combination of four factors: low unemployment, a strong union, poor communication between workers and management, and the introduction of new production technology opposed by workers. Suppose there are 91 instances of this combination of conditions and 70 of these instances result in strikes. The actual success rate is 70/91 or .769 (76.9%). Suppose the researcher wants to tests the hypothesis that this combination of conditions is "usually" sufficient for strikes, using .65 to define this benchmark. The observed proportion (.769) is greater than the

6. Bruce Western (1998, personal communication) points out that these benchmarks would not work for outcomes with very low baseline probabilities. To address such phenomena, much lower benchmarks must be used. However, the lower the benchmark, the greater the analytic distance to the concepts of necessity and sufficiency.

.65 used as the benchmark proportion, but is it significantly greater than .65?

To assess this difference, the researcher can use a simple z test for the difference between an observed proportion and a "population" proportion. The benchmark proportion provides the population proportion (.65); the observed proportion is .769. The general format for this test is described by Hays (1981:211–214):

$$z = \frac{(P - p) - \dfrac{1}{2N}}{\sqrt{\dfrac{pq}{N}}},$$

where P is the observed proportion, N is the number of cases displaying the causal combination, p is the benchmark proportion, and q equals $1 - p$. Essentially, this formula assesses the degree to which the observed proportion exceeds the benchmark proportion relative to the standard error of the benchmark proportion. The calculation is predicated on having an observed proportion that is larger than the benchmark proportion and includes a correction for continuity (see Hays 1981:214). Notice that according to the formula, the greater the gap between the observed proportion and the benchmark proportion, the larger the z value. Also, the greater the number of cases, the larger the z value because a large number of cases will result in a small denominator in the formula.

Using the hypothetical data just described, the calculation of the relevant z value,

$$z = \frac{(.769 - .65) - \dfrac{1}{2 * 91}}{\sqrt{\dfrac{.65 * .35}{91}}},$$

gives $z = 2.27$.

The next step is to evaluate the z value just calculated. How large must z be to assure the researcher that the observed proportion is significantly greater than the benchmark proportion? If the researcher is willing to take a one-in-twenty chance of reaching wrong conclusions about the null hypothesis (i.e., 95% confidence or .05 significance), then the z value must be greater than 1.65 (the z score corresponding to a one-tailed α of .05). If the researcher is willing to take a one in ten chance of being wrong, then the z value must be greater than 1.28 (the z score corresponding to a one-tailed α of .10). It is clear in this hypothetical analysis that the test of sufficiency succeeds, using either .05 or .10 significance. The gap between the observed proportion of successes (.769) and the benchmark proportion (.65) is great enough to provide clear evidence that the causal combination in question is "usually" sufficient for the outcome (strikes).

When the number of cases displaying the causal combination is 30 or fewer, a binomial probability test should be used instead of the z test. After all, the z test is a large-N approximation of the binomial test. Essentially, the binomial test assesses the probability of observing a specific range of "successful" outcomes, given an expected probability of success, which in turn is provided by the benchmark selected by the investigator (e.g., "sufficient more often than not" or .5). For example, a researcher might assess the probability of observing four or more successes in six trials, when the underlying probability of success is .5 (as in a coin toss). The binomial probability formula is

$$\binom{N}{r} p^r q^{N-r},$$

where N equals the number of cases displaying the causal combination, p equals the benchmark proportion, $q = 1 - p$, and r equals the number of cases displaying the outcome. Note that this formula is applied not only to the observed frequency of cases with the outcome but also to all frequencies that are superior to the observed frequency. These probabilities are then summed.

For purposes of illustration, assume that the researcher studying strikes observes only 13 instances of a causal combination, and 10 of these instances also display the outcome (strikes). In this analysis, the observed proportion of successes is the same as in the previous example (10/13 = 70/91 = .769), but now the number of cases is much smaller ($N = 13$). Essentially, the binomial test asks, What is the probability of observing 10 *or more* successes, out of 13 trials, if the underlying probability of success is the benchmark proportion? To maintain continuity with the earlier example, I use an underlying probability of .65 (i.e., "usually sufficient") in the demonstration of the binomial test. Using the binomial formula just described the probability of 10 successes is .1651; the probability of 11 successes is .0836, the probability of 12 successes is .0259; and the probability of 13 successes is .0037

(Hays 1981:647–51). In short, the probability of 10 or more successes in 13 trials is .2783.

This probability is far in excess of most conventional significance levels for this type of evidence (.05 and .10). It exceeds even the .20 level, which is used occasionally in small-N research. Thus, the researcher in this example would refrain from making any inference about sufficiency. That is, the researcher could not claim that the evidence supports the conclusion that the causal combination is "usually sufficient" for the outcome (using .65 as the appropriate benchmark proportion). This example shows that sufficiency tests are strongly influenced by the number of cases displaying the combination. With fewer cases, the researcher has less confidence that the observed proportion (.769) is superior to the benchmark proportion (.65).

To make the problem interesting, assume the researcher again finds only 13 instances of the causal combination in question and, again, only 10 display the outcome (strikes). Instead of using the benchmark proportion for "usually" sufficient (.65), the researcher decides to use a more generous benchmark, "sufficient more often than not" (.5) and sets the significance level at .05. Summing the relevant probabilities from the binomial test yields a probability of .0461, which indicates that the probability of observing 10 or more successes, when the underlying probability is .5, is smaller than the significance level, .05. Thus, the researcher could argue that even though the evidence does not lend support to the claim that the causal combination in question is "usually sufficient," it does lend support to the claim that the causal combination is "sufficient more often than not."

Finally, consider a common small-N situation: the pattern of results is "perfect" but the number of cases is very small. In this example, the researcher locates only four instances of the causal combination in question, but all four instances display the outcome in question. From a "veristic" as opposed to a probabilistic perspective, perfect sufficiency has been established: there are no "cell 4" cases. (A veristic evaluation of the evidence is a search for disconfirming cases. If any negative cases are found, even one, the test fails.) But how does it pan out using probabilistic criteria? Is an observed proportion of 1.0 based on four cases strong enough evidence to support the claim that the causal combination is "usually sufficient" ($p = .65$)? The binomial calculation yields a probability of .1785. These results show that even though there are no cell 4 cases (see table 4.6), we cannot reject the null hypothesis that the observed proportion (1.0) is the same as or less than the benchmark

Table 4.9
Number of Consistent Cases Needed to Pass Probabilistic Test of Sufficiency or Necessity for Different Ns

Benchmark Proportion

	.50			.65			.80		
N	$\alpha = .10$	$\alpha = .05$	$\alpha = .01$	$\alpha = .10$	$\alpha = .05$	$\alpha = .01$	$\alpha = .10$	$\alpha = .05$	$\alpha = .01$
4	4	...	...	...	...	...	...	...	...
5	5	5	...	...	...	...	...	...	...
6	6	6	...	...	...	...	...	...	...
7	6	7	7	7	7	...	...	...	...
8	7	7	8	8	8	...	...	...	...
9	7	8	9	9	9	...	...	...	...
10	8	9	10	9	10	...	...	...	...
11	9	9	10	10	11	11	11	...	...
12	9	10	11	11	11	12	12	...	...
13	10	10	12	12	12	13	13	...	...
14	10	11	12	12	13	14	14	14	...
15	11	12	13	13	14	15	15	15	...
16	12	12	14	14	14	15	16	16	...
17	12	13	14	14	15	16	17	17	...
18	13	13	15	15	16	17	17	18	...
19	13	14	15	16	17	18	18	19	...
20	14	15	16	17	17	19	19	20	...
21	14	15	17	17	18	19	20	21	21
22	15	16	17	18	19	20	21	21	22
23	16	16	18	19	20	21	22	22	23
24	16	17	19	20	20	22	23	23	24
25	16	17	19	20	21	22	23	24	25
26	17	18	20	21	22	23	24	25	26
27	17	19	20	22	23	24	25	26	27
28	18	19	21	22	23	25	26	27	28
29	19	20	22	23	24	26	27	28	29
30	19	20	22	24	25	26	28	28	30

proportion (.65), using either .05 or .10 significance. Thus, when using probabilistic criteria, "perfect" evidence based on small Ns (four confirming cases, no disconfirming cases) may not be strong enough to support the argument that a causal combination is "usually sufficient." It should be noted, however, that the evidence just described (four positive cases, no negative cases) does support the claim that the causal combination is "sufficient more often than not" (benchmark = .5) using a significance level of .10 (binomial probability = .0625).

Table 4.9 presents the number of positive cases (i.e., the number of cases in cell 2 of table 4.6) needed to pass sufficiency for different size Ns (i.e., the number of cases in cells 2 and 4 of table 4.6 combined). For each N (shown in column [1]), the number of positive cases needed to pass nine different tests is shown, using three sufficiency benchmarks (.50, .65, and .85) and three significance levels (.10, .05, and .01). The table shows both the difficulty of passing probabilistic sufficiency tests when Ns are very small and the moderating effect of both lower benchmarks and more lenient significance levels. The calculations presented in table 4.9 are all based on the binomial test. (These figures apply to probabilistic tests of necessity as well; see chapter 8.)

The incorporation of probabilistic criteria sketched here offers an important alternative to the veritistic standard depicted in table 4.6— "no cell 4 cases allowed." Using the probabilistic techniques just described, it is possible to assess causal complexity while making allowances for the randomness and error inherent in both human social life and the work of social scientists. Also, as I have just demonstrated, by incorporating probabilistic criteria it is possible to take advantage of linguistic qualifiers such as "more often than not" and "usually" and thereby enlarge and sharpen the assessment of the sufficiency of causal combinations. Using the concept of quasi-sufficiency, it is possible as well to expand the discourse surrounding the nature of causation and establish an important new tool for the study of causal complexity and social diversity.

ASSESSING SUFFICIENCY: A SUMMARY OF THE DIFFERENT TESTS

The assessment of sufficiency can take either one of two general forms: veristic, with no tolerance for discordant outcomes among the cases conforming to a causal combination, or probabilistic, using benchmarks and linguistic qualifiers, as just demonstrated. In *The Comparative Method* and most applications of the techniques I present in that book, the assessment of the sufficiency of causal combinations is veristic: In order to be considered sufficient for an outcome, *all* the cases conforming to a particular causal combination must display the outcome in question. When the number of relevant cases is small, as in most macrosocial research, this method is the only one available. The other general type of sufficiency test is probabilistic. There are two versions of this test. The first is the small-N version based on the binomial probability test, used with Ns of 30 or fewer cases. The second is the large-N version based on the z test for the significance of the positive difference between a sample proportion and a benchmark proportion, used with values of $N > 30$.

It should be noted that the veristic approach may be modified to include evaluation of the strength of the evidence (see, e.g., Ragin 1995). As already explained, if a causal combination includes *any* negative cases of the outcome, it fails the veristic test of sufficiency. In addition, the investigator may establish a *frequency threshold* for the number of positive instances. If a causal combination embraces one positive instance of the outcome and zero negative instances, does the evidence support the claim that the causal combination in question is sufficient for the outcome? Is two positive instances enough? How many does it take? The researcher must justify the frequency threshold used to evaluate sufficiency in each investigation. In some studies, especially small-N comparative studies of large-scale macrosocial processes and events, a claim of sufficiency may be based on a single positive instance. This standard is the de facto norm in comparative case-study research. In studies with moderate-sized Ns, more positive instances may be required. Thus, there are two forms of the veristic test of sufficiency, one involving no frequency threshold (in essence, a threshold of one positive case), the other incorporating a frequency threshold specified by the investigator. Table 4.10 summarizes the four major types of sufficiency tests. (These four types apply to tests of necessity as well.)

Table 4.10
Types of Sufficiency Tests

Veristic: No Disconforming Cases Allowed		Probabilistic: Disconfirming Cases Permitted; Researcher Sets Benchmark and Significance Level	
No use of frequency criteria: One case is enough to pass test	Use of frequency criteria: Researcher sets threshold for pass	Small-N: Use of binomial test with 30 or fewer cases	Large-N: Use of z test with greater than 30 cases

CONTRASTS WITH CONVENTIONAL,
VARIABLE-ORIENTED PRACTICES

Social scientists generally avoid discussing causal complexity. Consequently, they rarely have much to say about either necessity or sufficiency. The reasons they avoid these topics are straightforward.

The first is the simple fact that the language of necessity and sufficiency evokes absolute standards, for example, the idea that a single disconfirming case refutes a claim of sufficiency or necessity. Social scientists work with imperfect evidence drawn in imperfect ways from a social world that not only is very complex, but that is also subject to a great deal of chance and randomness. The play of the weather alone on what people do and how they feel is enormous and unpredictable. Thus, the very nature of social phenomena makes social scientists shy away from the absolute standards that are an integral part of most discussions of causal necessity and sufficiency. In this chapter, I have shown various ways to relax these standards and bring necessity and sufficiency back into social science discourse (see also Dion 1998).

The second reason has less to do with the nature of social phenomena and more to do with conventional practices in variable-oriented research. Generally, when variable-oriented researchers address causal complexity, they do so by examining the many single causes that they believe may affect some outcome. The implicit model they use is that every single cause is a sufficient cause.[7] In this approach, the goal is to identify all the relevant single causes and then assess their relative importance. Consider the cross-case analysis of strikes one last time. The conventional approach would be to elaborate a list of possible causes (among them, wage levels, unemployment rates, inflation, and union strength), and then assess the relative importance as each cause as an "independent" cause of strikes. The key question would be, Does each cause significantly increase the odds of a strike, holding the others constant, and if so, how much?

Without going into the details of statistical procedures, a researcher using these techniques might find that the introduction of new technology opposed by workers increases the odds of a strike by 5 or 10 per-

---

7. While not a central concern here, it is worth noting that in the conventional approach causal necessity and sufficiency are approximated, probabilistically speaking, by the model or prediction equation *considered as a whole,* assuming this model has been completely and correctly specified.

cent, the exact figure does not matter, controlling for the impact of other relevant conditions (e.g., wage levels, unemployment rates, union strength). The effects of these other conditions are "held constant" using statistical techniques designed to calculate the "independent" effect of each causal variable.[8] For example, if the introduction of new technology opposed by workers often occurs when there is poor communication between workers and managers, and if poor communication, by itself, also has a positive effect on the odds of a strike, then the estimate of the impact of new technology on the odds of a strike must be downwardly adjusted to take account of its frequent association with poor communication. Conventional statistical procedures are designed to make such adjustments with great precision.

Researchers using conventional techniques almost never examine causal combinations. Their emphasis, instead, is on individual causes and assessing their relative strength. Thus, it is usually difficult to incorporate the consideration of necessity and sufficiency into these analyses because the examination of these aspects of causation usually entails the analysis of combinations of conditions, as sketched in this chapter. In the conventional statistical approach every cause is thought to be capable of acting alone to influence the outcome (i.e., the common bias is toward causal additivity), and every causal variable is usually thought to be causally relevant in the same way for all cases (i.e., the usual bias is also toward causal homogeneity). Thus, researchers using conventional quantitative techniques make very strong assumptions about the nature of the causes they study. They also make very strong assumptions about the homogeneity of the cases that are embraced by their populations.

These practices are antithetical to the study of social diversity, especially as manifested in causal complexity. As I show in this chapter, it is possible to allow causation to be complex, to avoid making assumptions about its specific character, and still study it in a systematic way.

8. In the conventional approach, the assessment of a cause's impact basically involves comparing the odds of the outcome in the first column of table 4.2 (the frequency of cases in cell 1 is divided by the frequency of cases in cell 3) with the odds of the outcome in the second column of table 4.2 (the frequency of cases in cell 2 is divided by the frequency of cases in cell 4) after adjusting for the impact of other causes on the difference in the odds of the outcome. Thus, the conventional statistical assessment of the impact of a cause on an outcome involves all four cells of the simple cross-tabulation presented in table 4.2.

LOOKING BACK, LOOKING AHEAD

Chapters 1–4 establish the basic elements of the diversity-oriented approach, mostly by contrasting this approach with variable-oriented and case-oriented strategies. As I demonstrate in these chapters, the diversity-oriented approach does the following:

1. It treats the constitution of populations as an ongoing process laden with potential for obscuring diversity.
2. It sees cases as complex configurations and recognizes the possibility that a single difference between two cases may signal a difference in kind.
3. It allows for maximum causal complexity in social processes, especially for the possibility that no single causal condition may be either necessary or sufficient for an outcome.

Configurational thinking is at the core of the diversity-oriented approach. Central to configurational thinking, in turn, is the notion of the property space, an analytic device showing all combinations of relevant conditions. In Lazarsfeld's approach to property spaces, the key concern is the elaboration and reduction of types. As I show in these chapters, the property space notion can be extended to the analysis of causal conditions, where it can be used to guide and structure the examination of causal complexity, especially as manifested in causal conditions that are sufficient only in combinations.

The usual lesson that social scientists draw from the observation that no single cause is either necessary and sufficient in the study of social phenomena is that necessity and sufficiency have no place in social research. This chapter demonstrates otherwise, first by showing the importance of studying causation that is both conjunctural and multiple and then by showing how to do so. Chapter 5 provides a detailed example of the study of causal complexity, based on the techniques I present in this chapter. I present two analyses of the same evidence, one using probabilistic criteria, as just discussed, and the other using the "no cell 4 cases" rule (i.e., veristic criteria).

FIVE

THE LOGIC OF
DIVERSITY-ORIENTED RESEARCH

INTRODUCTION

This chapter describes a data analytic strategy known as *qualitative comparative analysis* (QCA; see Ragin 1987; Drass and Ragin 1992), originally developed as a formalization and extension of the comparative case-study approach. In a nutshell, QCA provides analytic tools for comparing cases as configurations of set memberships and for elucidating their patterned similarities and differences.[1] With QCA it is possible to view cases as configurations, examine complex patterns of causation, and reconstitute populations based on the patterns that cases exhibit (Ragin 1995). QCA frees social scientists from many of the restrictive, homogenizing assumptions of conventional variable-oriented research without giving up the possibility of formulating statements about broad, cross-case patterns. This alternative approach to cross-case analysis provides the set-theoretic foundation for diversity-oriented research.[2]

1. Only some of the procedures described in this chapter are implemented in QCA 3.0 (Drass and Ragin 1992). All are implemented in FS/QCA 1.0 (Drass and Ragin 1999). Procedurally speaking, QCA 3.0 is a subset of FS/QCA 1.0. The new program separates the analysis of necessity and sufficiency, incorporates the use of probabilistic criteria, and fully implements all fuzzy-set procedures. Both QCA 3.0 and FS/QCA 1.0 can be downloaded from the Web site http://www.nwu.edu/sociology.

2. The exact operation of QCA, as described in this chapter, is *not* identical to the description presented in *The Comparative Method* (Ragin 1987). I have altered the procedure slightly so that the parallel to fuzzy-set techniques, presented in part 2 of this work, is enhanced. Specifically, the approach presented in this chapter considers not only all logically possible combinations of conditions—the

Most of this chapter is devoted to describing the application of QCA to *dichotomous* social data reflecting the memberships of cases in conventional, crisp sets. In contrast to statistical methodology, which is based on linear algebra, QCA is based on Boolean algebra, the algebra of sets and logic. QCA treats social categories as sets and views cases in terms of their multiple set memberships. In Boolean algebra a case is either in or out of a set and QCA uses binary-coded data, with 1 indicating membership and 0 indicating nonmembership. Combinations of crisp-set memberships, represented as arrays of binary data, are compared and contrasted to identify decisive cross-case patterns.

Because there is no allowance in QCA for the partial membership of cases in sets, QCA does not directly address one of the main objectives of this book, namely, the introduction of fuzzy sets to the social sciences and the development of fuzzy-set techniques for the analysis of social data. As I detail in part 2 of this work, with fuzzy sets the membership of cases in sets can be partial, with membership scores ranging from 0 (nonmembership) to 1 (full membership). (For example, an Eastern European country might have a membership score of .68 in the set of "rich countries.") This scheme offers a major advance over Boolean algebra and crisp sets.

Boolean algebra, the foundation of QCA, may appear inadequate from the perspective of fuzzy sets—especially given the ubiquity of partial membership in sets. Recall from the introduction, however, that it is impossible for social scientists to take full advantage of the power of fuzzy sets without also adopting techniques of data analysis that focus on set-theoretic relationships. Most quantitative techniques of data analysis eschew the examination of such relationships. However, the analysis of set-theoretic relationships is the core of QCA. Thus, the discussion of QCA offered in this chapter is essentially the presentation of a data analytic strategy that provides a basis for the integration of fuzzy sets into social research. It is important to understand and appreciate the set-theoretic principles that are central to QCA in order to understand how to take full advantage of the power of fuzzy sets. The analytic procedures that I present in part 2 using fuzzy sets parallel those discussed in this chapter.

---

emphasis of *The Comparative Method*—but also all possible "groupings" of cases. Also, rather than use what is known as a "prime implicant chart" to logically simplify results, in this chapter I show how to use the "containment" rule. Finally, this chapter demonstrates how to incorporate probabilistic criteria into the analysis of set-theoretic relationships, building on the discussion presented in chapter 4.

WORKING WITH CASES AS CONFIGURATIONS

In QCA cases are examined in terms of their multiple memberships in sets, viewed as configurations. This interest in how different aspects or features combine in each case is consistent with an emphasis on understanding aspects of cases in context. For example, having many small- to medium-sized political parties (party "fractionalization") signifies different things about a country's political stability, depending on, among other things, the nature of its electoral system, its degree of sociocultural diversity, and the age of its political institutions. Take another example: having many debts can signal different things about a person's financial situation, depending on his or her other attributes, including age, income, employment status, assets, and career trajectory. By looking at combinations of aspects, it is possible to get a sense of a case as a whole, especially how its different aspects connect. As noted in chapter 3, this emphasis on how characteristics connect contrasts sharply with the variable-oriented view of aspects of cases as analytically separable, independent features.

In every social scientific investigation, the selection of cases and attributes to study is dependent on the substantive and theoretical interests of the researcher and his or her intended audiences. Sometimes a research literature is especially well developed, and the selection of cases and attributes is relatively unproblematic. In other situations, however, the researcher can formulate a worthwhile selection of attributes only through an in-depth analysis of cases (Amenta and Poulsen 1994). Sometimes researchers must constitute relevant cases and their key aspects through a systematic dialogue between ideas and evidence, as described in chapter 2. Researchers progressively refine their understanding of relevant cases and their key aspects as they sharpen the concepts appropriate for studying them.

Often the selection of aspects is shaped by the nature of the outcome to be investigated and the researcher's understanding of the causal conditions relevant to this outcome. The selection of causal conditions is usually broad because the concern is to identify not only the factors that seem connected to the outcome as proximate causes, but also the conditions that provide the contexts for the operation of these proximate causes. A fractionalized party system, for example, could be a proximate cause of political breakdown in some situations; in other situations, it might be irrelevant; still in others, it might contribute to long-term political stability. Thus, it is important to consider the contexts and conditions that enable and disable causal connections. This concern for the impact of context on causal connections is a key aspect of configurational thinking.

In QCA, once a set of causally relevant aspects has been identified, the researcher constructs a table listing the different logically possible combinations of these attributes ("configurations") along with the cases that conform to each configuration. As explained in chapter 3, this table can be seen as a "property space" (Lazarsfeld 1937). Each location within a property space, in turn, can be seen, potentially at least, as a different kind or type of case. In QCA, attributes are represented with presence/absence dichotomies, with 0 indicating absence (the case is not in the set in question), and 1 indicating presence (the case is in the set in question). Multichotomies (e.g., race/ethnicity at the individual level) are represented with multiple dichotomies, which can be coded in a variety of ways, depending on the interests of the investigator.

By examining the cases that conform to each configuration, represented as a row of the table, it is possible for the investigator to evaluate whether the best set of attributes has been identified. For each configuration, the researcher asks, Do these cases go together? Are they comparable instances, in the context of the present investigation? Thus, the configurational understanding of cases focuses on the equivalence of cases at the level of the configuration, not simply at the more global, population-wide level.

Consider, for example, table 5.1, which shows different configurations of conditions relevant to ethnic political mobilization among territorially based linguistic minorities in Western Europe. Four attributes define the property space: (1) whether the minority is large or small, (2) whether the minority has a weak or strong linguistic base, (3) whether the minority region is richer or poorer than the core region of the host country, and (4) whether the minority region is growing or declining (see Allardt 1979; Ragin 1987). There are 16 logically possible combinations ("configurations") of these four presence/absence dichotomies, and thus 16 mutually exclusive subsets of cases. For notational convenience in the discussion that follows, the presence of an attribute is denoted by the name of the attribute; the absence of the attribute (negation) is denoted with the "~" symbol preceding the attribute name. Thus, "large" indicates that the linguistic minority is large in size, while "~large" indicates that it is small; "fluent" indicates good linguistic ability; "afluent" indicates poor linguistic ability; "~wealthy" indicates that the minority region is wealthier than the core region; "~wealthy" indicates that it is poorer than the core region; "growing"

Table 5.1
Territorially Based Linguistic Minorities in Western Europe

Combination No.	Size[a]	Linguistic Ability[b]	Relative Wealth[c]	Growth[d]	Instance
1	~large	~fluent	~wealthy	~growing	Lapps, Finland
					Lapps, Sweden
					Lapps, Norway
					Finns, Sweden
					Albanian, Italy
					Greeks, Italy
2	~large	~fluent	~wealthy	growing	North Frisians, Germany
					Danes, Germany
					Basques, Frances
3	~large	~fluent	wealthy	~growing	Ladins, Italy
4	~large	~fluent	wealthy	growing	None
5	~large	fluent	~wealthy	~growing	Magyars, Austria
					Croats, Austria
					Slovenes, Austria
					Greenlanders, Denmark
6	~large	fluent	~wealthy	growing	None
7[e]	~large	fluent	wealthy	~growing	Aalanders, Finland
8[e]	~large	fluent	wealthy	growing	Slovenes, Italy
					Valdotians, Italy
9	large	~fluent	~wealthy	~growing	Sards, Italy
					Galicians, Spain
10[e]	large	~fluent	~wealthy	growing	West Frisians, Neth.
					Catalans, France
					Occitans, France
					Welsh, Great Britain
					Bretons, France
					Corsicans, France
11	large	~fluent	wealthy	~growing	None
12[e]	large	~fluent	wealthy	growing	Friulians, Italy
					Occitans, Italy
					Basques, Spain
					Catalans, Spain
13	large	fluent	~wealthy	~growing	Flemings, France
14[e]	large	fluent	~wealthy	growing	Walloons, Belgium
15[e]	large	fluent	wealthy	~growing	Swedes, Finland
					South Tyroleans, Italy
16[e]	large	fluent	wealthy	growing	Alsatians, France
					Germans, Belgium
					Flemings, Belgium

Note: The (~) sign preceding an attribute name indicates "not" or negation.
[a] Whether the minority is large or small (~large).
[b] Whether the minority has a strong (fluent) or weak (~fluent) linguistic ability.
[c] Whether the minority region is richer (wealthy) or poorer (~wealthy) than the core region of the country.
[d] Whether the minority region is growing or declining (~growing).
[e] Row with strong evidence of ethnic political mobilization.

indicates that the region is growing; "~growing" indicates that it is not growing. Superscripted "e" next to configuration numbers indicates minorities that have mobilized politically (configuration nos. 7, 8, 10, 12, 14, 15, and 16).

Table 5.1 also shows the cases conforming to each of the 16 logically possible combinations of these four dichotomies. By evaluating the comparability of the cases conforming to each configuration, the researcher can make a preliminary assessment of the adequacy of the aspects selected for investigation. For example, the first configuration (~large · ~fluent · ~wealthy · ~growing; note that midlevel dots are used to indicate combinations of characteristics) brings together Lapps in Finland, Lapps in Sweden, Lapps in Norway, Torne Valley Finns in Sweden, Albanians in Italy, and Greeks in Italy. Viewing these six cases together, the researcher asks whether it is reasonable to group these as similar cases in a study of ethnic political mobilization of linguistic minorities in Western Europe. If not, then additional attributes should be added to the list of relevant causal conditions, or perhaps the researcher should substitute different attributes for some of the listed attributes. For example, the investigator may believe that the four minorities in Scandinavia differ in some causally decisive way from the two minorities in Italy. If so, the causal condition that distinguishes these two groups should be added to the table. The cases conforming to each configuration in the property space (i.e., row of the table) should be evaluated in this manner.

When researchers view their evidence in terms of logically possible combinations of conditions along with the cases conforming to each configuration, as in table 5.1, they also evaluate the cases in each row to see if they all display the same outcome or at least roughly comparable outcomes. For example, the researcher would ask: Are the six cases in the first row similar with respect to their ethnic political mobilization? Each row is examined in this manner, so that the researcher can gain some confidence that a viable specification of relevant causal conditions, which comprise the property space for the outcome, has been realized. Obviously, if the cases in a row display widely divergent outcomes or if they are evenly split between contrasting outcomes, the researcher will examine these cases closely and reformulate his or her specification of causal conditions accordingly. This evaluation of cases with respect to outcomes is separate from the first evaluation, just described, where the researcher asks simply whether the cases grouped within each combination of attributes belong together as comparable cases regardless of their outcomes.

When making assessments of outcomes, it is unrealistic to expect that all the cases in each row will be perfectly consistent with respect to the outcome in question. It is very difficult to capture all causally relevant conditions in broad, cross-case analyses. Furthermore, mistakes can be made when assigning cases to sets or when evaluating the evidence with respect to the outcome in question. As an illustration of the general problem, consider the twelfth row of table 5.1. The Friulian and Occitan minorities of Italy occupy this row, along with the Basque and Catalan minorities of Spain. But the two minorities in Spain are more politically active than the two in Italy, and the Basque minority is more mobilized than the Catalan. This information could be used to identify a fifth causal condition, or perhaps even to reformulate the property space altogether, with a completely new set of causal conditions. Alternatively, the researcher might decide simply that there is enough evidence of ethnic political activity across the four cases in this row to justify treating them all as instances of ethnic political mobilization. In other words, the researcher might conclude that the discordance is not so great as to motivate any change in the specification of causal conditions.

The larger point is that the examination of outcomes is a central part of constructing a property space and generating configurations, especially when it comes to the selection of causally relevant aspects of cases. This interplay between theory and data analysis leads to a progressive refinement of the understanding of relevant cases and to a more nuanced elaboration of the ideas guiding the research. Again, perfect consistency in outcomes for the cases with the same combination of causal conditions is relatively rare. As demonstrated in chapter 4, however, it is possible to use probabilistic criteria when evaluating the links between causal conditions and outcomes. This tactic partially ameliorates the problem of contradictory outcomes and thus allows for some discordance in outcomes within configurations.

It is important to understand that in QCA the fundamental analytic unit is the configuration, along with the cases conforming to each configuration. Thus, table 5.1 should *not* be viewed as a presentation of four presence/absence dichotomies but rather as a specification of 16 qualitatively distinct conditions—that is, 16 kinds of cases. The principles of configurational thinking discussed in chapter 3 mandate allowance for the possibility that a single difference between two cases may signal a difference in kind. This thinking provides the conceptual basis for constructing and evaluating evidence in terms of logically possible combinations of causes (i.e., as configurations). Thus, the table should be viewed as a property space with 16 separate locations. Each of the 16 configurations constitutes, potentially at least, a qualitatively distinct constellation. Note that if five dichotomies had been used, there would have been 32 configurations ($2^5 = 32$); 6 dichotomies would yield 64 configurations, and so on. Using dichotomies, the number of logically possible combinations is equal to 2^k, where k is equal to the number of attributes.

The four dichotomies presented in table 5.1 can be presented not only as 16 configurations (the logically possible combinations of the four presence/absence attributes), but also as 80 logically possible *groupings*. The 16 configurations presented in table 5.1 provide basic groupings, that is, groupings that use all four presence/absence dichotomies. They correspond to the 16 cells of the property space that can be constructed from four dichotomies. Additional groupings can be formed by merging configurations that share one or more attributes. For example, the bottom two rows of table 5.1, linguistic minorities that are large·fluent·wealthy·~growing (the penultimate row) and those that are large·fluent·wealthy·growing (the bottom row), share three attributes and thus can be merged to form a larger grouping, minorities that are large·fluent·wealthy. In set terminology, the larger set is formed from the union of its two component sets. Still larger groupings can be formed from the union of more rows as long as the rows that are grouped contain at least one attribute in common. For example, the first eight rows display ~large. Merging these eight rows yields the set of cases that have ~large in common—that is, all the smaller linguistic minorities.

Just as it is possible to calculate the logically possible number of combinations (2^k), it is also possible to calculate the number of logically possible groupings. The formula is $3^k - 1$, where k again is the number of attributes ($3^4 - 1 = 80$). Table 5.2 shows the 80 logically possible groupings of the four dichotomies presented in table 5.1. Using the formula just described, the 80 possible groupings are formed as follows: 16 involve combinations of four attributes, 32 involve combinations of three attributes, 24 involve combinations of two attributes, and eight involve single attributes.

These 80 groupings are important because they are relevant to any conclusions about cross-case patterns the researcher may wish to construct using the property space presented in table 5.1. For example, the researcher might examine all minorities that are wealthy and growing (wealthy·growing) to see if they all display ethnic political mobilization. The 80 groupings listed in table 5.2 provide the basis for formulating

Table 5.2
Groupings Using Four Dichotomies

Initial Configurations (16 Combinations of Four Aspects) (1)	Groupings Involving Combinations of Three Aspects (32) (2)	Groupings Involving Combinations of Two Aspects (24) (3)	Groupings Involving a Single Aspect (8) (4)
~large·~fluent·~wealthy·~growing	~large·~fluent·~wealthy	~large·~fluent	~large
~large·~fluent·~wealthy·growing	~large·~fluent·wealthy	~large·fluent	large
~large·~fluent·wealthy·~growing	~large·fluent·~wealthy	large·~fluent	~fluent
~large·~fluent·wealthy·growing	~large·fluent·wealthy	large·fluent	fluent
~large·fluent·~wealthy·~growing	large·~fluent·~wealthy	~large·~wealthy	~wealthy
~large·fluent·~wealthy·growing	large·~fluent·wealthy	~large·wealthy	wealthy
~large·fluent·wealthy·~growing	large·fluent·~wealthy	large·~wealthy	~growing
~large·fluent·wealthy·growing	large·fluent·wealthy	large·wealthy	growing
large·~fluent·~wealthy·~growing	~large·~fluent·~growing	~large·~growing	
large·~fluent·~wealthy·growing	~large·~fluent·growing	~large·growing	
large·~fluent·wealthy·~growing	~large·fluent·~growing	large·~growing	
large·~fluent·wealthy·growing	~large·fluent·growing	large·growing	
large·fluent·~wealthy·~growing	large·~fluent·~growing	~fluent·~wealthy	
large·fluent·~wealthy·growing	large·~fluent·growing		

large·fluent·~wealthy·growing
large·fluent·wealthy·~growing
large·fluent·wealthy·growing

large·~fluent·growing
large·fluent·~growing
large·fluent·growing
~large·~wealthy·~growing
~large·~wealthy·growing
~large·wealthy·~growing
~large·wealthy·growing
large·~wealthy·~growing
large·~wealthy·growing
large·wealthy·~growing
large·wealthy·growing
~fluent·~wealthy·~growing
~fluent·~wealthy·growing
~fluent·wealthy·~growing
~fluent·wealthy·growing
fluent·~wealthy·~growing
fluent·~wealthy·growing
fluent·wealthy·~growing
fluent·wealthy·growing

~fluent·wealthy
fluent·~wealthy
fluent·wealthy
~fluent·~growing
~fluent·growing
fluent·~growing
fluent·growing
~wealthy·~growing
~wealthy·growing
wealthy·~growing
wealthy·growing

Note: From table 5.1.

any statement that can be made regarding cross-case patterns using this property space. As I show subsequently, the examination of these different groupings is central to the assessment of causal complexity, especially the evaluation of the *sufficiency* of different combinations of causal conditions.

Note also that the 80 groupings in table 5.2 represent all logically possible *selections* on the four causal conditions used in this analysis. Recall from chapter 4 that to assess the sufficiency of a combination of causal conditions, the researcher selects cases with a given combination of conditions and then evaluates whether these cases display the same or roughly the same outcome. If they all (or virtually all) display the outcome in question, then the evidence supports the argument that the combination of causal conditions in question is sufficient for the outcome. The $3^k - 1$ logically possible selections, in this light, can be seen as an attempt to implement an exhaustive examination of causal sufficiency. Each grouping constitutes a different logically possible selection, and each grouping can be evaluated with respect to the outcome. In short, the groupings specify multiple selections on the relevant causal conditions and thus multiple tests of sufficiency.

ANALYZING CAUSAL COMPLEXITY

Usually, social research begins with the goal of explaining an outcome. For example, a researcher might ask why some territorially based linguistic minorities participate in politics on an ethnic basis while others do not. Table 5.1, for example, shows that linguistic minorities in row nos. 7, 8, 10, 12, 14, 15, and 16 (as indicated by the superscripted "e" attached to the row numbers in the table) offer consistent evidence of ethnic political mobilization, while those in the other rows offer weak or no evidence of such mobilization. How should the researcher describe the key differences between these two sets of minorities (mobilized versus not)? In other words, what combinations of causal conditions are linked to ethnic political mobilization?

Recall that in diversity-oriented research, investigators assume maximum causal complexity. This concern for causal complexity is best implemented by allowing for the possibility that no single causal condition may be either necessary or sufficient for the outcome in question. When no single causal condition is either necessary or sufficient, researchers anticipate finding that different *combinations* of causal conditions are sufficient for the outcome. This emphasis on causal complexity, however, does not preclude the possibility of finding necessary causes. As noted in chapter 4, it is important in any analysis to first test for necessary conditions before examining sufficiency, especially when there is "limited diversity" (i.e., logically possible combinations of causal conditions lacking empirical instances). Necessary conditions may be obscured if researchers focus *exclusively* on sufficiency.

Assessing Necessity

To evaluate necessity, researchers examine instances of the outcome to see if they share any theoretically or substantively relevant causal conditions (see chapter 4). Table 5.3 lists relevant instances of the outcome—the rows from table 5.1 that contain cases with consistent evidence of ethnic political mobilization (seven rows with a total of 19 mobilized minorities). It is clear from simple inspection of the table

Table 5.3
Analysis of Necessary Conditions Using Instances of Ethnic Political Mobilization

Combination No.[a]	Size[b]	Linguistic Ability[c]	Relative Wealth[d]	Growth[e]	Instance
7	~large	fluent	wealthy	~growing	Aalanders, Finland
8	~large	fluent	wealthy	growing	Slovenes, Italy
					Valdotians, Italy
10	large	~fluent	~wealthy	growing	West Frisians, Neth.
					Catalans, France
					Occitans, France
					Welsh, Great Britain
					Bretons, France
					Corsicans, France
12	large	~fluent	wealthy	growing	Friulians, Italy
					Occitans, Italy
					Basques, Spain
					Catalans, Spain
14	large	fluent	~wealthy	growing	Walloons, Belgium
15	large	fluent	wealthy	~growing	Swedes, Finland
					South Tyroleans, Italy
16	large	fluent	wealthy	growing	Alsatians, France
					Germans, Belgium
					Flemings, Belgium

Note: The (~) sign preceding an attribute name indicates "not" or negation.
[a] From table 5.1, show strong evidence of ethnic political mobilization.
[b] Whether the minority is large or small (~large).
[c] Whether the minority has a strong (fluent) or weak (~fluent) linguistic ability.
[d] Whether the minority region is richer (wealthy) or poorer (~wealthy) than the core region of the country.
[e] Whether the minority region is growing or declining (~growing).

that there is no single cause (and thus no combination of causes) that is uniformly present in all instances of the outcome, ethnic political mobilization. The two that come closest are "large size" and "growing," with 16 out of 19 mobilized minorities exhibiting each condition. Thus, based on simple inspection of this table, the researcher would conclude that there are no necessary conditions present among the four conditions that comprise this property space. This evaluation is based on "veristic" criteria. That is, it is based on the simple query: Is it true that the mobilized minorities *uniformly* exhibit one or more causal conditions?

As noted in chapter 4, it is possible to incorporate probabilistic criteria not only into the evaluation of sufficient conditions, as sketched in that chapter, but also into the evaluation of necessary conditions. For example, a researcher might argue that if significantly greater than 65% of the instances of an outcome exhibit the same causal condition, then that condition is "usually necessary" for the outcome. Using this benchmark (.65) and a significance level .05, however, neither "large size" nor "growing" passes the test of "usually necessary." The probability of observing 16 or more successes in 19 trials, with an underlying probability of success equal to .65, is .0591, which exceeds the .05 significance level. To pass .05 significance with nineteen cases, only two cases may deviate (see table 4.9). Thus, even using probabilistic criteria— and thereby permitting disconfirming cases—it is reasonable to conclude that there are no necessary conditions for ethnic political mobilization present in this property space.

Assessing Sufficiency

To assess the sufficiency of a cause or causal combination, the researcher examines the cases conforming to the cause or the combination and evaluates whether they agree in displaying the outcome in question. For example, the evidence presented for row 10 of table 5.1 (cases conforming to the combination ~large·~fluent·wealthy·growing) indicates that this causal combination may be sufficient for ethnic political mobilization because all six cases with this combination display ethnic political mobilization. Of course, researchers must establish standards for evaluating sufficiency and state them clearly. Is six positive cases and no negative cases enough to establish the sufficiency of a causal combination? What about two positive cases and no negative cases, or only one positive case? In each investigation, the investigator must justify the method used to assess sufficiency based on, among other things, the nature of the evidence, previous research, the state of relevant theoretical and substantive knowledge, and the intended audience for the research.

Because the example presented here, ethnic political mobilization among linguistic minorities, involves a moderate number of cases (36), I present both types of sufficiency tests, veristic and probabilistic (see discussion of table 4.10). I focus first on the probabilistic approach, building on the strategies presented in chapter 4. After presenting the probabilistic approach, I present the veristic approach and then contrast the two general ways of assessing sufficiency.

The core of the probabilistic approach to the assessment of sufficiency is to test the significance of the difference between the observed proportion of positive instances and a benchmark proportion specified by the investigator. As explained in chapter 4, the benchmark proportion is linked to linguistic qualifiers, such as "almost always sufficient" (.80) and "sufficient more often than not" (.50). When the number of cases conforming to a causal combination is modest, 30 or fewer, researchers should use an exact probability test; otherwise, the z test for the difference between two proportions will suffice (Hays 1981: 211–14, 647–51). To conduct either the z test or the exact probability test, the researcher must set a benchmark proportion and a significance level before making these assessments. For example, a researcher might argue that if the proportion of cases displaying the outcome in question is significantly greater than .65, using a .05 significance level (one-tailed test), then the causal combination in question is "usually sufficient" for the outcome.

The sufficiency test is applied not only to the original 16 configurations listed in table 5.1 but also to the remaining 64 groupings listed in columns (2)–(4) of table 5.2. In essence, by applying the test to each of the 80 groupings in table 5.2, the researcher examines all logically possible causal expressions that can be constructed from the four presence/absence dichotomies that make up the property space showing causal conditions relevant to ethnic political mobilization. Alternatively, these groupings can be viewed as all possible "selections" on the causal conditions. Table 5.4 summarizes the 80 tests of sufficiency using a benchmark of .65 and a significance level of .05 (one-tailed test). The first column of Table 5.4 lists the 80 groupings. The second column shows the number of cases conforming to each grouping. The third column shows the proportion of cases with strong evidence of ethnic political mobilization (calculated only for groupings with at least two cases). The last column shows the results of the binomial probability tests. Probability levels .05 or lower in the fourth column indicate

Table 5.4
Sufficiency Tests for the 80 Groupings

Grouping (1)	Case (2)	Proportion (3)	Probability (4)
~large·~fluent·~wealthy·~growing	6	.00	
~large·~fluent·~wealthy·growing	3	.00	
~large·~fluent·wealthy·~growing	1		
~large·~fluent·wealthy·growing	0		
~large·fluent·~wealthy·~growing	4	.00	
~large·fluent·~wealthy·growing	0		
~large·fluent·wealthy·~growing	1		
~large·fluent·wealthy·growing	2	1.00	.4225
large·~fluent·~wealthy·~growing	2	.00	
large·~fluent·~wealthy·growing	6	1.00	.0754
large·~fluent·wealthy·~growing	0		
large·~fluent·wealthy·growing	4	1.00	.1785
large·fluent·~wealthy·~growing	1		
large·fluent·~wealthy·growing	1		
large·fluent·wealthy·~growing	2	1.00	.4225
large·fluent·wealthy·growing	3	1.00	.2746
~large·~fluent·~wealthy	9	.00	
~large·~fluent·wealthy	1		
~large·fluent·~wealthy	4	.00	
~large·fluent·wealthy	3	1.00	.2746
large·~fluent·~wealthy	8	.75	.4278
large·~fluent·wealthy	4	1.00	.1785
large·fluent·~wealthy	2	.50	
large·fluent·wealthy	5	1.00	.1160
~large·~fluent·~growing	7	.00	
~large·~fluent·growing	3	.00	
~large·fluent·~growing	5	.20	
~large·fluent·growing	2	1.00	.4225
large·~fluent·~growing	2	.00	
large·~fluent·growing	10	1.00	.0135
large·fluent·~growing	3	.67	.7182
large·fluent·growing	4	1.00	.1785
~large·~wealthy·~growing	10	.00	
~large·~wealthy·growing	3	.00	
~large·wealthy·~growing	2	.50	
~large·wealthy·growing	2	1.00	.4225
large·~wealthy·~growing	3	.00	
large·~wealthy·growing	7	1.00	.0490
large·wealthy·~growing	2	1.00	
large·wealthy·growing	7	1.00	.0490
~fluent·~wealthy·~growing	8	.00	
~fluent·~wealthy·growing	9	.67	.6089
~fluent·wealthy·~growing	1		
~fluent·wealthy·growing	4	1.00	.1785
fluent·~wealthy·~growing	5	.00	
fluent·~wealthy·growing	1		
fluent·wealthy·~growing	3	1.00	.2746
fluent·wealthy·growing	5	1.00	.1160

Table 5.4 *continued*

Grouping (1)	Case (2)	Proportion (3)	Probability (4)
~large·~fluent	10	.00	
~large·fluent	7	.43	
large·~fluent	12	.83	.1513
large·fluent	7	.86	.2338
~large·~wealthy	13	.00	
~large·wealthy	4	.75	.5630
large·~wealthy	10	.70	.5138
large·wealthy	9	1.00	.0207
~large·~growing	12	.08	
~large·growing	5	.40	
large·~growing	5	.40	
large·growing	14	1.00	.0024
~fluent·~wealthy	17	.35	
~fluent·wealthy	5	.80	.4284
fluent·~wealthy	6	.17	
fluent·wealthy	8	1.00	.0319
~fluent·~growing	9	.00	
~fluent·growing	13	.77	.2783
fluent·~growing	8	.38	
fluent·growing	6	1.00	.0754
~wealthy·~growing	13	.00	
~wealthy·growing	10	.70	.5138
wealthy·~ growing	4	.75	.5630
wealthy·growing	9	1.00	.0207
~large	17	.18	
large	19	.84	.0591
~fluent	22	.45	
fluent	14	.64	
~wealthy	23	.30	
wealthy	13	.92	.0296
~growing	17	.18	
growing	19	.84	.0591

Note: From table 5.2.

which causal combinations pass the sufficiency test. As table 5.4 shows, 8 of the 80 groupings pass the sufficiency test.[3]

3. Of course, from a hypothesis-testing viewpoint, many tests, some involving overlapping sets of cases, have been applied to the same "sample" of cases. From a textbook point of view (e.g., Leamer 1978; von Eye 1990), these tests should be adjusted to take this fact into account. I am not opposed to such adjustments. Recall, however, that these techniques are presented primarily as a way to explore data, to enrich the dialogue between theory and evidence. Thus, the ultimate test of the value of this interrogation of the data is its intellectual return: Does it advance understanding of these cases?

Note first that none of the 16 groupings using all four conditions (the configurations from table 5.1) passes the sufficiency test. For a proportion of 1.0 to be significantly greater than .65, with a one-tailed significance level of .05, a grouping needs to have at least 7 cases (see table 4.9). Because none of the 16 configurations has this many cases (6 is the maximum), none passes the sufficiency test. For 6 positive cases and no negative cases to pass a sufficiency test, either the benchmark must be lowered (e.g., to "sufficient more often than not" or .50), or the significance level must be raised (e.g., to .10 significance). Second, observe that the 8 groupings that pass the sufficiency test all have very high proportions: 7 are 1.0; the eighth is .92. Thus, even though the benchmark proportion is relatively modest ("usually sufficient" or .65), only very high proportions with seven or more cases actually pass the test. This result follows from the use of a relatively stringent significance level for evidence of this type.

The eight groupings that pass the sufficiency test are (1) large·~fluent·growing, (2) large·~wealthy·growing, (3) large·wealthy·growing, (4) large·wealthy, (5) large·growing, (6) fluent·wealthy, (7) wealthy·growing, and (8) wealthy. While it is possible to use minimization algorithms to simplify these eight groupings into a logical equation for ethnic mobilization (see Ragin 1987; Drass and Ragin 1992; Drass and Ragin 1999), it is not necessary to do so in this example because the pattern is straightforward. A logically minimal equation can be derived using the *containment rule*. Some groupings are contained within other groupings and thus are logically redundant. For example, linguistic minorities that are large·wealthy·growing (no. 3) are a subset of minorities that are large·wealthy (no. 4), which in turn are a subset of minorities that are wealthy (no. 8). Thus, the third and fourth groupings are *contained within* grouping no. 8 and thus can be eliminated. Altogether, four groupings (nos. 3, 4, 6, and 7) are contained within no. 8, and three are contained within no. 5 (nos. 1, 2, and 3). These logically redundant groupings can be dropped. Eliminating these groupings yields the following simplified statement of the causal conditions sufficient for ethnic political mobilization (as noted previously, in logical statements addition indicates logical *or*):

large·growing + wealthy → ethnic political mobilization.

Using a probabilistic approach to the assessment of causal sufficiency thus produces a relatively parsimonious statement of the conditions for ethnic political mobilization: Linguistic minorities that are wealthy and those that combine large size and growth are the ones that mobilize.

These results confirm that there are no necessary conditions for ethnic political mobilization. However, being wealthy, relative to the core region of the host country, is "usually" sufficient, by itself, for such mobilization. Using this logical statement as a prediction equation yields only one incorrect assignment: Ladins of Italy are a false positive. According to the equation they should offer strong evidence of ethnic political mobilization, but in fact they do not. This deviating case is very complex. Ladins live in a region of Italy that is populated by another territorial minority, South Tyroleans. Unlike Ladins, South Tyroleans are mobilized politically. While every ethnic situation can be considered unique, the situation of Ladins in Italy is clearly more complex than most.

Just as the probabilistic approach to the assessment of sufficiency entails specification of benchmarks and significance levels, the alternative, veristic approach may involve an evaluation of the strength of the evidence using a frequency threshold. In order to enhance the potential for contrast with the probabilistic approach with its implicit frequency threshold of seven positive cases when there are no negative cases, the example of the veristic approach that follows uses a relatively low frequency threshold: If a grouping has no negative instances of the outcome and two or more positive instances of the outcome, it is judged sufficient for ethnic political mobilization. Applying these criteria to the 80 groupings listed in table 5.3 yields the following 23 groupings that pass sufficiency:

1. ~large·fluent·wealthy·growing,
2. large·~fluent·~wealthy·growing,
3. large·~fluent·wealthy·growing,
4. large·fluent·wealthy·~growing,
5. large·fluent·wealthy·growing,
6. ~large·fluent·wealthy,
7. large·~fluent·wealthy,
8. large·fluent·wealthy,
9. ~large·fluent·growing,
10. large·~fluent·growing,
11. large·fluent·growing,
12. ~large·wealthy·growing,
13. large·~wealthy·growing,
14. large·wealthy·~growing,
15. large·wealthy·growing,
16. ~fluent·wealthy·growing,

17. fluent·wealthy·~growing,
18. fluent·wealthy·growing,
19. large·wealthy,
20. large·growing,
21. fluent·wealthy,
22. fluent·growing, and
23. wealthy·growing.

The containment rule described previously can be applied to this list to simplify these 23 causal combinations into a single logical statement. Alternatively, the minimization algorithm I describe in *The Comparative Method* may be used; the results are the same. Applying either technique results in the following logical statement for the causal combinations linked to ethnic political mobilization:

large·growing + fluent·wealthy → ethnic political mobilization.

In short, the results are very similar, though not identical, to those obtained using the probabilistic approach. The equation states that territorially based linguistic minorities that combine either large size and growth or a strong linguistic base and greater relative wealth are the ones that exhibit substantial ethnic political mobilization. In this equation, it is clear that no single condition is either necessary or sufficient because both terms are combinations formed from different causal conditions. These results duplicate those in *The Comparative Method*, where I present a somewhat different, though compatible, approach.

While not as parsimonious as the results using the probabilistic approach, it is easy to see that the two equations differ precisely because the veristic test does not allow false positives. Thus, Ladins of Italy are not covered by the equation that follows from the application of the veristic test of sufficiency. They are excluded because of their weaker linguistic ability, compared with the positive instances of mobilization.

It is not productive at this point to ask, Which solution is correct? because *correctness* is not intrinsic to analytic techniques. Analytic techniques offer social scientists different ways of describing and representing social phenomena (Ragin 1994a). The two equations just presented are alternate presentations of the same evidence on ethnic political mobilization using different techniques for assessing sufficiency. In social research, different techniques almost always result in different portraits of the phenomenon. Which approach is "best" depends on the criterion applied. For example, if the criterion is "no false positives," then the veristic approach may be best. If the criterion is "makes allowance for imperfect evidence," then the probabilistic approach may be best. As a general rule, when the number of cases is small and researchers can gain in-depth knowledge of cases, the first criterion is more important. When the number is large, the second criterion is more important.

Ultimately, the question of "correctness" can be addressed only through case-level analysis. For example, the investigator might take a close look at the positive instances of ethnic political mobilization where greater relative wealth seems important as a causal factor and examine whether linguistic ability also seems important in these cases. In addition, the researcher could ask whether weaker linguistic ability seems to be the main factor interfering with the development of strong ethnic political mobilization among Ladins in Italy. More generally, as I stress repeatedly in *The Comparative Method* and elsewhere, representations of this type, where large amounts of evidence are reduced to broad patterns summarized in an equation (or using some other shorthand), must be evaluated in terms of their utility for understanding cases. Broad representations are best viewed as maps or guides to help a researcher through difficult terrain (Becker 1986). They cannot show many details, only the most important. As Charles Tilly (1997:54) would argue, representations of this type "discipline our thinking about . . . complex phenomena in preparation for genuine explanatory efforts" at the case level.

CAUSAL COMPLEXITY AND SIMPLIFYING ASSUMPTIONS

While it might seem that producing an equation that provides a summary statement of broad causal patterns concludes the analysis of causal complexity, it does not. No analysis is complete without an examination of the "simplifying assumptions" embedded in a summary statement. As explained in chapters 3 and 4, simplifying assumptions take advantage of limited diversity. Limited diversity exists when one or more of the logically possible combinations of causal conditions specified in an analysis does not exist empirically—a common situation in the study of naturally occurring social phenomena—or when the number of cases attached to a configuration is too small to permit a sufficiency test. In effect, simplifying assumptions assert that cases with these combinations of conditions would pass sufficiency—if, in fact, enough of them existed to conduct the test. In practical terms, investigators make simplifying assumptions whenever one or more of the initial groupings included in an analysis (e.g., the 16 configurations listed in table 5.1) has too few cases to permit a sufficiency test yet is covered by the equation that follows from the analysis of causal complexity. It is not "wrong" to make simplifying assumptions. However, it is hazardous to make them without assessing their plausibility. Thus, it is important for researchers to identify the simplifying assumptions they have incorporated into summary statements and to evaluate them.

For illustration, consider again the results just presented, using the veristic approach to the assessment of sufficiency:

large·growing + fluent·wealthy → ethnic political mobilization.

The first causal combination brings together 4 of the original 16 configurations:

$$
\begin{aligned}
\text{large·growing} = \; &\text{large·}{\sim}\text{fluent·}{\sim}\text{wealthy·growing} + \\
&\text{large·}{\sim}\text{fluent·wealthy·growing} + \\
&\text{large·fluent·}{\sim}\text{wealthy·growing} + \\
&\text{large·fluent·wealthy·growing.}
\end{aligned}
$$

The second causal combination also brings together 4 of the original 16 configurations:

$$
\begin{aligned}
\text{fluent·wealthy} = \; &{\sim}\text{large·fluent·wealthy·}{\sim}\text{growing} + \\
&{\sim}\text{large·fluent·wealthy·growing} + \\
&\text{large·fluent·wealthy·}{\sim}\text{growing} + \\
&\text{large·fluent·wealthy·growing.}
\end{aligned}
$$

At a minimum, the researcher should be able to point to at least one case that displays both the causal conditions and the outcome for each configuration that is covered by an equation. Inspection of table 5.1 shows that this minimum threshold is met by all the configurations covered by the equation for ethnic political mobilization. Thus, the results presented above do not incorporate simplifying assumptions.

Note, however, that if the researcher were to study the combinations of conditions linked to an absence of ethnic political mobilization, which would involve all the rows not covered by the results for ethnic political mobilization, then he or she would find that simplifying assumptions are incorporated into the results of this analysis.[4] Table 5.1 shows clearly that rows 4, 6, and 11 (configurations not covered by the equation for ethnic political mobilization) lack empirical instances.

4. Assumptions about configurations not covered by an equation (e.g., configurations not covered by the equation for ethnic political mobilization) are not as critical or as important as assumptions made about configurations covered by an equation. Each equation constitutes a logically minimal expression of the causal combinations linked to a specific outcome.

Thus, the results of the analysis of the absence of ethnic political mobilization would incoporate the assumption that if found, instances of these absent causal configurations would provide little or no evidence of ethnic political mobilization.

From the perspective of conventional variable-oriented research, the fact that results may be extrapolated to configurations that lack empirical instances is not a serious problem. In this approach, causal conditions are viewed as "independent variables" that have separate effects on the outcome. All that matters is a variable's net effect, controlling for the effects of its competitors. In a configurational approach, however, the basic analytic unit is not the "variable," but the "configuration" and the cases conforming to each configuration. Recall that the key principle undergirding the configurational approach is the idea that a single difference between two cases may signal a difference in kind. When inclusive groupings are formed (e.g., the grouping of minorities that are large · growing), configurations that embrace cases differing on one or more attributes are joined together as equivalent instances. If it can be shown that the component configurations that make up a grouping display the outcome in question, then this merging is justified because the researcher has demonstrated that the configurations are, in fact, equivalent with respect to the outcome. But when larger groupings involve configurations that lack empirical instances altogether, researchers can include these configurations in the summary statement only if they are willing to make assumptions about what these cases' outcomes would be, if in fact such cases existed.

Once an equation showing sufficient combinations of conditions has been derived, therefore, the researcher should examine the simplifying assumptions it incorporates to see if these assumptions are warranted. This evaluation, in turn, should be based on the investigator's substantive and theoretical understanding of the outcome in question. If the simplifying assumptions are not warranted, then the equation should be reformulated excluding the configurations that involve unwarranted assumptions (Ragin 1995).

THE MULTIPLE CONSTITUTION OF POPULATIONS

One hallmark of the diversity-oriented approach is its allowance for both the constituted nature of social scientific populations and the fragility of these constructions. This concern permeates the discussion of QCA presented so far. For example, rather than seeing the 36 territorially based linguistic minorities as a single population, table 5.1 constructs them as 16 different kinds of minorities. Furthermore, in the construction of these 16 different kinds, each configuration is evaluated with respect to the cases that conform to it and also with respect to the outcomes they exhibit. First the researcher asks of each configuration, Do these cases belong together in this study? If they do not, a new scheme is formulated. Second, the researcher asks, Do these cases all have the same outcome or at least roughly comparable outcomes? If there is too much discordance, new causal conditions may be selected, which in turn provide the basis for generating new configurations. When making these evaluations the researcher continually reassesses and reconstructs the property space that defines "kinds" of cases.

This understanding of populations also permeates the evaluation of sufficiency. Tests of sufficiency are conducted for each configuration and for every possible grouping that can be formed from these configurations. In the end, configurations are joined together as similar only if they pass relevant sufficiency tests. Furthermore, once a summary equation is derived, it is evaluated with respect to simplifying assumptions. The researcher must indicate which configurations covered by the equation lack adequate evidence.

In the empirical analysis presented in this chapter, no discussion of the initial selection of the 36 territorially based linguistic minorities was offered. In effect, this set was taken more or less as fixed. However, it is important to emphasize that this larger population is also open to reconstitution in the course of the research. For example, when evaluating the cases that conform to each logically possible combination of conditions, the researcher might decide that some of the smaller minorities are too small and thus do not belong in the same study with the other minorities. Or the investigator might decide that minorities with very weak linguistic ability do not belong. Alternatively, after examining the 36 cases closely the researcher might broaden the analysis to embrace territorially based minorities defined by regional dialects and not just those defined by language differences.

When evaluating the outcomes associated with each configuration, the researcher might also use this as an opportunity to restrict or enlarge the set of cases included in the study. For example, the researcher might find that mobilization is muted or distinct in some other way when the minority speaks a language that is dominant in a neighboring country (Rothschild 1981), for example, speakers of Swedish in Finland. These minorities might be dropped from the investigation. (Alternatively, the researcher might add this contextual factor to the analysis.) More generally, the detailed, case-level evaluations that go into the construction of a property space and the generation of configurations (as in table 5.1) often prompt the investigator to reconsider the set of cases initially chosen for investigation.

Finally, it is also possible to use summary equations, like the equation for ethnic political mobilization, to reconstitute populations. Essentially, a summary equation shows, in a logically shorthand manner, the different combinations of conditions linked to an outcome. These different combinations provide a basis for describing alternate paths to a given outcome, and cases can be classified according to the paths they travel. For illustration, consider again the results of the analysis using the veristic assessment of sufficiency:

$$large \cdot growing + fluent \cdot wealthy \rightarrow ethnic \ political \ mobilization.$$

In essence, the equation states that there are two sets of conditions linked to ethnic political mobilization: large size combined with growth, and linguistic strength combined with greater relative wealth. Table 5.5 shows the different linguistic minorities conforming to each combination of conditions. (Three minorities, listed in the third column of table 5.5, conform to both causal combinations.)

While far beyond the scope of this chapter, a researcher might find important differences between the nature of the ethnic political mobilization present in these different sets of cases. In fact, an important way to reinforce the results would be to examine the cases to see if differences in the character or course of ethnic mobilization can be traced to differences in relevant causal conditions. In the end, the researcher might be able to differentiate types of ethnic political mobilization and

Table 5.5
Conformity of Cases to Causal Combinations

Minorities That Are large·growing	Minorities That Are fluent·wealthy	Minorities That Conform to Both
W. Frisians, Neth.	Aalanders, Finland	Alsatians, France
Catalans, France	Slovenes, Italy	Germans, Belgium
Occitans, France	Valdotians, Italy	Flemings, Belgium
Welsh, Great Britain	Swedes, Finland	
Bretons, France	South Tyroleans, Italy	
Corsicans, France		
Friulians, Italy		
Occitans, Italy		
Basques, Spain		
Catalans, Spain		
Walloons, Belgium		

assign cases to types (including mixed types) based on these results. Thus, the results provide a basis for reconstituting cases in terms of broad types, based on their causally relevant features. This construction of broad types dovetails with some of the key analytic concerns of diversity-oriented research.

Note that the decision about whether to include or drop a case from an investigation is essentially a dichotomous choice: A case is either "in" or "out" of the study. As I show in part 2 of this work, however, it is possible to apply fuzzy-membership criteria to this assessment so that researchers are not limited to crisp, "in-or-out" decisions. For example, a researcher could gauge the degree to which the evidence justifies including a collectivity in the set of "territorially based linguistic minorities" and operationalize such assessments as a fuzzy set, with membership scores ranging from 0 to 1. This fuzzy set, in turn, could be manipulated as a causally relevant condition, just like any other fuzzy set (see chapter 7). Thus, as I elaborate in part 2, even the degree to which a case warrants inclusion in a study can be evaluated as a fuzzy set and used in the analysis as a contextual factor.

SUMMARY: USING QCA

There are three distinct phases in the application of QCA to cross-case evidence: (1) selecting cases and constructing the property space that defines kinds of cases (initial configurations), (2) testing the necessity and the sufficiency of causal conditions, and (3) evaluating the results, especially with respect to simplifying assumptions. As already noted, the summary equations that result from the application of QCA should be viewed as part of the larger dialogue between ideas and evidence (see also Ragin 1987:164–71). The real test of any representation of evidence is how well it helps the researcher and his or her audiences understand specific cases or sets of cases. Broad representations of cross-case patterns provide maps that guide and facilitate in-depth investigation; they are not substitutes for this type of investigation. Thus, QCA has an implicit fourth phase involving the application of the results to specific cases, but this phase does not belong to QCA proper.

In many respects the first phase is the most difficult (see also Griffin et al. 1991). The dimensions of the property space (i.e., relevant aspects of cases) must be clarified and refined to see if the resulting scheme sorts cases in a way that makes sense. At the same time, the researcher must study the cases initially chosen for the investigation and evaluate whether the set as a whole has integrity. Dropping or adding cases may help the researcher refine the property space while at the same time increase the comparability of the cases in the study. The researcher also examines cases conforming to each configuration with respect to the outcomes they display. If cases differ too greatly on the outcome, then either the property space must be reformulated or the relevant set of cases must be reconstituted, or both.

Once the researcher successfully stabilizes the relevant cases and the property space that sorts them into types, then the assessment of causal complexity can proceed. In this phase, a key issue is the definition of sufficiency: How should the tests be structured? The answer to this question is shaped in large part by the nature of the evidence and the criteria that are most important to the investigator. Still, in most analyses, it is probably best to work with several definitions of sufficiency and conduct tests favoring competing criteria. Once these tests are complete, QCA can be used to analyze and simplify the patterns.[5]

In the third phase the summary equation itself is examined, especially with respect to simplifying assumptions. The configurational understanding of social phenomena that undergirds diversity-oriented research mandates careful attention to the assumptions that enter into the production of summary statements. Investigators must use their substantive and theoretical knowledge to evaluate these assumptions. Some assumptions may be accepted and others rejected. In the end, the researcher crafts a representation of evidence that reflects both the diversity of cases included in the investigation and the researcher's knowledge.

5. Fuzzy-Set/Qualitative Comparative Analysis or FS/QCA (Drass and Ragin 1999) is a new version of QCA that implements all the features described in this book, including the fuzzy-set methods. It can be downloaded from <http://www.nwu.edu/sociology>.

PART II

Fuzzy-Set Methods

SIX

FUZZY SETS AND THE
STUDY OF DIVERSITY

INTRODUCTION

Diversity exists not only in the different configurations of set member-ships that social phenomena exhibit but also in the degree to which they belong to such sets and configurations. For example, two countries can both be described as advanced industrial, capitalist democracies, as instances of a specific intersection of sets, and they can also differ in the degree to which they belong to this intersection. The first aspect of diversity is captured by the notion of differences in kind and the many different configurations of memberships that arise from multiple distinctions. The second aspect of diversity is captured by the notion of degree of membership and is based on the idea that virtually all categorical distinctions in the social sciences also involve variation by degree.

In this chapter, I show that by using fuzzy instead of crisp sets it is possible to address this second aspect of diversity—the varying degree to which cases belong to sets, without forsaking the first aspect—the idea of differences in kind. While this chapter builds on the configura-tional thinking developed in part 1, it focuses primarily on the nature of fuzzy sets and shows how they resonate with basic social scientific aims and principles. To lay the groundwork for my argument, I first explore the concept of diversity and argue that it is "dual" in nature because it simultaneously embraces qualitative and quantitative varia-tion. That is, it refers both to differences in kind (i.e., qualitative dis-tinctions) and to differences in degree of membership (i.e., quantitative differences) at the same time. I then argue that fuzzy sets are especially appropriate for the study of diversity precisely because they capture both kinds of difference, qualitative and quantitative, in a single instrument.

After showing the parallels between the dual nature of diversity and fuzzy sets, I address a range of issues in the construction and use of fuzzy sets. To aid this presentation, at various points in the discussion I contrast fuzzy sets and fuzzy-set analysis with conventional variables and variable-oriented research. One strong and enduring difference between variables and fuzzy sets is that fuzzy sets are more demanding. Researchers must establish a very close correspondence between fuzzy membership scores (which range from 0 to 1) and their concepts. That is, they must carefully calibrate fuzzy scores to reflect degree of membership in the empirical categories that reflect their concepts. The better this parallel, the more useful the fuzzy set. After presenting several examples of fuzzy sets and discussing issues surrounding the measurement of fuzzy membership, I show that fuzzy sets offer powerful tools for evaluating complex conceptual formulations (e.g., social theories). With fuzzy sets, researchers can take advantage of analytic devices based in Boolean algebra (e.g., negation, intersection, and union), as well as devices that are specific to fuzzy sets, for example, the use of verbal modifiers such as "very" and "more or less" to recalibrate fuzzy membership scores.

EXTENDING THE CONCEPT OF DIVERSITY

Diversity has two main facets. In some respects, these dual aspects are contradictory. The first is diversity in kind, as indicated in categorical distinctions. The second is diversity in degree of membership in categories, which reflects, in part, the indeterminateness of categorical distinctions and the artificiality of force-fitting social objects into categories.

The first facet of diversity is readily apparent in everyday social life. Consider racial categories. It is clear that racial categories are important social categories. They exist as fixed "givens" on census, employment, and application forms, and they pervade the collective social consciousness. Their fixity as social constructs is further reinforced by the many reified representations of race appearing in the mass media. Rigid racial categories are reified in social research as well. Survey researchers, for example, typically do not pause to reconsider common schemes for categorizing people according to race when they construct such items for questionnaires. Even elaborate schemes are often collapsed into three categories (White, Black, and other) when the results of research are reported.

But we know that the understandings of race reflected in these categorical schemes are gross simplifications. People are not "Black," "White," or "other." Scholars who study human genetics, for example, have long noted that it is impossible to locate race genetically. There is no race gene or even an identifiable set of race genes. In the social realm, we know that there is much more diversity than can be captured in any categorical scheme. Are recent dark-skinned immigrants from the Caribbean "African Americans"? How should Arab Americans be classified? What about Asians from India and Pakistan? According to many right-wing groups, Jews are nonwhites. In the early part of this century, immigrants from southern and eastern Europe were described as belonging to a "different race." And, of course, all such "racial" distinctions ignore the massive amounts of "racial mixing" that has taken place and that continues at a dramatic pace.

The dual nature of race is often acknowledged in everyday social life. For example, people often make statements about how "White" or how "Black" others are. An African American can be "too Black" or "not Black enough;" a European American can be "Waspy." A person can "look" Black, "sound" White, but "be" Hispanic. These examples of the dual nature of race show that the everyday conception of diversity recognizes "degrees of membership" while at the same time invoking important "differences in kind." In short, diversity simultaneously embraces both *categories* and *different degrees of membership* in categories. The dual nature of diversity indicates, in the language of social research, that it involves differentiation that is simultaneously "qualitative" and "quantitative." That is, diversity involves variation that is both nominal-scale and interval-scale at the same time. A person can be "in" a category (e.g., Protestant) in the sense of being more in than out of the set in question, but also can be less "in" that category than those who are *fully* in it (i.e., not as Protestant as those who are fully and unquestionably Protestant).

Everyday social categories like race and religion provide easy examples of the dual nature of diversity and the challenge of studying it. The problem of how to conceptualize and study diversity is not limited, however, to the categories that social scientists and others apply to individuals. The issue of "dual diversity" is relevant to virtually all social science concepts used in cross-case analyses. Consider, for example, the category *democracy,* which is conceived by most political scientists as one of several distinct "kinds" of political systems. Scholars describe some countries as democracies and some as not, but the category is inherently indeterminate. Is Russia a democracy? Is Indonesia?

Is Mexico? Is the United States a democracy? Compared with some democracies, the United States is surprisingly undemocratic: The U.S. Senate gives small-population states incredible power over national policy; its structure radically violates the fundamental democratic notion of one person, one vote. Some political scientists argue that presidential veto and judicial review are undemocratic. The U.S. electoral system, based on single-member simple-plurality voting districts, seems rigged so that there are only two parties, each pushing more or less the same agenda as they struggle to dominate the middle ground. Voters have little real choice. Perhaps most important of all is the simple fact that powerful interest groups control the electoral process through their campaign contributions. Politicians must keep a close eye on the flow of donations from the rich and powerful and adjust their positions accordingly. In the end, it seems that dollars count more than people.

The problem is not one of simply acknowledging that countries vary in how democratic they are and that the United States is less democratic than many of the other countries conventionally labeled "democratic." It is also one of specifying what is meant by democracy and then assessing which countries are fully democratic, which are not democratic, and which are only partially democratic. Among those that are only partially democratic, there is the additional issue of specifying their different degrees of membership in the set of democratic countries, ranging from slight to almost full membership. Would the United States end up in the fully democratic set or in the partially democratic set? It depends on how democracy is defined. Still, the qualitative breakpoint separating fully democratic and partially democratic is an important distinction. It matters a great deal, for example, to people in the United States who want to live in a *fully* democratic country.

Another example of the dual nature of diversity comes from the study of organizations. Some organizations are described as for-profit and some as not-for-profit. Still, the boundary between these two types is often blurred, and there are many organizations that are mixed in a variety of different ways. To address the diversity of organizations, it is not sufficient (or even possible) to sort organizations into these two broad categories, nor is it enough simply to rank them on a for-profit/not-for-profit continuum. As with democracy, it is important to establish qualitative breakpoints on the continuum. For example, a policymaker might wish to reserve certain tax benefits only for organizations that are "fully" not-for-profit or to apply certain tax penalties only to organizations that are "fully" for-profit. Thus, it would be necessary to establish qualitative breakpoints on the for-profit/not-for-profit continuum to justify these distinctions.

The key feature of these examples is that they involve careful attention to the dual nature of diversity. The central point is that whenever social scientists use terms like "White," "Hispanic," "democratic," "for-profit," and so on, they invoke distinctions that involve differences in kind and differences in degree at the same time. In fact, virtually all social science concepts that address differences across cases have this dual character. Thus, rather than seeing diversity as differences in kind (i.e., categorical distinctions) or as differences in degree (i.e., distinctions that permit cases to be ranked), the study of diversity should address both kinds of difference simultaneously.

The understanding of diversity just sketched provides a good context for introducing fuzzy sets. Fuzzy sets are central to the study of diversity precisely because they integrate qualitative and quantitative assessment and thus can be used to address diversity's dual character.

FUZZY SETS

The Concept of Fuzzy Sets

Conventional, crisp sets allow only two mutually exclusive states, membership and nonmembership. An object or element (e.g., a person) within a domain (e.g., persons) is either in or out of a set that exists within a domain (e.g., the set of male persons). In short, crisp sets establish distinctions that are wholly qualitative. Usually, membership in a set is indicated with a Boolean value of 1 (or "yes"); nonmembership is indicated with a Boolean value of 0 (or "no"). In the example just mentioned (the set of males), the crisp-set formulation conforms well to conventional bipolar thinking about gender, that a person must be either crisply in the set of males or crisply in the set of females (i.e., the set of not males).

Crisp logic is not exclusively binary, of course. Multichotomies are possible as well, but the principle of crispness still holds. Membership scores may be only one of two values, 1 (yes, the object is in the set) or 0 (no, the object is not in the set). In the multichotomous case, a person might be assigned to one of several mutually exclusive categories (e.g., using race/ethnicity: European American, Native American, African American, Asian American, and so on). With crisply defined multichotomies, each object scores 1 on membership in one of the relevant sets and 0 on membership in the other sets defined by the multichotomy.

Fuzzy sets extend crisp sets by permitting membership scores in the interval between 0 and 1. For example, a person might receive a membership score of .35 in the set of European Americans and a score of .83 in the set of Protestants. The basic idea behind fuzzy sets is to permit the scaling of membership scores and thus allow partial or fuzzy membership. A membership score of 1 indicates full membership in a set; scores close to 1 (e.g., .8 or .9) indicate strong but partial membership in a set; scores less than .5 but greater than 0 (e.g., .2 and .3) indicate that objects are more "out" than "in" a set, but still weak members of the set; a score of 0 indicates full nonmembership in the set. Thus, fuzzy sets combine qualitative and quantitative assessment: 1 and 0 are qualitative assignments ("fully in" and "fully out," respectively); values between 0 and 1 (noninclusive) indicate degree of membership.

Superficially, the idea of crisp-set versus fuzzy-set membership appears to be a mere measurement issue involving the familiar problem of information loss that occurs when a variable with different levels is turned into a dichotomy (i.e., a crisp set). Shades of gray (i.e., fuzziness) are constrained to be either black or white (i.e., crisp). Thus, it is tempting to see the concept of fuzzy membership as a simple restatement of the common idea that it is a mistake to use categorical variables to represent phenomena that are better represented with ordinal-, interval-, or ratio-scale measures in social research. However, this similarity is only skin-deep. Fuzzy sets are simultaneously qualitative and quantitative. They address the varying degree to which different cases belong to a set (including the two qualitative states, full membership and full nonmembership), not how they differ from one another along quantifiable dimensions of open-ended variation. Thus, fuzzy sets pinpoint qualitative states while at the same time assessing degrees of membership. In this sense, a fuzzy set is a continuous set that has been carefully calibrated to indicate degree of membership.

Note how the concept of fuzzy sets challenges conventional thinking about "levels of measurement." The usual argument, reproduced in most textbooks on social research, is that the lowest form of measurement is the nominal scale (i.e., crisp sets), followed by the ordinal scale (ranked categories), followed by the interval scale (equal intervals, represented with interpretable numerical values), followed by the highest form of measurement, the ratio scale (equal intervals, interpretable numerical values, plus a fixed and more or less meaningful zero point). How does the fuzzy set fit into this scheme? Like interval and ratio scales, fuzzy sets can have equal intervals, represented with interpretable numerical values. Because they are measures of the degree of membership in sets, however, fuzzy sets not only have a fixed and meaningful zero point (0 = nonmembership) like a ratio scale, but they also have a fixed and meaningful maximum (1 = full membership). In this light, it could be argued that fuzzy-set membership is a *higher* form of measurement than the conventional ratio scale—it is a ratio scale with a fixed and meaningful minimum *and maximum*.[1] Still, the purpose of a fuzzy set is parallel to that of the nominal scale—to indicate set membership.

Types of Fuzzy Sets

For illustration of the general idea of fuzzy sets, first consider a simple three-value logic that allows cases to be in the gray zone between "in" and "out" of a set. Instead of using only two scores, 0 and 1, three-value logic adds a third value .5 indicating objects that are neither fully in nor fully out of the set in question (see columns [1] and [2] of table 6.1). As an example, consider the set of people employed by a firm. Suppose managers lay off a substantial number of workers on what they believe is a temporary basis. That is, the managers hope to put these employees back to work in the very near future, but they are not absolutely certain that they will be able to do so. Are the laid-off workers in the set of people employed by the firm? Yes and no. They are in the gray zone separating people employed by the firm and people not employed by the firm.

This three-value logic (using 0, .5, and 1 to indicate nonmembership, partial membership, and full membership, respectively) is a rudimentary form of fuzzy set. A more elegant but still simple form of fuzzy set uses five numerical values, as shown in column (3) of table 6.1 Consider the researcher conducting a cross-national study of the involvement of nonprofit organizations in the provision of primary and secondary education. Essentially, this researcher wants to determine for each country included in the study: Are nonprofit organizations important providers of primary and secondary education? Are they major actors in this arena? Because the nature of the evidence differs from one country to the next (e.g., enrollment data versus expenditure data versus interview data, versus anecdotal evidence), the researcher might use a five-value scheme to summarize the evidence. Specifically, he or

1. Normally, quantitative scholars view variables with restricted or limited ranges as problematic. For example, a limited dependent variable poses estimation problems because predicted values may exceed the maximum empirically possible value. As I show in subsequent chapters, fuzzy-set analysis does not share this problem with conventional quantitative analysis.

Table 6.1
Crisp versus Fuzzy Sets

Crisp Set (1)	Three-Value Fuzzy Set (2)	Five-Value Fuzzy Set (3)	Seven-Value Fuzzy Set (4)	"Continuous" Fuzzy Set (5)
1 = fully in	1 = fully in	1 = fully in	1 = fully in	1 = fully in
		.75 = more in than out	.83 = mostly but not fully in .67 = more or less in	Numerical scores indicating that degree of membership is more "in" than "out" $(.5 < x_i < 1)$
	.5 = not fully out or fully in	.50 = crossover: neither in nor out	.5 = crossover: neither in nor out .33 = more or less out	.5 = crossover: neither in nor out
		.25 = more out than in	.17 = mostly but not fully out	Numerical scores indicating that degree of membership is more "out" than "in" $(0 < x_i < .5)$
0 = fully out	0 = fully out	0 = fully out	0 = fully out	0 = fully out

she would use the numerical values 0, .25, .5, .75, and 1.0 to indicate "definitely not a major actor," "probably not a major actor," "may be/ may not be a major actor," "probably a major actor," and "definitely a major actor," respectively. Essentially, the five-value logic scheme uses what is known as a "crossover point" (a fuzzy membership score of .5) to separate cases that are "more in" from those that are "more out" and also distinguishes between cases that are "mostly in" versus "fully in" and between cases that are "mostly out" versus "fully out." The five-value scheme is especially useful in situations where researchers have a substantial amount of information about cases, but the evidence is not systematic or strictly comparable from case to case.

A still more fine-grained fuzzy set uses seven values, as shown in column (4) of table 6.1. Like the five-value fuzzy set, the seven-value fuzzy set utilizes two qualitative states ("fully out" and "fully in") and the .5 crossover point. However, the seven-value fuzzy set inserts two intermediate levels between "fully out" and the crossover point ("mostly out" and "more or less out") and two intermediate levels between the crossover point and "fully in" ("more or less in" and "mostly in").

At first glance, the five-value and seven-value fuzzy sets might seem equivalent to ordinal scales. In fact, however, they are qualitatively different from such scales, and it is important to emphasize their distinctiveness. An ordinal scale is a mere ranking of categories, usually without reference to external criteria such as set membership. In constructing ordinal scales, researchers typically do not peg categories to degree of membership in sets; rather, the categories are simply arrayed relative to each other, yielding a rank order. For example, a researcher might develop a seven-rank ordinal scheme of religiosity and apply it to individuals, using categories that range from antireligious to religious zealots. It is unlikely that this scheme would translate automatically to a seven-value fuzzy set, with the lowest rank set to 0, the next rank to .17, and so on (see column [4] of table 6.1). Assume the relevant fuzzy set is the set of "religious individuals." The lower three ranks of the ordinal variable might all translate to "fully out" of the set of religious individuals (fuzzy score = 0). The next rank up might translate to the crossover point (.5, neither more out nor more in). The top two ranks might translate to "fully in" (fuzzy score = 1), and so on. In short, the specific translation of ordinal ranks to fuzzy membership scores depends on the fit between the *content* of the ordinal categories and the researcher's *conceptual understanding* of the fuzzy set. This point underscores the principle that fuzzy sets must be carefully calibrated with respect to the sets they reference.

Finally, a "continuous" fuzzy set permits cases to take values any-
where in the interval from 0 to 1 (inclusive), as shown in column (5)
of table 6.1. The continuous fuzzy set, like all fuzzy sets, utilizes the
two qualitative states (fully out and fully in) and also uses the crossover
point to distinguish between cases that are more out from those that
are more in. Consider as an example of a continuous fuzzy set the
membership of countries in the set "rich." A conventional variable like
GNP per capita offers a good starting point for assessing membership
in this set, but the translation of this variable to fuzzy membership
scores is neither automatic nor mechanical. It would be a serious mistake, for instance, to score the poorest country 0, the richest country
1.0, and then to array all the other countries between 0 and 1, depending on their positions in the range of GNP per capita values. Instead, the first task in this translation would be to specify three important qualitative anchors: the point at which full membership is reached
(i.e., definitely a rich country, membership score = 1), the point at
which full nonmembership is reached (i.e., definitely not a rich country, membership score = 0), and the point of maximum ambiguity in
whether a country is "more in" or "more out" of the set of rich countries
(a membership score of .5, the crossover point). When specifying these
qualitative anchors, the investigator should offer an explicit rationale
for each breakpoint.

For illustration, consider table 6.2 and figure 6.1, which show one
possible translation of GNP per capita values to fuzzy membership in
the set of rich countries. In this example, countries with GNP per capita
values of $2,000 and less are definitely out of the set of rich countries;
countries with values between $2,000 and $8,000 are more out than
in, but not fully out; $8,000 is the crossover point, where there is maxi-
mum ambiguity in whether a country is more in or more out; countries
with values between $8,000 and $18,000 are more in than out of the

Table 6.2
Fuzzy Membership in the Set of "rich countries"

GNP/Capita (U.S. $)	Membership (M)	Verbal Labels
100 → 1,999	M = 0	Clearly not rich
2,000 → 7,999	0 < M < .5	More or less not rich
8,000	M = .5	In between
8,001 → 17,999	.5 < M < 1.0	More or less rich
18,000 → 30,000	M = 1.0	Clearly rich

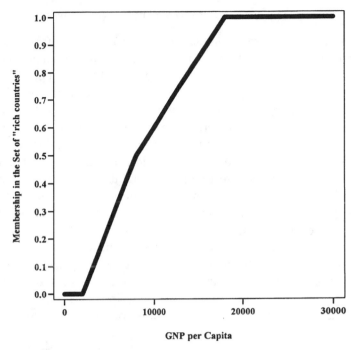

Figure 6.1 Plot of membership in "rich countries" against GNP per capita.

set of rich countries but not fully in; and countries with values of $18,000 or more are fully in the set of rich countries. All GNP per capita values below $2,000 are compacted into the fuzzy score of 0 because these cases are all equally "out" of the set of rich countries. Likewise, all GNP per capita values greater than $18,000 are compacted into the fuzzy score of 1 because these cases are all equally "in" the set of rich countries. In this way, fuzzy membership scores for the set of rich countries operationalize both qualitative categories (countries fully in and countries fully out of the rich set—the fuzzy scores of 1 and 0) and quantitative differences in degree of membership (countries with fuzzy scores between 0 and 1). The crossover point provides an additional qualitative anchor, separating countries than are more in the set from those that are more out of the set.[2]

2. As I show subsequently, the crossover point also can involve a range of raw-scale values. It is not restricted to a single raw-score value.

FUZZY SETS AND SOCIAL SCIENTIFIC CONCEPTS

The examples just presented illustrate the consistency of fuzzy sets with the dual nature of diversity. In fact, there is a virtual mathematical identity between the understanding of diversity as a dual concept, sketched at the outset of this chapter, and the constitution of fuzzy sets. Recall that the social scientific conception of diversity emphasizes the fact that diversity involves differences that are simultaneously qualitative and quantitative. There is a straightforward correspondence between this conception of diversity and the constitution of fuzzy sets. When constructing a fuzzy set, the researcher must establish criteria for full membership in a set (membership score = 1); criteria for determining partial membership in the set (membership scores greater than 0 and less than 1, with .5 separating cases that are more "in" than "out" of the set); and criteria for exclusion from the set (membership score = 0). In short, to construct a fuzzy set it is necessary to specify qualitative breakpoints on continua, thus linking the measurement of fuzzy-set scores to substantive and theoretical criteria. In effect, substantive and theoretical knowledge provide the means for calibrating continuous measures as fuzzy sets.

More generally, the compatibility of fuzzy sets with the analysis of diversity stems from its development as a mathematical system designed to join formal logic, which is crisp and precise, and verbal concepts, which are not. As designed by the founder of fuzzy logic, Lotfi Zadeh (1965, 1972, 1982), fuzzy sets bring formal logic and verbal formulations much closer together. In essence, fuzzy logic offers a mathematical system that makes allowances for the pliable nature of verbal concepts (e.g., the adjectives "short" and "old"). Virtually all social science concepts are verbal formulations. Thus, fuzzy sets are useful not only for representing membership in social categories but for operationalizing any social science concept that addresses differences across cases or instances.

The Issue of Correspondence

In any operationalization of a concept as a fuzzy set, it is important for the fuzzy-membership scores generated by the investigator's procedures to be as faithful as possible to the concepts they reference. That is, the correspondence between theoretical concepts and the measurement of set membership is decisively important. The researcher must pay careful attention to the meaning of the concept, the empirical evidence used to index membership, and the criteria used to establish qualitative breakpoints. Thus, investigators who use fuzzy sets must maintain a much tighter coupling of theory and analytic technique than is typical of empirical social science. Paradoxically, the use of fuzzy sets requires a degree of specificity that is beyond the reach of conventional practices, especially the use of interval-scale and ratio-scale variables to index theoretical concepts.

Consider, for example, an investigator who wishes to evaluate a theoretical statement pertaining to "democratic countries"—that they have interest-based political organizations. Conventionally, social scientists would test this argument by developing an index of democracy and assessing its association with some measure of the prevalence of interest-based political organizations. All that matters in this approach is that the relevant cases vary on both measures. From the perspective of fuzzy-set social science, however, such conventional measures are only loosely coupled to the concepts they index. The formulation in question concerns "democratic countries" and "countries with interest-based political organizations," which are both fuzzy sets. While an index of democracy might be a useful starting point for assessing degree of membership in the set of democratic countries (see, e.g., Bollen 1993), it is the start of the journey, not its conclusion. The researcher in this investigation would need to establish qualitative anchors for the set of democratic countries—breakpoints separating the fully democratic from the mostly democratic, the more democratic from the less democratic, and so on. These breakpoints would define the fuzzy set of democratic countries, the key focus of the theoretical formulation.

Relevant versus Irrelevant Variation

Qualitative anchors, in effect, distinguish between relevant and irrelevant variation. Variation in democracy scores among the unambiguously democratic countries is *not* relevant to the theoretical formulation just stated, at least from the perspective of fuzzy sets. If a country is unambiguously democratic, the theoretical formulation should apply with full force. Similarly, variation in democracy scores among the unambiguously not democratic countries is also *not* relevant. After all, the statement is about democratic countries, not about unambiguously not democratic countries that happen to fake some of the elements of democracy. Thus, in fuzzy-set social science it is not enough simply to develop scales that show the *relative positions* of cases on distributions (e.g., a conventional index of democracy). It is necessary also to use qualitative anchors to map the links between specific scores on continuous variables (e.g., an index of democracy) and fuzzy-set membership (e.g., degree of membership in the set of democratic countries, including nonmembership).

An even more forceful example of the importance of qualitative anchors for distinguishing between relevant and irrelevant variation comes from the literature on state formation. Social scientists often distinguish between countries that experienced "early" versus "late" state formation (see, e.g., Rokkan 1975). Those that developed "early" had certain advantages over those that developed "late," and vice versa. David Laitin (1992:xi), for example, notes that coercive nation-building practices available earlier to monarchs (e.g., the forceful imposition of a common language) are not available to leaders of new states today, in part because of the international outrage these policies would generate. But what is "early" state formation? The timing of state formation, of course, can be dated. Thus, it is possible to develop a relatively precise measure of the "age" of a state. But most of the variation captured by this measure is not relevant to the concept of "early" versus "late" state formation. Suppose, for example, that one state has been around for 400 years, and another for 200 years. The first is twice as old as the second, but both are fully "early" from the perspective of state formation theory. Thus, much of the variation captured by the ratio-scale variable "age" is simply irrelevant to the distinction between "early" versus "late" state formation. To convert "age" to fuzzy membership in the set of "early," it would be necessary to truncate irrelevant variation using qualitative breakpoints. These qualitative breakpoints, in turn, must be anchored in theoretical and substantive criteria.

This example underscores several key features of the fuzzy-set approach to the operationalization of social science concepts. The first is that the fidelity of membership scores to concepts in very important. Scores should show, as closely as possible, the degree to which cases belong to the sets that are implicated in the concepts used in theoretical statements (e.g., "early states"). The second is that researchers must use qualitative anchors to establish a close correspondence between raw measures (such as GNP per capita in dollars and state age in years) and membership in fuzzy sets (such as "rich countries" and "early state formation"). Qualitative anchors truncate irrelevant variation and establish criteria for determining whether cases are more in or more out of sets. The third and most important feature underscored by the example is that fuzzy sets are fundamentally *interpretive tools*—they operationalize theoretical concepts in a way that enhances the dialogue between ideas and evidence. With fuzzy sets it is possible to establish a much closer fit between theory and data than is possible using conventional procedures. If, as I have argued in this work and elsewhere (see especially Ragin 1994a), social research is fundamentally an effort to represent empirical social phenomena using social theory as a guide, then the close correspondence between fuzzy sets and concepts makes the fuzzy-set approach ideally suited for this undertaking.

The Contrast between Fuzzy Sets and Conventional Measures

The use of qualitative anchors to identify key breakpoints on continua contrasts sharply with conventional social science, where the usual concern is to *maximize* the variation of all variables used in an investigation. Thus, the use of fuzzy sets challenges the implicit assumption of much conventional work that all variation is meaningful. From the perspective of fuzzy logic, conceptual formulations (e.g., "democratic countries" or "early state formation") are paramount, and the central problem is to assess the membership of relevant cases in such sets using substantive and theoretical criteria. Some portions of the range of a conventional variable used as an indicator of a concept may be completely irrelevant. From the perspective of fuzzy-set social science, to operationalize social science concepts with conventional variables containing unknown amounts of irrelevant variation adds error to ambiguity. The practice of truncating irrelevant variation, central to the fuzzy-set approach, is also consistent with everyday practice. For example, people who are unambiguously "not female" can vary in how feminine they are, but this variation is irrelevant to the assessment of statements about the set of females.

The importance of having an interpretable correspondence between theoretical concepts and fuzzy membership scores can be illustrated dramatically in a simple contrast between variable-oriented research and fuzzy-set social science. Consider the investigator who wishes to assess two different theoretical statements. The first is that rich countries are politically stable. The second is that poor countries are economically dependent on rich countries. To assess the first statement, the investigator would examine the correlation between a measure of national wealth such as GNP per capita and some measure of political stability to see if there is a statistically significant, positive correlation between them. To assess the second statement, the investigator would examine the correlation between the same measure of country wealth, GNP per capita, and a measure of economic dependence to see whether there is a statistically significant, negative correlation between them. In short, two very different verbal formulations—one involving the set of rich countries and the other involving the set of poor countries—would be operationalized using exactly the same independent variable, GNP per capita, without altering it in any way to fit the two different verbal theories.

From the perspective of fuzzy-set social science, however, the set of poor countries is not simply the inverse of the set of rich countries. Referring back to table 6.2 and figure 6.1, countries with GNP per capita value less than $2,000 are unambiguously "not rich" and thus receive membership scores of 0 in the set of rich countries. But are countries that are unambiguously "not rich" also unambiguously poor? Of course not. There are many countries that are in the definitely not-rich set (fuzzy membership in the set of rich countries = 0), which nevertheless have membership scores in the set of poor countries that are less than 1.0. In the language of fuzzy-set social science, the qualitative anchors for the set of "poor" countries are very different from the qualitative anchors for the set of "rich" countries. One set of anchors is not the reverse of the other. Plausible anchors for the set of poor countries are shown in table 6.3 and figure 6.2. (As before, GNP per capita varies between $100 and $30,000.) Countries with GNP per capita values below $500 are unambiguously poor, and those with values greater than $5,000 are unambiguously not poor. The crossover point is $1,000.

The lack of mathematical symmetry between "rich" and "poor" in fuzzy-set social science provides an important contrast with variable-oriented social science. In the variable-oriented approach, very different verbal formulations (one about "poor" countries and the other about "rich" countries) would be operationalized using the same exact measure of country wealth, GNP per capita. In fuzzy-set social science, by contrast, operationalizations of set memberships must adhere closely to concepts, which, in this example, means that the investigator must construct appropriately *asymmetrical* anchors for measuring fuzzy membership. Furthermore, the fuzzy-set approach defines the subset

Table 6.3
Fuzzy Membership in the Set of "poor countries"

GNP/Capita (U.S. $)	Membership (M)	Verbal Labels
100 → 499	M = 1.0	Clearly poor
500 → 999	.5 < M < .1	More or less poor
1,000	M = .5	In between
1,001 → 4,999	0 < M < .5	More or less not poor
5,000 → 30,000	M = 0	Clearly not poor

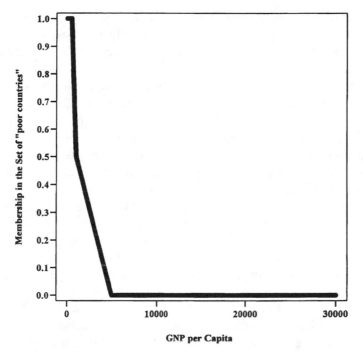

Figure 6.2 Plot of membership in "poor countries" against GNP per capita.

of countries that are unambiguously not rich as irrelevant to statements about rich countries, and it defines the subset of countries that are unambiguously not poor as irrelevant to statements about poor countries. Thus, from the perspective of fuzzy-set social science, the conventional approach is ungrounded, uncalibrated, and imprecise.

MEASURING FUZZY MEMBERSHIP

Fuzzy membership scores indicate the degree to which relevant cases (e.g., "families") belong to the sets that social scientists use to describe and analyze them (e.g., "traditional").[3] These fuzzy sets, in turn, reflect the concepts appearing in theoretical statements (e.g., "the traditional family is declining in 'postmodern' society"). The strength of fuzzy-set analysis derives from the close correspondence between the content of theoretical concepts, on the one hand, and the assessment of fuzzy

---

3. The category "families" also can be treated as a fuzzy set. See chapter 7, where I discuss fuzzy membership in domains.

membership scores, on the other. In order to achieve this correspondence, it is important for researchers to view the measurement of fuzzy membership as a fundamentally interpretive act, not as a mechanical exercise.

There are several steps in the assessment of fuzzy membership. The steps I sketch here assume that researchers have a solid understanding of the concepts appearing in their theories and that they have an extensive base of relevant substantive knowledge as well. Using this knowledge, they can (1) identify pertinent evidence for assessing fuzzy membership scores and (2) specify appropriate qualitative anchors defining full membership, full nonmembership, and the crossover point. In the course of assigning fuzzy membership scores to cases, researchers may find that they need to clarify their concepts, deepen their substantive knowledge, or study their cases more intensively. Much of the discussion that follows seems deductive and prescriptive in emphasis. It is important to point out, however, that in most investigations there is rich interplay between theory, data collective, data analysis, and conceptualization that is not linear or step-by-step in any way. Thus the steps that I list here could just as well be seen as different aspects of a complex, ongoing process that reaches a conclusion only once researchers complete their representations of social life in the form of some kind of representation or report.

The first step in the assessment of fuzzy membership scores is to specify the relevant domain of the assessment. Every empirical analysis is an application of ideas to evidence. In fuzzy-set analysis the key domain issue is the set of cases that have been selected for analysis and the resonance of these cases with the investigator's theory. In essence, the researcher must answer the question, What are these cases, or observations, cases of? The answer to this question has a large impact on the analysis of cases because the specification of the domain, in effect, may magnify the importance of some concepts and diminish others. For example, the relative importance of being a "rich" country diminishes if the investigator's domain is the advanced industrial societies. The specification of the domain also has important implications for the operationalization of concepts as fuzzy sets.

The second step in the assessment of fuzzy membership scores is to define the fuzzy sets that follow from the concepts guiding the investigation. This step may seem obvious and straightforward, like listing the variables to be used in an analysis. However, there is a subtle and important difference between specifying fuzzy sets and specifying variables. When assessing fuzzy membership, the researcher's goal is to assess each case's degree of membership in a set, not simply to determine its position on a continuum, relative to other cases, as in variable-oriented social research. For example, instead of measuring "household income" (a variable), a researcher might want to assess degree of membership in the set of "households that are financially secure." Instead of measuring crime rates at the neighborhood level (a variable), the investigator might want to assess degree of membership in the set of "dangerous neighborhoods."

It is important to shift thinking and analytic procedures in this way, toward sets and away from variables, for two reasons. First, the concepts central to social scientists' theories are often best understood as sets, not as variables (e.g., financial security instead of income, dangerous neighborhoods instead of crime rates, rich countries instead of GNP per capita, and so on). The second reason is that when concepts are understood as sets and not as variables, it becomes very clear that some of the range of a variable that might be used to index membership in a set may be irrelevant. For example, if a theoretical statement really pertains to "financially secure households," then the extensive variation that exists in the upper ranges of "household income" may not be relevant to the investigation. Thus, in this step the researcher focuses on the sets that are implicit, and very often explicit, in theoretical statements and avoids the common practice of reformulating them as open-ended variables.

The third step is to determine the type of fuzzy set that is feasible for each concept. For some concepts, it may not be possible to implement fine-grained distinctions, and researchers may be limited to three-value or five-value schemes (see table 6.1). In others, investigators may be able to peg fuzzy membership scores to existing interval- or ratio-scale measures, as in the example of crime rates and the fuzzy set of "dangerous" neighborhoods. Two main considerations enter into these assessments: (1) the definition of the set in question, and (2) the quality, amount, and consistency of evidence that is available to the researcher. The first consideration is primarily theoretical. Some sets, while still fuzzy, have only a limited number of theoretically relevant values, as in the example of the three-value fuzzy set mentioned previously (involving the employees of a firm). It would be pointless to create fine-grained distinctions that are theoretically irrelevant. The second consideration is the more important. Most theoretical concepts translate to fuzzy sets with continuous degrees of membership and thus permit fine-grained distinctions. However, the available evidence may be too weak to support such distinctions. Customary indicators may be too crude or too indirect; the nature of the evidence may be inconsistent from one case to the next; the available data may be entirely qualitative and thus difficult to quantify in a conventional manner; and so on. Generally, if the data are too weak to support fine-grained distinctions, then researchers should summarize their evidence using five- or seven-value schemes.

The fourth step is to determine the likely *range* of fuzzy membership scores. It is second nature for social scientists to assign low scores (fuzzy membership < .10) to cases at the bottom of a distribution and high scores (fuzzy membership > 90) to cases at the top of a distribution. This deeply ingrained habit is inappropriate in many fuzzy-set analyses. Suppose, for example, that a researcher studying the welfare state in advanced industrial democracies wants to assess the membership of existing welfare states in the ideal-typic Social Democratic welfare system (Kvist 1999). While Scandinavian countries might well receive the top membership scores in this set (say, .7–.8), no country would be "fully in" this set (with membership scores of 1.0).[4] The ideal-typic social democratic welfare system is a lofty goal that no country is likely ever to achieve. Thus, membership in this set might range from 0 to a maximum of about .8.

It is also possible for fuzzy membership scores to be pushed in the other direction. This same welfare state researcher might be interested in the membership of the 18 or so advanced industrial democracies in the set of "rich" countries, based on the argument that being a "rich" country is a necessary condition for having a "social democratic" welfare state. *All* of the advanced industrial democracies have membership scores exceeding .5, the crossover point, in the set of "rich" countries. These countries' scores in the set of "rich" countries might range from about .65 to 1.0. It is also possible for membership scores to be concentrated in the middle range of fuzzy membership (say, .35–.65), with no cases fully in or fully out of the set in question. For each fuzzy set used in an investigation, the researcher should ask, Are any cases fully out of the set? Are any fully in? What is likely to be the maximum membership score? What is likely to be the minimum membership score? Are most cases more in or more out of the set?

These considerations underscore an important contrast between fuzzy-set analysis and conventional variable-oriented analysis. The conceptual midpoint of every fuzzy set is .5, the crossover point. It does not matter that all the cases may have scores greater than this value

4. Zadeh (1972) refers to such sets as "subnormal."

(as in the set of "rich" countries, just mentioned) or less than this value. The crossover point is a qualitatively defined anchor, a point in the distribution of membership scores that is established by the investigator. A conventional variable, by contrast, is anchored by the mean, an empirically derived measure of central tendency. In a given data set, values less than the mean are "low"; value greater than the mean are "high." No theoretical or external substantive criteria enter into the designations of "low" or "high." In conventional variable-oriented analysis, these designations are entirely data-driven and sample-specific. In fuzzy-set analysis, by contrast, these designations are specific to criteria established by the investigator. In other words, variables are calibrated according to sample means and standard deviations; fuzzy sets are calibrated according to theoretical and substantive knowledge.

The fifth step is to identify empirical evidence that is appropriate for indexing fuzzy membership scores. Sometimes a conventional variable can be used, as in the example of using GNP per capita to index membership in the set of "rich" countries. Sometimes, it may be necessary to use several conventional variables at once to index membership in a single fuzzy set. For example, a researcher might argue that an "efficient" bureaucracy brings together several traits and thus would assess the degree to which bureaucracies *combine* these characteristics. To receive a high score on "efficiency," a case would have to display high scores on *all* the relevant component variables. A low score of any one of the traits would give the case a low score on the index of efficiency. Another researcher might have several crude but *substitutable* indicators of the same concept and use factor-analytic procedures to develop and refine a composite index (Nunnally 1967). In many investigations, it may prove impossible to identify conventional variables that could be used to index fuzzy-set membership. Researchers may rely instead on qualitative evidence, in-depth knowledge of cases, and other less systematic forms of evidence to help them construct five- and seven-value fuzzy sets.

Fuzzy-membership scores also can be derived more directly. For example, a survey researcher might ask respondents to rate their degree of membership in sets, using the labels from the seven-value scheme presented in table 6.1. Survey respondents also could be asked to rate things like occupations, and these rating could be averaged and then used as fuzzy membership scores. For example, respondents might be asked, using the seven-value scheme, to rate the degree to which occupations belong in the set "prestigious." Another direct method for deriving fuzzy membership scores is to query experts or insiders (e.g., Cas-

Table 6.4
Translating from Raw Scores to Verbal Labels to Fuzzy Membership Scores

Raw Scores of Population Size	Verbal Labels	Fuzzy Membership Score
≤100,000	Fully out	.000
100,001–250,000	Mostly out	.001–.250
250,001–400,000	More or less out	.251–.499
400,001–600,000	Neither out nor in	.500
600,001–800,000	More or less in	.501–.750
800,001–1,000,000	Mostly in	.751–.999
≥1,000,001	Fully in	1.000

tles and Mair 1984). For example, foreign policy experts might be asked to assign fuzzy membership scores for the set of countries with "pro-U.S. foreign policies." Fuzzy membership scores could also be derived from ethnographic investigation. The goal of this tack would be to understand fuzzy sets from the point of view of the actors who use them and to assign membership scores accordingly.[5]

The sixth and final step in the assessment of fuzzy membership scores is the translation of empirical evidence into scores. To accomplish this translation, it is necessary to establish connections between "raw" scores (or specific kinds of evidence—if the evidence is qualitative in nature) and verbal labels, which, in turn, are linked to different fuzzy membership scores. For purposes of illustration, I present a simple example, involving the use of a single ratio-scale variable to index membership in a fuzzy set. This translation is relatively straightforward because there is a single input (a conventional ratio-scale variable) and the output is a continuous fuzzy set. Table 6.4 shows the translation of the variable "city population" into the set "major urban area." The first column of the table shows various ranges of city population; the second column shows the verbal labels relevant to different fuzzy scores (from table 6.1); and the third column shows the fuzzy scores specific to these verbal levels. The verbal labels sort raw scores according to substantive criteria and thus establish qualitative breakpoints on a continuum of raw scores.

To translate city population to fuzzy membership in the set "major urban area," the researcher asks a series of questions, structured by the

5. It is also possible to use a "neural net" approach to derive fuzzy membership scores. In general, however, it is better for social scientists to base their fuzzy membership scores on theoretical and substantive knowledge as much as possible and to avoid surrendering too much scholarly authority to computer algorithms.

last two columns of the table, including the following: What population size places a city "fully" out of the set of major urban areas? What population size places a city "mostly but not fully" out of the set of major urban areas? What population size places a city "more or less" out of the set of major urban areas? In essence, the verbal labels in the second column serve as guides and thereby structure the translation of city sizes (first column) to fuzzy membership scores (third column). Various mathematical functions can be used to smooth or shape a translation (e.g., a logarithmic versus an S-shaped curve), depending on the ideas guiding the construction of the fuzzy set. It is important to point out as well that different functions might be applied to scores above versus below the crossover point. However, it is important not to focus on mathematical functions. The key consideration is the linking of raw scores to verbal labels, which in turn are pegged to specific fuzzy scores.

Once membership scores have been assigned to cases, they should not be viewed as fixed and permanent. In the course of using fuzzy sets, investigators, in effect, assess the utility and plausibility of their scoring of cases. Sometimes an anomalous finding or pattern signals that the researcher should reconsider the assessment of fuzzy membership scores. In short, the coding of fuzzy membership scores should be seen as an important part of the dialogue between ideas and evidence in this approach.

OPERATIONS ON FUZZY SETS

Unlike variables, fuzzy sets are strongly coupled to theoretical concepts. This strong coupling places new demands on researchers, namely, that they pay careful attention to the meaning of the concepts they use and to the specification of appropriate qualitative anchors. The analytic rewards from using fuzzy sets, however, far outweigh these costs. *Because fuzzy sets are closely coupled to theoretical concepts, they can be manipulated in a variety of ways and thus offer new possibilities for representing and evaluating social theories.* Before illustrating these features, I first discuss some common operations on fuzzy sets: negation, logical *or*, logical *and*, concentration, and dilation. Many other operations on fuzzy sets are possible (see, for example, Zadeh 1972; Lakoff 1973), but the operations described here are the most basic and the most useful.[6]

6. Other operations include contrast intensification, where scores are transformed so that they move away from the crossover point and toward 1 or 0, and fuzzification, where scores are transformed so that they move away from 1 and 0 and toward .5.

Negation

Like crisp sets, fuzzy sets can be negated. In crisp logic, negation switches membership scores from 1 to 0 and from 0 to 1. The negation of the crisp set of males, for example, is the crisp set of not males. If a case has a Boolean score of 1 in the set of males, then it has a Boolean score of 0 in the set of not males. Likewise, a case with a Boolean score of 0 in the set of males has a Boolean score of 1 in the set of not males. This simple mathematical principle holds in fuzzy algebra as well. The relevant numerical values are not restricted to the Boolean values 0 and 1 but extend to values between 0 and 1 as well. To calculate the membership of a case in the negation of fuzzy set A, simply subtract its membership in set A from 1, as follows:

fuzzy membership in set not $A = 1 -$ fuzzy membership in set A.

This can also be displayed as $\sim A_i = 1 - A_i$, where the subscript "i" indicates the "ith" case, the set "not A" is represented as $\sim A$, and the symbol "$\sim$" denotes negation. Thus, for example, if the United States has a membership score of .79 in the set of "democratic countries," it has a score of .21 in the set of "not democratic countries." That is, the United States would be mostly but not fully out of the set of not democratic countries. An individual with a membership score of .35 in the set of Roman Catholics has a membership score of .65 in the set of not Roman Catholics; a city with a score of .5 in the set of racially divided cities has a score of .5 in the set of cities that are not racially divided, and so on.

Negation is useful in part because it serves as a subtle reminder of the restricted nature of bipolar thinking. Just as "rich" is not the mathematical inverse of "poor," at least not from the perspective of fuzzy sets, many other conventional binaries loosen when reformulated as fuzzy sets. For example, many people are neither "White" nor "Black" and resist this common bipolarity. Given the opportunity to code their own fuzzy racial membership, they might give themselves low membership scores in all conventional racial categories and thus high membership scores in not White, not Black, or not Asian categories, and so on. Others might feel the same way about conventional bipolar gender categories. Beyond these common issues of identity, fuzzy sets offer social scientists great flexibility in how they conceive social categories. For example, just as fuzzy membership in the set of females is not exactly equivalent to fuzzy membership in the set of not males, fuzzy membership in the set of not females is not exactly equivalent to fuzzy membership in the set of males. Some theoretical statements might apply only to not females; others might apply only to males (a subset of not females), and so on.

Logical and

Compound sets are formed when two or more sets are brought together in some way. The most common compound set involves the intersection of two sets, joined together by "logical *and*." For example, a researcher interested in the fate of democratic institutions in relatively inhospitable settings might want to draw up a list of countries that are "democratic *and* poor." Conventionally, these countries would be identified using crisp sets by cross-tabulating the two dichotomies, poor versus not poor and democratic versus not democratic, and seeing which countries are in the democratic/poor cell of this two-by-two table. This cell, in effect, shows the cases that exist in the intersection of the two component sets.

With fuzzy sets, logical *and* is accomplished by taking the *minimum* membership score of each case in the sets that are intersected. For example, if a country's membership in the set of poor countries is .34 and its membership in the set of democratic countries is .91, its membership in the set of countries that are poor *and* democratic is the smaller of these two scores, .34. This operation is consistent with everyday experience. Consider the set of people who are young *and* blond. An excess of blondness cannot compensate for very low membership in the set of young people, just as an excess of youth or "youngness" cannot compensate for very low membership in the set of people with blond hair. In either case, the resulting membership score in the set of people who are young *and* blond is ruled by the minimum.

For further illustration of this principle, consider table 6.5, which shows a range of hypothetical membership scores for the set of countries that are "democratic and poor." The first four rows of this table demonstrate that the fuzzy operation of finding the minimum produces correct Boolean values when membership scores are crisp. That is, only cases that have scores of 1 on both "democratic" and "poor" receive scores of 1 on the intersection of these two sets; otherwise, membership scores are 0. For the remainder of the hypothetical cases a wide range of membership scores is possible, but in each row the result reported in the last column is ruled by the minimum. That is, if a country has a very low score in one set, it does not matter how high its score is in the

Table 6.5

Using the Minimum to Show Membership in Intersecting Fuzzy Sets
(Logical *and*)

Country	Membership in the Set of Democratic Countries	Membership in the Set of Poor Countries	Membership in the Set of Democratic and Poor Countries
A	0.0	0.0	0.0
B	0.0	1.0	0.0
C	1.0	0.0	0.0
D	1.0	1.0	1.0
E	.1	.9	.1
F	.7	.9	.7
G	.9	.9	.9
H	.1	.1	.1
I	.5	.2	.2
J	.9	.4	.4
K	.5	.5	.5

other set. It still receives a low membership score in the intersection. All countries receiving scores greater than .5 in the last column are more in than out of the set of countries that are democratic and poor.

Logical *or*

Two or more sets also can be joined through logical *or*—the union of sets. For example, a researcher might be interested in countries that are "developed" *or* "democratic" based on the conjecture that these two conditions might offer equivalent bases for some outcome (e.g., bureaucracy-laden government). Conventionally, crisp categories would be used to compile a complete list of countries that are "developed or democratic" (i.e., countries that have one or both characteristics). With fuzzy sets, the researcher focuses on the *maximum* of each case's memberships in the component sets. That is, membership in the set formed from the union of two or more component sets is the maximum value of the case's memberships in the component sets. Thus, if a country has a score of .15 in the set of democratic countries and a score of .93 in the set of developed countries, it has a score of .93 in the set of countries that are "democratic *or* developed." This operation is also consistent with everyday experience. A young person with black hair has a high score in the set of people who are "young *or* blond," despite having black hair.

For illustration of the use of the maximum, consider table 6.6, which shows a range of hypothetical membership scores for the set of coun-

Table 6.6
Using the Maximum to Show Membership in the Union of Fuzzy Sets
(Logical *or*)

Country	Membership in the Set of Developed Countries	Membership in the Set of Democratic Countries	Membership in the Set of Developed and Democratic Countries
A	0.0	0.0	0.0
B	0.0	1.0	1.0
C	1.0	0.0	1.0
D	1.0	1.0	1.0
E	.1	.9	.9
F	.5	.9	.9
G	.9	.9	.9
H	.1	.1	.1
I	.7	.4	.7
J	.9	.1	.9
K	.5	.5	.5

tries that are "developed or democratic." The first four rows show that the fuzzy operation of finding the maximum produces correct Boolean values when the membership scores are crisp. That is, cases that have scores of 1 on either "developed" or "democratic" receive scores of 1 on the union of these two sets. Membership in the union of these two sets is 0 only if membership in both component sets is 0. For the remainder of the hypothetical cases a wide range of membership scores is possible, but in each row the result reported in the fourth column is ruled by the maximum. That is, if a country has a high score in one set, it does not matter how low its other score is. It still receives a high score on the union. All countries with scores greater than .5 in the last column are more in than out of the set of countries that are democratic or developed.

A detailed example of logical *or* and logical *and* with five countries and three sets is offered in table 6.7, using hypothetical membership scores. The first column lists the five countries; the next three columns list, in turn, their membership scores in three sets: "capitalist," "democratic," and "ethnically diverse." The fifth column lists their resulting membership scores in the set defined by the intersection of these three sets (i.e., the set of countries that are capitalist *and* democratic *and* ethnically diverse). The last column lists their scores in the set defined by the union of these three sets (i.e., the set of countries that are capitalist *or* democratic *or* ethnically diverse).

Table 6.7
Illustration of Fuzzy Logic's Minimum and Maximum

Country (1)	Capitalist (2)	Democratic (3)	Ethnically Diverse (4)	Capitalist · Democratic · Diverse[a] (5)	Capitalist + Democratic + Diverse[b] (6)
Germany	.95	.95	.15	.15	.95
United States	1.00	.80	.85	.80	1.00
United Kingdom	.90	.90	.60	.60	.90
Sweden	.80	1.00	.20	.20	1.00
Russia	.30	.40	.95	.30	.95

[a] Midlevel dots (·) are used to indicate logical *and*. Thus, the fifth column shows membership scores in the set of countries that are ethnically diverse capitalist democracies (the intersection of the three sets).
[b] Addition (+) is used to indicate logical *or*. Thus, the sixth column shows membership scores in the set of countries that are capitalist *or* democratic *or* ethnically diverse (the union of the three sets).

The fifth column (defined by intersection) could be considered a measure of the conformity of these five countries to an ideal typically democratic, capitalist, ethnically diverse country. According to these hypothetical data, the United States conforms most closely to this ideal type; the United Kingdom comes in second; and Russia is third. The sixth column has a less straightforward interpretation. It could be considered a list of membership scores in a set defined by the potential for chaos emanating from alternate sources: the anarchy of the market (capitalism), the collective expression of mass whims (democracy), or the heterogeneity of the people living within a single country (ethnic diversity). According to these hypothetical data, all five countries exhibit a substantial potential for chaos.

Concentration

Because they are verbal constructs, most social science concepts can be altered with conventional modifiers, just as everyday concepts accept modification. For example, the everyday concept "tall" can be modified with the adverb "very" to produce "very tall;" the concept "bureaucratic" can be modified with "very" to produce "very bureaucratic;" the concept "traditional" can be modified with "very" to produce "very traditional;" and so on. The use of modifiers has direct implications for fuzzy membership scores. For example, membership in the fuzzy set "very tall" is not the same as membership in the fuzzy set "tall," but the two series of values should display some sort of systematic, monotonic correspondence.

As Lotfi Zadeh has shown, the impact of the verbal modifier "very" is to lower membership scores. For example, a person with a membership of .8 in the set of "tall" people may have a membership of .64 in the set of "very tall" people. The adverb "very" sets a higher standard; thus, fuzzy membership scores should be correspondingly lower. Zadeh (1972) refers to its effect as "concentration" and suggests the following function as a rough approximation

$$\text{Concentration } A_i = A_i^2.$$

In short, to calculate membership in "very" A (e.g., "very rich"), square membership in A (e.g., "rich"). Thus a person with a membership of .9 in the set of "rich" people has a membership of .81 in the set of "very rich" people. A country with a membership of .5 in the set "ethnically diverse," has a score of .25 in the set "very ethnically diverse." An organization that is almost fully in the set "bureaucratic" (membership = .99) is also almost fully in the set "very bureaucratic" (membership = .98). Notice also that "very" can be combined with negation to yield "not very." Thus, a neighborhood has .8 membership in the set "safe," then it has a score of .64 in the set "very safe" and a score of .36 in the set "not very safe."

The formula for "very" is powerful and simple. Its main liability is that any case that is fully in the original (unconcentrated) set is also fully in the concentrated set. For example, a state that is fully authoritarian (membership = 1.0) is also fully in the "very authoritarian" set (membership = 1.0). Thus, researchers who wish to use this formula to concentrate membership scores (and thereby apply the modifier "very") should reevaluate cases that are fully in the unconcentrated set because they may wish to exclude some that are fully in the unconcentrated set (e.g., "authoritarian") from full membership in the concentrated set (e.g., "very authoritarian"). Likewise, there may be cases that receive very low but still nonzero scores in the concentrated set, which nevertheless should receive scores of 0 in the concentrated set. For example, suppose India has a membership score of .05 in the set of authoritarian countries and should have a score of 0 in the set of "very authoritarian" countries, at least from the researcher's perspective. However, the square of .05 is .0025, not 0. Thus, researchers should reevaluate the assignment of cases at the lower end of a concentrated fuzzy set, as well.

Dilation

Another simple operation on fuzzy sets is known as dilation. In direct contrast to concentration and the modifier "very," dilation sets a lower standard. A common verbal translation of dilation is "more or less."[7] It is easier to be "more or less" rich than it is to be "rich." Similarly, the standard "more or less" democratic is lower and thus easier to meet than the standard "democratic." In short, dilation is a loosening of criteria. Zadeh (1972) offers the following simple, rough formula for dilation:

$$\text{Dilation } A_i = A_i^{1/2}.$$

In short, to calculate membership in "more or less" A (e.g., "more or less rich"), take the square root of membership in A (the square root of "rich"). Thus a person with .36 membership in the set of "rich" people has .6 membership in the set of people who are "more or less rich." A country that has .81 membership in the set "developed" has .9 membership in the set "more or less developed."

Like concentration, dilation creates scores that are problematic at the extremes. It is only a rough approximation. For example, according to the formula, a country that is fully out of the set "economically dependent" is also fully out of the set "more or less economically dependent." In fact, however, a country could be fully out of the first but weakly in the second. Thus, the researcher should pay close attention to the codings of cases at the extremes of membership when a set is dilated. More than likely, cases at or near the extremes of the dilated set will need to be recoded, in line with qualitative anchors that are consistent with the researcher's substantive and theoretical criteria.

Complex Theoretical Statements

These five principles—logical *and*, logical *or*, negation, concentration, and dilation—can be used to evaluate membership in complex theoretical statements. Consider, for example, the following statement about "anomie." Suppose a theory states that anomie occurs in societies that are very capitalist and ethnically diverse and in societies that are more or less capitalist but not very democratic. In essence, the theory speci-

---

7. A more precise translation would be "at least somewhat," as in the phrase, a person who is "at least somewhat" rich. The semantic problem with "more or less" is that some might interpret a "very" rich person as having less than full membership in the set of "more or less" rich people.

fies two combinations of conditions thought to spawn anomie. This statement can be expressed algebraically as follows:

very capitalist·diverse +
　　　　more or less capitalist·~very democratic → anomie.

Midlevel dots indicate logical *and*—the intersection of conditions; plus signs indicates logical *or*—alternate combinations of conditions; and the "~" sign indicates negation or "not."

Using the principles of fuzzy logic just sketched and the membership scores shown in table 6.7, it is possible to calculate countries' membership scores in the formulation just presented (i.e., the left-hand side of the statement). In essence, these membership scores show the relevance of the verbal formulation to different cases. Consider Russia's score, computed according to the principles of fuzzy logic:

$$\text{Russia} = \max \{\min \{(.30)^2, .95\}, \min \{(.30)^{1/2}, (1 - (.40)^2\}\},$$
$$= \max \{\min \{.09, .95\}, \min \{.55, .84\}\},$$
$$= \max \{.09, .55\},$$
$$= .55.$$

In the first combination, Russia's scores in the set of capitalist countries (.3) is squared to get its membership in the set of very capitalist countries (.09). The minimum of this score and Russia's membership in the set of ethnically diverse countries (.95) is .09. In the second combination, the square root of Russia's membership in the set of capitalist countries, provides its membership in the set of more- or less capitalist countries (.55). Its membership in the set of democratic countries (.40) is squared to get its membership in the set of very democratic countries (.16). This score is subtracted from 1 to derive Russia's membership in the set of countries that are not very democratic (.84). The minimum of the two scores in the second combination (.55 and .84) is .55. Because the two combinations are alternates (denoted with addition, logical *or*), Russia's value in the statement for anomie is the maximum of the value of the two combinations (.09 and .55). Thus, Russia has a membership of .55 in the statement.

The purpose of these calculations is to illustrate the utility of fuzzy sets for evaluating complex verbal statements, not to construct a model of anomie. The exercise shows that by using fuzzy membership scores, it is possible to evaluate the degree to which cases adhere to the conditions specified in relatively complex theoretical statements. Such membership scores could be used subsequently to assess the empirical adequacy of the argument. For example, the scores just calculated could be compared with an independently conducted assessment of anomie to see if the conditions specified in the verbal formulation have any set-theoretic relationship with anomie. I demonstrate these and other techniques in chapters 7–11.

THE POWER OF FUZZY SETS

Fuzzy sets offer powerful new tools for social scientists. By combining qualitative and quantitative assessment in the same analytic instrument, they provide a new way for researchers to operationalize social science concepts. Because they demand a close coupling of theory and analysis, apparent in the calibration of fuzzy membership scores, fuzzy sets prod researchers to pay careful attention to the meaning of their concepts and to the criteria they use to establish qualitative breakpoints. Because they are strongly coupled to concepts, fuzzy sets offer new possibilities for evaluating complex theoretical arguments and, more generally, for establishing a close connection between theory and data analysis.

SEVEN

USING FUZZY SETS TO
CONSTITUTE CASES AND
POPULATIONS

INTRODUCTION

Configurational thinking is the core of the diversity-oriented approach. Central to configurational thinking, in turn, is the property space, an analytic device that focuses on different kinds of cases, conceived as combinations of qualitative attributes (Lazarsfeld 1937). Can property spaces accommodate fuzzy sets, analytic tools that combine qualitative and quantitative assessment? This chapter shows that they can. The discussion moves back and forth between brief reviews of the crisp-set approach to property spaces and the fuzzy-set approach. By comparing the two, I demonstrate the unique advantages of fuzzy-set methods and at the same time show how they extend and deepen diversity-oriented research.

In the fuzzy-set approach, a property space is much more than an elaboration of combinations of categories. Instead, it is conceived a multidimensional vector space with as many dimensions as fuzzy sets (see also Kosko 1993). Fuzzy-membership scores position cases along each dimension and thus locate cases within the multidimensional vector space. The corners of this vector space correspond to the cells of a crisp-set property space; the area within the vector space provides an infinity of possible points for locating cases. This alternative, "fuzzified" conception of the property space has important implications for social research because there is no longer a simple one-to-one correspondence between property-space locations and categories of cases as there is in the crisp-set approach (and in Lazarsfeld's approach to typology construction). In other words, with fuzzy sets the property space is no longer a simple sorting of cases into detailed subpopulations. Rather, it is an analytic frame that permits cases to have *par-*

tial memberships in types, represented by the corners of the vector space.

This added sophistication brings new richness and new analytic possibilities to the study of cases as configurations and to the constitution of populations and types. For example, with fuzzy sets a given case may have partial membership in all the types specified in a property space. If all cases have partial membership in a type, conceived as an intersection of set memberships, then they may all be used to evaluate that type. Thus, as I show in this chapter, the fuzzy-set approach brings a greater volume of information to the construction and evaluation of property spaces. I also discuss the implications of the fuzzy-set approach for the assessment of limited diversity—the fact that social phenomena rarely, if ever, display all logically and empirically possible combinations of relevant causal conditions. With fuzzy sets, limited diversity exists when a specific *region* of the vector space is void, or virtually void, of cases. I demonstrate fuzzy-set techniques for identifying these voids.

VIEWING CASES AS CONFIGURATIONS

Before presenting the fuzzy-set approach to cases as configurations, I briefly review the crisp-set approach. This summary provides important background for understanding key elements of the fuzzy-set approach and for grasping the advantages that follow from using fuzzy sets.

Combinations of aspects and conditions, viewed as crisp set memberships, are the basic analytic units of crisp configurational analysis. The idea that each location in the property space specified by the researcher may constitute a different kind or type of case captures the essence of this approach. In this view, two cases that differ on only one aspect may be as different from each other as two that differ on many aspects. The analysis of property space locations as types of cases establishes each combination of crisp set memberships as a separate and potentially distinct subpopulation. In the crisp-set approach, cases are sorted into subpopulations according to their different crisp set memberships. In other words, the set of cases included in a study is neatly divided into configurationally defined types in the early stages of the investigation. In a given investigation there are as many potential kinds of cases as there are logically possible combinations of crisp set memberships.

With fuzzy sets there is, potentially at least, an infinity of locations in a property space. Thus, it is impossible to sort cases into crisply delineated subpopulations, defined by specific property-space locations, because cases have varying degrees of membership in the sets that comprise the property space. In the extreme, no two cases may have the same profile of membership scores in the relevant fuzzy sets. To sort cases according to their membership scores could yield as many kinds of cases as the number of cases.

Instead of sorting cases into subpopulations, in the fuzzy-set approach each case is evaluated relative to its *degree* of membership in "crisply defined property-space locations." Such locations correspond to the logically possible combinations of *full membership* (membership score = 1) and *full nonmembership* (membership score = 0) in the fuzzy sets that comprise a property space. The idea of crisply defined locations can be grasped by viewing the property space as a multidimensional vector space with 2^k corners, where k is the number of attributes or conditions appearing in the property space. The 2^k corners of the vector space correspond to its "crisply defined locations"—logically possible combinations of full membership and full nonmembership in the sets that comprise the space. With two fuzzy sets there are four corners; with three fuzzy sets, there are eight corners; with four sets, there are sixteen corners; and so on.

A simple, two-dimensional property space is presented in figure 7.1. This plot shows the fuzzy membership scores of a sample of countries in two sets—the set of "democratic countries" and the set of "advanced industrial countries." This two-dimensional property space has four corners (with $k = 2$, $2^k = 4$): democratic and advanced industrial, democratic and not advanced industrial, not democratic and advanced industrial, and not democratic and not advanced industrial. The four corners of this property space represent the fuzzy membership scores corresponding to the different combinations of full membership and full nonmembership in the two sets, democratic and advanced industrial. Of course, most empirical cases fall short of full membership (and full nonmembership) in these two sets and thus are plotted in the interior of the vector space. In most fuzzy-set analyses, most cases have partial membership in most crisply defined property-space locations. Full membership in a crisply defined property-space location is reached only by cases displaying the appropriate combination of full membership in the sets that comprise a location.

Using the principles of fuzzy-set analysis, it is possible to calculate the degree of membership of each case in each corner—in each crisply defined property-space location. As explained in chapter 6, the membership of a case in an intersection of fuzzy sets is determined by its minimum membership score in the sets that comprise the intersection.

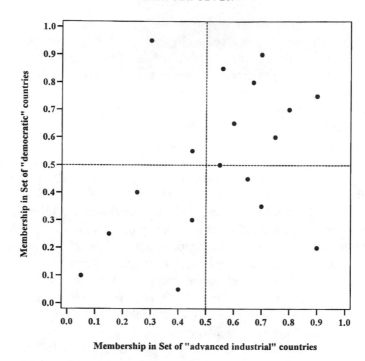

Figure 7.1 Two-dimensional property space showing "democratic" against "advanced industrial."

For example, the country near the lower right corner of figure 7.1 has a membership of .2 in the set of democratic countries and .9 in the set of advanced industrial countries. Its membership in the set of countries that are democratic and advanced industrial is .2, the minimum of these two scores. Its membership in the set of countries that not democratic and advanced industrial is .8, the minimum of its membership in the set of not democratic countries ($1 - .2 = .8$) and its membership in the set of advanced industrial countries (.9). Its membership in the set of not democratic not advanced industrial societies is .1, and its membership in the set of democratic not advanced industrial societies is also .1. Every case plotted in figure 7.1 has partial membership in each of the corners—the four crisply defined property-space locations.

Table 7.1 offers a somewhat more advanced illustration of these same principles. This table reports fuzzy membership scores for 8 community organizations in three sets (yielding a three-dimensional property space with eight crisply defined locations, or corners). Columns (2)–(4) show these organizations' fuzzy memberships in the three sets

Table 7.1
Using Fuzzy Sets to Derive Memberships in Crisply Defined Property-Space Locations

Case No. (1)	Multiracial (M) (2)	Cross-Class (C) (3)	Hierarchical (H) (4)	M·C·H (5)	M·C·~H (6)	M·~C·H (7)	M·~C·~H (8)	~M·C·H (9)	~M·C·~H (10)	~M·~C·H (11)	~M·~C·~H (12)
1	.1	.2	.4	.1	.1	.1	.1	.2	.2	.4	.6
2	.2	.3	.8	.2	.2	.2	.2	.3	.2	.7	.2
3	.1	.9	.4	.1	.1	.1	.1	.4	.6	.1	.1
4	.4	.8	.9	.4	.1	.2	.1	.6	.1	.2	.1
5	.7	.4	.1	.1	.4	.1	.6	.1	.4	.1	.3
6	.6	.3	.7	.3	.3	.6	.3	.3	.3	.4	.3
7	.9	.7	.3	.3	.7	.3	.3	.1	.1	.1	.1
8	.8	.8	.9	.8	.1	.2	.1	.2	.1	.2	.1

that constitute the property space: the set of "multiracial" community organizations (column [2]), the set of "cross-class" community organizations (column [3]), and the set of "hierarchically structured" community organizations (column [4]). Columns (5)–(12) show these organizations' membership scores in eight crisply defined property-space locations—the 8 corners of the three-dimensional vector space. (The 8 corners are shown in the headings of columns [5]–[12] of table 7.1.) Membership scores in each crisply defined location (the eight corners of the vector space) are derived using the principles of fuzzy negation and fuzzy intersection.

As table 7.1 shows, if a case is not fully in or fully out of any of the sets that make up a property space, then it has partial membership in *all* crisply defined property-space locations. That is, its membership in each crisply defined location will be greater than 0 and less than 1. Most such cases also have a *single* property space membership score exceeding .5. That is, even though such cases have partial membership in *all* crisply defined property-space locations, most cases will be more in than out of only one of the 2^k crisply defined property-space locations which form the corners of the k dimensional vector space. (Exceptions to this general rule are explained subsequently.) This pattern is shown across the eight rows of table 7.1. It follows that cases like these can be sorted according to their maximum membership scores, with each case assigned to the corner of the vector space that it is closest to.

There are exceptions to these general rules. Any case with a membership score of .5 (the crossover point) in one or more fuzzy sets will have a maximum membership score of .5 in the crisply defined property-space locations. If a case has a membership score of .5 in *one* of the fuzzy sets that make up a property space, then it scores .5 membership as its maximum in *two* of the crisply defined locations; if a case has a membership score of .5 in two fuzzy sets, then it scores .5 membership as its maximum in four locations; and so on. The pattern is shown in rows 1 through 3 of table 7.2, again using hypothetical data on community organizations. Note also that if a case is fully in *one* of the fuzzy sets that comprise a property space (membership = 1.0), then it will be fully out (membership score = 0) of half of the crisply defined property-space locations (i.e., half of the 2^k corners). If a case is fully in *two* of the fuzzy sets that comprise a property space, then it will be fully out of three-fourths of the crisply defined property-space locations, and so on. This result follows from the use of the principles of fuzzy negation and intersection. This pattern is illustrated in rows 4–6 of table 7.2.

Table 7.2
Fuzzy Memberships in Crisply Defined Property-Space Locations: Special Patterns

Case No.	Multiracial (M)	Cross-Class (C)	Hierarchical (H)	M·C·H	M·C·~H	M·~C·H	M·~C·~H	~M·C·H	~M·C·~H	~M·~C·H	~M·~C·~H
With scores at the crossover point:											
1	.8	.3	.5	.3	.3	.5	.5	.2	.2	.2	.2
2	.1	.5	.5	.1	.1	.1	.1	.5	.5	.5	.5
3	.5	.5	.5	.5	.5	.5	.5	.5	.5	.5	.5
With full membership in one or more fuzzy sets:											
4	.4	.8	1.0	.4	0.0	.2	0.0	.6	0.0	.2	0.0
5	.7	1.0	1.0	.7	0.0	0.0	0.0	.3	0.0	0.0	0.0
6	1.0	1.0	1.0	1.0	0.0	0.0	0.0	0.0	0.0	0.0	0.0

As I demonstrate in subsequent chapters, the fact that most cases have at least partial membership in most crisply defined locations in fuzzy-set analysis provides a great boon to the investigation of causal complexity. Using crisp sets, each test of sufficiency is limited to the cases that conform exactly to the configuration. With fuzzy sets, however, many cases may be involved in each assessment. Specifically, all cases with nonzero membership in a given combination of conditions can be included in an assessment of the sufficiency of that combination. Chapters 9 and 10 show that this increase in the number of relevant cases greatly enhances the utility of probabilistic criteria in the assessment of sufficiency.

In fuzzy-set social science, the idea that "a single difference between two cases may constitute a difference in kind" still holds, but the definition and constitution of "difference in kind" involve fuzzy-set criteria. In the crisp-set approach, a potential difference in kind is easy to identify. If two cases do not have the same exact combination of crisp set membership scores (1s and 0s), then they are potentially different kinds of cases. In the fuzzy-set approach, however, no two cases may have the same exact combination of membership scores. At first glance, therefore, it appears that there are many, many potential differences in kind in the fuzzy-set approach because each cases may differ in some way from all other cases in their membership profiles. However, as I show in tables 7.1 and 7.2, most cases have a maximum membership value in only *one* crisply defined property-space location. From the perspective of fuzzy-set social science, cases that have maximum membership scores in *different* crisply defined locations are potentially different kinds of cases; cases that have maximum membership scores in the same crisply defined location can be considered the same "kind" of case.

For illustration, consider the four community organizations presented in table 7.3. From a simple accounting point of view, these four

Table 7.3
Using Fuzzy Sets to Assess the Comparability of Instances

Case No.	Multiracial (M)	Cross-Class (C)	Hierarchical (H)	$M \cdot C \cdot H$	$M \cdot C \cdot \sim H$
1	.8	.9	.8	.8	.2
2	.8	.9	.6	.6	.4
3	.8	.9	.1	.1	.8
4	.8	.9	.3	.3	.7

cases are very similar because they have identical membership scores in the first two fuzzy sets and differ only in the third. However, their fuzzy membership scores for the combination "multiracial, cross-class, and hierarchical" are quite different. The first two cases have very high membership scores in this set; the other two cases are clearly more "out" than "in" this combination. The third case's score in the crisply defined location is especially low because of its very low membership in the set of hierarchical community organizations. Thus, based on the evidence presented, it is reasonable to treat the first two cases as differing in kind from the third and fourth cases, potentially at least, even though the four cases have identical membership scores for two of the three sets. Note that their fuzzy membership scores in the set of "multiracial, cross-class, and not hierarchical" community organizations reveal that the third and fourth cases can be treated as more-or-less the same kind. This is because both have membership scores exceeding .5 for this combination. The third case has a higher score in this combination of attributes and thus is more "in" this set than the fourth case, but both cases have scores greater than .5 and thus can be treated as comparable instances.

At first glance, it might seem radical to let the minimum "rule" when assessing the degree of membership of a case in a combination of fuzzy sets. Why not average the membership scores in some way? Recall the everyday logic on which the use of the minimum is based. A person's membership in the set of people who are "tall *and* redheaded" is ruled by the minimum. An excess of height cannot make up for having black hair, just as having bright red hair cannot compensate for being short. The minimum rules these everyday assessments, not the average. Note also that from a strictly mathematical perspective the use of the minimum in fuzzy algebra applies to the crisp sets of Boolean algebra as well, where membership scores are constrained to be either 0 or 1. If a case is "out" (membership $= 0$) of one of the sets that make up a combination of crisp sets, then its membership in the combination of sets is equal to 0, the minimum of its scores in the component sets. Thus, the use of the minimum in fuzzy algebra can be seen as an extension of the principles of Boolean algebra.

CONSTITUTING POPULATIONS

Again it is useful to briefly review the crisp-set approach to the constitution of populations before presenting the fuzzy-set approach. This review helps to establish the distinctiveness of fuzzy-set methods.

The crisp-set approach. Using crisp-set techniques researchers can constitute and reconstitute populations in the course of their research. In this approach, the researcher first constructs a property space using theory and substantive knowledge as guides. The property space is composed of attributes or aspects, which in turn, are used to specify different combinations of crisp set memberships. Each combination of memberships—each property-space location—is viewed, in effect, as a different kind of case. Thus, in the initial stages of the research there is not a single population but many subpopulations—many different kinds of cases. The researcher's task is to evaluate the utility of a given property space as a way of providing a conceptual map for a given set of cases. This set of cases, initially at least, contains an unknown degree of heterogeneity. The researcher refines and reconstitutes the property space based on how well it creates homogeneous groupings, as viewed through the lens of his or her property space. Ultimately, the evaluation of groupings is based on the researcher's broader knowledge of cases.

To evaluate a property space, the researcher examines cases located in each cell of the property space he or she has constructed and asks: Do the cases in each location belong together? Are they in fact comparable instances? If so, the investigation can proceed. If not, then the property space, and thus the constitution of subpopulations, must be revised. The space may be expanded with additional aspects, or some aspects may be dropped and new ones added. Alternatively, whole categories of cases may be dropped or added. For example, the property space may seem to work well only for certain subsets of cases (e.g., military coups in Third World countries *before* the fall of Soviet-style communism). The process of evaluating a property space is iterative and ongoing, and the researcher may devise several different versions of his or her property space before selecting a particular specification.

Once researchers are confident that the cases in each cell of a property space belong together, they can assess their comparability with respect to the outcome (or outcomes) under investigation. Here the guiding question is: Are the cases located in each cell of the property space similar (or similar enough) to each other with respect to the outcome in question? This evaluation can take various forms, depending on the interests of the investigator and the nature of the evidence. If the discordance in outcomes is not too great, then the investigation can proceed. Otherwise, the researcher may be forced to reconstitute the property space altogether. The investigator then returns to the previous step, just described, with new ideas about how the property space should be constituted or about which kinds of cases should be added or dropped. Alternatively, the conceptualization or definition of the outcome may be revised in light of the discordant evidence.

Each combination of set memberships—each location in the property space that results from these operations—is understood initially as a distinct kind. That is, the investigator has as many distinct kinds of cases—subpopulations—as there are locations in the property space. Thus, these locations are viewed simultaneously as qualitative states and as combinations of conditions, expressed as configurations of crisp set memberships. Different configurations are subsequently pooled into larger sets only if they display the same outcome.

The use of fuzzy sets brings depth and new possibilities to the constitution of populations. I discuss three benefits here: (1) With fuzzy sets it is possible to array cases with respect to their conformity to crisply defined property-space locations. Arraying cases in this way enhances the evaluation of both the comparability of cases and the utility of the property space. (2) Membership in crisply defined property-space locations (i.e., the corners) and outcomes both vary by degree (i.e., they both are fuzzy sets). Thus, the evaluation of the property space with respect to its success in grouping cases with similar outcomes can be much more nuanced. And (3) fuzzy sets provide a means for incorporating the degree to which cases belong in a population, conceived as a fuzzy set, into all phases of the research.

The first benefit of fuzzy sets is related to evaluating the homogeneity of cases. Consider the impact of fuzzy sets on the evaluation of the success of a property space in grouping cases into subpopulations. With crisp sets, each case has a membership score of 1 or yes for one location in the property space and a score of 0 or no for all other locations. Using fuzzy sets, by contrast, most cases have partial membership in all locations. Thus, for example, a country that is mostly but not fully democratic and mostly but not fully developed has weak membership in the set of countries that are not democratic and not developed. Likewise, an individual who is mostly Protestant and mostly Southern, also has weak membership in the set of people who are not Protestant and not Southern.

As explained in the previous section, in the fuzzy-set approach a property space is best viewed as a multidimensional vector space with 2^k corners—the crisply defined property-space locations. In some respects, each corner of a property space can be seen as a different ideal-typic case, and each empirical case's degree of membership in a corner (i.e., in a crisply defined location) can be interpreted as its degree of conformity to the ideal type (Weber 1949; Kvist 1999) defined and represented by that corner. Researchers use the fuzzy-set principles of negation and intersection to compute measures of the conformity of each case to the ideal-typic instance that is represented by each crisply defined location.

For illustration of the fuzzy-set approach, consider again table 7.1, which shows hypothetical data on eight community organizations. The eight combinations shown in the headings of columns (5)–(12) can be viewed as different ideal-typic forms of community organization. The fuzzy membership scores in columns (5)–(12) show each case's conformity to the ideal-typic form specified in the column headings. This understanding contrasts sharply with the crisp-set approach, where every case is a full member of one and only one property-space location. The crisp-set approach, in effect, mandates that the investigator treat each case as a pure instance of a single type and thus "force-fit" cases into types and into the categories that make up types. By contrast, with fuzzy sets no case may conform perfectly to any ideal-typic location (the corners of the vector space). As table 7.1 illustrates, each case exhibits at least weak membership in every crisply defined location.

Because the fuzzy-set approach permits the assessment of degrees of membership in crisply defined property-space locations, researchers can use this information to aid the evaluation of property spaces, especially with respect to the way it locates cases relative to each other. Arraying cases according to their strength of membership in crisply defined locations greatly facilitates the assessment of their comparability as instances of that combination. Recall that this evaluation is an important step in the constitution of populations. If a property-space location brings together cases that do not seem to belong together, based on the investigator's broader knowledge of the cases in question, then either the property space or the specification of "relevant" cases needs to be revised. This evaluation, which is central to the configurational approach, is greatly enhanced with fuzzy sets.

For illustration, consider table 7.4, which shows the conformity of ten community organizations to a *single* location in the property space depicted in table 7.1. (The organizations listed in table 7.4 are not the same as those listed in tables 7.1 or 7.2.) The table reports these organizations' membership scores in the combination multiracial, not cross-class, and not hierarchically organized. The cases are ordered in terms of their strength of membership in this combination, which is reported in the last column of table 7.4. These results show that the first three cases can be considered instances of the combination because they are

Table 7.4
Using Fuzzy Sets to Assess Conformity to Crisp Property-Space Locations

Case No.	Multiracial (M)	Cross-Class (C)	Hierarchical (H)	M·~C·~H
1	.9	.1	.1	.9
2	.9	.1	.2	.8
3	.6	.4	.2	.6
4	.7	.5	.1	.5
5	.7	.4	.6	.4
6	.4	.3	.7	.3
7	.4	.8	.8	.2
8	.1	.8	.9	.1
9	.3	.0	.9	.1
10	.0	.5	.9	.0

more in than out of the intersection of these three sets. The fourth case resides on the crossover point separating cases that are more in from those that are more out (.5); the next five are more out than in; and the last is fully out.

Because the first three cases have membership scores above .5 in this combination (and, of mathematical necessity, only in this combination), they are the key instances involved in the assessment of comparability. The researcher asks, based on all available evidence, whether these three cases seem to be comparable instances. In addition, because these three cases vary in the degree to which they conform to the combination, the researcher also can ask whether their membership rankings make sense. Generally, the lower the membership score, the more the researcher may relax his or her membership standards. Cases 1 and 2 in table 7.4 both have moderately high membership scores in the combination and thus should be strong instances of the combination. Case 3 has a weaker membership score; thus, this case should be a weaker instance. A case with a membership score of .51 would constitute a still weaker instance. When making an assessment of membership rankings, the researcher also might want to include consideration of cases at the crossover point (e.g., the case in row 4). It is important to acknowledge, however, that such cases also have a membership score of .5 in at least one other corner of the property space. Finally, the cases with membership scores below .5 should seem distinctly different from the ones with membership scores above .5. These evaluations should be based on the investigator's broader knowledge of the cases and the substantive focus of the investigation, as represented in the specification of the property space.

When evaluating a property space, researchers should examine the array of membership scores for each corner. This evaluation parallels the examination of case groupings in crisp configurational analysis, where the researcher is concerned mainly with whether the property space sorts and groups cases appropriately. In the fuzzy-set approach, the fundamental goal is the same—to evaluate the property space and if necessary to provide a basis for reconstructing it. But the evaluation is richer because the researcher has an array of membership scores for each crisply defined location.

The second benefit of the fuzzy-set approach is that fuzzy sets also enhance the examination of the outcomes exhibited by the cases conforming to each crisply defined location in a property space. As in crisp configurational analysis, the construction and evaluation of a property space should also include consideration of the distribution of outcomes for each grouping of cases. If the cases with high membership scores in a crisply defined location exhibit very different outcomes, then the researcher should consider reconstructing the property space or reconstituting the set of relevant cases.

In the crisp-set approach, the evaluation of the distribution of outcomes is straightforward. The researcher simply examines all cases with a specific combination of crisp set memberships to see if they agree, more or less, on the outcome under investigation. The researcher sorts cases according to their crisp set memberships, and the outcomes displayed by cases with each combination of memberships are examined, one combination at a time. If one or more combinations exhibits strong discordance in outcomes, then the researcher may decide to reconstruct the property space or reconstitute the set of relevant cases.

With fuzzy sets this assessment is more nuanced for two reasons: (1) cases vary in the degree to which they conform to crisply defined locations and may have partial membership in every location, and (2) cases also vary in their degree of membership in the outcome. In this phase of the research—where the focus is on the construction and evaluation of the property space and the selection of relevant cases—it is important to examine the cases with strong membership in each crisply defined location (i.e., greater than .5, the crossover point), one location at a time. Among these cases, if there are many cases where membership in the outcome exceeds membership in the crisply defined location and many cases where membership in the outcome is less, then it may be necessary to revise the property space. The investigator evaluates each crisply defined location in this manner, comparing membership in the outcome with membership in the crisply defined location. Of course, the pattern does not have to be perfect. However, as I show in chapter 9, if membership scores in a crisply defined location are less than or equal to membership scores in an outcome, then the causal combination represented by the crisply defined location may be sufficient for the outcome. With crisp sets, this pattern would correspond to the situation where the cases found in a specific property-space location agree in displaying the outcome under investigation.

If the researcher finds many crisply defined location with discordant outcomes, as just described, then he or she should take this as a sign that the property space should be reformulated. Perhaps new dimensions should be added, or some dropped and others substituted. Perhaps whole categories of cases should be dropped or added. Maybe the outcome needs to be reformulated and new outcome membership scores derived. The general point is that the property space and the definition of relevant cases should be refined using information on outcomes, as in crisp-set analysis.

Of course, research situations vary greatly. In some situations, researchers have great flexibility in deciding which cases they study and how they structure their property spaces. In others, the cases may be fixed because of policy or other reasons (e.g., elementary schools in a specific district, European Union members). In still other situations, the property space may be more or less fixed or restricted in some way (e.g., when researchers use secondary data). The less control researchers have over cases and property spaces, the more they must resort to probabilistic criteria when conducting cross-case analysis. Such criteria provide the most common way of addressing the heterogeneity of cases and outcomes.

The third benefit that follows from using fuzzy sets to constitute populations goes well beyond enhancement and refinement of the crisp-set approach. The fuzzy-set approach offers analytic possibilities that are beyond the scope of *either* crisp configurational analysis or conventional variable-oriented analysis. In these latter two approaches, cases are either in or out of the set of relevant instances. They cannot be partially in or partially out. Of course, in crisp configurational analysis, the researcher can move cases back and forth between fully in and fully out, but cases cannot reside in the zone *between* fully in and fully out. This analytic restriction does not exist in fuzzy-set social science.

Consider again the community organizations listed in table 7.4. Note that this table asserts, in effect, that all ten community organizations are full members of the set of community organizations. That is, they are fully in the domain of the study—community organizations. But it is sometimes difficult to determine which cases are fully in a domain and which are not fully in. In other words, it is often difficult in many cross-case studies to make crisp domain distinctions. In the present study, for example, some community organizations also may be political fiefdoms; some may be surrogates for national organizations; some may be creations of local governments; some may be de facto auxiliaries of local unions; and so on. In short, the degree to which the community organizations included in an analysis fit the investigator's definition of *community organization* is likely to vary. Of course, most of the organizations included in the study should be more in the domain than out. Otherwise, the researcher's conclusions would be suspect. Still, the membership scores of some of the organizations studied could be very low, and some might be more out of the domain than in it.

In fuzzy-set social science, the differing degrees to which empirical cases belong to a domain can be included as a relevant feature of cases, both in the construction and evaluation of the property space and later in the analysis of outcomes. In other words, it is not necessary to assign all cases a membership score of 1.0 in the domain—the de facto convention in both variable-oriented research and crisp configurational analysis. Instead, cases can be assigned various scores, depending on their degree of membership in the domain, and these scores can be included in all phases of the investigation.

Suppose, for example, the researcher studying the ten community organizations listed in table 7.4 evaluated each one with respect to its degree of membership in the domain—the set of "community organizations," as defined by the investigator, based on his or her understanding of the relevant research literature. These scores are presented in column (2) of table 7.5 (most of table 7.5 reproduces the information presented in table 7.4). Note that in this example the scores reported in column (2) are all greater than .5, indicating that the organizations studied are all more in than out of the domain. Note also, however, that there is substantial variation in column (2) in how well these ten organizations conform to the researcher's definition of community organization, with scores ranging from .6 to 1.0. Of course, it is up to the researcher to develop a method for evaluating the degree to which empirical cases conform to the domain definition guiding an investigation.

As shown in the last column of table 7.5, information on domain membership, presented in the second column, can be included in the evaluation of the membership of cases in crisply defined property-space locations. After all, in this table the key assessment is the evaluation of the degree to which these cases conform to a particular form of *com-*

Table 7.5
Using Fuzzy Sets to Assess Membership in a Domain

Case No. (1)	Membership in Domain (D) (2)	Multiracial (M) (3)	Cross-Class (C) (4)	Hierarchical (H) (5)	M·~C·~H (6)	M·~C·~H·D (7)
1	.6	.9	.1	.1	.9	.6
2	.7	.9	.1	.2	.8	.7
3	.8	.6	.4	.2	.6	.6
4	.9	.7	.5	.1	.5	.5
5	1.0	.7	.4	.6	.4	.4
6	.8	.4	.3	.7	.3	.3
7	.8	.4	.8	.8	.2	.2
8	.9	.1	.8	.9	.1	.1
9	.7	.3	.0	.9	.1	.1
10	.9	.0	.5	.9	.0	.0

munity organization—that is, community organizations that are multiracial, not cross-class, and not hierarchical. Membership in the larger set of community organizations may be viewed as an *implicit* condition in this formulation. Thus, what appears initially as an intersection of three sets (as in table 7.4) can now be seen as an intersection of four.

Obviously, if all cases have very strong membership in the domain (i.e., scores of 1.0 or close to 1.0), little would be gained from adding this fourth condition. Domain membership would rarely, if ever, provide the minimum in any combination of conditions. However, when domain membership scores range toward .5, as they do in table 7.5, these scores may provide the minimum for some cases. In the first two rows, for example, both cases' membership scores in the crisply defined location are reduced when fuzzy membership in the domain is included as a condition. Further, comparing the last two columns reveals that their relative positions are reversed in the ranking of membership scores. Thus, the consideration of domain membership, as just illustrated, has important implications for assessing cases with respect to their degree of conformity to crisply defined property-space locations. Without an assessment of their membership in the domain, some cases may appear to be relatively close to a corner of the property space, when their conformity is in fact much less because of their relatively weak membership in the domain. Thus, by including domain membership in the calculation of the minimum, more conservative measures of conformity to crisply defined locations (i.e., ideal-typic cases) may result.

To constitute populations in most forms of social science, researchers must impose a fundamentally dichotomous judgement—a crisp
distinction between relevant and irrelevant cases. However, the degree
to which a case belongs to a domain is often a matter of degree: Some
cases are clearly relevant; some are only marginally relevant. In fuzzy-
set social science, as I have just demonstrated, the partial membership
of cases in a domain can be made an explicit part of an investigation.

FUZZY SETS AND LIMITED DIVERSITY

Part 1 of this book argues that limited diversity is common in naturally
occurring social phenomena and that researchers who study cases configurationally should acknowledge this fact in their empirical generalizations. Generalizations based on analyses of cross-case patterns often
incorporate assumptions about combinations of conditions that lack
empirical instances. For example, a researcher studying personality factors linked to the rise of top corporate executives might find that his
or her sample lacks managers who are African American *and* male. If
this researcher presents the study's conclusions as relevant to the rise
of any manager hoping to become a top corporate executive, then he
or she has incorporated assumptions about race and gender—factors
linked to the upward mobility of managers—in the study's conclusion.
Specifically, the researcher assumes that if a similarly situated African
American male were to display these personality factors, his rise to the
top would be greatly facilitated. The literature on race and gender casts
serious doubts on this assumption.

This example makes the issue seem simple and the lesson, obvious:
Don't generalize if you don't have the evidence. But the bare truth is
that social researchers almost never have evidence on all logically and
empirically possible combinations of conditions. In almost every respect, the empirical social world is the exact opposite of a fully elaborated experiment designed to test all combinations of relevant causal
conditions. When social scientists study naturally occurring data, most
use multivariate statistical methods and attempt to assess the separate,
independent effect of each causally relevant condition on some outcome (e.g., the effect of X_1 on Y, controlling for the effects X_2, X_3, and
X_4). These techniques rarely, if ever, take account of the vast regions
of the property space, as defined by the relevant independent variables,
that are void or virtually void of empirical instances. Indeed, these statistical techniques are most often used to estimate additive, linear models, which, in turn, assume (1) that the impact of a causal condition

on an outcome is the same regardless of the state or level of other causal conditions, and (2) that the impact of a change in the value of an independent variable is the same at all levels of the variable. In effect, these techniques assume that the *context* of a given causal factor, as defined by other relevant causal conditions, is irrelevant to its effect and that changing the state or condition of other causal conditions has no impact on the effect of the causal condition in question. Consequently, when this approach is used to construct empirical generalizations, it routinely incorporates an extraordinary volume of simplifying assumptions. These assumptions are usually hidden from both the investigator and, more importantly, his or her audiences.

The crisp configurational approach described in part 1 provides tools for analyzing limited diversity and for identifying the simplifying assumptions embedded in empirical generalizations. With crisp sets, it is a simple matter to identify such assumptions. They are drawn from logically possible combinations of conditions (i.e., cells of a crisply defined property space), lacking cases (or, depending on the criteria used, cells lacking an adequate number of cases). The researcher simply identifies which cells from the property space covered by a generalization lack cases (e.g., the cells for "African American males" in the example presented in the opening paragraphs of this section). These simplifying assumptions can then be listed and evaluated. If some (or all) of these assumptions seen unwarranted, based on other substantive or theoretical knowledge, then the researcher must revise his or her empirical generalization accordingly.

In the fuzzy-set approach, the identification of causal combinations lacking empirical instances is less straightforward. As already noted, when membership in the component sets of a property space is fuzzy, cases may have partial membership in every crisply defined property-space location. Thus, it could be argued, following this observation, that all crisply defined locations may have empirical instances, at least to a partial degree, and that diversity, therefore, is not limited. On the other hand, it is also true that no empirical instance may display full membership (i.e., a membership of 1.0) in any crisply defined location. Following this reasoning, it could be argued that when crisply defined locations lack pure instances (i.e., instances with full membership), diversity is limited.

The most reasonable alternative to these two extremes is to view a case as an instance of a crisply defined location if its fuzzy membership in that location is greater than .5, the crossover point. Thus, a case is an instance of a crisply defined location only if its memberships in the sets that comprise the location all exceed .5 (i.e., the case is more in than out of the sets defining the location). Recall as well that in the fuzzy-set approach each case is mathematically constrained to have a membership score greater than .5 in only one crisply defined location at most. (As noted previously, cases with .5 membership in one or more of the sets that comprise a property space will have no membership scores greater than .5 in the crisply defined locations.) Thus, with fuzzy sets cases can be sorted according to crisply defined locations. Each case will be an instance (with membership score greater than .5) of only one crisply defined location, assuming it has no scores of .5 in any of the component sets that comprise the space.

Armed with this information, it is possible derive frequency scores for each location. These frequencies, in turn, provide the necessary raw material for specifying which property-space regions are vacant or, using probabilistic criteria, virtually vacant. For illustration, consider table 7.6, which shows membership scores of a set of schools districts in two fuzzy sets, "resource-rich" and "traditional." Resource-rich school districts are those that have maintained high levels of expenditures per pupil over a long period of time. "Traditional" school districts are those that emphasize core disciplines and basic skills in their curricula. Columns (2) and (3) show school districts' fuzzy membership scores in these two component sets. Columns (4)–(7) show their membership scores in the four crisply defined locations that form the corners of the property space. Note that the first four districts have maximum

Table 7.6
Fuzzy Sets and Limited Diversity

Case No. (1)	Resource-Rich (R) (2)	Traditional (T) (3)	R·T (4)	~R·T (5)	R·~T (6)	~R·~T (7)
1	.9	.3	.3	.1	.7	.1
2	.8	.1	.1	.2	.8	.2
3	.75	.4	.4	.25	.6	.25
4	.65	.35	.35	.35	.65	.35
5	.45	.2	.2	.2	.45	.55
6	.4	.35	.35	.35	.4	.6
7	.2	.2	.2	.2	.2	.8
8	.1	.4	.1	.4	.1	.6
9	.4	.6	.4	.6	.4	.4
10	.35	.9	.35	.65	.1	.1
11	.2	.65	.2	.65	.2	.35
12	.1	.8	.1	.8	.1	.2

membership in the resource-rich/not traditional corner of the property space. Districts five through eight have maximum membership in the not resource-rich/not traditional corner, and districts nine through twelve have maximum membership in the not resource-rich/traditional corner. No district has maximum membership in the resource rich/traditional corner. This property space is plotted in figure 7.2.

Table 7.6 and figure 7.2 show clearly that diversity is limited—one of the crisply defined locations lacks cases with membership scores greater than .5. If a researcher wished to construct general statements using this property space, this limitation on diversity should be taken into account. Suppose, for example, that this investigator wishes to conclude, based on available evidence, that school districts with traditional curricula have a problem with "dropouts." The researcher lacks information on students in resource-rich districts with traditional curricula—such school districts do not exist. To draw this conclusion from this property space, the researcher therefore must *assume* that if such districts did in fact exist, they too would have a problem with dropouts.

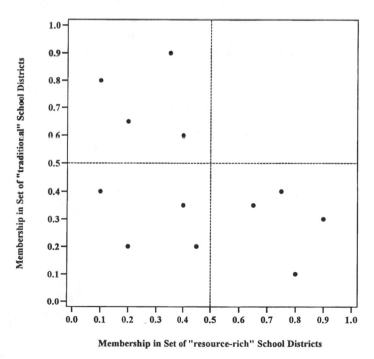

Figure 7.2 Two-dimensional property space showing "traditional" against "resource-rich."

Note that if the researcher were to assume an additive causal model, the assumption about resource-rich school districts with traditional curricula, just noted, is bypassed and thus obscured from the researcher's view. In a conventional additive model, the estimated effect of traditional curricula on dropouts is *assumed* to be the same regardless of the level of resources. The configurational view of cases, by contrast, argues that causal additivity is the exception, not the rule, in the study of social phenomena. Thus, in this approach, the researcher maps limited diversity and evaluates the assumptions that are embedded in empirical generalizations.

CONCLUSION

The procedures described in this chapter for constituting cases and populations with fuzzy sets rely heavily on the property-space approach (Lazarsfeld 1937). In essence, the property space provides a way to link the researcher's theory and data. This linkage must be well established before any analysis of cross-case patterns, especially the analysis of causal complexity, can proceed. This chapter also shows that the use of fuzzy sets greatly enhances the property-space approach and thus strengthens the dialogue between ideas and evidence that is central to discovery. By bringing together fuzzy sets and property spaces, it is possible to evaluate the comparability of cases in a more in-depth manner and to incorporate assessment of their degree of domain membership directly into the study of cross-case patterns.

EIGHT

FUZZY SETS AND
NECESSARY CONDITIONS

INTRODUCTION

Necessary conditions are very important to social theory. If a theoretically relevant causal condition is necessary, then it is present in all instances of an outcome. Any causal condition that is this general is worthy of the focused attention of social scientists. Necessary conditions provide important theoretical signposts and can bring clarity to large bodies of social science thinking. For example, the observation that "state breakdown" is a necessary condition for "social revolution" (as indicated in Skocpol 1979) has important implications not only for theories of revolution but also for the conceptualization of social revolution and the delineation of types of revolution.

Another good reason to study necessary conditions is the fact that they have very powerful policy implications. The identification of manipulable necessary conditions is especially important in social science subdisciplines that are concerned with social intervention. Imagine, for example, that a researcher successfully identifies a necessary condition for ethnic conflict. If political leaders can manipulate this condition, perhaps eliminate it altogether, then they may be able to prevent ethnic conflict. Any social scientist interested in social intervention, especially preventive measures, therefore, should have a strong interest in identifying necessary conditions. It is important to point out that while necessary conditions may both constrain and enable outcomes, enablement is much more difficult to achieve than constraint. To set the stage for an outcome—to create a situation where it can occur—all the necessary conditions for that outcome must be in place. To prevent an outcome, by contrast, all that is required is to remove or interfere with a single necessary condition. It is clear that enablement requires a much greater depth of knowledge about social life than constraint. To focus on necessary conditions, especially with prevention in mind, is to highlight the fragility of social accomplishment and the ubiquity of disruption.

Finally, the study of necessary conditions is also important because of its very long tradition in many forms of qualitative social inquiry.[1] As I argue in *Constructing Social Research* (Ragin 1994a), the search for commonalities shared by a set of purposefully selected cases is the quintessential qualitative research act. At the microsocial level, this practice is central both to analytic induction (Angell [1936] 1965; Becker 1953; Lindesmith 1947; Robinson 1951; Turner 1953) and to various grounded-theory and other approaches (e.g., Glaser and Strauss 1967; Strauss 1987). The identification of commonalities is important not only because of the insights they provide regarding possible necessary conditions, but also because they help researchers sharpen both their empirical categories and their theoretical concepts. At the macrosocial level, the study of causal conditions shared by multiple instances of an outcome (typically labeled, somewhat erroneously, the "method of agreement" and credited to John Stuart Mill [1843] 1967) is often the very first analytic step taken by comparatively oriented scholars in their investigations.[2] Another form of the search for commonalities is called the "most different cases" design. According to one version of this design, if two cases are very different from one another with respect to causal conditions yet experience the same outcome, then the few causal conditions they share should be considered decisive for the outcome in question (De Meur and Berg-Schlosser 1994; Dogan

---

1. Another justification for studying necessary conditions is procedural. Recall that chapter 4 demonstrates that if researchers focus exclusively on the sufficiency of combinations of causal conditions, they run the risk of overlooking necessary conditions. The more limited the available evidence with respect to the diversity of causal combinations, drawn from the investigator's property space, the greater the likelihood that the researcher will overlook necessary conditions. Thus, the examination of possible necessary conditions should precede the analysis of sufficient conditions.

2. Mill argued that the method of agreement was not appropriate for social phenomena, in large part because he intended it as a method for identifying *single* causes (i.e., the *one cause* of an outcome). Social causation, to use Mill's terms ([1843] 1967), is almost always chemical (i.e., conjunctural) and plural (i.e., multiple-conjunctural).

and Pelassy 1984; Dogan and Kazancigil 1994; Przeworski and Teune 1970; Ragin, Berg-Schlosser, and De Meur 1996).[3]

For these reasons, it should come as no surprise that there are many research designs in the social sciences that address commonalities, even though most social scientists are uncomfortable discussing necessary conditions per se. In the first part of this chapter I provide a brief sketch of several research designs that address necessary conditions in some way. To facilitate my sketch, I use a tactic first deployed in part 1 and open the discussion with an examination of the single-case study. Subsequently, I examine the technique commonly known as "the method of agreement" and then look at several extensions of this design. I then briefly review crisp-set procedures for identifying necessary conditions and demonstrate parallel procedures using fuzzy sets. Along the way, I address a variety of issues central to the analysis of social data using fuzzy sets, for example, problems of measurement error and randomness.

NECESSARY CONDITIONS AND THE DESIGN OF SOCIAL RESEARCH

The Single-Case Study

A single case may be chosen for in-depth study because it seems unique, extreme, or special in some way. It may display an unusual outcome or an uncommon mixture of causally relevant conditions. If a case is chosen for either of these reasons, then the arguments presented in chapter 4 concerning the study of causal complexity are relevant because the case is a selection on an outcome or on causal conditions.

Most often, when a single case is selected for in-depth study, it is chosen because of its unique or unusual outcome. This type of selection is especially common when researchers study novel happenings or events, the historical emergence of new institutional arrangements or practices, or the coalescence of a cultural form that signals a departure from or break with the past. As explained in chapter 4, when researchers select on the outcome and then examine causes, they focus on necessary conditions. Note, however, that the "search for common causal

3. Of course, this design is flawed from the perspective of diversity-oriented research because it assumes causal homogeneity—that there is only one way to generate or reach an outcome.

conditions" that follows "selecting on the outcome" is relatively mean-ingless when there is only one case. After all, a case has *everything* in common with itself. Instead, the researcher must rely on theoretical and substantive knowledge to structure the search for causally relevant conditions.[4]

Usually, researchers look for causal conditions that seem essential to the outcome and that *set the case apart* from possible comparison cases (e.g., Lipset 1963). In essence, they look for a unique combina-tion of causal conditions, following the common sense logic that a unique outcome must follow from a unique combination of causal con-ditions (or from a unique single cause). Thus, comparisons with nega-tive cases (i.e., cases lacking both the relevant causes and the outcome) may come into play, but only in an indirect and implicit way. Because there is only one instance of the outcome and only one instance of the relevant combination of causes, both unique, the researcher could claim to have illustrated both necessity and sufficiency. But it would be a very weak illustration. In the end, the success of most single-case studies depends on how well they articulate and advance existing theo-retical and substantive knowledge, in addition to knowledge of specific cases.

Multiple Positive Cases

The next step up, logically speaking, from the single-case study is the investigation of multiple instances of the same outcome (i.e., "positive" cases), a design conventionally but mistakenly identified with John Stu-art Mill's ([1843] 1967) "method of agreement."[5] The causally relevant conditions shared by these cases can be considered necessary condi-tions, assuming theory and auxiliary evidence support this interpreta-tion. There are two main versions of the "positive cases–only" research design. In both versions, researchers typically examine *all* instances of the outcome in question (i.e., all relevant positive cases). If only a sub-set of positive cases is studied, then the researcher must provide a ratio-

4. Alternatively, the researcher might follow Donald Campbell's (1975) advice and try to transform a single case into multiple observations (see chapter 3) or gain analytic leverage through empirical disaggregation (King et al. 1994). How-ever, most attempts to gain leverage through disaggregation undermine the ques-tion that inspired the investigation in the first pace (Ragin 1997; Griffin et al. 1997).

5. Mill ([1843] 1967) proposed the method of agreement as a technique to be used to identify the *single* cause of an effect. He based his proposal on the curious, pre-social scientific notion that each effect has one and only one cause.

nale for this restricted focus. For example, the researcher might argue that the cases included in the subset—the selected cases—are as diverse as the cases in the larger set of instances.

In the first version of this design, the researcher simply explores commonalities shared by positive cases, with no direct concern for "negative" cases (i.e., relevant comparison cases lacking the outcome). This version of the design is concerned exclusively with necessary conditions and typically is exploratory in nature. For example, the main goal might be to refine understanding of the outcome. A researcher might argue that if important causal commonalities cannot be identified, then perhaps the outcome is not really the same across all positive cases and thus should be disaggregated into types. Alternatively, a researcher may simply wish to compare positive cases to deepen the analysis. Insights from one case may highlight previously overlooked factors in other cases, and a more compelling portrait of causally relevant conditions may emerge from this cross-fertilization of case studies.

In the other main version of the "positive cases–only" design, researchers seek to identify common causal conditions that set the positive cases apart from possible comparison cases. That is, they search for a specific combination of conditions shared only by the positive cases. In this version of the design, there is no need to examine negative cases in any great depth because the goal is to identify causal conditions shared by the positive cases that set them apart and make them unique—as a set. If researchers succeed in identifying a combination of conditions that is uniquely shared by positive cases, then they may argue that this combination of conditions is also sufficient. The strength of the demonstration rests on (1) the degree to which the commonalities identified by the researcher do, in fact, set the positive cases apart from possible comparison cases and (2) the coherence of these commonalities as jointly necessary and sufficient conditions for the outcome.

Designs Using Negative Cases Directly

The next step up from "positive cases–only" designs are those that involve explicit examination of negative cases. These designs, in effect, complement the analysis of necessary conditions with the explicit evaluation of the sufficiency of these conditions using negative cases. Once again, there are two main versions.

The first version takes the definition of negative cases as unproblematic, usually because the population of relevant cases, both positive and negative, is either quasi-given or taken for granted. For example, a researcher might be interested in the causal commonalities shared by the member nations of the European Union that support a specific policy regarding agricultural exports. After identifying the causally relevant commonalities shared by supporters (i.e., causes that make sense as necessary conditions), it is a natural next step to examine whether this combination of causally relevant conditions is found in any of the non-supporters (i.e., the negative cases). If the combination of causally relevant conditions is found among nonsupporters, then the researcher may conclude that the combination is necessary but not sufficient. He or she may then return to the study of positive cases and try to identify additional factors, which might be specific to each case, that distinguish the positive cases from the relevant negative cases (i.e., those sharing the necessary but not sufficient conditions). If, on the other hand, there are no negative cases with the combination, the researcher might argue that the combination of necessary conditions identified in the first step is also sufficient.

The second version of this design does not use a quasi-given or taken for granted population but instead constitutes relevant negative cases after investigating positive cases. The researcher identifies causally relevant commonalities shared by positive cases and then searches for instances of these commonalities among negative cases. In effect, the set of relevant negative cases is defined as those that share the relevant commonalities with positive cases. In this research design, the investigator does not expect to identify causal commonalities that reveal the "uniqueness" of the positive cases. Instead, researchers expect to find negative cases that share relevant commonalities with the positive cases. Once researchers successfully identify such cases, then they can explore causal sufficiency. Specifically, they try to identify differences in causal conditions that account for differences in outcomes.

The interpretation of a set of causal conditions as necessary and sufficient conditions, no matter what the analytic context, adds new interpretive tasks for the investigator. That is, the researcher must marshal additional arguments and evidence to justify interpreting conditions as both necessary and sufficient. Furthermore, it is important to remember that researchers extend their investigations to negative cases only to assess sufficiency. Such extensions to negative cases assume the following: (1) that all positive cases (or at least all relevant "kinds" of positive cases) have been identified and studied; (2) that relevant negative cases can be identified, because they are either given or can be found—using the causal commonalities shared by positive cases as guides; and (3) that the causal conditions identified by the researcher after comparison of positive and negative cases make sense, both theoretically and substantively.

Many different research designs build upon the study of commonalities shared by positive cases, often with extensions to the study of negative cases. However, it is important not to lose sight of the fact that some of the most useful applications of this research strategy do not involve negative cases in any way. Often, the study of commonalities is used as a tool to help researchers bring clarity to their research. It helps them sharpen both their empirical categories and their theoretical concepts, often at the same time (Ragin 1994a). The cross-fertilization of case studies is central to this enterprise, as is theoretically informed judgements about whether two cases are cut from the same cloth—are they instances of the same phenomenon or different phenomena? The interplay of categorization and conceptualization that is central to this strategy makes it a powerful tool for theory construction (see also Collier 1993, 1998; Collier and Levitsky 1997).

"MAKING SENSE" OF CAUSAL CONDITIONS: THE IMPACT OF LIMITED DIVERSITY

The idea that the researcher must "make sense" of causal conditions identified as necessary, or as both necessary and sufficient, is very important. The importance of this principle, and the theory and knowledge dependence of social research in general, can be illustrated with a simple example. Suppose a researcher studies all relevant instances of an outcome and finds that they share causal conditions A, B, and C and that these three conditions "make sense" as jointly necessary conditions. Suppose further that the investigator then searches for other instances of the conjunction of these three conditions (i.e., searches for relevant negative cases) and finds none. The researcher might then conclude that the available evidence supports the argument that the three shared causal conditions are jointly necessary and sufficient. He or she then marshals arguments and evidence to support this conclusion. Suppose another researcher believes that the first researcher's argument is needlessly complex and that even though all positive cases share condition C, it is superfluous. All that really matters, according to the second researcher, is the coincidence of conditions of A and B. Suppose further that the second investigator's search for relevant negative cases (i.e., instances of the combination of A and B that lack the outcome in question) also comes up empty, providing support for the argument that A and B are jointly necessary and sufficient. Condition C indeed appears to be superfluous.

Which argument is correct? Some might argue that the second is correct because it is more parsimonious. Others, however, might argue that the first argument is correct because it provides a richer and fuller account of the nature of the causal forces behind the outcome. Ultimately, the argument that makes "better sense" from the viewpoint of the larger social science community will prevail. The dispute cannot be settled otherwise, without elevating one criterion (i.e., "parsimony" versus "explanatory richness") above the other, when clearly both are important.

Ideally, the first researcher—the one who argues that three conditions A, B, and C must be combined for the outcome to occur—should buttress his or her argument with negative cases that display as many competing combinations of conditions as possible (e.g., only A and B present, only A and C present, only B and C present, and so on). However, because naturally occurring social phenomena are characteristically *limited* in their diversity, such demonstrations are usually impossible.[6] The great diversity of cases needed to fortify evidence-based generalizations rarely, if ever, exists.

EVALUATING NECESSARY CONDITIONS: THE CRISP-SET APPROACH

As previously noted, to study necessary conditions the researcher first selects cases with the outcome in question and then determines whether these cases agree in displaying one or more causally relevant conditions. As table 8.1 illustrates, necessity concerns only the top row of the cross-tabulation of an outcome against a cause. Thus, it does not matter if there are cases in cell 4 of this table (cause present, outcome absent), because a cause can be necessary without being sufficient. For example, assume "state breakdown" is a necessary condition for "social revolution." This fact does not imply that wherever we find state break-

---

6. Consider, for example, Theda Skocpol's (1979) study *States and Social Revolution: A Comparative Analysis of France, Russia, and China*. Unlike many such studies, Skocpol makes a serious effort to examine negative cases. Unfortunately, however, the negative cases she studies have too little in common, causally speaking, with her positive cases. This "causal distance" between positive and negative cases undercuts the value of such comparisons.

Table 8.1
Cause Is Necessary but Not Sufficient

Outcome	Cause Absent	Cause Present
Present	[cell 1] no cases	[cell 2] cases
Absent	[cell 3] not relevant	[cell 4] not relevant

down we also will find social revolution. All that matters is that every instance of social revolution should involve state breakdown as a causal condition (i.e., cell 1 in table 8.1 should be empty).

It follows logically that if a condition is necessary but not sufficient for an outcome, then instances of the outcome will constitute a *subset* of instances of the cause. Using the example just mentioned, if state breakdown is a necessary but not sufficient condition for social revolution, then instances of social revolution should constitute a subset of instances of state breakdown. Of course, not every commonality shared by positive cases is a necessary condition. Any commonality identified must be a causally relevant condition; it must make sense as a necessary condition from the perspective of the researcher's theory; and, if possible, the claim that the condition is necessary should be supported by whatever additional argumentation and evidence the investigator can muster.

It is important to understand that *jointly* necessary conditions can be identified one at a time. In other words, the fact that there may be several necessary conditions for an outcome does not interfere with the evaluation of the necessity of a single condition. If a single condition is necessary, it will be present in all instances of the outcome; if several conditions are necessary, then each condition will be present in all instances of the outcome. After identifying all necessary conditions, one at a time, the researcher can view them as jointly necessary conditions and evaluate their plausibility as a combination or conjuncture. Even if researchers are able to identify a large number of jointly necessary conditions, this accomplishment, by itself, does not permit them to make any claims about causal sufficiency. Instances of the outcome are a subset of the cases displaying a combination of necessary but not sufficient conditions, just as they are a subset of the cases displaying a single necessary but not sufficient condition. Thus, there may be instances that display all the necessary but not sufficient conditions but that nevertheless fail to display the outcome.

Finally, it is important to note that the assessment of necessity may incorporate probabilistic criteria. Chapter 4 presents a probabilistic approach to the evaluation of *sufficiency,* using benchmarks and significance levels. For example, a researcher might argue that a cause is "usually sufficient" for an outcome if significantly greater than 65% of the instances of the cause also display the outcome, using a significance level of, say, .05. Parallel procedures can be applied to the evaluation of necessary conditions. For example, a researcher might argue that a cause is "usually necessary" for an outcome if significantly greater than 65% of the instances of the outcome also display the cause in question. The selection of the specific benchmark proportion (e.g., .5 versus .65 versus .80 and so on) and significance level (.10 versus .05 versus .01 and so on) is determined by the investigator, who must provide an explicit rationale for his or her choices.

As an illustration of the probabilistic approach to the assessment of necessary conditions, consider the investigator who wants to test the argument that "a breakdown in communications" between workers and management is "almost always" a necessary condition for "wildcat strikes" in the auto industry in the United States during the late twentieth century. The investigator collects data on 20 strikes (i.e., all relevant strikes) and finds that 17 provide evidence of communication breakdown as a cause. The observed proportion of outcomes with the cause in question is 17/20 or .85. Using a benchmark of .80 ("almost always necessary") and a significance level of .10, the observed proportion (.85) is not significantly greater than the benchmark proportion (.80). Thus, this investigator would conclude that the evidence does *not* support the claim that "communication breakdowns" are "almost always" necessary for wildcat strikes.

STUDYING NECESSARY CONDITIONS WITH FUZZY SETS

In the crisp-set approach to the assessment of necessity, the researcher selects cases displaying the outcome in question and then looks for causal commonalities, based on the property space developed for that outcome. In effect, the researcher selects cases with crisp-set scores of 1 on the outcome and then checks to see if any of the possibly relevant causal conditions are constant (or more or less constant, using probabilistic criteria) across these cases. But what if the membership of cases in the cause and the outcome are both fuzzy? For example, the distinction between a wildcat strike and a regular (i.e., not wildcat) strike is not crisp. Many strikes are not fully in one category or the other but instead have many, though not all, of the elements of a wildcat strike. Likewise, the evaluation of communication breakdowns is not a simple yes/no matter. There can be partial breakdowns, and minor miscommunications are common. What does it take to qualify as a full-fledged breakdown? What should the investigator do with cases that exhibit many but not all of the features of a communication breakdown? Like so many social science concepts, the cause and the outcome in this example do not involve simple dichotomous judgements. For most cases, it would not be possible to do a simple sorting into presence/absence of wildcat strike and presence/absence of communication breakdown.

Suppose instead that the investigator had used use fuzzy membership scores to characterize the degree to which strikes were wildcat strikes and the degree to which communication between workers and management had broken down before the strike. This measurement strategy solves the conceptual issue—the fact that the concepts cannot be operationalized as clear-cut dichotomies. But it seems to pose substantial obstacles to the assessment of necessary conditions. How can the investigator select cases with the outcome when they vary in the degree to which they exhibit the outcome, with many cases scoring in the interval between 0 and 1? How can the researcher look for commonalities across instances of an outcome when the instances vary in the degree to which they express causal conditions? The solution to this problem is to address the set-theoretic relation between fuzzy sets.

The Subset Principle

Recall the initial crisp example of necessity—the argument that state breakdown is a necessary condition for social revolution. As already noted, if this statement is true, then instances of social revolution should constitute a subset of instances of state breakdown. More generally, whenever a causal condition is necessary but not sufficient for an outcome, instances of the outcome will form a subset of instances of the causal condition. In fact, it is possible to argue that a causally relevant condition is necessary but not sufficient only if it can be demonstrated that instances of the outcome are a subset of instances of the cause. Thus, every test of necessity conducted in a crisp-set analysis is also a test of the set-theoretic relationship between a causal condition and an outcome.

Another way to understand the subset relationship is in terms of the *arithmetic* relationship between crisp-set membership scores (1s and 0s). Suppose a researcher studies 100 countries and finds that 50 of them experienced state breakdown. Suppose further that all known instances of social revolution ($N = 10$) are among these 50 instances of state breakdown and that in each of these 10 cases social revolution followed the coincidence of state breakdown with other revolution-inducing conditions. The cross-tabulation of the presence/absence of social revolution against the presence/absence of state breakdown for these 100 countries would show that there are cases in only three of the four cells because the social revolution/no state breakdown cell would be empty. If the researcher were to code both state breakdown and social revolution with 1 = yes and 0 = no, then he or she would find that countries' scores on social revolution are all less than or equal to their scores on state breakdown. This result occurs because there are no cases where social revolution equals 1 and state breakdown equals 0. It follows that the subset principle can be expressed in simple arithmetic terms: If instances of the outcome are a subset of instances of the cause, then the Boolean value of the outcome (1 versus 0) will be less than or equal to the Boolean value of the cause. This example illustrates the seamless translation first of the idea of necessity to the subset principle, and then from the subset principle to a simple arithmetic relationship.

Fuzzy Subsets

Now suppose that the researcher studying these 100 countries had used fuzzy sets for the causal condition and for the outcome. The use of fuzzy sets, in fact, would be much more appropriate in this hypothetical investigation because the characteristics under investigation reflect theoretical (i.e., verbal) formulations. With fuzzy sets, as already noted, it would be difficult to "select" countries with the outcome (the usual first step in the crisp-set analysis of necessary conditions) because countries vary in their degree of membership in the set displaying social revolution (see, e.g., Walton 1984). Likewise, it would be very difficult to evaluate cases' agreement with respect to the relevant causal condition (state breakdown) because they vary in their membership in this set as well. How can the subset principle, which is central to the assessment of necessity in the crisp-set approach, be implemented with fuzzy sets?

Fortunately, the subset principle and the arithmetic relationship between membership scores just described for crisp sets holds for fuzzy sets as well. With fuzzy sets, set A is a subset of set B if the membership scores of cases in set A are less than or equal to their respective membership scores in set B. Consider, for example, two fuzzy sets relevant to beginning basketball players, membership in "practices shooting baskets a lot" and membership in "scores a lot of points in games." Obviously, practice shooting baskets is a necessary condition for scoring many points in basketball games—even professional basketball players espouse this idea. But practicing shots is not a sufficient condition for scoring many points. Some players lack the competitiveness or basic shooting talent to score many points in games, despite countless hours of practice. Therefore, there are likely to be many individuals who practice a lot but nevertheless fail to score a lot. It follows that membership in the fuzzy set "scores a lot" is a subset of the fuzzy set "practices a lot."

This general relationship in depicted in figure 8.1. The lower-triangular plot shows this fuzzy subset relationship, where membership in the outcome (scores many points in games) is less than or equal to membership in the cause (practices shooting baskets). Cases in the lower right-hand corner of the plot are individuals who practice a lot but nevertheless do not score many points in games. From the evidence in the figure, it would be reasonable to conclude that membership in "practices a lot" is necessary but not sufficient for membership in "scores a lot."

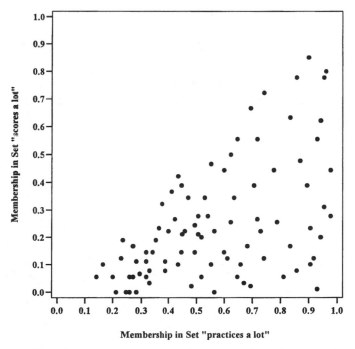

Figure 8.1 Plot of "scores a lot" against "practices a lot" showing subset relationship.

Return now to the example involving state breakdown and social revolution. If the goal is to show that state breakdown is a necessary condition for social revolution, and both state breakdown and social revolution are represented with fuzzy sets, the evidence should show that membership scores in the outcome, social revolution, are less than or equal to membership scores in the causal condition, state breakdown. Table 8.2 reports hypothetical data consistent with this argument, using data on 20 cases with nonzero membership in the set of social revolutions. A scatterplot showing the relationship between fuzzy membership in the causal condition and fuzzy membership in the outcome is presented in figure 8.2.

The lower-triangular plot shown in figure 8.2 is a direct reflection of the fact that all membership scores in the fuzzy set "social revolution" are less than or equal to membership scores in the fuzzy set "state breakdown." When membership scores for "state breakdown" are low, membership scores for "social revolution" must be low. However, when membership scores for "state breakdown" are high, membership scores for "social revolution" can take on a wide range of values. This lower-

Table 8.2
Fuzzy Membership Scores for "social revolution" (Outcome) and "state breakdown" (Necessary Condition)

Case No.	Fuzzy Membership In "Social Revolution"	Fuzzy Membership In "State Breakdown"
1	.10	.41
2	.34	.69
3	.13	.72
4	.10	.78
5	.04	.15
6	.11	.36
7	.49	.54
8	.81	.85
9	.76	.93
10	.35	.36
11	.47	1.00
12	.28	1.00
13	.81	.81
14	.39	.69
15	.72	.82
16	.10	.54
17	.22	.25
18	.46	.48
19	.54	.86
20	.28	.73

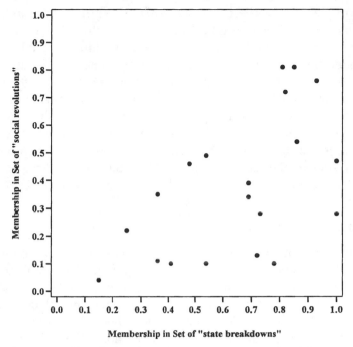

Figure 8.2 Plot of "social revolution" against "state breakdown."

triangular pattern of results is in accord with the simple idea that because state breakdown is a necessary condition for social revolution,
membership in the fuzzy set "state breakdown" sets a ceiling on membership in the fuzzy set "social revolution." Thus, the cases in the lower
right-hand corner of the plot in figure 8.2 are not "errors"; they are
simply cases that lack one or more of the conditions that must be combined with state breakdown for social revolution to occur.

This example illustrates the core of the fuzzy-set approach to necessary conditions. The key is to understand that when fuzzy membership
scores in the outcome are less than or equal to fuzzy membership in
the cause, then it is possible to argue that instances of the outcome are
a subset of instances of the cause. When researchers find this pattern,
they may cite this evidence as support for an argument of causal necessity. As always, the claim that a causal condition is necessary must be
supported with corroborating arguments and evidence.

This discussion has important practical implications for the study
of causal necessity using fuzzy sets. Rather than select on instances of
an outcome, the first step in the crisp-set approach to necessary condi-

tions, the researcher selects all cases with nonzero membership in the outcome.[7] Next, the researcher studies the set-theoretic relation between membership in the outcome and membership in possible necessary conditions, using theory and substantive knowledge—as represented in his or her property space for the outcome—to guide the selection of causal conditions. The key is to identify causal conditions producing a lower-triangular plot when arrayed against the outcome, as shown in figure 8.2. Thus, the researcher does not search for causal conditions that are the same across all cases, as in the crisp-set approach. Rather, the search is for causal conditions with membership scores that are consistently greater than outcome membership scores.

EXAMINING MULTIPLE NECESSARY CONDITIONS

As previously noted, the relationship between necessary conditions and an outcome can be tested one at a time, even if there are several jointly necessary conditions for the outcome in question. It does not matter how many necessary conditions there are; the outcome will be a subset of each necessary condition and a subset of their intersection—if they are all necessary conditions. This principle holds for both crisp and fuzzy sets. If there are several necessary conditions for an outcome, then fuzzy membership in the outcome will be less than or equal to fuzzy membership in each causal condition and less than or equal to fuzzy membership in the *intersection* of the relevant conditions. This principle can be conceived in terms of the *limits* that necessary conditions place on degree of membership in an outcome: Just as a case's degree of membership in a single necessary condition sets a ceiling on its degree of membership in the outcome (as in figure 8.2), its degree of membership in the intersection of jointly necessary conditions sets a *combined limit* on its degree of membership in the outcome.

It is important to recall at this juncture that a case's fuzzy membership in an intersection or combination of two or more fuzzy sets is the minimum of its fuzzy membership scores in the component sets. For

7. Note that cases with zero membership in the outcome provide evidence consistent with *any* necessity test. When a case's membership in the outcome is equal to zero, it will pass all necessity tests because its membership score in the outcome (0) must be less than or equal to its membership scores on all causal conditions (fuzzy membership scores range from 0 to 1). In effect, this observation is simply a restatement of the argument that noninstances of an outcome (membership = 0) are not directly relevant to statements about the outcome (as in the second row of table 8.1).

example, if a person has a fuzzy membership score of .8 in the set "young" and a fuzzy membership score of .4 in the set "blond," then he or she has a fuzzy membership score of only .4 in the set "young and blond." The use of the minimum applies just as well to crisp sets; the only difference is that with crisp sets, membership values are constrained to be either 1 or 0. With crisp sets, if a case scores 0 on any of the component sets, then it scores 0, the minimum, on their intersection.[8]

The importance of the minimum for the analysis of multiple necessary conditions using fuzzy sets can be illustrated with a simple example. Consider the argument that both "state breakdown" and "popular insurrection" are necessary conditions for "social revolution." Assume that membership in these three sets is fuzzy, with membership scores ranging from 0 to 1. Table 8.3 lists hypothetical membership scores for the three sets, using 20 instances (i.e., 20 cases with nonzero membership in the set of social revolutions). Observe in table 8.3 that fuzzy membership scores for social revolution (reported in column [2]) are all less than or equal to fuzzy membership scores for state breakdown (column [3]) and less than or equal to fuzzy membership scores for popular insurrection (column [4]). These two comparisons support the argument that the two causal conditions, considered one at a time, are necessary. Column [5] reports cases' fuzzy membership in the intersection of these two necessary conditions—their degree of membership in the set of cases combining state breakdown and popular insurrection, which is the minimum of columns (3) and (4). Note that each case's fuzzy membership in social revolution is also less than or equal to its membership in the intersection of state breakdown and popular insurrection.

Figure 8.3 illustrates the impact of identifying an additional necessary condition, in this case, popular insurrection. This scattergram

---

8. One issue not addressed in this chapter is the possibility that two conditions may be "substitutable" as necessary conditions. For example, suppose a certain level of "financial security" is a necessary condition for some outcome and this can be satisfied either by "high salary" or "extensive assets." A case's membership in the higher-order construct "financial security" in the *maximum* its memberships in the two conditions "high salary" and "extensive assets" because they are substitutable routes to "financial security" (see chapter 11). The presentation in this chapter assumes that the researcher has already considered the possibility that causal conditions may be substitutable as necessary conditions and modified the property space accordingly, using the higher-order construct in place of its components.

Table 8.3
Multiple Necessary Conditions and the Use of the Minimum

Case No. (1)	Membership in "social revolution" (2)	Membership in "state breakdown" (3)	Membership in "popular insurrection" (4)	Membership in Intersection of Cols. (3) and (4) (5)
1	.10	.41	.83	.41
2	.34	.69	.42	.42
3	.13	.72	.71	.71
4	.10	.78	.34	.34
5	.04	.15	.47	.15
6	.11	.36	.15	.15
7	.49	.54	.69	.54
8	.81	.85	.95	.85
9	.76	.93	.98	.93
10	.35	.36	.65	.36
11	.47	1.00	.75	.75
12	.28	1.00	.35	.35
13	.81	.81	.85	.81
14	.39	.69	.50	.50
15	.72	.82	.85	.82
16	.10	.54	.15	.15
17	.22	.25	.38	.25
18	.46	.48	.54	.48
19	.54	.86	.86	.86
20	.28	.73	.39	.39

shows the plot of fuzzy membership in social revolution against fuzzy membership in the intersection of state breakdown and popular insurrection, using data from table 8.3. By comparing figures 8.3 and 8.2 it is possible to observe the impact of identifying additional necessary conditions. Including a second necessary condition (popular insurrection) and intersecting it with the first condition (state breakdown) moves many of the plotted cases closer to the diagonal (where membership in the outcome equals membership in the intersection of the causal conditions). A case's membership in a combination of conditions is the minimum of its memberships in the component conditions. The impact of including additional necessary conditions, therefore, is to move the points in a lower-triangular plot to the left, toward the diagonal.[9] In this analysis, membership in the outcome, by definition, must be less

9. If the membership scores in the newly identified necessary condition were all greater than or equal to membership scores in an existing necessary condition, there would be no impact on the points in the plot.

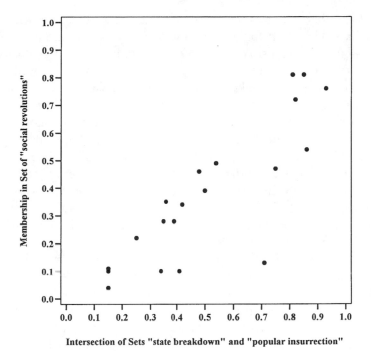

Figure 8.3 Plot of "social revolution" against intersection of "state breakdown" and "popular insurrection."

than or equal to membership in each necessary condition. Thus, membership in the intersection of necessary conditions can approach but not cross the diagonal.

As researchers identify more of the necessary conditions for an outcome, they place tighter constraints (i.e., a lower ceiling) on the degree of membership of each case in the outcome. This result follows because a case's membership in a combination of necessary conditions is the minimum of its memberships in the component conditions.

USING NECESSARY CONDITIONS TO "ACCOUNT FOR" OUTCOMES

One tantalizing implication that could be drawn from figure 8.3 is that it might be possible, ultimately, to identify all the relevant conditions for an outcome and thereby align all, or virtually all, of the points on the diagonal of the plot, or at least very close to the diagonal. It might be inferred, further, that when researchers successfully achieve this rough alignment, they have established not only necessity but also sufficiency. They have accounted for the varying degree to which an outcome is expressed across cases. For example, a researcher might find that the degree to which communities have "drug problems" (conceived as a fuzzy set) is shaped entirely by two conditions: having a "steady supply of drugs" and having a "stable network of drug dealers" (two jointly necessary conditions, conceived as fuzzy sets). These two causal conditions could be interpreted as enabling conditions, with membership in the set of communities with "drug problems" determined, in effect, by degree of membership in the intersection of these two enabling conditions. All cases, in this example, would line up on or just below the diagonal of the plot of membership in "communities with drug problems" against the intersection of the two necessary conditions, "steady supply of drugs" and "stable network of dealers."

Unfortunately, there are many factors that interfere with the neat alignment of degree of membership in an outcome with degree of membership in relevant causal conditions. I discuss three here: causal complexity, measurement error, and case-specific factors that are manifested as "prediction error" and "randomness" in cross-case analyses.[10]

Causal complexity is quite common in the study of social phenomena. Often there are many different paths to the same outcome (e.g., having a drug problem in a community), and it may be difficult to identify even a single necessary condition, much less a set of jointly necessary conditions that accounts for the varying degrees to which cases express a particular outcome. As chapter 4 demonstrates, when causation is complex, no single cause may be either necessary or sufficient. In such situations it would not be possible to intersect necessary conditions and line up cases on or near the diagonal for the simple reason that no condition might pass the investigator's test of necessity.

The second issue centers on the fact that measurement is not precise. Consider the task of measuring the membership of cases in the fuzzy set "communities with drug problems." Presumably, membership in this set would be pegged to such measures as the number of drug users

---

10. There is also a procedural issue, namely, the fact that when studying necessity, researchers select on the outcome and search for commonalities. In fuzzy-set analysis, researchers select cases with nonzero scores on the outcome and then examine their membership in possible necessary conditions. Omitted from these analyses are cases that are central to the assessment of sufficiency—cases with nonzero scores on relevant causal conditions that nevertheless have zero scores on the outcome.

in a community, relative to the size of the community—a calculation that would yield some sort of rate of drug use or addiction. However, the number of users is notoriously difficult to determine, especially given the widespread reluctance of individuals to admit to illegal activity. There is also the additional task, in fuzzy-set social science, of translating the *rate* of drug use in a community to degree of membership in the set of "communities with drug problems." There are several ways to anchor this translation, and each way of anchoring it may have different social and political implications. Because of these and other measurement issues, it would be unrealistic to expect cases to plot neatly on or near the diagonal in any plot of fuzzy membership in an outcome against fuzzy membership in one or more causes.

The third issue is randomness. Even with precise measures and well-reasoned translations to fuzzy membership scores, the researcher is still likely to confront ill-fitting data. The social world is multicausal, and a variety of causal conditions unique to each case, including exogenous events like snowstorms and flu epidemics, affect every outcome. Thus, cases almost never plot exactly where they "should." Consider again the hypothetical analysis of communities with drug problems. Some communities may be more resistant or more vulnerable to drug problems than others, depending on their histories. Community-specific differences may be very difficult to detect, much less to operationalize and measure in a meaningful cross-case manner. Thus, factors relevant to each specific community are likely to be left out of the analysis altogether, increasing the lack of fit between membership in the outcome and membership in relevant causal conditions.

I return to the first issue, causal complexity, in chapter 9, where I present fuzzy-set procedures for the assessment of multiple combinations of sufficient conditions. In the remainder of this chapter, I offer solutions to the problems of imprecision and randomness.

PROCEDURES FOR ADDRESSING THE PROBLEM OF IMPRECISE MEASUREMENT

In the analysis of necessary conditions, the key issue is the set-theoretic relationship between the outcome, on the one hand, and causally relevant conditions, on the other, examined individually. If it can be shown that membership in the outcome is a subset of membership in a relevant cause, then this relationship can be cited, along with other evidence, as support for an interpretation of causal necessity. As explained in detail in this chapter, with fuzzy sets the subset relation can be demonstrated by showing that the membership scores of relevant cases in the outcome are less than or equal to their corresponding membership scores in a causal condition.

Often, researchers lack complete confidence in their measurement of fuzzy membership and may wonder if a condition that fails the test of necessity might pass using better measures. This question is especially vexing in situations where there is a single "near miss"—a case has an outcome membership score that exceeds its membership in a causal condition by only a small margin. For example, suppose in a study of the necessary conditions for social revolution, one case has a membership score of .6 in the set of social revolutions, but a score of only .55 in the set of cases exhibiting state breakdown. Assume also that for other relevant cases, membership in state breakdown exceeds membership in social revolution, a pattern consistent with an interpretation of necessity. Should this one inconsistent case void the interpretation of state breakdown as a necessary condition?

From a strict set-theoretic viewpoint, it should. But social scientists often lack confidence in their measures. They are likely as well to lack complete confidence in their calibration of fuzzy membership scores, especially the specification of qualitative breakpoints. Furthermore, it is likely that measurement in the middle range of most fuzzy sets will be more imprecise than it is at either extreme. That is, it may be easier to say, with confidence, that a case's membership in the set of social revolutions is .90 versus 1.0 than it is to say that its membership is .45 versus .55. Perhaps most researchers are willing to ignore or explain away one "near miss" and argue that a causal condition is necessary, despite the one inconsistent case. But what if there are several near misses?

Consider the researcher studying beginning basketball players who is interested in demonstrating what all the evidence indicates, that practicing baskets is a necessary but not sufficient condition for scoring many points in games. A conventional scatterplot of two ratio-scale measures, "hours spent practicing" against "number of points scored in games," is likely to reveal a rough, lower-triangular plot—and perhaps a healthy number of outliers as well. Even after using this plot of ratio-scale measures to guide the translation of raw scores to fuzzy membership scores (and thus maximizing the plotting of the points in the lower triangle), the researcher is likely to find a few points residing stubbornly above the diagonal.

One way to take account of known, or suspected, imprecisions in the measurement of fuzzy membership scores is to incorporate an "adjustment factor" when assessing the set-theoretic relation between an outcome and possible necessary conditions. In effect, as a substitute for better measures, which in any case might not be available, researchers can implement a more lenient test of necessity. For example, suppose a researcher believes that his or her assessment of fuzzy membership in a cause is precise within .10 fuzzy-membership units. This researcher might argue, based on this evaluation, that if no case's score on the outcome exceeds its score on a causal condition by more than .10 fuzzy-membership units, then the pattern is consistent with an interpretation of causal necessity.

In effect, this adjustment shifts the line separating consistent and inconsistent cases in a more lenient direction, as shown in figure 8.4. With this adjustment in place, near misses no longer violate necessity. To constitute a violation, a case's membership in the outcome must exceed its membership in the causal condition by more than .10 fuzzy-

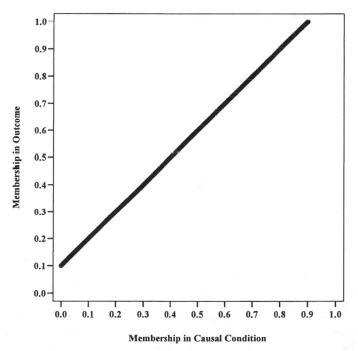

Figure 8.4 Adjusting test of necessity for measurement and translation imprecision.

membership units. Expressed as an equation, causal condition X can be interpreted as a necessary condition for outcome Y, with an adjustment of .10 fuzzy-membership units, if

$$Y_i \leq X_i + .10.$$

It is also possible to formulate a nonlinear adjustment equation that allows for the possibility that the researcher has *less* confidence in the measurement of fuzzy membership in the middle range (i.e., in the vicinity of .5) than at either extreme (i.e., near 1 or 0).

It is important to understand that adjustments are not mechanistically applied simply to bring about a better fit. As I have emphasized throughout part 2, fuzzy sets serve best as aids to interpretive analysis. They establish closer ties between concepts, on the one hand, and empirical analysis, on the other. The adjustment proposed here serves these interpretive aims by increasing the number of conditions likely to pass the researcher's test of necessity. As always, any condition that passes this test must also make sense as a necessary condition—that is, the interpretation of necessity must be consistent with the researcher's understanding of the phenomenon.[11]

PROCEDURES FOR ADDRESSING THE PROBLEM OF RANDOMNESS

Often cases do not plot where they "should" (i.e., according to predictions) because of case-specific factors that are outside the scope of the theories that investigators bring to their analyses. Generally, these case-specific conditions are conceived as proof of the randomness of the phenomena that social scientists study. Of course, sometimes the guiding theoretical perspectives themselves are simply wrong, and it is not "randomness" that produces a poor fit, but ignorance and specification error. Whatever the source, the bare truth is that it is difficult to model social phenomena with precision even when using measures that are error free.

---

11. There are more technical approaches to the measurement and translation issues raised here. For example, it might be possible to examine a variety of different functional forms of both causal conditions and outcomes (before or after converting them to fuzzy membership scores), with an eye toward maximizing the triangularity of the way they plot. A lower-triangular plot also could be viewed as a special case of heteroscedasticity or regression through the origin, and "outliers" (i.e., cases outside the triangle) could be evaluated relative to these models. These strategies are not examined here because of the importance attached to maintaining empirical intimacy, gained through familiarity with one's data at the case level.

One way to address randomness is to use probabilistic criteria to undergird assessments of necessity and sufficiency, as demonstrated in part 1 and echoed in this chapter. As shown in the discussion of the crisp-set approach to necessary conditions, probabilistic criteria can be incorporated into the assessment of necessity using benchmarks and significance levels. In that discussion, a researcher tested the necessity of "communication breakdowns" for "wildcat strikes" using a benchmark of "almost always necessary" (i.e., at least 80% of instances of the outcome should also have the causal condition) and a significance level of .10. In the crisp-set approach, the investigator selects on the outcome (e.g., wildcat strikes) and then uses probabilistic criteria to evaluate the proportion of these instances with a given causal condition (e.g., communication breakdowns).

In the fuzzy-set approach, by contrast, the investigator first selects all instances with nonzero membership in the set defining the outcome. He then evaluates, using probabilistic criteria, the proportion of these cases with outcome membership scores that are less than or equal to their membership scores in a given causal condition. Note that because the investigator selects all instances with nonzero membership in the outcome, the relevant number of cases is likely to be much greater than in a crisp-set analysis of the same data. This larger number of cases, in turn, makes probabilistic analysis of the evidence more feasible. Note also that the key question is not the proportion of cases displaying the cause in question, but the proportion of cases where membership in the outcome is less than or equal to membership in the cause, which is also a fuzzy set, with values ranging from 0 to 1. In short, to use probabilistic criteria to assess necessity with fuzzy sets, the researcher calculates the proportion of cases that are consistent with the argument of necessity and evaluates this proportion relative to the benchmark proportion. The evidence for an individual case is compatible with the argument of necessity if its membership score in the outcome is less than or equal to its membership score in the cause. If its score in the outcome is greater than its score in the cause, then the case contradicts the argument of necessity.

Consider a fuzzy-set analysis of the necessity of "communication breakdowns" for "wildcat strikes." The researcher would do the following: (1) identify all strikes with nonzero membership in the set of "wildcat strikes," (2) plot their membership in this set against their membership in the set "communication breakdowns between workers and management preceded the strike," (3) calculate the proportion of cases that fall on or below the diagonal of this plot (at the diagonal, membership in the outcome equals membership in the cause; below the diagonal it is less), and (4) test the significance of this proportion against the benchmark proportion (for example, the researcher might assess whether the observed proportion is significantly greater than the "usually necessary" benchmark of .65, using a .05 significance level). Of course, if measurement imprecision is a pressing concern, then the researcher would adjust the line separating concordant and discordant cases in an upward direction (e.g., .05 or .10 fuzzy-membership units), as discussed in the previous section, before calculating the proportion of cases that pass the necessity test (see figure 8.4).

For illustration of the probabilistic approach to the assessment of necessity using fuzzy sets, examine figure 8.5. This figure shows a plot of membership in the set of wildcat strikes (the outcome) against membership in the set of strikes preceded by a communication breakdown between workers and management (the causal condition). The plot has the characteristic lower-triangular shape, suggesting necessity without sufficiency, and all but four of the cases are below the main diagonal. The cases above the diagonal contradict the argument of necessity. Note

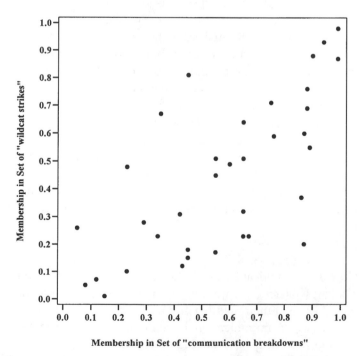

Figure 8.5 Plot of "wildcat strike" against "communication breakdown."

that adding an adjustment of .10 for measurement imprecision would not change the assessment of these cases. All four are more than .10 fuzzy-membership units above the diagonal.

The proportion of cases consistent with an argument of necessity is 31/35 or .886. Using the "usually necessary" benchmark of .65 and a .05 significance level, the observed proportion is significantly greater than the benchmark proportion. The investigator could interpret this finding as support for the argument that communication breakdowns are "usually" necessary for wildcat strikes.[12] Of course, this interpretation should be bolstered by appropriate theoretical and substantive argumentation and auxiliary evidence. As always, it is up to the researcher to establish both the necessity benchmark and the significance level.

CONCLUSION

Necessary conditions are important to both social theory and social policy. However, variable-oriented researchers rarely frame their investigations in terms of either necessity or sufficiency. Most are content to study general patterns of covariation without delving into the subtleties of causation. Furthermore, the language of necessary conditions seems antithetical to variable-oriented social science. This language seems to imply (1) that necessity applies only to presence/absence conditions and (2) that a single disconfirming case disproves necessity.

This chapter demonstrates otherwise. Using fuzzy sets, it is possible to gauge the degree to which a necessary condition is present and to make this variation a key part of the analysis. I demonstrate as well that with the aid of probabilistic criteria, researchers can allow for randomness in the assessment of necessity. Finally, I show that this assessment, in essence, is a test of a set-theoretic relationship. By adopting fuzzy-set analysis and viewing necessity in set-theoretic terms, it is possible to introduce the analysis of necessary conditions into the study of broad, cross-case patterns.

12. It is important to add a word of caution regarding the application of probabilistic criteria to multiple necessary conditions. Examined separately, two causal conditions may pass the researcher's probabilistic test of necessity. When joined together as a combination (and taking the minimum), however, the combination may not pass the same test. This would happen, for example, if both conditions, examined separately, barely passed the investigator's probabilistic test and they had nonoverlapping disconfirming cases.

NINE

USING FUZZY SETS TO STUDY
SUFFICIENT CONDITIONS

INTRODUCTION

The study of sufficiency is central to the study of causal complexity, which, in turn, is central to diversity-oriented research. When causation is complex, no single condition may be either necessary or sufficient. Instead, causes are sufficient only in combinations. In this chapter, I show how to unravel causal complexity using fuzzy sets (see also Ragin 1998). First, I briefly review crisp-set procedures for assessing causal complexity and show how the subset principle is central to this assessment. Specifically, the finding that a cause or causal combination is a subset of an outcome supports the argument of sufficiency. I then extend this thinking with fuzzy sets and present a fuzzy-set analysis of sufficient conditions using a simple data set.[1] I also address several practical problems in using these procedures (e.g., measurement imprecision and randomness). Finally, I discuss the strengths of the fuzzy-set approach compared with both the crisp-set approach and correlational methods.

THE CRISP-SET APPROACH TO CAUSAL COMPLEXITY

The best way to study causal complexity is to assess the sufficiency of *combinations* of causal conditions, drawn from the researcher's property space for an outcome. In the crisp-set approach, the assessment of sufficiency is relatively straightforward. Assuming the investigator has

---

1. All the procedures I discuss in this chapter are implemented in the computer program Fuzzy-Set/Qualitative Comparative Analysis (FS/QCA 1.0; Drass and Ragin 1999).

tested for necessary conditions and found none, he or she may then sort cases according to combinations of crisp set memberships and then assess the sufficiency of each combination. In effect, the researcher examines all possible selections on the independent variables (which number $3^k - 1$, where k is the number of dichotomies). Various rules can be used to structure sufficiency assessments, veristic or probabilistic, depending on the nature of the evidence, the goals of the researcher, and the intended audience for the research. In some investigations, researchers may use probabilistic criteria applied to specific benchmark proportions; in others, they may use the veristic "no negative cases" rule, with or without frequency thresholds (see table 4.10). It is very important for investigators to state and justify the specific sufficiency criteria they use.

Once the investigator has derived a list of combinations of conditions that pass the sufficiency test, the researcher then simplifies this list algebraically. The most common and useful algebraic rule concerns combinations of causal conditions that can be absorbed into other combinations because they are logically contained within them, the *containment rule*. Suppose, for example, that a researcher finds that three combinations of causal conditions pass the sufficiency test: $A \cdot B$, $A \cdot B \cdot C$, and $A \cdot B \cdot \sim D$. The second and third combinations ($A \cdot B \cdot C$ and $A \cdot B \cdot \sim D$) can be eliminated because they are absorbed by combination $A \cdot B$. That is, the second and third terms cover cases that are logically contained within the set of cases covered by the first term ($A \cdot B$), just as the set of tall redheads (tall $\cdot$ redheaded) is contained within the set of redheads. Thus, the terms $A \cdot B \cdot C$ and $A \cdot B \cdot \sim D$ are logically redundant. Essentially, this rule asserts that simpler, more inclusive causal arguments are preferred to those that are more complexly combinatorial and thus narrower in scope.[2]

The terms that remain after the researcher has algebraically simplified the list are then joined together using logical *or* (Boolean addition)

2. As explained in chapter 4, in any application of these techniques it is important for the researcher to evaluate the plausibility of any simplifying assumptions that have been incorporated into the final summary statement describing sufficient combinations of causal conditions. The general rule is, If one or more of the component configurations of an expression lacks cases or has too few cases to permit a sufficiency test, then the researcher must evaluate the plausibility of the implicit assumption that these component configurations would pass the sufficiency test, if in fact it could be conducted. Because of the nature of the configurational approach, as presented in part 1 of this work, it is important to document all such implicit assumptions.

to form a statement describing the combinations of conditions that are sufficient for the outcome. In the end, the researcher derives a concise logical statement of causal complexity, as seen through the lens of the researcher's property space.

SUFFICIENCY AND THE SUBSET PRINCIPLE

In order to understand the fuzzy-set approach to sufficiency, it is important to grasp the set-theoretic principles behind the crisp-set approach. Consider a brief example of a single sufficiency test using crisp sets. Suppose a researcher is interested in explaining the presence/absence of ideological conflict in community organizations and believes that this type of conflict emerges when the membership of an organization is homogeneous with respect to both class and race. The researcher also believes that there are other combinations of conditions that engender ideological conflict but chooses to focus initially on only this single combination. The researcher collects data on 50 community organizations and classifies them, crisply, according to their presence/absence of class homogeneity (cross-class versus not cross-class), presence/absence of racial homogeneity (multiracial versus not multiracial), and presence/absence of ideological conflict.

Because the presence/absence of ideological conflict is the outcome, not a causal condition, the property space is composed of the two crisp causal conditions, cross-class versus not cross-class and multiracial versus not multiracial. With two crisp sets there are eight causal expressions to test (using the formula $3^k - 1$, where k is the number of dichotomies; see chapter 5). Thus, the researcher would conduct eight separate tests of sufficiency. Using the same notation as in previous chapters, the researcher would test each of the following causal expressions:

~cross-class · ~multiracial,
~cross-class · multiracial,
cross-class · ~multiracial,
cross-class · multiracial,
~cross-class,
cross-class,
~multiracial, and
multiracial.

Consider only the sufficiency test that addresses the investigator's main concern—the idea that ideological conflict emerges in community organizations that are homogeneous with respect to both race and class (i.e., organizations that are ~cross-class·~multiracial). To conduct this sufficiency test, the researcher would focus only on the organizations that combine these two traits and evaluate whether they exhibit ideological conflict. Suppose that 12 of the 50 community organizations have this combination of characteristics and that all 12 exhibit ideological conflict. Using either a probabilistic test (with benchmark = .65 and significance level = .01) or a veristic test, this causal expression would pass, and the researcher would conclude that this combination of conditions is sufficient for ideological conflict in community organizations.

It is important to note that the evaluation of sufficiency just described also can be seen as a test of whether the cases displaying the causal conditions form a *subset* of the cases displaying the outcome. Suppose the researcher looks at evidence on all 50 community organizations. The cross-tabulation of presence/absence of ideological conflict against presence/absence of the causal combination in question (not cross-class and not multiracial) would reveal cases in three of the four cells of the table, as shown in table 9.1. Because there are no cases in cell 4 (causal combination present and outcome absent), the table shows, in effect, that cases with the causal combination in question (i.e., those displaying class and race homogeneity) are a subset of the cases with the outcome (ideological conflict).

The subset principle is central to the assessment of causal sufficiency because this assessment addresses whether a cause or combination of causes is one of the (possibly) many ways to produce or reach some outcome. In Boolean terms, we can say that community organizations that are homogeneous with respect to both race and class have ideological conflict precisely because the set of community organizations with these characteristics is a subset of the set of the community organizations with ideological conflict. Thus, every test of sufficiency conducted

Table 9.1
Cross-Tabulation Showing Sufficiency of the Combination of Class and Racial Homogeneity for "ideological conflict"

Ideological Conflict	Cross-Class *or* Multiracial (0)	Not Cross-Class *and* Not Multiracial (1)
Present (1)	[cell 1] 20 cases	[cell 2] 12 cases
Absent (0)	[cell 3] 18 cases	[cell 4] 0 cases

in a crisp-set analysis of causal complexity is also a test of the set-theoretic relationship between a causal combination and the outcome in question.

As shown in chapter 8, another way to understand the subset relationship is in terms of the arithmetic relation between membership scores (1s and 0s in crisp-set analysis). In the hypothetical study just described, the 50 organizations have scores of 1 and 0 on both the cause (presence/absence of the combination of class *and* race homogeneity) and the outcome (presence/absence of ideological conflict). When the value of the cause equals 0, the value of the outcome can be 1 or 0. However, when the value of the cause is 1, then the value of the outcome is equal only to 1 (present), not to 0 (absent). In short, there are no cases scoring 1 on the cause and 0 on the outcome. Consequently, membership scores in the cause are *less than or equal to* membership scores in the outcome. This simple arithmetic relationship between membership scores defines the subset relationship.

Thus, the crisp-set approach uses the subset principle to evaluate sufficiency. According to this basic set-theoretic idea, sufficiency exists when instances of the cause can be shown to be a subset of instances of the outcome, as shown in table 9.1. Note the important difference between the application of the subset principle to the assessment of sufficiency and its application to the assessment of necessity. To demonstrate necessity the researcher must show that the outcome is a subset of the cause. To support an argument of sufficiency, the researcher must demonstrate that the cause is a subset of the outcome.

THE FUZZY-SET APPROACH TO SUFFICIENCY

In the crisp-set approach, the researcher sorts cases according to their different combinations of memberships in the causal conditions and then conducts sufficiency tests on all possible selections on the independent variables (i.e., on all combinations of causal conditions). As noted previously, with fuzzy sets it is difficult to sort cases in this manner because each case may have a unique profile of membership scores, and cases may display varying degrees of membership in every crisply defined property-space location. Note also that in the fuzzy-set approach, cases have fuzzy membership not only in the sets that comprise the property space for an outcome (i.e., the causal conditions), but also in the outcome.

These features of fuzzy-set analysis, at first glance, might seem to pose insurmountable obstacles to the assessment of sufficiency as outlined for crisp sets. In fact, however, with fuzzy sets researchers can conduct a far more elegant and thorough examination of causal complexity than is possible using crisp sets. The key to grasping the fuzzy-set approach to causal complexity is to understand how its techniques for assessing causal sufficiency parallel those with crisp sets. Specifically, both approaches use the subset principle: If it can be shown that a causal condition or combination of conditions is a subset of the outcome, then the investigator may use this evidence to support an argument of causal sufficiency. To show fuzzy subsets, researchers use the arithmetic relationship *less than or equal to.*

For illustration of the subset principle in the fuzzy-set analysis of causal sufficiency, consider two fuzzy sets relevant to students in a course: those who "studied hard" and those who "performed well on the exam." Obviously, studying hard is only one of several ways to do well on an exam. There are likely to be individuals (e.g., geniuses, cheaters, students who successfully bribe the grader) who perform well on exams without studying hard. Assume what all professors assume, namely, that all those who study hard perform well on exams. It follows that membership in the fuzzy set "studied hard" will be a subset of membership in the fuzzy set "performed well on the exam." This general relationship is depicted in figure 9.1. The upper-triangular plot shows the fuzzy subset relationship, where fuzzy membership in one set (studied hard) is less than or equal to fuzzy membership in another (performed well on the exam). Cases in the upper left-hand corner of the plot are individuals who performed well on the exam without studying hard. From the evidence in the figure, it would be reasonable to argue that "studying hard" is sufficient but not necessary for "performing well on the exam."

Return now to the example involving the 50 community organizations. Suppose that the researcher studying community organizations had used fuzzy sets for the two causal conditions and for the outcome. Using fuzzy sets, as already noted, it would be difficult to select community organizations displaying a specific combination of characteristics, those that are homogeneous with respect to both class and race, because the organizations vary in their degree of membership in these two sets. Likewise, it would be difficult to evaluate cases' agreement with respect to the outcome because they also vary in their degree of membership in the outcome, organizations that exhibit ideological conflict. However, it is possible to evaluate whether the causal combination is a subset of the outcome by examining the arithmetic relation between the two sets of scores.

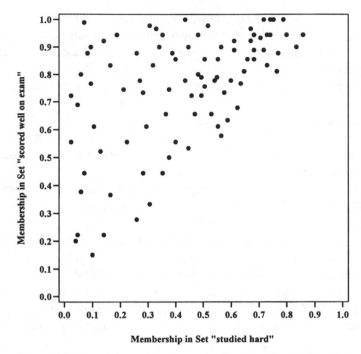

Figure 9.1 Plot of "scored well on exam" against "studied hard."

Because the goal is to show that the combination of race and class homogeneity provides one of several possible bases for ideological conflict in community organizations, the evidence should show that membership scores in the combination of causal conditions, not cross-class and not multiracial, are less than or equal to membership scores in the outcome, ideological conflict. Table 9.2 show hypothetical data consistent with this argument, reporting data on 20 of the 50 community organizations. A scatterplot showing the relationship between fuzzy membership in the causal combination and fuzzy membership in the outcome is presented in figure 9.2.

The upper-triangular plot shown in figure 9.2 is a direct reflection of the fact that membership scores in the fuzzy set "race and class homogeneity" (i.e., ~cross-class · ~multiracial) are less than or equal to membership scores in the fuzzy set "ideological conflict." When membership scores for "race and class homogeneity" are high, membership scores for "ideological conflict" must be high because the causal combination is sufficient for the outcome. However, when membership scores for "race and class homogeneity" are low, membership scores for "ideological

Table 9.2
Fuzzy-Set Analysis of "ideological conflict" in Community Organizations

Case No.	Multiracial (M)	Cross-Class (C)	~M·~C	Ideological Conflict
1	.17	.70	.30	.35
2	.86	.21	.14	.80
3	.22	.89	.11	.23
4	.75	.42	.25	.82
5	.61	.65	.35	.61
6	.48	.14	.52	.88
7	.50	.57	.43	.48
8	.04	.93	.07	.38
9	.59	.38	.41	.78
10	.33	.90	.10	.60
. . .				
41	.48	.34	.52	.70
42	1.00	.69	.00	.32
43	.24	.52	.48	.50
44	.92	.13	.08	.95
45	.13	.25	.75	.95
46	.11	.46	.54	.78
47	.83	.75	.17	.31
48	.37	.27	.63	.77
49	.55	.88	.12	.15
50	.76	.95	.05	.11

conflict" can take on a wide range of values. This upper-triangular pattern is in accord with the simple idea that there may be several different combinations of conditions that give rise to ideological conflict.

The fact that there are other combinations of conditions that are sufficient for ideological conflict is not directly relevant to the evaluation of a statement about organizations that combine race and class homogeneity. Thus, the cases in the upper-left corner of the plot in figure 9.2 are not errors. Because these cases have low scores on the causal combination, they are not of central relevance to the investigator's argument. More generally, it is important to understand that a sufficient causal condition or combination of conditions establishes a *floor* for the expression of the outcome—a minimum level for the observed outcome. A case's score on the outcome should not be lower than the level set by its score on relevant sufficient conditions. Note the contrast here with necessity. As discussed in chapter 8, fuzzy-set statements describing necessary conditions place a ceiling on the outcome, that is, a case's score on the outcome should not exceed the level set by a necessary condition.

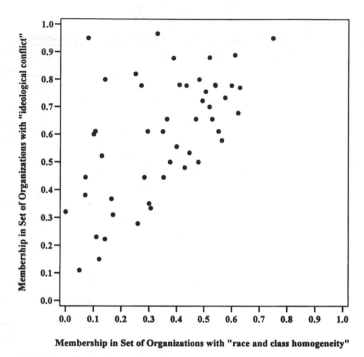

Figure 9.2 Plot of "ideological conflict" against "race and class homogeneity."

To summarize: a researcher could cite the evidence presented in table 9.2 and figure 9.2 to support the argument that the combination of class and racial homogeneity is sufficient for ideological conflict in community organizations. As always, such empirical demonstrations should be supported with auxiliary arguments and evidence. This example illustrates the core of the fuzzy-set approach to causal sufficiency. The key is to understand that when fuzzy membership scores in a cause or causal combination are less than or equal to fuzzy membership scores in the outcome, then it is possible to argue that instances of the cause are a subset of instances of the outcome. When researchers find this pattern, they may cite it to support the argument that the causal condition or combination of causal conditions is sufficient for the outcome.

COMPLETING THE FUZZY-SET ANALYSIS
OF CAUSAL COMPLEXITY

While the evidence in the hypothetical analysis just presented supports the researcher's central argument, the analysis is not complete. Recall that with two conditions, there are eight $3^k - 1$ selections on the independent variables to test in a full evaluation of sufficient conditions. It is possible that there are other causal expressions that are sufficient for the outcome besides ~cross-class·~multiracial. For example, either class homogeneity (~cross-class) *or* race homogeneity (~multiracial) alone might be sufficient for ideological conflict. If so, then either of these would logically eliminate the *combination* of race and class homogeneity (~cross-class·~multiracial) as a sufficient cause of ideological conflict.

Conducting the Tests

As previously noted, the eight causal expressions to test in this hypothetical analysis are ~cross-class·~multiracial, ~cross class·multiracial, cross-class·~multiracial, cross-class·multiracial, ~cross-class, cross-class, ~multiracial, and multiracial. To test these eight arguments, the researcher derives membership scores in the eight causal expressions using the principles of negation (subtracting membership scores from 1) and intersection (finding the minimum) described in chapters 6 and 7. These scores are reported in table 9.3. This table reproduces the information contained in table 9.2 and adds the relevant fuzzy membership scores for the remaining causal expressions. Once again, to streamline the tables, information on only 20 of the 50 community organizations is reported.

Comparing scores in columns (2)–(9) (i.e., the columns showing membership in the eight causal expressions), on the one hand, with column (10) (membership in the outcome, ideological conflict), on the other, reveals that scores in columns (5) and (6) (causal arguments ~cross-class and ~multiracial·~cross-class) are uniformly less than or equal to the outcome scores reported in column (10). Following the reasoning just presented, the investigator would conclude from this evidence that these two causal expressions (~cross-class and ~multiracial·~cross-class) are subsets of the outcome (ideological conflict). These set-theoretic relations, in turn, are consistent with the argument that ~cross-class and ~multiracial·~cross-class are sufficient for the outcome.

Logical Simplification

Note, however, that one of the causal arguments (~multiracial·~cross-class) can be absorbed by the other (~cross-class) using the containment rule because instances of a compound set are contained within the instances of its component sets (just as the set of

Table 9.3
Full Analysis of Conditions Sufficient for "ideological conflict" in Community Organizations

Case No. (1)	M (2)	C (3)	~M (4)	~C (5)	~M·~C (6)	~M·C (7)	M·~C (8)	M·C (9)	I (10)
1	.17	.70	.87	.30	.30	.70	.17	.17	.35
2	.86	.21	.14	.79	.14	.14	.79	.21	.80
3	.22	.89	.78	.11	.11	.78	.11	.22	.23
4	.75	.42	.25	.58	.25	.25	.58	.42	.82
5	.61	.65	.39	.35	.35	.39	.35	.61	.81
6	.48	.14	.52	.86	.52	.14	.48	.14	.88
7	.50	.57	.50	.43	.43	.50	.43	.50	.48
8	.04	.93	.96	.07	.07	.93	.04	.04	.38
9	.59	.38	.41	.62	.41	.38	.59	.38	.78
10	.33	.90	.67	.10	.10	.67	.10	.33	.60
: : :									
41	.48	.34	.52	.66	.52	.34	.48	.34	.70
42	1.00	.69	.00	.31	.00	.00	.31	.69	.31
43	.24	.52	.76	.48	.48	.52	.24	.24	.50
44	.92	.13	.08	.87	.08	.08	.87	.13	.95
45	.13	.25	.87	.75	.75	.25	.13	.13	.95
46	.11	.46	.89	.54	.54	.46	.11	.11	.78
47	.83	.75	.17	.25	.17	.75	.25	.75	.31
48	.37	.27	.63	.73	.63	.27	.37	.27	.77
49	.55	.88	.45	.12	.12	.45	.12	.55	.15
50	.76	.95	.24	.05	.05	.24	.05	.76	.11

short Protestants is contained within the set of Protestants). Thus, ~multiracial·~cross-class is logically redundant and can be eliminated. This simplification also follows the simple algebraic principle, which holds in both Boolean and fuzzy algebra, that more-complex terms can be absorbed by less-complex terms as long as all the elements of the less-complex term (e.g., ~cross-class) appear in the more-complex term (e.g., ~multiracial·~cross-class).[3]

The elimination of ~multiracial·~cross-class also holds arithmetically. Consider the following statement:

$$\sim\text{cross-class} + \sim\text{multiracial}\cdot\sim\text{cross-class} \rightarrow \text{ideological conflict}$$

(where "→" means *is sufficient for*). In fuzzy algebra, the statement indicates that the value of the left-hand side is the maximum of ~cross-class and ~multiracial·~cross-class. Plus signs indicates logical *or*, which in fuzzy algebra is the same as taking the maximum value of the expressions that are joined by *or*. Observe that the maximum of the left-hand side of the statement is never supplied uniquely by the more complex expression, ~multiracial·~cross-class. If the value of ~multiracial is greater than or equal to the value of ~cross-class, then the value of ~multiracial·~cross-class is equal to the value of ~cross-class, the same as the other term in the statement. If the value of ~multiracial is less the value of ~cross-class, then the value of ~multiracial·~cross-class is equal to ~multiracial. However, when ~multiracial is less than ~cross-class, the first term in the statement, ~cross-class, will provide the value of the left-hand side because the two expressions are joined by logical *or*. In other words, because logical *or* dictates the use of the maximum in fuzzy algebra, a term that is contained within another is not only logically redundant but is also arithmetically redundant.

After eliminating the term ~multiracial·~cross-class, the statement

---

3. It is very important to point out that not all of Boolean algebra can be transported directly to fuzzy algebra. For example, in Boolean algebra the formula $A + aB$ can be simplified to $A + B$ because A can be decomposed into $Ab + AB$ and then AB and aB can be joined to form B ($AB + aB = B$). Take a simple example: Suppose a statement is true for all Protestants and for all non-Protestants who are blond. The statement is also true for all blonds. This simplification is impossible in fuzzy algebra because $AB + aB$ is *not* equal to B in fuzzy algebra. Instead, it is equal to $B(A + a)$. In fuzzy algebra $a + A$ is equal to the maximum of A and a, which in turn is equal to 1 only when A or a equals 1. For example, if a case has a membership of .7 in A, it has a membership of .3 in a, and thus a membership of .7 in $A + a$.

describing the results of the hypothetical analysis presented in table 9.3 can be simplified to

$$\sim\text{cross-class} \rightarrow \text{ideological conflict.}$$

The investigator would conclude from this analysis that class homogeneity by itself is sufficient for ideological conflict; it does not have to be combined with racial homogeneity.[4]

Other Eliminations

Before moving on to a discussion of this solution and how to evaluate it, it is important to describe a further simplification of results that is possible in some fuzzy-set analyses. Sometimes a causal expression that survives algebraic simplification (i.e., application of the containment rule) still may be arithmetically redundant and therefore should be dropped from the list of sufficient causal expressions. While there are no such causal expressions in the current example, it is important to look for such terms because eliminating them from the list of sufficient causal expressions may greatly simplify the solution. The specific rule is, Any causal expression on the left-hand side of a logical statement describing sufficient conditions that fails to provide a unique maximum can be eliminated.[5] Such expressions are arithmetically useless because they have no impact on the numerical value of the left-hand side of the statement and thus provide no unique or useful information.

Suppose, for illustration, that the researcher includes condition "z"

─────────────────

4. It might seem reasonable to infer in this hypothetical study that $\sim$cross-class is not only sufficient but also necessary, based on its solo appearance in the solution just presented. After all, it is the only cause in the statement. Note, however, that there are cases in Exhibit 10.6 with high scores on the outcome ideological conflict but relatively low scores on class homogeneity ($\sim$cross-class). Thus, these cases of ideological conflict are not explained by class homogeneity. Because they are located in the upper left corner of the plot of ideological conflict against class homogeneity ($\sim$cross-class), they must be seen as instances of ideological conflict in community organizations explained by conditions that are not included in the property space the researcher has constructed for this investigation. Thus, in any analysis of causal sufficiency it is unwise to jump from a statement describing sufficiency to any conclusions about causal necessity.

5. This rule should not be applied blindly or mechanistically. Suppose that (1) two expressions both supply the same maximum for a case, (2) no other expression supplies this maximum, and (3) neither of these two expressions supplies a unique maximum for any case. To eliminate both terms would be to eliminate the terms that supply the maximum for the case in question, thus degrading the overall strength of the results.

in the truth table for ideological conflict and that the causal expression $z \cdot$cross-class (the combination of condition "z" and class heterogeneity) passes the researcher's sufficiency test. Suppose also that this combination fails to provide a unique maximum on the left-hand side of the statement:

$$z \cdot \text{cross-class} + \sim\text{cross-class} \rightarrow \text{ideological conflict.}$$

That is, for every case, membership in $\sim$cross-class exceeds membership in $z \cdot$cross-class. (The expression $\sim$multiracial$\cdot\sim$cross-class already has been algebraically eliminated from this statement.) Because $z \cdot$cross-class never provides a unique maximum, it can be eliminated from this statement without affecting any case's score on the left-hand side. To assess whether a term provides a unique maximum, it is necessary to check the scores of each case. In contrast to the elimination of $\sim$multiracial$\cdot\sim$cross class (which is algebraically, logically, and arithmetically justified), the elimination of terms that fail to supply unique maximums, such as $z \cdot$cross-class in this example, is empirically and pragmatically justified.

Evaluating the Results

After eliminating all redundant or useless causal expressions, the researcher should examine, as a final step, a plot of scores on the outcome against scores on the left-hand side of the sufficiency statement. As a general rule, logical statements describing sufficient conditions contain several causal expressions on the left-hand side (indicating the alternate combinations of conditions that are sufficient for an outcome), and most cases have nonzero membership scores on more than one of these expressions. Fuzzy logic, specifically, the operation of logical *or,* ensures that each case's score on the left-hand side of the statement will be its best (highest) score—the one that is closest to, without exceeding, its score on the outcome. It follows that a scattergram showing the plot of outcome scores against "left-hand side" scores generally will be superior to the plot of outcome scores against any single sufficient expression. Its superiority derives from the fact that the points in this plot will be closer to the diagonal than in the other plots. When a case plots close to the diagonal, the investigator has, in effect, established the highest possible floor for the expression of the outcome.

The degree to which cases line up on or near the diagonal is a crude indicator of the success of an analysis of causal complexity. Cases on or near the diagonal have outcome scores consistent with the floor specified in the logical statement describing sufficiency. Cases well above the diagonal have outcome scores that exceed this floor. These unexplained cases (in the upper left region of the plot) have high membership in the outcome due to factors that are outside the scope of the researcher's property space. They are not "errors" in the conventional sense. Rather, they are simply cases that display high membership in the outcome due to the operation of causal conditions not included in the researcher's property space.[6] If all cases plot close to the main diagonal, then researchers may advance the claim that they have identified the different ways an outcome might be achieved, for they have accounted for its varying degrees of expression in relevant cases.

Note the contrast here with the analysis of necessity presented in chapter 8. In the analysis of necessary conditions, if several conditions are found to be necessary, they are joined by logical *and*. After all, if a condition is necessary it must be present in *every* case. Joining necessary conditions by logical *and* (intersection) dictates the use of the *minimum* of a case's memberships in these conditions. Thus, when there are several necessary conditions, the effect of using the minimum is to push cases to the left—toward the diagonal—in a scatterplot of membership in the outcome against membership in necessary conditions, as shown in figure 8.3. (Recall that in the analysis of necessary conditions, researchers study lower-triangular plots. Pushing cases to the left in a lower-triangular plot pushes them toward the diagonal.) In the analysis of sufficiency, by contrast, alternate causal expressions are joined by logical *or* because they represent different ways of reaching a given outcome. The operation of logical *or* dictates the use of the maximum. In an upper-triangular plot (the characteristic sufficiency plot) this has the impact of moving points to the right—toward the diagonal. In short, logical *and* pushes cases to the left—toward the diagonal—in a fuzzy-set analysis of necessity, while logical *or* pushes cases to the right—also toward the diagonal—in a fuzzy-set analysis of sufficiency.

A STEP-BY-STEP SUMMARY OF THE FUZZY-SET APPROACH TO CAUSAL COMPLEXITY

This extended discussion of fuzzy-set procedures for the analysis of causal complexity presents the core of the approach. While the hypo-

---

6. It is quite possible that measurement, translation, and specification error, as well as case-specific and random factors, will confound the evaluation and interpretation of any results. These issues are addressed in the next section.

thetical finding in this example is very simple (the isolation of a single sufficient cause, ~cross-class), the broad outline of the research strategy is clear. Remember that this presentation assumes that the researcher already has completed the difficult tasks of (1) constituting relevant cases, (2) constructing a useful property space for the outcome, and (3) specifying the fuzzy membership scores of cases in both the outcome and the sets that comprise the property space. It is also worth noting that this sketch of the fuzzy-set approach to causal complexity does not address the connection between the assessment of necessary conditions and the assessment of sufficient conditions, a topic I address subsequently in this chapter and also in chapter 10 with an empirical example.

The basic steps in the assessment of sufficiency using fuzzy sets are the following:

1. Specify the causal expressions to be tested. The number of logically possible arguments to test is given by the formula $3^k - 1$, where k is the number of causal conditions in the property space the researcher has constructed for the outcome.
2. Compute the membership of each case in each causal expression. These computations use the principles of negation (subtracting from 1) and intersection (finding the minimum).
3. Compare membership scores in each causal expression with membership scores in the outcome. Identify which causal expressions are subsets of the outcome by determining which have membership scores that are consistently less than or equal to membership scores in the outcome. Apply the same test to each of the $3^k - 1$ causal expressions. Expressions that are subsets of the outcome may be considered sufficient.
4. Algebraically simplify this list. The primary algebraic principle is the containment rule: more-complex expressions can be absorbed by less-complex expressions as long as all the elements that appear in the less-complex expression also appear in the more-complex expression.
5. Check to see if any of the remaining causal expressions fail to supply a unique maximum in the logical statement that results from the previous step. Any expression that fails this test can be eliminated.
6. Form a statement describing causally sufficient conditions using the expressions that remain after step 5, using logical *or* to join them. The resulting summary statement is a representation of the sufficient

conditions for the outcome, expressed as alternate causal combinations.

7. Examine a scattergram showing the plot of membership in the outcome against membership in the left-hand side of the statement that summarizes the results of the sufficiency analysis. Cases that are close to the diagonal of the scattergram are consistent with the ideas operationalized in the researcher's property space. Cases in the upper left region of the plot display the outcome due to causal conditions not included in the property space.

It is important to recognize that deriving an algebraic statement describing causal complexity is only one phase in the dialogue between ideas and evidence in fuzzy-set analysis. In many respects, it is the midpoint of the investigation. In addition to the extensive preparatory work that leads up to the analysis of sufficiency, there is also substantial follow-up. Once a statement describing causal complexity has been derived, it is still necessary to evaluate it. Does it make sense? Are the results consistent with theory? Do they advance or refine theory in some way? Are the findings consistent with substantive knowledge? Is there any auxiliary evidence to corroborate the argument that the causal expressions identified in the algebraic statement are sufficient? Do the results advance substantive knowledge of cases? Do they help us make sense of cases?

PRACTICAL ISSUES IN THE FUZZY-SET ANALYSIS OF CAUSAL COMPLEXITY

The example just presented is straightforward. The property space has only two dimensions, and the results are monocausal, revealing little in the way of causal complexity. The example is also unrealistically simple because it skirts several important issues in the fuzzy-set analysis of causal complexity. These issues include the following: (1) the problem of making adjustments for measurement error and for imprecisions in the translation of raw data to fuzzy membership scores; (2) the problem of randomness and the associated issue of incorporating probabilistic criteria into the assessment of sufficiency; (3) the issue of limited diversity, especially with respect to implicit, simplifying assumptions that may be embedded in the results of a fuzzy-set analysis; and (4) the problem of incorporating necessary conditions into the analysis of sufficiency. The discussions of the first two issues (imprecision and randomness) build on arguments presented in chapter 8 for the assessment of necessary conditions. The latter two issues are specific to the analysis of sufficiency.

Adjusting for Measurement and Translation Imprecisions

As explained in chapter 8, researchers often lack complete confidence in their measures or in the translation of their measures from raw data to fuzzy membership scores. Consider, for example, the measurement of the membership of community organizations in the fuzzy set "cross-class." The researcher would first devise a measure of the heterogeneity of the members of a community organization with respect to social class and then develop a scheme for translating these heterogeneity scores to fuzzy membership scores in the set "cross-class." Unfortunately, there are many opportunities for imprecision, biases, and distortions to enter into this process. Furthermore, different ways of translating raw measures of class heterogeneity into fuzzy membership scores have different theoretical, interpretive, and political implications. These problems are especially irksome when researchers find that one or a small number of cases fall just below the diagonal in a sufficiency test. (Recall that in the analysis of sufficiency, if a case falls below the diagonal, it contradicts the argument that the causal expression is sufficient for the outcome.)

As explained in chapter 8, it is possible to use an adjustment factor to counteract these imprecisions. In the analysis of necessity, the adjustment factor in effect moves the diagonal in an upward direction to capture cases that are near misses from the perspective of necessity. In the analysis of sufficiency, by contrast, the adjustment factor moves the diagonal downward to capture cases that are near misses from the perspective of sufficiency. Figure 9.3 illustrates the operation of the adjustment factor, showing a diagonal that has been shifted .10 fuzzy-membership units. With this adjustment in place, near misses no longer violate sufficiency. To constitute a violation in this plot, a case's membership in the causal expression must exceed its membership in the outcome by more than .10 fuzzy-membership units.

Expressed as an equation, causal condition X can be interpreted as a sufficient condition for outcome Y, with an adjustment of .10 fuzzy-membership units, as shown in figure 9.3, if

$$X_i - .10 \leq Y_i.$$

It is also possible to formulate a nonlinear adjustment equation that allows for the possibility that the researcher has less confidence in the measurement of fuzzy membership in the middle range of fuzzy mem-

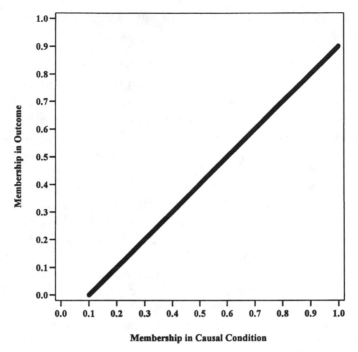

Figure 9.3 Adjusting the test of sufficiency for measurement and translation imprecision.

bership (i.e., in the vicinity of .5) than at either extreme (i.e., near 1 or 0).

Of course, it is incumbent upon investigators to explain and justify any adjustment factor they might use. For example, a researcher might wish to counteract known biases in the measurement of fuzzy membership in the outcome or one or more causal conditions. Generally, the use of an adjustment factor will increase the number of causal expressions that pass the investigator's sufficiency test, which in turn will enhance interpretive opportunities. This fact underscores the argument, presented in chapter 6, that fuzzy sets are most usefully seen as interpretive devices, not as mechanistic transformations of conventional variables (see also chapter 11).

Adjusting for measurement and translation imprecisions alters only slightly the seven-step procedure for assessing sufficiency sketched in the previous section. Between steps 2 and 3, the researcher should adjust membership scores using whatever adjustment formula seems appropriate.

Incorporating Probabilistic Criteria

The examples presented so far in this chapter all use a veristic test of sufficiency. As discussed above, the veristic test of sufficiency does not permit *any* nonconforming cases (i.e., cases that fall below the diagonal in the plot of membership in the outcome against membership in a causal expression). As noted in chapter 8, however, there are often causal factors specific to individual cases that make them outliers, at least from the perspective embodied in the researcher's property space. Thus, the veristic test may fail because of a relatively small number of inconsistent cases. When these cases are not near misses resulting from imperfect measurement or translation but true outliers, they may not be captured when the diagonal is altered with an adjustment factor, as sketched in the previous section. For example, a community organization that is fully homogeneous with respect to class composition (i.e., with a membership score of 1 or close to 1 in the fuzzy set ~cross-class) might yet have very low membership in the set of community organizations displaying ideological conflict. Suppose this organization is the only inconsistent case; all others are near or above the diagonal. Should the researcher reject sufficiency based on this one case?

Fortunately, it is possible to inject probabilistic criteria into the evaluation of sufficiency using fuzzy sets. As explained in part 1, to assess sufficiency using probabilistic criteria, the investigator specifies both a sufficiency benchmark and a significance level. (As always, it is up to the researcher to establish and justify both the sufficiency benchmark and the significance level.) Using crisp sets, for example, a researcher might argue that if significantly greater than 65% of the cases displaying a specific causal condition or combination also display the outcome (using a one-tailed significance level of .05), then the causal expression is "usually sufficient" for the outcome.

Note that in the crisp-set approach researchers examine only cases that display the causal expression in question (crisp set membership = 1). When using fuzzy sets, researchers examine all cases with nonzero membership in the causal expression and focus on the varying degree of membership of all relevant cases in both the cause and the outcome. Thus, the fuzzy-set approach addresses a greater number of cases and thus a much larger volume of evidence. The key question in this assessment is the set-theoretic relation between the cause and the outcome. The researcher calculates the proportion of cases that are consistent with the argument of sufficiency and evaluates this proportion relative to the benchmark proportion. The evidence for an individual case is consistent with the argument of sufficiency if its membership score in the cause is less than or equal to its membership score in the outcome.[7] If its score in the cause is greater than its score in the outcome, then the case contradicts the argument of sufficiency. Referring back to figures 9.1 and 9.2, cases on or above the diagonal are consistent with the argument of sufficiency; cases below the diagonal contradict it.

When making a probabilistic assessment of sufficiency, it is important to exclude cases that have membership scores of 0 in a causal expression. There are two main reasons for this exclusion. First, recall from part 1 that to test an argument of sufficiency, it is necessary to select on instances of the cause. Any case with a crisp set membership score of 0 in a causal expression is completely out of the set of cases displaying the relevant causes. Such cases are irrelevant to any statement about the causal expression. The same holds in fuzzy-set analysis. Any case with a score of 0 in the causal expression is completely out of the set displaying the causal expression and thus is not relevant to statements about the causal expression. Thus, the exclusion of cases with fuzzy membership scores of 0 parallels the exclusion of cases in the first column of the cross-tabulation of a cause and an effect in a crisp-set analysis. Second, if cases with fuzzy membership scores of 0 were not excluded, they would artificially inflate the proportion of conforming cases and thus bias the test of sufficiency in a positive direction. If a case's membership in a causal expression is equal to 0, then its score is automatically less than or equal to the case's membership score in the outcome, which, after all, must be between 0 and 1. Thus, all cases with membership scores of 0 in a causal expression conform artificially to any statement about the expression. Clearly, these cases should not enter into a probabilistic assessment of sufficiency. Not only would their inclusion bias the proportion of conforming cases in an upward direction, it would also shrink the estimate of the standard error of the benchmark because the number of cases included in the test would be artificially inflated.

In practice, relatively few cases in a fuzzy-set analysis may have membership scores of 0 in a causal expression. Indeed, the researcher may argue that no case is "completely out of" or "completely in" any of the sets that comprise a property space. Still, the irrelevance of cases with membership scores of 0 underscores the importance of the integration of qualitative and quantitative thinking that undergirds fuzzy-

---

7. Cases with membership scores of 0 in a causal expression are not relevant to the evaluation of its sufficiency; this issue is addressed subsequently.

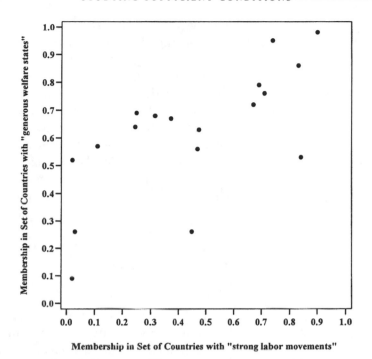

Figure 9.4 Plot of "generous welfare state" against "strong labor movement."

set analysis, especially the specification of qualitative anchors on continua (full membership, full nonmembership, and the crossover point).

For a very simple illustration of the probabilistic approach to the assessment of sufficiency using fuzzy sets, consider figure 9.4. This figure shows a plot of membership in the set of countries with "strong labor movements" (the cause) against membership in the set of countries with "generous welfare states" (the outcome), using data on 18 advanced industrial democracies. This plot has the characteristic upper-triangular shape, suggesting sufficiency without necessity, but 2 of the 18 cases are below the main diagonal. These two cases contradict the argument of sufficiency because they have relatively greater membership in the set of countries with strong labor movements than in the set of countries with generous welfare states. Thus, in this example the veristic test of sufficiency fails. Using probabilistic criteria, however, this cause passes the test of "usually sufficient." The probability of finding 16 consistent cases and 2 inconsistent cases, or better, given a benchmark proportion of .65, is less than .05.

The incorporation of probabilistic criteria alters only slightly the seven steps for assessing sufficiency with fuzzy sets described in the previous section. The third step is modified so that each causal expression is evaluated to see if the evidence supports the idea that it is a qualified subset of the outcome, not a strict subset of the outcome. Thus "usually sufficient," according to this reasoning, translates into "membership in the cause is 'usually' less than or equal to membership in the outcome." Using probabilistic criteria, the researcher is very likely to increase the number of causal expressions that pass sufficiency (unless, of course, the number of cases is very small). It is important to note, however, that sufficiency itself is compromised in this approach. That is, rather than being able to state that a causal expression is "sufficient" for an outcome, researchers must qualify their conclusions when using probabilistic criteria, stating that a causal expression is "almost always sufficient," "usually sufficient," or "sufficient more often than not," depending on the benchmark they select.

Limited Diversity and Implicit Assumptions

Part 1 of this book emphasizes the diversity of social phenomena and the use of configurational methods to address this diversity. In the configurational view, different combinations of case characteristics constitute, potentially at least, different kinds of cases. Statements about necessity and sufficiency often have direct implications for unobserved configurations of causal conditions. In any analysis of naturally occurring phenomena, it is very likely that the investigator will be unable to observe all logically possible combinations of causal conditions (i.e., all kinds of cases) and thus will have only a limited view of social diversity. Consequently, general statements about causation may incorporate simplifying assumptions about unobserved cases. Investigators should make these assumptions explicit and evaluate their plausibility.

For illustration, consider again the fuzzy-set analysis of ideological conflict in community organizations. Recall that this analysis concludes with the argument that being ~cross-class (i.e., homogeneous with respect to class) is sufficient for ideological conflict in community organizations, based on an analysis of a two-dimensional property space, with multiracial versus ~multiracial as the other dimension. Suppose, for example, there are no cases combining class homogeneity and race heterogeneity (i.e., cases with greater than .5 membership in the crisp property-space location, multiracial·~cross-class). In other words, community organizations that are homogeneous with respect to class also tend to be homogeneous with respect to race. How does this limitation on diversity affect the researcher's conclusion that class homogeneity (i.e., membership in ~cross-class) is sufficient for ideological conflict?

The conclusion that class homogeneity (~cross-class) is sufficient for ideological conflict implies that the combination multiracial · ~cross-class is also sufficient for ideological conflict because this latter expression is contained within the former. Thus, the simplifying assumption that being multiracial · ~cross-class is sufficient for ideological conflict is embedded in the conclusion that being ~cross-class is sufficient for ideological conflict. Yet the researcher has no organizations of this type (i.e., there are no organizations with greater than .5 membership in this crisp location). As explained in chapter 5, it is important to document and evaluate such simplifying assumption. The researcher might decide that the simplifying assumption is plausible based on the available evidence. However, if the researcher were to conclude that this simplifying assumption is not plausible, then he or she should modify the results of the fuzzy-set analysis accordingly. Specifically, the researcher would conclude that for class homogeneity (~cross-class) to spawn ideological conflict, it must be combined with race homogeneity (~multiracial), as follows:

$$\sim\text{multiracial} \cdot \sim\text{cross-class} \rightarrow \text{ideological conflict.}$$

It is a simple matter to identify simplifying assumptions in fuzzy-set analyses involving small property spaces, as in the present example (a two-dimensional space). To identify simplifying assumptions in studies based on large, multidimensional property spaces, it is wise to use an algorithm specifically designed for this purpose, such as the one provided in FS/QCA (Drass and Ragin 1999). Basically, the researcher first derives a logical equation describing the regions of the property space that lack cases (or regions lacking adequate numbers of cases—using whatever criteria may be appropriate for this assessment). This equation, in essence, describes hypothetical cases—the kinds of cases that are not adequately represented in the investigator's data set. Next, the researcher intersects this equation with the logical statement describing sufficient combinations of conditions. The intersection of these two statements reveals the simplifying assumptions that have been incorporated in the investigator's solution. These assumptions, in turn, should be evaluated one at a time. Any simplifying assumption that is not plausible should be eliminated from the statement describing sufficient conditions, and the solution should be reformulated accordingly.

Incorporating Necessary Conditions

The analysis of necessary conditions is in many respects logically prior to the analysis of sufficient conditions. This analysis is also procedurally prior to the analysis of sufficient conditions because researchers may overlook necessary conditions if they study sufficient conditions without first testing for necessary conditions (see discussion of table 4.8). This problem of "missed necessary conditions" stems ultimately from the limited diversity of social phenomena, which, in turn, poses serious problems for all forms of social scientific inquiry. When social phenomena exhibit limited diversity, which is the usual situation, it is impossible to conduct a thorough assessment all combinations of causal conditions. Consequently, researchers must rely on theory, substantive knowledge, and auxiliary empirical evidence (e.g., in-depth knowledge of cases) to support their causal generalizations.

The examples presented in this chapter, so far, all bypass the assessment of necessary conditions. How should researchers modify their analysis of sufficiency if they do in fact find that one or more causal conditions is necessary? As it turns out, the relevant modifications are relatively minor. If a causal condition passes the researcher's test of necessity, then this condition should be made a component of every causal expression that the researcher examines subsequently in the analysis of sufficiency. This way, the necessary condition appears in every causal expression in the logical statement summarizing patterns of causal sufficiency. If several conditions pass the test of necessity, they are all inserted into the causal expressions that are subsequently tested for sufficiency.

For illustration, suppose that the researcher interested in ideological conflict in community organizations had examined three causes: multiracial versus ~multiracial, cross-class versus ~cross-class, and mobilized versus ~mobilized. Suppose further that the third condition (mobilized) passed the test of necessity. That is, this researcher demonstrates that the fuzzy set of organizations with ideological conflict is a subset of the fuzzy set of mobilized community organizations (a mobilized organization is one that has garnered substantial commitments of time and resources from its constituency). Assume the researcher accepts the idea that mobilization is a necessary condition for ideological conflict. Before proceeding to the analysis of sufficient conditions, the investigator would insert the necessary condition (mobilized) into each causal expression formed from the remaining components of the property space (multiracial versus ~multiracial and cross-class versus

~cross-class). The sufficiency phase of the analysis thus would involve the assessment of eight causal expression ($3^k - 1$, where $k =$ the number of remaining dimensions), with the term *mobilized* inserted into each of the eight expressions, as follows:

mobilized·~cross-class·~multiracial,
mobilized·~cross-class·multiracial,
mobilized·cross-class·~multiracial,
mobilized·cross-class·multiracial,
mobilized·~cross-class,
mobilized·cross-class,
mobilized·~multiracial, and
mobilized·multiracial.

In short, the eight causal expressions that are formed from multiracial versus ~multiracial and cross-class versus ~cross-class are modified so that each now includes the necessary condition mobilized as an additional component. Thus, the finding that mobilization is a necessary condition for ideological conflict is integrated into the analysis of sufficiency. This list of causal expressions becomes the appropriate starting point for the analysis of sufficiency.[8]

Finally, note that because the condition mobilized appears in each of the eight causal expressions to be tested, any case that is fully out of the set of mobilized community organizations (fuzzy membership = 0) will be excluded from the sufficiency analysis. Such a case would score 0 on each of the combinations to be tested. This exclusion is consistent with the simple idea that cases that are fully out of the set of cases displaying a necessary condition for an outcome are not candidates for the outcome.[9]

8. It is important to note that because being mobilized is a necessary condition for ideological conflict, membership scores in mobilized are greater than membership scores in ideological conflict. Consequently, if the term mobilized yields the minimum in any of the above expressions, it will constitute a violation of sufficiency (except when the score in a necessary condition equals the outcome score). Thus, when strict criteria are used (i.e., no adjustment factor, no use of probabilistic criteria), the insertion of the term mobilized in the causal expression will have an insubstantial impact on the results of the sufficiency analysis. However, if the analyses of necessity and sufficiency make use of adjustment factors or probabilistic criteria, then insertion of a necessary condition into the terms to be tested in the sufficiency analysis may have a minor impact on these results.

9. If probabilistic criteria are used to assess necessity, then the actual standard for the evaluation of necessity is relaxed (e.g., a condition may be "usually" necessary). Thus, when using probabilistic criteria, a researcher may decide not to drop

ADVANTAGES OF THE FUZZY-SET APPROACH
OVER THE CRISP-SET APPROACH

The fuzzy-set approach to the analysis of sufficiency, just sketched, offers several distinct advantages over the crisp-set approach. These advantages follow directly from the use of degrees of membership in sets instead of the simple "in or out" crisp distinction.

The first and most obvious advantage of the fuzzy-set approach is that it makes much better use of available evidence than the crisp-set approach, resulting in more precise assessments. For illustration, consider a possible alternate treatment of the fuzzy membership scores presented in table 9.2. A researcher could use the crossover point (.5) as a cutoff value, recode the fuzzy membership scores in table 9.2 into simple dichotomies (i.e., turn fuzzy sets into crisp sets), and then use the procedures described in chapter 5 for the analysis of crisp sets.

But what if a case that is almost fully in the set of ~cross-class and ~multiracial community organizations (fuzzy membership = .98) displays much weaker membership in the set of community organizations with ideological conflict (fuzzy membership = .55)? From a crisp-set perspective, this case is compatible with the argument that the combination of class and race homogeneity is sufficient for ideological conflict in community organizations. After all, it scores above the crossover point (.5) on both the causal expression and the outcome. But from a fuzzy-set perspective, this case contradicts the argument of sufficiency. It is almost fully in the set of community organizations that are homogeneous with respect to both class and race, but it is barely more in than out of the set of community organizations with ideological conflict. Thus, it clearly contradicts the argument that organizations that are homogeneous with respect to race and class are a subset of those that display ideological conflict. By analogy, imagine a student with a membership of .98 in the set "studied hard" and a membership of .55 in the set "performed well on the exam." This student would surely object to the statement that "studying hard is sufficient for doing well on the exam."

The second advantage of the fuzzy-set approach over the crisp-set approach concerns the sheer volume of evidence involved in each assessment of sufficiency. In the crisp-set approach, the investigator *selects* cases with a specific combination of set memberships and then

---

cases with 0 membership in a condition that passes this less stringent test of necessity, especially when the number of cases is substantial.

assesses whether they agree in displaying the outcome. Thus, each assessment of sufficiency involves a specific subset of cases. Referring back to table 9.1 for illustration, in a crisp analysis the investigator would focus only on the twelve organizations in the second column of the table to assess the sufficiency of the causal combination in question. In a fuzzy-set analysis, by contrast, the investigator examines all cases with nonzero membership in the causal expression and then evaluates their degree of membership in the set defined by the causal conditions relative to their degree of membership in the set defined by the outcome.[10] This evaluation is illustrated in table 9.2 and figure 9.2, which shows that almost all of the fifty community organizations are involved in the assessment. Thus, the fuzzy-set approach utilizes information on many more cases in each assessment, providing a much stronger empirical base.

The third advantage follows from the use of a larger body of evidence. In the crisp-set approach, researchers can conduct probabilistic assessments of sufficiency only when there are many cases conforming to a given causal expression. For example, using a benchmark proportion of .80 ("almost always sufficient") and a one-tailed significance level of .05, the researcher must have at least fourteen positive cases and no negative cases to pass the test (see table 4.9). Consequently, in a crisp-set analysis many causal combinations will have too few cases to permit a probabilistic assessment. In the crisp-set analysis of ethnic political mobilization presented in chapter 5, most of the eighty probabilistic tests of sufficiency failed or could not be conducted because of an inadequate number of cases.

This problem is remedied in the fuzzy-set approach. Every case that has nonzero membership in a causal expression is included in the assessment of the sufficiency of that expression. Thus, almost every assessment involves a substantial number of cases, and in most investigations researchers can apply probabilistic tests of sufficiency to all causal expressions.[11] As is well known, the larger the number of cases involved in a probabilistic assessment, the more useful and more powerful the

10. Cases with membership scores of 0 in a causal expression are not relevant to the assessment of the sufficiency of that expression and thus are not included in its assessment. If a case has a membership score of 0 in a causal expression, then, of mathematical necessity, its score in the causal combination will be less than or equal to its score in the outcome.

11. The number of cases with zero membership in a causal expression is equal to the number of cases with zero membership in one or more of the sets comprising the expression.

assessment. Thus, the use of fuzzy sets dovetails neatly with the use of probabilistic criteria to assess sufficiency.

ADVANTAGES OF THE FUZZY-SET APPROACH OVER CORRELATIONAL METHODS

The fuzzy-set approach offers several distinct advantages over correlational methods, as well. These advantages derive primarily from the set-theoretic properties of fuzzy membership scores.

At first glance, fuzzy membership scores appear to resemble interval-scale measures commonly used in conventional quantitative analysis. After all, both kinds of measures place cases on a continuum from low to high, and their units of measurement are both relatively meaningful, not mere rankings. Because of this superficial similarity, it might seem reasonable simply to correlate fuzzy membership scores. For example, a researcher might calculate the correlation between membership in a causal expression and membership in an outcome. A strong correlation between these two would seem to be relevant to the issue of causation, just as it is in conventional quantitative analysis. However, correlations between fuzzy membership scores by themselves reveal very little of value to researchers interested in unraveling causal complexity.

Consider, for example, the correlation between fuzzy membership in the set of community organizations that are homogeneous with respect to both class and race, on the one hand, and fuzzy membership in the set of organizations displaying ideological conflict, on the other. This correlation would show the degree to which membership in the set of "community organizations with ideological conflict" parallels membership in the set of "community organizations that are homogeneous with respect to both race and class." Suppose the correlation is perfect, $r = 1.00$. Does this mean that all the cases are on the diagonal and that, consequently, the causal expression is sufficient (and, in this example, necessary) for the outcome?

At first glance, this conclusion might seem reasonable, especially given the common practice of aligning a perfect positive correlation on the main diagonal of a scatterplot. But what if fuzzy membership scores for the causal expression range from .26 to .74, while fuzzy membership scores for the outcome range from 0 to 1.0? With these scores, the researcher would find roughly half the cases below the diagonal and half above the diagonal. In short, despite a perfect correlation, it is not possible to construct an argument of necessity or sufficiency directly from this evidence. From a set-theoretic point of view, membership in the causal expression is not a subset of membership in the outcome (sufficiency), nor is membership in the outcome a subset of membership in the causal expression (necessity).

Of course, the researcher might decide to rescale fuzzy membership in the causal conditions so that scores in the causal expression range from 0 to 1.0 (not .26 to .74). In the world of correlational analysis, linear rescalings are mathematically inconsequential—correlations are not affected. However, such rescalings have important substantive and theoretical consequences in fuzzy-set analysis, in effect changing the theoretical and substantive status of cases. For example, a case that was only "partially in" a set might become "fully in" a set, after rescaling membership scores. As noted previously, such rescalings often call for reconceptualizing the set that is rescaled (e.g., using modifiers such as "very" or "more or less"—see chapter 6).

When the main diagonal is used to indicate *equality* between membership in a causal expression and membership in the outcome, it is clear that a perfect correlation could show many different things about the nature of the link between a causal expression and an outcome. The exact placement of the regression line (i.e., the straight line showing the linear relationship between variables) relative to this diagonal is crucially important. Not only may the regression line fall completely above or below the diagonal, it may also cross the diagonal, as in the example just presented. Thus, one advantage of fuzzy-set analysis over correlational analysis is the fact that correlations, by themselves, reveal nothing about sufficiency or necessity. They indicate the degree to which two series of scores parallel each other, not their set-theoretic relationship.

The second advantage of the fuzzy set approach follows from a different shortcoming of the correlational approach. In the example presented in table 9.2 and figure 9.2, the researcher's argument asserts simply that organizations that are homogeneous with respect to class and race have ideological conflict. The argument does not state that only these organizations have ideological conflict. Instead, it leaves open the possibility that there are other conditions or combinations of conditions that may provide fertile settings for ideological conflict. Thus, it is quite possible, according to this reasoning, that there are many cases with strong membership in the set of organizations with ideological conflict but weak membership in the set of organizations that are homogeneous with respect to race and class.

While the existence of such organizations does not violate the researcher's argument in any direct way, these cases would seriously deflate any correlation between membership in the relevant causal expression and membership in the outcome. From a correlational point of view, cases that have strong membership in the outcome but weak membership in the causal expression (i.e., those in the upper left corner of figure 9.2) are outliers. Thus, they contribute substantially to the error sums of squares, to use the language of correlation and regression. While not inconsistent with the investigator's theoretical formulation, at least from a set-theoretic perspective, such cases would greatly weaken the correlation. The fuzzy-set approach makes it clear that such cases are not errors. Cases in the upper left corner of figure 9.2 are not errors because they do not contradict the argument of sufficiency. Viewed in this light, it is clear that correlation is not a useful tool for the analysis of sufficiency or, more generally, for the investigation of set-theoretic relationships.

SUMMARY

The examination of causal complexity, especially as manifested in causation that is multiple and conjunctural, is central to the study of social diversity. Everyday experience and qualitative research both indicate that this form of causation, where the same outcome may follow from several different combinations of conditions, is common. This chapter demonstrates how to unravel causal complexity using fuzzy sets to assess combinations of conditions. These procedures culminate in logical statements describing the different combinations of conditions that are sufficient for an outcome. The key to the derivation of these statements is the examination of fuzzy subset relationships. I also show that the fuzzy-set approach to the assessment of sufficiency can make much better use of probabilistic criteria than the crisp-set approach.

The only way to address causal complexity using quantitative techniques is with models that estimate complex interaction effects. However, most quantitative researchers in the social sciences today stick to additive models and avoid assessing complex interaction effects. Not only are complex interaction models difficult to interpret, but most of the data sets that social scientists use are too weak to support a thorough examination of these effects (see Ragin 1987, 1997). It is also worth noting that the variable-oriented approach to interaction effects works best when the researcher formulates a well-specified hypothesis involving interaction and then constructs an explicit test of that hypothesis. Thus, the variable-oriented approach of examining statistical interaction is most useful as a tool for testing well-specified theories, not as a tool of discovery.

TEN

CAUSAL COMPLEXITY

APPLYING FUZZY-SET METHODS

INTRODUCTION

This chapter presents detailed examples of fuzzy-set methods using data from previously published studies. Because these applications involve empirical data, and not data constructed specifically to illustrate a point, they address data analysis problems that social researchers routinely face. Presenting detailed applications of these techniques also provides a way to bring together the various pieces of the fuzzy-set approach presented in chapters 6–9, especially techniques for the analysis of causal conditions.

The first application is a reanalysis of evidence on "IMF protest" (mass protest against austerity measures mandated by the International Monetary Fund), based on a study originally published in *American Sociological Review* (Walton and Ragin 1990). This analysis provides a platform for addressing a range of issues in fuzzy-set analysis. The outcome, IMF protest, is truly a fuzzy set. Some countries experienced repeated periods of riots; others experienced only a few peaceful demonstrations. Thus, constituting the set of positive cases (countries with IMF protest) is not a simple matter. The constitution of the set of relevant *negative* cases is an even greater challenge. Should the study include all countries? All less-developed countries? Only less-developed debtor countries? Researchers must pay careful attention to the constitution of negative cases because these cases have important implications for the assessment of causal conditions.

The second example is an analysis of evidence on the welfare state in advanced-industrial, democratic countries, especially their different degrees of membership in the set of countries with "generous" welfare states. The main focus of this application is the problem of constructing causal generalizations in situations of limited diversity. The advanced-industrial, democratic countries differ substantially in their member-ship in the set of countries with generous welfare states. The causal conditions that account for their different levels of membership, how-ever, are highly confounded. Most of the conditions that further the development of generous welfare states are concentrated in Scandina-vian countries. They are only weakly present in such countries as the United States, Canada, and Australia. What should researchers do when they are confronted with limited diversity? What are the causal implica-tions?

While both examples offer substantive findings, they are constructed and presented in ways that highlight methodological issues. The anal-ysis of IMF protest highlights the problem of constituting popula-tions, especially negative cases. This analysis could have been based on a more or less "given" or taken-for-granted population (e.g., "less-developed debtor countries," as identified in IMF publications) and the problem of constituting the set of relevant negative cases would evapo-rate. As I have emphasized, however, it is often hazardous to base social science on taken-for-granted populations. Likewise, the selection of causal conditions in the second example, the analysis of "generous wel-fare states," is skewed toward causal conditions that are known to be confounded. Following Huber, Ragin, and Stephens (1993), this prop-erty space could be modified to include less-confounded conditions, for example, the fuzzy set of countries with strong Christian Democratic parties. However, the purpose of the second example is to address the problem of limited diversity, as manifested in strongly confounded causal conditions.

EXAMPLE ONE: IMF PROTEST

Background

Over the post–World War II period, and at an accelerating rate, the World Bank and its sister institution the IMF have become a dominant force in world financial restructuring and economic integration. As national economies have become more open to trade and investment, they also have become more closely tied to, and dependent upon, in-ternational financial institutions. Today, it is not trade and foreign investment alone that encourage the "liberalization" of national eco-nomies, but also the direct influence of the World Bank and the IMF, especially in developing countries. These countries periodically run into serious economic and financial difficulties, and their leaders often propose relatively drastic remedies such as radical currency devaluation or the imposition of tight restrictions on foreign capital. To forestall radical economic measures and the further erosion of investor confidence, the IMF steps in, coordinating a new loan package that typically involves a consortium of banks and devising a plan for restructuring existing debt (Walton and Ragin 1990; Walton and Seddon 1994).

IMF help is usually welcomed, but it comes at a price. As a condition for a new loan package and the restructuring of existing debt, the IMF typically makes substantial demands on the governments of debtor countries. In Russia in 1998, for example, the IMF demanded that the government set up a effective system of tax collection so that it would have some means for generating the revenue necessary not only for debt repayment but also for funding the day-to-day operations of government. Different conditions for new loans were placed on East Asian countries. In Indonesia, for example, the IMF demanded economic and financial reforms that would undercut the "cronyism" that is believed to be at the heart of this country's economic system. The net effect of conditions mandated by the IMF has been to further the "liberalization" of the economies of debtor countries, making them more like the advanced countries in their financial structures and also more open to international capital. IMF "conditionality," a relatively arcane topic in previous decades, became a matter of public discussion in the late 1990s, as economic crises spread from East Asia to Russia and then to Latin America.

IMF "conditionality" is not new. In fact, the IMF has long used debt renegotiation as a lever for economic and even political reform. In the 1980s many Third World countries experienced economic difficulties and called on the IMF for help. The IMF's conditions for new loan packages during this period were, in most instances, more severe than those typically imposed today. For example, in the 1980s the IMF often demanded the privatization of government enterprises, sharp reductions in government budgets, the removal of government price supports for everyday commodities such as fuel oil (used for cooking) and foodstuffs such as grains (used for making bread), and many other harsh measures. These "austerity" programs, as they become known, created great hardship in all sectors of debtor countries, but especially for the poor. In defense of the IMF, it should be noted that these strict austerity programs came at a time when *many* Third World countries were experiencing repayment difficulties and bank funds for restructuring debt were scarce. Still, many of these austerity programs were very strict, and they were sometimes counterproductive, dampening or delaying economic recovery.

One thing the IMF learned in the 1980s was that severe austerity programs sometimes spawn mass protest. In fact, a wave of "IMF riots" swept debtor countries in the 1980s. In some countries, austerity measures were rescinded, at least partially, in response to these protests; in others, governments fell. Some protestors declared, "Let the ones who stole the money pay the debt," a reference to the fact that some of the easy money that could be borrowed by Third World governments in the 1970s was either squandered or diverted to Swiss bank accounts. For a while, it appeared the IMF was more a source of political disruption than an agent of economic stabilization.

Defining IMF Protest

It is difficult to say exactly how many countries had IMF protest in the 1980s. Part of the problem is the fact that the category "IMF protest" is a fuzzy set. Virtually all countries have mass protest from time to time, and the IMF is a popular target of protest in Third World countries, whether or not the organization is connected in a direct way to any specific government policy or action. After all, the IMF is unquestionably an instrument of international capitalism, which, in turn, is considered by some political activists to be the root cause of human suffering around the globe. Another problem in defining and identifying IMF protest is the simple fact that IMF conditions for debt renegotiation are kept secret. There is no way to know for sure if a new government austerity measure is put into place to satisfy the IMF or for some other reasons. Thus, not all protest in Third World countries is austerity- or even debt-related, and not all austerity is IMF-mandated. On the surface a mass protest might appear to be against the IMF (with protestors carrying signs that read "OUT WITH THE IMF"), when neither austerity nor the IMF may be involved directly. Walton and Ragin (1990) address this problem by developing a relatively strict definition of IMF protest, weeding out other kinds of protest.

Measurement problems also abound. The most common data source for cross-national studies of mass political protest is newspapers, which are known to be biased sources. Suppose mass protest occurs in a relatively obscure country (i.e., from the viewpoint of U.S. journalists) on the same day that a national political scandal is discovered, and newspapers are filled with domestic news. An IMF protest easily could go unreported. Suppose a riot occurs in Mexico one day, and a copycat demonstration occurs in Guatemala the next, on a day when there is little in the way of important domestic news. The protest in Guatemala might well be over-reported and given special prominence. These issues of timing and coverage compound the usual shortcomings of journalistic data—the simple fact that reporters' accounts are often full of errors of omission and of interpretation.

In this example of the application of fuzzy-set methods, I assess countries' membership in the set with severe IMF protest, thus insuring that only the clearest instances of IMF protest receive high membership scores. I construct this and all other fuzzy sets in this example as seven-value fuzzy sets. With seven-value fuzzy sets, it is possible to transform relatively unsystematic qualitative evidence into a fuzzy set with seven levels of membership:

1.00: fully in,
.83: mostly but not fully in,
.67: more or less in,
.50: neither in nor out,
.33: more or less out,
.17: mostly but not fully out, and
.00: fully out.

To translate newspaper accounts to fuzzy membership in the set of countries with severe IMF protest, I consider both the number of separate events reported (frequency) and the severity of those events, restricting the temporal focus to the 1980s—the period of relatively harsh IMF-mandated austerity programs. Severity assessments incorporate several factors—number of reported deaths, number of reported cities involved, journalistic reporting of events as riots, and so on. Frequency ratings are based on simple counts of major protest episodes whether or not these events involved violence or rioting. To receive a high fuzzy-membership score in the set of countries with severe IMF protest in the 1980s, the evidence for a country must show both high severity and high frequency—that is, these two aspects of IMF protest must be combined. This approach to the assessment of membership in the set of countries with severe IMF protest sets a high standard. Only countries with strong evidence of repeated mass protest against the IMF receive scores of .5 or greater.[1]

1. Countries with episodes of less-violent protest (e.g., peaceful demonstrations and labor strikes) receive scores of less than .5.

Based on the available evidence, countries were assigned the following membership scores in the set with severe IMF protest:

1.00: Argentina, Peru
 .83: Brazil
 .67: Bolivia, Chile
 .50: Dominican Republic, Ecuador, Haiti, Jamaica, Morocco, Po-
       land, Sudan, Yugoslavia, Zaire
 .33: Costa Rica, Egypt, India, Nigeria, Philippines, Romania, Sierra
       Leone, Tunisia, Turkey, Venezuela, Zambia
 .17: El Salvador, Ghana, Guatemala, Hungary, Ivory Coast, Jordan,
       Liberia, Mexico, Niger, Panama

Note that there are *no* countries assigned the fuzzy score = 0. The
constitution of the set of relevant negative cases (i.e., countries without
IMF protest that nevertheless might be considered good candidates for
protest) is a separate analytic task. As I show subsequently, the specification of this set follows logically from the analysis of necessary conditions.

Causal Conditions Relevant to IMF Protest

It is not possible in one chapter to do justice to the complex topic of
the causes of IMF protest. A thorough examination of causes would
require a book-length manuscript based on years of study. Each case
presents a different configuration of political and economic factions and
groups, and each country has its own history—of state building, of
contention, of political-economic interplay, and so on. Instead, I offer
a broad-stroke investigation of structural conditions. Obviously, this
analysis is not a substitute for in-depth study of individual cases. However, my goal is to demonstrate fuzzy-set techniques, not to offer a
thorough examination of IMF protest. Thus, the analysis should be
viewed primarily as a reanalysis of the general structural conditions
examined in a previously published study (Walton and Ragin 1990)
and secondarily as a possible basis for further research on IMF protest.
This examination goes beyond the previously published report, however, in offering a more systematic consideration of political liberalization and government activism.

The original study demonstrates that two general conditions predict
IMF protest: "overurbanization" and "IMF pressure" (Walton and Ragin
1990). Based on quantitative analyses of evidence on protest in sixty
Third World countries over the 1980–87 period, the study shows that
these two conditions are the best predictors of (1) which countries ex-

perienced IMF protest and (2) which countries had the most severe IMF protest among those countries that experienced protests. In unpublished analyses of IMF protest incorporating data on protest events occurring over the entire decade of the 1980s (i.e., adding events from the late 1980s), we found that a conventional measure of urbanization performed better than the measure of overurbanization used in the published study. Because the analysis reported in this chapter uses evidence from the whole period, including the late 1980s, the simpler urbanization measure is used.[2]

There are various mechanisms that link high levels of urbanization to IMF protest, ranging from mobilization factors (urban populations are easier to mobilize for collective action), to political-economic factors (urban populations suffer the brunt of austerity measures), to basic social structural conditions (many Third World countries have experienced a concentration of poor people in urban areas). Thus, there are many different ways to explain the impact of urbanization on IMF protest. The interpretation of the impact of IMF pressure is more straightforward; after all, IMF protest occurred mostly in response to IMF-mandated austerity programs. Still, it is worth pointing out that in linear-additive models, IMF pressure overwhelms the direct effects of debt, economic hardship, and other indicators of economic conditions on IMF protest (Walton and Ragin 1990). Thus, it can be argued that it is not economic conditions per se that are immediately responsible for these events. Although economic conditions are correlated with IMF pressure, the proximate cause of IMF protest is IMF pressure.

IMF pressure is difficult to measure. As noted previously, negotiations between debtor countries and the IMF are secret, and there is no way to know exactly which conditions the IMF has imposed. To remedy this problem, the previous study uses evidence on number of debt renegotiations and restructurings, along with related evidence of actions that usually provoke or signal IMF conditionality, among them a high ratio of funds received by a country relative to its "quota," set by the IMF; use of the IMF's Extended Fund Facility; and the exercise of Special Drawing Rights. These various measures were combined to create an index of IMF pressure (Walton and Ragin 1990). This same evidence is used in the present analysis to assign countries different degrees of membership in the set of countries subject to IMF pressure. As with membership in the set of countries with severe IMF protest,

2. In any event, these two measures, urbanization and overurbanization, are highly correlated.

Table 10.1
Fuzzy Membership Scores for Countries with "IMF protest" (35 Positive Cases)

Country	Severe IMF Protest	IMF Pressure	Urbanized	Economic Hardship	Investment-Dependent	Political Liberalization	Government Activism
Argentina	1.00	.83	1.00	1.00	.33	1.00	1.00
Bolivia	.67	.83	.67	1.00	.50	.50	.33
Brazil	.83	1.00	1.00	1.00	.50	.50	.83
Chile	.67	1.00	1.00	.83	.50	.33	1.00
Costa Rica	.33	.83	.67	.50	.83	.00	.83
Dominican Republic	.50	.83	.67	.17	.67	.00	.33
Ecuador	.50	.83	.67	.50	.33	.67	.83
Egypt	.33	.33	.67	.17	.00	.17	.50
El Salvador	.17	.17	.50	.17	.33	.33	.33
Ghana	.17	.50	.50	.83	.67	.00	.50
Guatemala	.17	.17	.33	.17	.50	.17	.17
Haiti	.50	.50	.83	.17	.33	.17	.00
Hungary	.17	.33	.33	.00	.00	.33	1.00
India	.33	.50	.33	.17	.00	.00	.33
Ivory Coast	.17	1.00	.50	.17	.83	.00	.67

Jamaica	.50	1.00	.50	.50	1.00	.17	.67
Jordan	.17	.17	.83	.17	.17	.17	.17
Liberia	.17	1.00	.33	.00	1.00	.00	.33
Mexico	.17	1.00	1.00	.83	.17	.17	.67
Morocco	.50	1.00	.50	.00	.17	.00	.50
Niger	.17	.50	.17	.17	.33	.17	.50
Nigeria	.33	.33	.33	.33	.67	.00	.67
Panama	.17	.50	.83	.00	1.00	.00	.67
Peru	1.00	1.00	1.00	1.00	.50	.67	.67
Philippines	.33	.83	.50	.33	.17	.83	.33
Poland	.50	.50	.83	.50	.00	.17	1.00
Romania	.33	.83	.67	.17	.00	.00	1.00
Sierra Leone	.33	.83	.33	.67	.67	.17	.17
Sudan	.50	1.00	.33	.50	.00	.17	.00
Tunisia	.33	.17	.83	.17	.50	.17	.83
Turkey	.33	1.00	.67	.83	.00	.17	.67
Venezuela	.33	.33	1.00	.17	.83	.00	.83
Yugoslavia	.50	1.00	.67	.67	.00	.17	.83
Zaire	.50	1.00	.50	.83	.67	.00	.50
Zambia	.33	.83	.67	.33	.83	.00	.50

the evidence used in this assessment is indirect and multiple. Precision beyond seven levels of membership would exaggerate the strength of the evidence. Table 10.1 reports fuzzy membership in the set of countries subject to IMF pressure for the thirty-five countries with nonzero membership in the set with severe IMF protest.

While easier to measure, urbanization poses conceptualization issues. As a variable, it is usually conceived as "level of urbanization" and calculated as a ratio-level measure—the percentage of a country's population living in major urban areas. It is important to recall, however, that fuzzy-set techniques emphasize degree of membership in defined sets, not relative levels. In a conventional quantitative analysis, a difference of 20 percentage points on level of urbanization has the same causal impact regardless of whether this 20 points is between 0 and 20 or between 80 and 100. By contrast, with fuzzy sets it is necessary to define the relevant set and then assess degree of membership in that set. Thus, the impact of urbanization must be examined in terms of degree of membership in the set of urbanized countries.

To translate "percentage living in urban areas" to "degree of membership in the set of urbanized countries," it is necessary to define three qualitative breakpoints on the level of urbanization continuum: the point at which countries are fully in the set (fuzzy membership = 1), the point at which they are fully out of the set (fuzzy membership = 0), and the point or region of maximum ambiguity in whether they are more in or more out of the set (fuzzy membership = .5). As noted previously, all fuzzy sets in this example are seven-value sets. Thus, even though it would be possible to assess membership in the set of urbanized countries with some precision (as in the last column of table 6.1), in this analysis I convert urbanization to a seven-value fuzzy set. Fortunately, the distribution of level of urbanization is somewhat lumpy, especially once the three qualitative breakpoints are specified, and the conversion to seven values is straightforward. Table 10.1 reports degree of membership in the set of urbanized countries for the thirty-five countries with nonzero membership in the set with severe IMF protest.

Other Causal Conditions

The original study examined a variety of causal conditions, in addition to urbanization and IMF pressure, that might be linked to IMF protest: economic hardship, international economic dependence, and political conditions, among others (Walton and Ragin 1990). These different conditions can be linked to a range of arguments and perspectives, including resource mobilization theory, dependency/world-systems theory, and relative deprivation theory. As noted previously, these causal conditions are correlated to varying degrees with urbanization and IMF pressure; however, none has a consistent, direct effect on IMF protest in multivariate quantitative analyses (Walton and Ragin 1990).

In the reanalysis that follows, these different conditions are operationalized as seven-value fuzzy sets. Specifically, four fuzzy sets are examined as causal conditions, in addition to the two already mentioned (IMF pressure and urbanized):

1. *The set of countries experiencing economic hardship.* To assess countries' degree of membership in this set, a variety of economic indicators were examined, focusing especially on those relating to inflation and consumer prices from the late 1970s through the mid-1980s.
2. *The set of countries dependent on foreign investment.* Various sources detailing the amount and sectoral distribution of foreign capital formation, especially by multinational corporations based in developed countries, were used to assess countries' degree of membership in this set.
3. *The set of countries with activist governments.* Membership in this set is based on the size of the public sector (government revenue as a proportion of gross domestic product [GDP]), the role of direct taxation in public finance, and the accumulated years of experience of governments with the provision of social security programs.
4. *The set of countries that experienced political liberalization (1978–88).* Membership in this set is scaled according to the number of civil and political rights gained over the decade from 1978 to 1988. Countries that experienced a net decrease or no increase in political and civil rights were assigned membership scores of 0 in this set.

Fuzzy-membership scores for these four sets are reported in table 10.1, which shows the values for the thirty-five countries with nonzero membership in the set with severe IMF protest.[3] The membership scores for negative cases are reported subsequently.

Analysis of Necessity

As explained previously, the analysis of necessary conditions focuses on positive cases—instances of the outcome. The investigator, in effect, selects instances of the outcome and then searches for common ante-

3. Note that when deriving fuzzy membership scores for the six causal variables, all sixty countries examined in Walton and Ragin (1990) were evaluated.

cedent conditions. With crisp sets, the key question is, What causal conditions, if any, do the positive cases share? With fuzzy sets, the question is modified only slightly. The investigator asks, Do instances of the outcome constitute a subset of one or more causal conditions? If so, then the relevant causal conditions may be considered necessary for the outcome.

As shown in chapter 8, the subset relation between fuzzy sets can be determined by assessing the arithmetic relation between fuzzy-membership scores. If fuzzy-membership scores in the outcome are uniformly less than or equal to fuzzy-membership scores in the cause (yielding a "lower triangular" scatterplot), then the cause may be considered a necessary condition for the outcome and evaluated as such. The assessment of necessity may be conducted with or without the aid of probabilistic criteria, and it may include an adjustment factor to take account of measurement and translation imprecisions.

Table 10.1 contains all the raw material needed for conducting tests of causal necessity. With six causal conditions, there are twelve tests to conduct. Each causal condition is tested both in its original form (as reported in table 10.1) and in its negated form. It is important to test not only whether each condition (e.g., government activism) is a necessary condition for severe IMF protest, but also whether the absence of each condition is a necessary condition (e.g., the absence of government activism). Thus, the six causal conditions in table 10.1 were negated (i.e., their membership scores were subtracted from 1), and necessity tests were applied to the negated values as well. In this example of fuzzy-set methods, I use a probabilistic test of necessity with "almost always necessary" (.80) as the benchmark and .01 as the significance level.

Of course, with seven-value fuzzy sets, the assessment of set membership is very rough, and there are many opportunities for measurement and translation imprecisions. To make allowance for these imprecisions, the twelve tests of necessity were recomputed, with an adjustment factor of one level in the seven-value fuzzy scheme. With the adjustment factor in place, a case is not counted as a violation of necessity if its score on the outcome exceeds its score on a cause by *only one* membership level. For example, suppose a case's membership in the set of countries with economic hardship is .67 ("more or less in" the set with hardship). This case would be counted as a violation of necessity only if its membership in the set of countries with severe IMF protest is 1.00. A score of .83 ("mostly in" the set with severe IMF protest) would not count as a violation of necessity because this score

Table 10.2
Results of Analysis of Necessity, Applied to Countries with "IMF protest"
(N = 35)

Causal Condition	Proportion of Cases: Cause ≥ Outcome	Significance of Proportion > .80	Adjusted Proportion of Cases: Cause ≥ Outcome	Significance of Adjusted Proportion > .80
IMF pressure	.94	.03	1.00	.003
Urban	.94	.03	1.00	.003
Investment-dependent	.51	. . .	.69	. . .
Economic hardship	.69	. . .	.91	.07
Political liberalization	.26	. . .	.49	. . .
Activist government	.83	.42	.89	.15
~IMF pressure	.66	. . .	.80	. . .
~Urban	.40	. . .	.63	. . .
~Investment-dependent	.63	. . .	.89	.15
~Economic hardship	.77	. . .	.83	.42
~Political liberalization	.83	.42	.91	.07
~Activist government	.63	. . .	.77	. . .

is only one fuzzy level higher than this case's membership in the set with hardship (.67). Table 10.2 reports the results of necessity tests with and without the adjustment for measurement and translation imprecision.

Altogether, table 10.1 reports the results of twenty-four necessity tests: Each of the six causal conditions is tested in both its original and its negated form, and each of these twelve tests is conducted with and without an adjustment factor of one fuzzy level. Columns (2) and (3) of table 10.2 report the results without the adjustment factor; columns (4) and (5) report the results with the adjustment factor. Two conditions pass the test of necessity (with benchmark = .80 and significance level = .01): IMF pressure and urbanized. Without the adjustment factor 94% of the thirty-five cases have membership scores in these two conditions that are greater than or equal to their membership scores in severe IMF protest; with the adjustment factor in place, all thirty-five cases pass. With thirty-five cases a proportion of 1.0 easily exceeds the benchmark proportion (.80), using a .01 significance level (p = .003).

The next step in the fuzzy-set analysis is to evaluate the plausibility of these two conditions as necessary conditions. (Technically, it is an evaluation of the argument that these two conditions are "almost always" necessary for severe IMF protest.) Clearly, it is reasonable to argue that IMF pressure is a necessary condition for severe IMF protest.

Assuming the membership scores for these two fuzzy sets have been assessed appropriately, it is plausible to argue that the analysis should show that the fuzzy set of countries with severe IMF protest is a subset of the fuzzy set of countries with IMF pressure. A finding to the contrary would undermine confidence in the procedures. The finding that the fuzzy set of countries with severe IMF protest is also a subset of the fuzzy set of urbanized countries is less expected, but interpretable. As noted previously, the link between urbanization and IMF protest is, in a sense, causally overdetermined. There are many different mechanisms connecting urbanization to IMF protest, including basic enabling conditions integral to mobilization (e.g., the physical concentration of the primary victims of austerity and the simple massing of potential participants). As noted in chapter 8, necessary conditions often have an enabling character. That is, such conditions sometimes provide the context or setting needed to generate an outcome without producing the outcome in a more direct manner.

Note that the two conditions that pass the necessity test, IMF pressure and urbanized, are the same two conditions identified in the original study as the best predictors of IMF protest, using conventional quantitative techniques (Walton and Ragin 1990). Essentially, the fuzzy-set analysis of necessary conditions shows that these two conditions are not mere "predictors" of IMF protest but that in fact they are "almost always" necessary conditions for severe IMF protest. Thus, the analysis of necessary conditions just presented provides an important clarification of the previously published results. These two conditions place a *ceiling* on countries' level of membership in the set of countries with severe IMF protest. A country with weak membership in the set of countries with IMF pressure or in the set of urbanized countries can have, at best, weak membership in the set of countries with severe IMF protest.

An additional benefit of the fuzzy-set approach is that once necessary conditions have been identified and evaluated, they can be combined as jointly necessary conditions, using the principle of the minimum. As explained in chapter 6, membership in a compound set (e.g., the set of politically liberal Protestants) is the minimum of a case's memberships in the component sets (e.g., the set of politically liberal people and the set of Protestants). Using the fuzzy-set scores in table 10.1, it is possible to compute each country's membership in the intersection of the two necessary conditions, urbanized and IMF pressure.

The analysis of necessary conditions is outside the scope of conventional quantitative methods. There are two main obstacles. The first is that correlational methods conflate the analysis of necessity and sufficiency. These methods fail to distinguish between two very different kinds of error. The second obstacle is that it is impossible to assess necessity (or sufficiency) without the aid of qualitative anchors that define full membership, full nonmembership, and the crossover point. These breakpoints, established by the investigator, provide the means for arraying membership scores in a substantively meaningful manner. Without these qualitative anchors there is no way to assess set-theoretic relationships between aspects of cases. The conventional interval-scale variable, the cornerstone of multivariate statistical methods, lacks these important features. The conventional variable is anchored only by its mean, which is inductively derived and sample specific.

Identifying Negative Cases

The examination of necessary conditions just presented provides an important means for identifying negative cases—candidates for IMF protest that nevertheless did not experience protest. The basic argument is simple: If a country displays the necessary conditions for IMF protest (i.e., membership in the set of countries that are urbanized and subject to IMF pressure) but did not experience IMF protest, then it is a good negative case. With fuzzy sets it can be argued further that any country with nonzero membership in both fuzzy sets, IMF pressure and urbanized, is a plausible candidate for nonzero membership in the set of countries with severe IMF protest.

Altogether, twenty-five less-developed countries were considered for possible inclusion in the set of relevant negative cases.[4] Of these six had fuzzy membership scores of 0 on either IMF pressure or urbanized and thus were excluded from further consideration. A fuzzy membership score of 0 on either necessary condition yields a score of 0 on their intersection and thus a ceiling score of 0 on severe IMF protest— the fuzzy membership scores these cases actually displayed. Cases that score 0 on a necessary conditions and 0 on the outcome do not warrant further consideration. These cases could be considered "explained" and would be treated as such in a conventional quantitative analysis of data on "less-developed countries," conceived as a population. The inflation of the proportion of explained variation that results from these conventional practices, however, is somewhat artificial. In the fuzzy-set ap-

---

4. The search for relevant negative cases was limited in part by data availability. Any country lacking evidence on one or more fuzzy sets used in the analysis was excluded from the study.

proach, cases that display neither the outcome nor the necessary conditions are simply considered irrelevant.

This exclusion of cases lacking at least minimal membership in the necessary conditions for an outcome has virtually no parallel in conventional quantitative analysis. The closest analogue is the use of cutoff values to define populations (e.g., a random sample of "adults employed at least twenty hours per week" or a study of "countries with at least one million inhabitants and GNP per capita values not greater than $1,000 per year"). The use of such criteria is roughly comparable to using necessary conditions as filters, but the establishment of such criteria in conventional research is usually done on an ad hoc basis, with little consideration or analysis of possible necessary conditions. Typically these ad hoc criteria are employed simply to maximize the homogeneity of the cases included in a study and thereby minimize the number and influence of statistical outliers.

Table 10.3 lists the nineteen negative cases and shows their degree of membership in the seven fuzzy sets used in this analysis. Of course, these cases all have zero membership in the set of cases with severe IMF protest during the 1980s, and they all have nonzero scores in both IMF pressure and urbanized. Their scores in the other fuzzy sets (i.e., the four causal conditions that did not pass the necessity test) range from full nonmembership (0) to full membership (1). Judged from the perspective of their scores on the two necessary conditions, the "best" negative cases are Nicaragua, Uruguay, Honduras, and South Korea—cases with strong membership in both IMF pressure and urbanized.[5]

Note that these preliminary findings could just as well provide the basis for an in-depth, case-oriented comparative analysis. The best positive cases are the five cases with strong membership in both severe IMF protest and the necessary conditions for IMF protest: Peru, Argentina, Brazil, Chile, and Bolivia. These five cases could be compared most fruitfully with the four cases with high scores in the necessary conditions but full nonmembership in the set of countries with severe IMF protest (Nicaragua, Uruguay, Honduras, and South Korea). This case-

5. One issue not addressed in this analysis is the problem of identifying negative cases when no causal condition passes the necessity test. In this situation, the researcher is more dependent on theoretical and substantive knowledge. For example, a researcher might argue, based on theory, that any one of the conditions comprising his or her property space might be sufficient for nonzero membership in the outcome. Thus, according to this reasoning, any case with nonzero membership in at least one of the fuzzy sets found in the property space is a candidate for the outcome and thus a plausible negative case.

Table 10.3
Fuzzy Membership Scores for Countries Lacking "IMF protest" (19 Negative Cases)

Country	Severe IMF Protest	IMF Pressure	Urbanized	Economic Hardship	Investment-Dependent	Political Liberalization	Government Activism
Burma	.00	.17	.33	.17	.00	.00	.17
Central African Rep.	.00	.33	.33	.17	.83	.33	.17
Ethiopia	.00	.17	.17	.00	.17	.17	.00
Honduras	.00	.83	.50	.17	.83	.67	.33
Kenya	.00	.67	.17	.17	.33	.00	.50
Madagascar	.00	.83	.17	.50	.33	.00	.17
Mali	.00	.17	.17	.17	.00	.33	.33
Nicaragua	.00	.83	.83	.67	.50	.17	.33
Pakistan	.00	.83	.33	.17	.00	.83	.17
Portugal	.00	.33	.33	.50	.33	.17	.83
South Africa	.00	.17	.67	.17	.50	.00	.83
South Korea	.00	.50	.83	.17	.00	.83	.17
Senegal	.00	1.00	.33	.17	.67	.00	.33
Somalia	.00	.50	.33	.50	.17	.00	.17
Sri Lanka	.00	.50	.33	.33	.17	.00	.17
Thailand	.00	.33	.17	.17	.17	.67	.00
Togo	.00	.83	.33	.17	.83	.17	.83
Uruguay	.00	.50	1.00	.83	.17	1.00	.83
Zimbabwe	.00	.17	.33	.33	.50	.00	.50

oriented comparative analysis would provide important insights into key causal conditions, especially those that are sufficient for IMF protest.[6]

Analysis of Sufficiency

It must be admitted, first off, that the analysis of the general, structural conditions linked to IMF protest cannot pinpoint sufficient conditions in a strict sense. It is probably impossible to identify all the conditions sufficient for *any* social outcome. As in the analysis of necessary conditions, the analysis of sufficient conditions focuses on possible subset relationships between general causal conditions and the outcome. The key is to identify set-theoretic patterns consistent with an argument of sufficiency. Specifically, if it can be shown that fuzzy membership in a causal condition or combination of conditions is less than or equal to fuzzy membership in the outcome, then the researcher may argue that instances of the causal expression constitute a subset of instances of the outcome. This evidence, in turn, can be used to support an interpretation of sufficiency.

Of special interest in the analysis of sufficiency is the possibility that several different combinations of causal conditions may be linked to the outcome (multiple-conjunctural causation). If the investigator suspects that different combinations of conditions are sufficient for an outcome, then the analysis of sufficiency should address all possible combinations of causal conditions. The investigator evaluates the plot of membership in the outcome against membership in each causal expression to see if any conforms to the upper-triangular pattern. Points that fall above the main diagonal are consistent with sufficiency; those that fall below the diagonal violate sufficiency. The identification of patterns consistent with sufficiency provides a basis for pinpointing causal complexity, as expressed in multiple conjunctural causation, which in turn provides important keys for understanding diversity.

Because the analysis of necessity presented above reveals two necessary conditions, these two conditions are included as causal conditions in every combination of conditions subjected to the sufficiency test. If a condition is shown to be necessary, then logically it must be a part of every combination of conditions subjected to sufficiency analysis. In

---

6. David Collier (1998) argues that case-oriented comparative analysis can be seen as an analytic arena that researchers can return to at many different points in the research process. In this way case-oriented comparative analysis can work in tandem with both single-case studies and large-N studies.

the examination of sufficiency that follows, therefore, the two necessary conditions, IMF pressure and urbanized, are included in each evaluation. For example, when testing the sufficiency of the combination of economic hardship and investment dependence for severe IMF protest, IMF pressure and urbanized are included as joint conditions. A case's fuzzy membership in this combination of conditions is the minimum of its memberships in these four sets.

It should be noted that the inclusion of necessary conditions in the evaluation of sufficient conditions has only a very minor impact, if any, on the sufficiency analysis. Recall that the goal of the analysis of necessary conditions is to identify causal conditions with fuzzy membership scores that are greater than or equal to fuzzy membership in the outcome. The goal of the analysis of sufficient conditions (especially, sufficient combinations of conditions), by contrast, is to identify causal expressions with scores that are less than or equal to membership in the outcome. Thus, when necessary conditions are included with other causal conditions in sufficiency analyses, they rarely, if ever, provide a valid minimum because their scores are greater than or equal to membership in the outcome. Strictly speaking, the one situation in which a necessary condition would provide a minimum consistent with sufficiency is when (1) a case's membership in the necessary condition is equal to its membership in the outcome and (2) its memberships in all the other conditions in the causal expression are greater than its membership in the necessary condition.[7]

With four conditions, there are eighty sufficiency tests to conduct (a total of $3^k - 1$ tests, where k is the number of conditions remaining in the property space—the four conditions that did not pass necessity). Table 10.4 reports the results of these tests using probabilistic criteria. I use a benchmark of "almost always sufficient" (.80) and a significance level of .01, the same test used in the analysis of necessity.[8] To stream-

7. The use of probabilistic criteria, which permit a small number of violations of necessity and a small number of violations of sufficiency, complicates this picture somewhat. However, the general point remains, namely, that the inclusion of necessary conditions in the analysis of sufficient conditions has only a modest impact on the results of these analyses.

8. Note that the benchmark (.80) and significance level (.01) are relatively stringent. A more generous benchmark or a more forgiving significance level would allow more causal expression to pass sufficiency. These stringent criteria are warranted in part to counterbalance the generous allowance for measurement and translation imprecisions (one level in the seven-value fuzzy scheme). However, less stringent criteria would reveal more causal complexity and might provide a better basis for examining cases in terms of their diversity.

Table 10.4
Results of Analysis of Sufficiency: Causes of "IMF protest"

Causal Expression (N)	Proportion of Cases: Outcome ≥ Causal Expression	Significance of Proportion > .80	Adjusted Proportion: Outcome ≥ Causal Expression	Significance of Adjusted Pro- portion > .80
press·urban·dependent·activist·liberalization·hardship (21)	.714	...	1.00	.009
press·urban·dependent·~activist·liberalization·hardship (21)	.667	...	1.00	.009
press·urban·dependent·liberalization·hardship (23)	.696	...	1.00	.006
press·urban·~dependent·~activist·liberalization·hardship (26)	.614	...	1.00	.01
press·urban·~activist·liberalization·hardship (27)	.630	...	1.00	.009
press·urban·~dependent·activist·liberalization·~hardship (23)	.565	...	1.00	.006

line the presentation, I report sufficiency results only for combinations of conditions that passed. I present the results with and without an adjustment for measurement and translation imprecisions. As in the analysis of necessary conditions, the adjustment factor allows for an error of one level in the seven-value fuzzy scheme. For example, if a case has an outcome score of .50 and a score of .67 on a combination of causal conditions, it is not treated as a violation of sufficiency because its score on the causal expression exceeds its outcome score by only one level. However, a score of .83 (i.e., an error of two fuzzy levels in the seven-value scheme) on the causal combination would constitute a violation. (Recall that when testing sufficiency, the goal is to identify causal combinations that are subsets of the outcome—the reverse of the necessity test.) Columns (2) and (3) of table 10.4 report the results of sufficiency tests without the adjustment for measurement and translation imprecisions; columns (4) and (5) report the results with this adjustment.

Recall that when testing sufficiency with crisp sets, the researcher selects on the causal condition or causal combination in question and tests whether cases exhibiting that cause or combination of causes agree on the outcome. With fuzzy sets this is accomplished by selecting cases with nonzero membership in a causal expression and assessing whether their membership scores in the causal expression are less than or equal to their membership scores in the outcome. If they are, then the researcher may argue that the causal expression is a subset of the outcome, which in turn may be cited in support of an interpretation of causal sufficiency. Any case with a membership score of 0 in a causal expression is irrelevant to the evaluation of the sufficiency of that expression. Thus, the number of cases included in each sufficiency test varies according to the number of cases with nonzero scores in the expression. The relevant counts are reported in column (1), along with the name of the causal expression tested.

No causal combination passes the sufficiency test without the adjustment factor (see columns [2] and [3] of table 10.4). With the adjustment factor, six combinations pass:

press·urban·dependent·activist·liberalization·hardship,
press·urban·dependent·~activist·liberalization·hardship,
press·urban·dependent·liberalization·hardship,
press·urban·~dependent·~activist·liberalization·hardship,
press·urban·~activist·liberalization·hardship, and
press·urban·~dependent·activist·liberalization·~hardship,

where "press" stands for IMF pressure, "urban" stands for, urbanized, "dependent" stands for investment-dependent, "activist" stands for activist government, "liberalization" stands for political liberalization, "hardship" stands for economic hardship, the ~sign stands for not (negation), and midlevel dots (·) stand for intersection (combined conditions). The two necessary conditions are listed first in each causal expression.

It is possible to simplify this list using the containment rule. The first and second causal expressions are contained within the third and thus may be eliminated. Likewise, the fourth expression is contained within the fifth and also may be eliminated. After these simplifications, the remaining three expressions are the following:

press·urban·dependent·liberalization·hardship,
press·urban·~activist·liberalization·hardship, and
press·urban·~dependent·activist·liberalization·~hardship.

Simply put, the analysis of sufficiency shows that in addition to the two necessary causes, IMF pressure and urbanized, there are three combinations of conditions that are "almost always" sufficient: (1) political liberalization combined with economic hardship and investment dependence, (2) political liberalization combined with economic hardship and government *in*-activism, and (3) political liberalization combined with government activism, *not* being investment-dependent, and *not* experiencing economic hardship. Normally, the next step in the analysis would be to identify and evaluate the simplifying assumptions that have been incorporated into these results. However, the analysis of limited diversity is bypassed here because it is the key focus on the second example.[9]

Discussion of the Results

The first two sufficient combinations are very similar and can be combined into a single expression:

press·urban·liberalization·hardship·(dependent + ~activist).

This way of representing these two combinations highlights the causal equivalence of being investment-dependent and not having an activist

---

9. With seven-value fuzzy sets, the analysis of limited diversity is constrained somewhat by the small number of possible values. One way to redress this limitation is to count a configuration as lacking in instances only if all membership scores are below the crossover point (.5).

government. In essence, this expression states that a subset of the countries with severe IMF protest combine political liberalization, economic hardship, and either investment dependence or government *in*-activism (along with the two necessary conditions) and that their substantial scores in this combination distinguish them from the negative cases. Countries with the highest membership scores in this causal expression are Peru, Brazil, and Bolivia, followed by Chile and Argentina. These five countries all have very strong membership in the set with severe IMF protest.

Of course, the real test of this finding would come in a case-level evaluation. Does this causal combination help the investigator make sense of these cases? Does it make "more sense" where it fits better—in the first three cases just listed? The image suggested by this combination of conditions is consistent with scholarly and journalistic representations of these cases, especially the key sufficient conditions—political liberalization combined with economic hardship. The general point that is worth emphasizing, however, is that this finding is not an endpoint; it is a midpoint. The finding offers an analytic structure for the case-level interpretations that should follow. It is not a substitute for these efforts, just as reading a detailed trail map is not a substitute for taking a hike in the mountains.

The third sufficient combination differs in several ways from the first two. It combines government activism, not being investment-dependent, and not experiencing economic hardship with political liberalization and the two necessary conditions. This expression is suggestive of a very different route to IMF protest, with the key difference being the combination of political liberalization and government activism. In these cases the debt crisis may threaten to undermine the benefits of having an activist government. Note, however, that there are only three countries with discernible membership in this expression: Ecuador, Hungary, and the Philippines. Again, the real test of this causal combination is its value as an aid to the interpretation of these cases, Ecuador especially.

It should be pointed out that even though political liberalization appears in every sufficient causal expression, it is not a necessary condition. The analysis of sufficiency, just presented, does not account for all cases with IMF protest. For example, the Dominican Republic, Morocco, and Zaire all have .5 membership in the set with severe IMF protest, but they have membership scores of 0 in the three sufficient causal expressions. Recall that in the analysis of the sufficiency of causal expressions, a case's score on the outcome may exceed its score on a given causal expression by a wide margin. This gap does not constitute a violation of sufficiency because the basic idea behind sufficiency is that there may be several routes to a given outcome. Ideally, in the end, the investigator identifies all the different routes and covers every case. To account for every positive case in this analysis, however, it would be necessary to have a better specification of relevant causal conditions. Close examination of the failures just listed (e.g., the Dominican Republic) would provide a good basis for reformulating and augmenting the property space and then conducting a reanalysis of the causal conditions relevant to IMF protest.

Table 10.5 summarizes the results of the fuzzy-set analysis of causal conditions, showing each case's score in the set of sufficient causal expressions, its membership in the set of countries with severe IMF protest, and its score in the set defined by the two jointly necessary conditions. Recall that each case's score in the set of sufficient causal expressions is the maximum of its memberships in the causal expressions that pass sufficiency. This result follows from the fact that sufficient combinations of conditions are joined by logical *or*. When two or more fuzzy sets are joined by logical *or* (represented with addition), the membership of a case in this union is the maximum of its memberships in the component expressions.

As noted previously, a case's score in the conditions that are sufficient for an outcome sets a floor for its membership in the outcome; its score in the conditions that are necessary for an outcome establishes a ceiling. In general, a case's membership in an outcome should fall between the floor established by the sufficiency analysis and the ceiling established by the necessity analysis. Exceptions to this pattern result from the use of probabilistic criteria or from the use of an adjustment factor to allow for measurement and translation imprecision. Because the analysis just presented uses an adjustment factor of one fuzzy level (in the seven-value scheme), the floor can be as much as one fuzzy level higher than it should be, and the ceiling can be as much as one fuzzy level lower than it should be. Still, most of the positive cases have outcome membership scores between their floor and ceiling values.[10]

Two kinds of departures stand out in table 10.5. Among the positive cases, the ones that stand out most are those whose sufficiency scores fall well below their observed degree of membership in the set of coun-

───────────

10. I note, for readers interested in evaluations based on correlations, that the correlation between the average of ceiling and floor scores, on the one hand, and outcome membership scores, on the other, is .70.

Table 10.5
Summary of Fuzzy-Set Analysis of "IMF protest"[a]

Country	Sufficiency Score	Membership in IMF Protest	Necessity Score	Country	Sufficiency Score	Membership in IMF Protest	Necessity Score
Peru	.50	1.00	1.00	Panama	.00	.17	.50
Argentina	.33	1.00	.83	Ghana	.00	.17	.50
Brazil	.50	.83	1.00	Liberia	.00	.17	.33
Chile	.33	.67	1.00	Hungary	.33	.17	.33
Bolivia	.50	.67	.67	Niger	.17	.17	.17
Ecuador	.50	.67	.67	El Salvador	.17	.17	.17
Dom. Rep.	.00	.50	.67	Jordan	.17	.17	.17
Yugoslavia	.17	.50	.67	Guatemala	.17	.17	.17
Jamaica	.17	.50	.50	Nicaragua	.17	.00	.83
Morocco	.00	.50	.50	Uruguay	.17	.00	.50
Zaire	.00	.50	.50	Honduras	.17	.00	.50
Poland	.17	.50	.50	South Korea	.17	.00	.50
Sudan	.17	.50	.33	Portugal	.17	.00	.50
Haiti	.17	.50	.33	Togo	.17	.00	.33
Costa Rica	.00	.33	.67	Senegal	.00	.00	.33
Turkey	.00	.33	.67	Sri Lanka	.00	.00	.33
Zambia	.00	.33	.67	Pakistan	.17	.00	.33
Romania	.00	.33	.67	Somalia	.00	.00	.33
Philippines	.33	.33	.50	Central African Republic	.17	.00	.33
Venezuela	.00	.33	.33	South Africa	.00	.00	.17
Nigeria	.00	.33	.33	Kenya	.00	.00	.17
Egypt	.17	.33	.33	Mali	.17	.00	.17
India	.00	.33	.33	Burma	.00	.00	.17
Sierra Leone	.17	.33	.33	Thailand	.17	.00	.17
Tunisia	.17	.33	.17	Ethiopia	.00	.00	.17
Mexico	.17	.17	1.00	Zimbabwe	.00	.00	.17
Ivory Coast	.00	.17	.50	Madagascar	.00	.00	.17

tries with severe IMF protest. Several positive cases score 0 in the sufficiency analysis, and .33 or better on the outcome: the Dominican Republic, Morocco, and Zaire, all with .50 on severe IMF protest; and Costa Rica, India, Nigeria, Romania, Turkey, Venezuela, and Zambia, all with .33 on severe IMF protest. These cases are important because it is clear that there are other combinations of conditions that are sufficient for IMF protest—combinations involving causes not examined here. In-depth study of these cases, especially the three with .5 on severe IMF protest, would help identify other routes to IMF protest, involving conditions omitted from the property space used here. The biggest gap between sufficiency score and observed membership in severe IMF protest, however, is Argentina (.33 versus 1.0). Peru's gap is also substantial (.50 versus 1.0). Argentina and Peru are the two cases with full membership in the set of countries with severe IMF protest. These gaps reinforce the conclusion just stated—that the sufficiency analysis is not complete and that further in-depth research is needed.

Among the negative cases, the most salient are those that have high scores in the two necessary conditions, but nonmembership (0 scores) in the outcome. As noted earlier, these countries are the "best" negative cases. In-depth study of these cases would also provide a good basis for reformulating the property space. Specific factors present in these cases may prevent or neutralize IMF protest. Provided these same conditions are more or less *absent* in the positive cases, they might prove essential to understanding the occurrence of protest. More than likely, the positive cases would display varying, though weak, membership in these protest-inhibiting conditions.

The analysis just presented provides clear guidance for further in-depth research, pinpointing key cases, key causal combinations, and a variety of analytic strategies for gaining a better understanding of the causal conditions behind IMF protest.

EXAMPLE TWO: THE GENEROSITY OF WELFARE STATES

Background

The advanced-industrial, democratic countries (AIDCs) all have relatively well-developed welfare programs. These programs provide citizens with a safety net to protect them from many of the common threats to material well-being—unemployment, old age, physical injury, and so on. While having a good safety net is more or less universal among the AIDCs, there is considerable variation in how these safety nets operate and in how much protection they actually provide. A common contrast in the welfare state literature is between the generous, social democratic welfare states of Scandinavian countries (e.g., Denmark), and less-generous, market-sensitive welfare states such as those found in the United States, Canada, and Australia (see Cameron 1978, 1984; Stephens 1979; Esping-Andersen 1990). In this literature, Scandinavian welfare states are portrayed as generous because coverage is broad (welfare is seen more as a right and less as public charity), benefits are relatively high, and the quality of support programs for recipients (e.g., day care services) is generally good. In market-oriented welfare states by contrast, coverage is limited, benefits are lower (to discourage welfare dependency), and support services are spotty.

There are many forces that might encourage greater uniformity among the AIDCs in the generosity of their welfare states. Not only do all the advanced countries, except Japan, share a "Western" cultural heritage, they also participate in the same global economy. The impact of economic forces alone should be considerable because countries compete with each other more and more each day as markets expand and national economies interpenetrate. Some scholars believe that these forces should push countries toward a rough equalization of welfare benefits. Specifically, competitive pressure should force high-benefit countries to reduce their benefits as a way to lower labor costs and thus remain competitive (Leibfried and Pierson 1995). However, this "rush to the bottom" has not occurred, at least not yet. The diversity of welfare states that emerged in the 1950s and 1960s persisted through the economic troubles of the 1980s and early 1990s (when many Western European countries experienced very high levels of unemployment), and they remain in place today despite increased European and global integration.

Explaining Welfare State Generosity

What accounts for these enduring differences? One popular explanation is politics. Generally, countries with more generous welfare states also have stronger left parties and longer periods of rule by left parties. This argument follows from a perspective that emphasizes "the democratic translation of the class struggle," which itself is a spin-off from Marxist social theory (Stephens 1979; Korpi 1983). The clearest evidence in support of this perspective comes from Scandinavia, a region of generous welfare states and strong left parties. Their experience is thought by some to show the future of the advanced industrial countries: a gradual and peaceful transition to market-tolerant socialism, with social democratic parties in the lead. Empirical support for the thesis that strong left parties promote the development of generous welfare states has accumulated since the 1970s (Huber et al. 1993). Most studies show a strong, robust relationship between years of rule by left parties over the post-World War II period and the generosity of welfare states.

While most adherents to this perspective emphasize the strength and success of social democratic parties, it is possible to argue, somewhat tangentially, that all that really matters is having strong unions. Whether or not unions exercise power through left parties, they exist as an organized block with reasonably well-articulated interests. Moderate and even conservative forces could see a generous welfare state as a way to appease a highly unionized work force and undercut both the political appeal of the left and the power of labor. Thus, from this perspective, countries with strong unions should have generous welfare states, whether or not left parties win elections. It is worth noting as well that some countries' electoral systems are constituted in ways that pose institutional obstacles to the emergence of strong left parties (Huber et al. 1993). Under these conditions, union pressure applied to all left-of-center and moderate political parties might offer the best route to a generous welfare state.

Of course, other explanations of the differences among welfare states abound (Quadagno 1987; Skocpol and Amenta 1986).[11] One explanation notes, for example, that the countries with the most generous welfare states tend to be relatively small countries with "corporatist" industrial systems (Lehmbruch 1984). Smaller industrialized countries tend to have a relatively larger proportion of trade to GDP. Thus, they are more vulnerable to the fluctuations of the international economy. In response, many such countries have instituted centralized "tripartite" bargaining systems, involving representatives of unions, employers, and the government at a national level (Katzenstein 1985). These corporatist institutions negotiate wages, employment, and other key aspects of labor and industrial policy. Tripartite bargaining ensures both labor peace and economic competitiveness, giving smaller countries a competitive edge vis-à-vis much larger economies. In countries with

11. Wilensky (1975), for example, focuses on the impact of economic development and the changes in wealth and its distribution that are associated with development. More developed countries also tend to have a larger proportion of aged individuals, which in turn increases welfare state expenditures. See also Cutright (1965).

corporatist systems, welfare policy is typically treated as an essential part of labor and industrial policy (Wallerstein 1989). Thus, the safety net provided by welfare programs in these countries tends to be more generous than in other countries. In fact, in several of the more corporatist countries some welfare state benefits (e.g., unemployment payments) are distributed directly by unions (Western 1997).

Another explanation of differences in welfare state generosity points to the greater social and cultural homogeneity of countries with generous welfare states (Ragin 1994b). The Scandinavian countries, for example, are much more homogeneous in language, religion, and ethnicity than such countries as the United States, Canada, and Australia, populated by immigrants from many different parts of the world. Why should homogeneity matter? First, it is more difficult to win electoral support for generous welfare programs when the likely recipients of these benefits are seen as "different." In heterogeneous countries, middle-class voters are often reluctant to vote benefits for "minorities." Second, countries that are more homogeneous tend to have fewer obstacles to majority party rule in their political systems (Huber et al. 1993). Obstacles to majority party rule include such institutions as a strong presidency with the power to veto legislation, a supreme court with the power to declare legislation unconstitutional, an upper legislative house that is not elected on the basis of one person, one vote (e.g., the U.S. Senate), and so on. These obstacles (some of which are specifically designed to protect "minority rights"), undercut the power of democratically elected majority parties. Generally speaking, countries that are more homogeneous tend to have fewer obstacles to majority party rule and thus fewer political-institutional impediments to the establishment of generous welfare programs.

These different explanations of welfare state generosity were chosen for examination here precisely because they cite conditions that are highly confounded empirically. Alternate explanations, citing factors that are less confounded (see, e.g., Huber et al. 1993 who discuss the role of Christian Democratic parties), have been deliberately bypassed. All four conditions (strong left parties, strong unions, corporatist industrial systems, and sociocultural homogeneity) are found in Scandinavian countries. The United States, Canada, and Australia, by contrast, exhibit substantial deficits on all four conditions. Is it possible to disentangle these different factors?

In conventional quantitative analysis, independent variables compete with each other to explain variation in the dependent variable. If a causal variable has the highest correlation with the dependent variable and low correlations with its competitors, it wins the contest. When independent variables are strongly correlated (a situation of "multicollinearity"), however, the competition to explain variation in the dependent variable is distorted and compromised, and often it is difficult to declare a winner or even to assess the relative strength of the competing independent variables. For example, suppose that left party strength exhibits the strongest correlation with the generosity of welfare states, but is correlated at the .8 level with other independent variables. Would it be reasonable in this situation to declare this variable the winner and to credit theories that emphasize political struggle?

In the demonstration of fuzzy-set methods that follows, I offer a different approach to the problem of multicollinearity. Rather than conceiving of independent variables as strongly correlated and therefore hopelessly confounded, I argue instead that researchers should focus on their cases and assess the limits on their "diversity." This shift in focus from variables to cases follows the discussion presented in part 1. There I argue that investigators should construct property spaces defining kinds of cases and that they should make the evaluation of the different kinds of cases that exist an explicit part of their analysis, especially when it is likely that the diversity of their cases is sharply limited. As I show in the demonstration that follows, information about the limited diversity of cases can be integrated into the analysis of causal conditions. Specifically, this information provides raw material for identifying the simplifying assumptions that are often embedded in empirical generalizations.

Constituting Cases: The Advanced Industrial, Democratic Countries

In the examination of IMF protest, the specification of the set of relevant cases was one of the central problems of the research. What is IMF protest? Which countries are members of the set with severe IMF protest? How should the set of negative cases be constituted? In the present analysis, the set of relevant cases—the advanced industrial, democratic countries (AIDCs)—is not problematic, in part because its definition has been conventionalized by social scientists. There is relatively little disagreement in the social science literature regarding which countries to study when addressing questions pertaining to the AIDCs. Generally, scholars study the same sixteen to nineteen countries in most such investigations, focusing on those that combine being (1) *advanced*, used most often as a euphemism for rich, (2) *industrial*, used as a substitute for the somewhat discredited term "modern," and (3) *democratic*, used in reference to Western-style democracy—political systems that combine representative institutions and protection of political and civil rights. The time frame for these evaluations is almost always restricted to the second half of the twentieth century, and only countries that have been continuously democratic over this period are included in these studies.

If the selection of cases for the present analysis were to follow the same tack used in the first example, the first task would be to define precisely what is meant by *generous welfare state*. Armed with this definition, the researcher could then identify cases with some degree of membership (i.e., substantially nonzero) in this set. After constituting this set (the "positive" cases), the analysis of necessary conditions could proceed. This in turn would provide the basis for identifying negative cases—good candidates for membership in the set of countries with generous welfare states, which nevertheless failed to produce them. It is likely, though by no means certain, that this exercise would lead to the identification of being advanced, industrial, and democratic as necessary conditions for having a generous welfare state. Of course, if all cases with nonzero membership in the necessary conditions for generous welfare states in fact have welfare states with some degree of membership in the set of generous ones, then there would be no pure "negative" cases, per se.

Alternatively, the investigator might consider these three aspects (advanced, industrial, and democratic) as theoretically given. These attributes, in turn, could be conceived as fuzzy sets, and the researcher could assess the membership of all possibly relevant cases in these three sets. Formulated in this way, the investigator in the end might restrict the analysis to cases with membership scores greater than .5 (the crossover point) in the intersection of these three sets. It is likely that this exercise would lead to the identification of the conventionally defined set of AIDCs as the set of relevant cases. These countries all have strong membership in the three relevant sets.

In the interest of streamlining the presentation, I simply accept the view of the existing literature that the eighteen cases included in the present analysis are the best instances of "advanced industrial, democratic countries." The purpose of this strategy is to maximize the resonance of the fuzzy-set analysis with the existing literature.[12] The memberships of these eighteen cases in the five fuzzy sets used in the

---

12. The eighteen cases are Australia, Austria, Belgium, Canada, Denmark, Finland, France, Germany, Ireland, Italy, Japan, the Netherlands, New Zealand, Norway, Sweden, Switzerland, the United Kingdom, and the United States.

Table 10.6

Fuzzy Membership Scores for Analysis of Countries with "generous welfare states" (18 AIDCs)

Country	Generous Welfare States	Strong Left Parties	Strong Unions	Corporatist Industrial System	Sociocultural Homogeneity
Australia	.26	.25	.40	.17	.25
Austria	.72	.70	.64	.83	.67
Belgium	.79	.54	.84	.83	.29
Canada	.26	.00	.06	.05	.10
Denmark	.86	.85	.81	.83	.86
Finland	.76	.56	.86	.83	.72
France	.57	.12	.10	.33	.31
Germany	.68	.43	.20	.67	.30
Ireland	.67	.11	.63	.67	.84
Italy	.64	.10	.39	.50	.55
Japan	.52	.00	.04	.33	.95
Netherlands	.69	.33	.17	.83	.27
New Zealand	.56	.40	.54	.17	.15
Norway	.95	.95	.53	.83	.95
Sweden	.98	.98	1.00	.95	.70
Switzerland	.53	.34	.13	.67	.10
United Kingdom	.63	.61	.34	.50	.15
United States	.09	.00	.04	.05	.05

analysis that follows is presented in table 10.6. The five fuzzy sets are the outcome (membership in the set of countries with generous welfare states) and the four causal conditions that comprise the property space for this outcome.

The first set is the set of countries with generous welfare states. The assessment of degree of membership in this set is based on measures used by Gøsta Esping-Andersen in *Three Worlds of Welfare Capitalism* (1990) to construct his index of "decommodification" (the separation of welfare state benefits from labor market participation) and his index of "liberalism" (the degree to which means-testing is attached to welfare state benefits). Welfare state generosity scores were derived by standardizing these two indexes (converting them to z scores), inverting liberalism (means-testing is usually viewed as "ungenerous"), and then averaging the two sets of scores. The resulting index was then transformed to fuzzy scores by assigning cases with the lowest index scores weak but nonzero membership in the set, cases with the highest index scores strong but slightly less than full membership in the set, and then arraying the remaining cases in between these values, according to their index scores. These procedures place the bulk of the AIDCs above the crossover point (more in than out of the set of countries with generous welfare states), a pattern that is consistent with substantive knowledge about these cases—most have relatively generous welfare states. In effect, this fuzzy set reflects the "liberal versus social democratic" dimension that inspires much research on the welfare state in AIDCs.

The second is the set of countries with strong left parties. The assessment of degree of membership in this set is based on a measure used by Huber et al. (1993). For each year of the post-World War II period, the "cabinet share" of left parties (which can range from 0 to 1) is calculated for each of the eighteen countries included in the study. These values are then summed across years for each country, yielding a measure of the number of years of "rule by left parties." (When left parties comprises only a fraction of a cabinet, they receive only partial credit for the year in question.) The resulting index ranges from 0 to about 30. To convert these values to fuzzy-set scores, countries with 0 on the index were assigned fuzzy scores of 0, while countries with the highest scores were assigned fuzzy scores close to 1.0. It might seem reasonable to peg fuzzy scores according to a maximum possible score (i.e., a hypothetical country with the left party continuously in power). This strategy would assign relatively lower scores (e.g., .7 instead of .95) to countries with the most years of left rule in the present sample. However, extended periods of uninterrupted one-party rule, stretching over decades, are extremely rare in AIDCs. In fact, this pattern of party dominance, if it existed, would challenge the label "democratic."

The third is the set of countries with strong unions. There is great variation among the AIDCs in the strength of unions. Furthermore, the pattern over time is one of divergence, with some countries increasing in level of unionization and others decreasing (Western 1997). The most commonly used measure of unionization is the percentage of wage and salary workers organized into unions (Ebbinghaus and Visser 1992). To convert this measure to fuzzy membership in the set of countries with strong unions, only countries with a clear majority of unionized workers (well in excess of 50%) were coded above the crossover point (.5) on membership in the set of countries with strong unions. The country with the highest level of unionization, Sweden, was coded as having full membership in the set of countries with strong unions. Countries with unionization rates substantially lower than 50% (e.g., the United States, Japan, and France) were coded as having very weak membership in this set.

The fourth is the set of countries with corporatist industrial systems. The primary basis for coding degree of membership in this set is Lehmbruch's (1984:65–66) index of corporatism. He divides the AIDCs into five ordinal categories, ranging from weak corporatism (e.g., Canada) to strong corporatism (e.g., Sweden). To create a finer-grained system, I also used information on degree of union centralization, a precondition for corporatism (Headey 1970; Stephens 1979; Wallerstein 1989; Western 1997). The resulting seven-value fuzzy set arrays countries from very weak membership in the set of countries with corporatist industrial systems (membership = .05) to very strong membership (membership = .95). The extreme values of full nonmembership (0) and full membership (1.0) were not used. Thus, in this scheme "fully corporatist" and "fully noncorporatist" are ideal-typic conditions, not reached by empirical cases.

The fifth is the set of countries displaying sociocultural homogeneity. To assess degree of membership in this set, two measures were combined: an index of religious homogeneity and an index of ethnic/racial homogeneity. Each index was calculated using data on the proportion of the population in different groups (e.g., in major religious groups). These proportions were squared and then summed. The two indexes were then converted to z scores and averaged, yielding a single measure of sociocultural homogeneity. The most homogeneous countries (Japan and Norway) were assigned fuzzy scores of .95, while the least homogeneous country (the United States) was assigned a fuzzy score of .05, with the other countries arrayed between these two values according to their index scores. This fuzzy set treats the two extremes, full membership and full nonmembership in the set of countries with sociocultural homogeneity, as ideal-typic states, not reached by empirical cases.

Note that the membership scores for four of the five fuzzy sets reported in table 10.6 take on many different values (as in the last column of table 6.1). Thus, this analysis is not restricted to the seven-value scheme used in the first example, the analysis of IMF protest. A "fully fuzzy" scheme is used for these sets for several reasons. First, using a fully fuzzy scheme offers a good contrast with the fuzzy-set analysis of IMF protest. Second, the use of this scheme reflects greater confidence in the accuracy and relevance of the measures used to index set membership. Third, the literature on the welfare state is much more extensive and developed than the literature on IMF protest. The use of a fine-grained fuzzy scheme reflects the greater consensus in this literature regarding which indicators to use and how to interpret them.

While the literature on welfare states is more developed than the literature on IMF protest, it is important to point out that this example was constructed primarily to demonstrate issues surrounding the problem of limited diversity. Thus, the outcome and the causal conditions have been selected to highlight this issue. A thorough examination of the causal conditions relevant to welfare state generosity is far beyond the scope of this chapter. Note also that I have constructed fuzzy membership scores in table 10.6 so that the scores for most sets range from slightly greater than full nonmembership (0) to slightly less than full membership (1). This strategy was adopted, in part, to dispel possible suspicion that the limited diversity of the AIDCs in this analysis is due to restrictions in the coding of their set memberships (e.g., skewing cases toward the low end or the high end of each set).

Fuzzy-Set Analysis of Conditions Relevant to Welfare State Generosity

Analysis of Necessity. The first task in the fuzzy-set analysis of causal conditions is to assess necessity. As explained in the analysis of IMF protest, there are $2k$ necessity tests to perform, where k is the number of causal conditions in the property space. (Each causal condition is tested in both its original and its negated form.) As in the analysis of IMF protest, I use a probabilistic test of necessity with a benchmark proportion of .80 ("almost always necessary"). In this analysis, however, I use a significance level of .05, not .01. With eighteen cases, a proportion of 1.00 is not significantly greater than the benchmark proportion of .80 using .01 significance (see table 4.9). Note also that because of greater confidence in the measures used in this study, I refrain from applying any adjustment for measurement or translation imprecision.

In tests of necessity, the key calculation in each of the tests is the proportion of cases with membership scores in the causal condition that are greater than or equal to their membership scores in the outcome. If this proportion is significantly greater than the benchmark proportion, then the researcher has detected a "lower-triangular pattern" consistent with an argument of necessity. (A lower-triangular pattern indicates that the outcome is a subset of the cause.) The eight tests of necessity reveal, however, that none of the conditions is necessary for generous welfare states (results not shown here). The closest any of the eight tests comes to the benchmark proportion (.80) is .50.

It should not be surprising that none of the conditions in the property space passes the test of necessity. Recall that the set of relevant cases in this example is well defined and tightly circumscribed—the set of advanced industrial, democratic countries. In essence, the constitution of this set of cases as a more or less "given" set, with well-elaborated conditions for membership, establishes de facto necessary conditions for having a generous welfare state. The condition for membership in the set of AIDCs that is most difficult for countries outside this set to satisfy is that the country must be democratic. Almost all existing studies of the welfare state in AIDCs examine only countries that have been continuously democratic over the post-World War II period. This criterion excludes, among many others, Spain, Portugal, and Eastern European countries.

Analysis of Sufficiency. The next step in the fuzzy-set analysis of causal complexity is to assess sufficiency. Recall that the key concern in the evaluation of sufficiency is the identification of causal expressions (usually, combinations of conditions) that are subsets of the outcome. If a causal expression is a subset of the outcome, then a scatterplot of their relationship will reveal an upper-triangular plot. When a combination of conditions is a subset of the outcome, the evidence supports the argument that the combination is one of possibly several ways to generate the outcome. I use a benchmark proportion of .80 and a significance level of .05, the same values used in the analysis of necessity. I avoid using an adjustment factor for possible measurement and translation imprecisions, again following the procedures used in the analysis of necessity. Sufficiency is indicated as a possibility whenever significantly greater than 80% of the cases have membership scores in a causal expression that are less than or equal to their membership scores in the outcome.

With four causal conditions, there are 80 causal expressions to test ($3^k - 1$, where k is the number of conditions). About half of the eighty causal expressions pass sufficiency. When many expressions pass sufficiency, as in this example, most can be eliminated using the containment rule. For example, many of the causal expressions that pass sufficiency are formed from combinations of "strong left party" with other conditions. Because having a strong left party is sufficient by itself for a generous welfare state, any condition combined with strong left party also passes sufficiency. (The membership of a case in a combination of conditions is always less than or equal to its membership in any one of the component conditions.) Thus, the containment rule can be used to eliminate these logically redundant causal expressions. Eliminating all redundancies results in the following simplified list of conditions "almost always" sufficient for generous welfare states:

left,
unions·homogeneity,
corporatist·homogeneity, and
unions·corporatist·~homogeneity,

where "left" stands for strong left parties, "unions" stands for strong unions, "corporatist" stands for corporatist industrial system, "homogeneity" stands for sociocultural homogeneity, midlevel dots (·) stands for intersection (conditions joined using logical *and*), and the "~" sign indicates negation.

These results are easiest to interpret through the lens of sociocultural homogeneity. The first path is unaffected by sociocultural homogeneity. It does not matter whether a country has strong or weak membership in the set of homogenous countries. If it has strong left parties, it has a generous welfare state. The next two paths are limited to countries with strong membership in the set of homogenous countries. If such countries have either strong unions or corporatist institutions, then they develop generous welfare states. The last path is limited to countries that are not homogenous. Such countries develop generous welfare states if they have both strong unions and corporatist institutions. In effect, the last path shows that when there is low membership in the set of homogenous countries (an unfavorable condition), it is possible to develop generous welfare states if two favorable conditions, strong unions and corporatist institutions, are combined. Using language consistent with the logic of fuzzy sets, the results indicate that the floor for membership in the set of countries with generous welfare states is set by the four causal expressions just listed. The greater a country's membership in any one of these four expressions, the higher its minimum membership in the set of countries with generous welfare states.

Discussion

Table 10.7 presents detailed results showing each country's scores on the four causal expressions, their scores on the maximum of these four expressions, and their scores on the outcome. I report the maximum of the four causal expressions because a case's score in the union of several causal expressions (which, as noted previously, constitute alternate routes to the same outcome) is the maximum of its memberships in the separate expressions. Overall, the scores provided by the maximum of the four causal expressions are very close to observed membership scores in the set of countries with generous welfare states. Figure 10.1 presents a scatterplot of these two sets of scores, showing their close correspondence.

The maximum of the four causal expressions is provided most often by membership in the set of countries with strong left parties. For ten out of the eighteen cases, membership in this set provides the maxi-

Table 10.7
Fuzzy Membership of Countries in Causal Expressions Passing Sufficiency

Country	Strong Left Parties	Strong Unions· Corporatist· ~Homogeneous	Strong Unions· Homogeneous	Corporatist· Homogeneous	Maximum of Causal Expression	Generous Welfare States
Australia	.25	.17	.25	.17	.25	.26
Austria	.70	.33	.64	.67	.70	.72
Belgium	.54	.71	.29	.29	.71	.79
Canada	.00	.05	.06	.05	.06	.26
Denmark	.85	.14	.81	.83	.85	.86
Finland	.56	.28	.72	.72	.72	.76
France	.12	.10	.10	.31	.31	.57
Germany	.43	.20	.20	.30	.43	.68
Ireland	.11	.16	.63	.67	.67	.67
Italy	.10	.39	.39	.50	.50	.64
Japan	.00	.04	.04	.33	.33	.52
Netherlands	.33	.17	.17	.27	.33	.69
New Zealand	.40	.17	.15	.15	.40	.56
Norway	.95	.05	.53	.83	.95	.95
Sweden	.98	.30	.70	.70	.98	.98
Switzerland	.34	.13	.10	.10	.34	.53
United Kingdom	.61	.34	.15	.15	.61	.63
United States	.00	.04	.04	.05	.05	.09

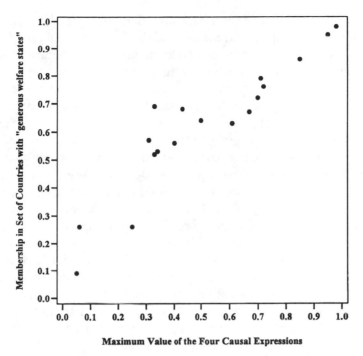

Figure 10.1 Plot of "generous welfare state" against maximum of the four causal expressions.

mum value of the four expressions, and nine of these maximums are unique. Membership in the set of countries with strong left parties provides maximum values close to outcome membership scores for Australia, Austria, Denmark, Norway, Sweden, and the United Kingdom. Next in the pecking order is the combination of a corporatist industrial system with sociocultural homogeneity, which provides the maximum for five of the eighteen cases. This combination of conditions provides maximum values for Finland, France, Ireland, Italy, and Japan. The remaining two causal expressions provide fewer maximum values. The combination of strong unions, corporatist industrial system, and low homogeneity provides the best account of Belgium's membership in the outcome, while the combination of strong unions and sociocultural homogeneity provides nonunique maximums for Australia and Finland. The United States and Canada have low scores on all four causal expressions.

Three countries have outcome membership scores that exceed their maximum score in the causal expressions by more than .20 fuzzy units:

the Netherlands, France, and Germany. The gaps are also relatively great for Canada, Japan, and Switzerland. In-depth study of causal conditions relevant to welfare state development in these countries would provide important clues for improving the property space used in this analysis. As noted already, the causal conditions examined in the present analysis reflect the strong contrasts between Scandinavian countries, on the one hand, and Australia, Canada, and the United States, on the other. As Gøsta Esping-Andersen (1990) has noted, the specific contrasts between these two sets of countries do not do a very good job of explaining continental welfare states such as France and Germany.

Overall, the results are consistent with dominant themes in the literature on the welfare state in AIDCs. If any single factor is emphasized in this literature, it is the importance of having strong left parties. However, as researchers in this field have noted, there are countries with relatively generous welfare states that nevertheless do not have strong left parties. The fuzzy-set analysis shows that having a strong left party is a sufficient but not necessary condition for having a generous welfare state; several combinations of conditions offer alternate routes.

While consistent with the existing literature, the fuzzy-set analysis just presented makes no allowance for the fact that the AIDCs are severely limited in their diversity. For example, the conclusion that having a strong left party is sufficient by itself for a generous welfare state extends well beyond the evidence. If a country has a strong left party but weak unions, will it have a generous welfare state? The conclusion that combining a corporatist industrial system with sociocultural homogeneity is sufficient for a generous welfare state also extends beyond the evidence. What if a country has these two characteristics but lacks strong unions? Will it have a generous welfare state? These and other important questions cannot be answered with the available evidence because there are no AIDCs with these specific combinations of characteristics. Thus, the results just presented incorporate assumptions about combinations of conditions that do not exist. What are the simplifying assumptions? Are they plausible? To answer these questions, an examination of the limits on diversity must be made an explicit part of the investigation.

THE LIMITED DIVERSITY OF THE ADVANCED INDUSTRIAL, DEMOCRATIC COUNTRIES

As noted at the outset, the various causal conditions that are thought to give rise to generous welfare states are highly confounded. The confounding of these factors is manifested in the "limited diversity" of the AIDCs. When diversity is substantially limited, as it is in this example, the researcher must assess its impact on the results of the analysis of causal complexity. In general, this assessment shows that simplifying assumptions involving combinations of conditions lacking empirical instances have been incorporated into the results of the analysis.

The assessment of limited diversity is always specific to the property space the researcher has constructed for an outcome. (The four causal conditions shown in table 10.6 constitute the property space for the present analysis.) The core of the assessment is the evaluation of the membership of cases in the different logically possible combinations of conditions defined by the property space. Recall from chapter 7 that a property space composed of fuzzy sets can be seen as a multidimensional vector space with 2^k corners, where k is the number of fuzzy sets. With four fuzzy sets, as in the present example, there are sixteen corners. Each corner, in turn, can be viewed as an ideal-typic pattern (Kvist 1999). For example, in one corner of the property space is the combination of full membership (scores of 1.0) in all four sets: strong left party, strong unions, corporatist industrial system, and sociocultural homogeneity. This corner, in effect, is the ideal-typic Scandinavian case. It is possible to measure the membership of each case in this corner—that is, to measure each case's conformity to the Scandinavian ideal type—by taking the minimum of its memberships in these four sets. In a similar manner, it is possible to assess the membership of every case in each of the sixteen corners, with each corner representing, in effect, a different ideal-typic pattern.

Analysis of the membership of each case in the sixteen corners (with each corner representing a different ideal-typic pattern) reveals that the following nine corners lack empirical instances. That is, no case scored greater than .5 membership in the following corners of the property space:

~left·~unions·corporatist·homogeneity,
~left·unions·~corporatist·homogeneity,
~left·unions·corporatist·~homogeneity,
left·~unions·~corporatist·~homogeneity,
left·~unions·~corporatist·homogeneity,
left·~unions·corporatist·~homogeneity,
left·~unions·corporatist·homogeneity,
left·unions·~corporatist·homogeneity, and
left·unions·~corporatist·~homogeneity.

Using a logical minimization algorithm such as QCA 3.0 (Drass and Ragin 1992) or FS/QCA (Drass and Ragin 1999), these nine configurations can be simplified to the following five expressions:

left · ~unions,
left · ~corporatist,
~left · unions · corporatist · ~homogeneity,
~unions · corporatist · homogeneity, and
unions · ~corporatist · homogeneity.

These expressions show explicitly which combinations of causal conditions lack strong instances. For example, there are no cases scoring greater than .5 in the combination of strong left parties and weak unions. Consequently, if a country has a strong left party, it has a strong union. Likewise, there are no cases with strong membership in the combination of strong left parties and weak corporatism. Thus, if a country has a strong left party, it has strong membership in the set of countries with corporatist industrial systems. The many other limitations on diversity are detailed in the list.

This list can be used to identify the simplifying assumptions that have been incorporated into the results of the sufficiency analysis. If a causal expression resulting from the sufficiency analysis overlaps with one or more of the nine combinations of conditions (corners) lacking good empirical instances, then it is only by making assumptions about these combinations that the researcher can argue that the causal expression is sufficient for the outcome. For example, the results indicate that having a strong left party is sufficient, by itself, for having a generous welfare state. However, the analysis of limited diversity reveals that among the AIDCs there are no empirical cases that combine having a strong left party with having weak unions. Likewise, there are no cases that combine having a strong left party with weak corporatism. Thus, the conclusion that having a strong left party by itself is sufficient for having a generous welfare state is valid only when accompanied by the simplifying assumption that if these other kinds of cases existed, they would have generous welfare states. In the language of fuzzy sets, the assumption is that if such countries existed, the floor for their membership in the set with generous welfare states would be governed only by their membership in the set of countries with strong left parties and not altered by their memberships in these other two sets. This is a very strong assumption.

Table 10.8 details all the simplifying assumptions that are incorporated into the four causal expressions identified in the analysis of suffi-

Table 10.8
Simplifying Assumptions Embedded in Sufficient Causes
for "generous welfare states"

Causal Expression	Simplifying Assumptions
left	left · ~unions · corporatist · ~homogeneity
	left · ~unions · corporatist · homogeneity
	left · ~unions · ~corporatist · ~homogeneity
	left · ~unions · ~corporatist · homogeneity
	left · unions · ~corporatist · ~homogeneity
	left · unions · ~corporatist · homogeneity
unions · corporatist · ~homogeneity	~left · unions · corporatist · ~homogeneity
unions · homogeneity	~left · unions · ~corporatist · homogeneity
	left · unions · ~corporatist · homogeneity
corporatist · homogeneity	~left · ~unions · corporatist · homogeneity
	left · ~unions · corporatist · homogeneity

ciency. I show all the configurations that are embedded as simplifying assumptions in each of the four causal expressions identified in the sufficiency analysis. Assumptions about six configurations are incorporated into the first causal expression (having strong left parties is sufficient for a generous welfare state). Assumptions about one or two configurations are incorporated into each of the remaining three expressions. The causal expression that incorporates the fewest simplifying assumptions is the second, the combination of strong unions, corporatist industrial systems, and nonhomogenous. The finding that the second causal expression incorporates only one simplifying assumption may make it seem more solid or trustworthy than the others. However, the important lesson to draw from table 10.8 is that simplifying assumptions play an important part in every sufficient causal expression derived in this analysis.

EVALUATING ASSUMPTIONS

One way to assess the impact of limited diversity on the results is to consider what the solution would have been if the analysis had been restricted to the seven configurations (corners) that have empirical instances with membership scores exceeding .5. Using this strategy, there are only twelve causal expressions to test, not 80. They are

left · unions · corporatist · homogeneity,
left · unions · corporatist · ~homogeneity,
~left · unions · corporatist · homogeneity,

left·unions·corporatist,
unions·corporatist·homogeneity,
~left·unions·~corporatist·~homogeneity,
~left·~unions·corporatist·~homogeneity,
~left·~unions·~corporatist·homogeneity,
~left·~unions·~corporatist·~homogeneity,
~left·~unions·~corporatist,
~left·~unions·~homogeneity, and
~left·~corporatist·~homogeneity.

Only the first five of these twelve causal expressions pass the test of "almost always" sufficient (benchmark = .80, significance = .05); three of these five, in turn, are contained within the other two. Using the containment rule to eliminate the redundant causal expressions results in the following alternate solution to the analysis of sufficiency:

left·unions·corporatist,
unions·corporatist·homogeneity.

These two expressions, in turn, can be factored for convenience to show

unions·corporatist·(left + homogeneity).

Far from confirming the causal power of having strong left parties, this solution highlights the importance of strong unions and corporatist industrial organization. In this solution, having strong left parties is but one of three conditions that must be present to produce generous welfare states, and it can be overruled, causally speaking, by sociocultural homogeneity. (When two conditions are joined by logical *or*, denoted by addition, the *maximum* of the two conditions provides the value of that part of the expression.)

Thus, limiting the investigation to the seven configurations with empirical instances leads to a much more restricted conclusion: To develop a generous welfare state, a country must have three ingredients: (1) strong unions, (2) a corporatist industrial system, and (3) either strong left parties or sociocultural homogeneity. This conclusion can be restated in a manner consistent with the logic of fuzzy sets as follows: The floor for a country's membership in the set of countries with generous welfare states is established by the minimum of its memberships in (1) the set with strong unions, (2) the set with corporatist industrial systems, and (3) either the set of countries with strong left parties or the set of socioculturally homogeneous countries, whichever is greater. In this more restricted view of the evidence, the path to developing a generous welfare state is much more difficult and demanding than the route shown previously (i.e., the path paved with simplifying assumptions, as shown in table 10.8).

While it might be tempting to avoid incorporating *any* simplifying assumptions and conclude the investigation with analytically prudent results, it is important to point out that simplifying assumptions can be used *selectively*. Their role in social research need not be all or nothing. In fact, the practice of case-oriented comparative analysis is dependent upon the selective use of simplifying assumptions (Ragin 1987, 1995; Hicks, Misra, and Tang 1995). Empirical cases rarely offer the case-oriented researcher the full diversity of causal conditions that would be needed to nail down a specific causal argument or generalization. Consequently, researchers often must engage in "thought experiments" involving combinations of conditions that do not exist empirically (see, e.g., Stephens and Huber forthcoming). In a thought experiment, researchers ask questions about combinations of conditions that lack empirical cases, constructing these combinations as hypothetical cases. They use their theoretical and substantive knowledge to answer their own questions. These answers, in turn, can be used to expand the scope of a causal generalization, adding hypothetical patterns to empirical cases. In effect, thought experiments provide case-oriented researchers with a rationale for incorporating simplifying assumptions.

Seen in this light, the combinations of conditions that lack empirical instances form a pool of *potential* simplifying assumptions. Each combination in this pool can be viewed as a separate thought experiment. Ultimately, the selection of simplifying assumptions for incorporation into a causal generalization must be grounded as much as possible in theoretical and substantive knowledge. The purpose of each evaluation—that is, each thought experiment—is to assess the plausibility of a nonexistent combination of conditions as a simplifying assumption. The researcher asks: If this combination of conditions existed empirically, would it generate the outcome? If the answer is "yes," then the simplifying assumption is permitted. Of course, if any simplifying assumptions are incorporated into a causal generalization, they should be carefully documented and thus made available for evaluation by the audience for the research.

Consider again the assumptions listed in the second column of table 10.8. After studying and evaluating these as potential simplifying assumptions, a researcher might conclude that several are plausible. For example, the researcher might argue, based on thought experiments, that the following combinations of conditions are permissible as simplifying assumptions. That is, if countries with these combinations of conditions existed, it is *assumed* that they would have generous welfare states:

left · ~unions · corporatist · homogeneity,
left · unions · ~corporatist · homogeneity.

Spelled out, this means that if a country has strong left parties and sociocultural homogeneity combined with either strong unions/weak corporatism or weak unions/strong corporatism, then it should have a generous welfare state. To add these two simplifying assumption to the solution, it is necessary simply to (1) expand the number of sufficiency tests, using the two new expressions; (2) determine which expressions pass sufficiency; and (3) use the containment rule to simplify the results.

With the two simplifying assumptions in place, it is now possible to test the sufficiency of the following four terms, in the addition to the twelve already listed for the analysis without simplifying assumptions:

left · unions · ~corporatist · homogeneity,
left · ~unions · corporatist · homogeneity,
left · union · homogeneity, and
left · corporatist · homogeneity.

All four expressions pass sufficiency. Adding these four to the five expressions that pass sufficiency without simplifying assumptions and then simplifying the results with the containment rule yields the following solution:

left · unions · corporatist,
left · unions · homogeneity,
left · corporatist · homogeneity,
unions · corporatist · homogeneity.

This new result reveals that if a country has strong membership in any three of the four causal conditions that constitute the property space, then it will have strong membership in the set of countries with generous welfare states. Thus, a country can have low membership in any one of the four sets but not two, and still have a generous welfare state. In more theoretical terms, the conclusion is that countries that are "mostly like" the ideal-typic Scandinavian country in terms of political economy—with strong memberships in at least three of the four key attributes—develop generous welfare states. Of course, the value of this conclusion hinges, in part, on the plausibility of the two simplifying assumptions that it incorporates. Other simplifying assumptions would lead to different solutions. It is important for the researcher to state and defend the simplifying assumptions that are incorporated into any causal generalization that he or she may derive.

This demonstration of the link between simplifying assumptions and causal generalizations may make the results of fuzzy-set analysis, and of configurational analysis in general, seem dependent on whatever simplifying assumptions the investigator is willing to make. There are several responses to this concern. First, it is important to note that the more limited the diversity, the greater the role of simplifying assumptions (and the greater the role of theoretical and substantive knowledge—via thought experiments). This connection is well known to case-oriented comparative researchers who routinely deal with very small Ns and a considerable number of causal conditions—situations of extreme limited diversity. Conversely, simplifying assumptions play no role when diversity is not limited. Second, while it is true that different simplifying assumptions yield different causal generalizations, an important benefit of the approach advocated here is that the connection between simplifying assumptions and causal generalizations is made explicit. Any simplifying assumption that is incorporated into a causal generalization must be documented. It can then be evaluated by the audience for the research. Third, note that the audience for the research is free to propose alternate simplifying assumptions and thus produce alternate causal generalizations. Fourth, it should be noted that all causal generalizations that might be produced from a property space for an outcome have as their core the causal expressions that pass sufficiency without simplifying assumptions. For the analysis just presented, these are

left · unions · corporatist,
unions · corporatist · homogeneity.

Thus, these two combinations of conditions will be shared by *all possible causal generalizations* that the researcher, or an audience for the research, might produce from this evidence.

The use of thought experiments to selectively incorporate simplifying assumptions underscores the interpretive nature of fuzzy-set analysis and of configurational analysis in general. These techniques are primarily intended as aids to the construction of portraits of social phenomena. These portraits, in turn, reflect the knowledge that investigators bring to their research. With fuzzy-set methods it is possible to uncover and evaluate the interpretive process that is at the heart of social research.

I should point out, as a way to conclude this example, that conventional quantitative methods routinely make de facto assumptions about combinations of conditions that do not exist. Further, these assumptions are rarely documented or evaluated by researchers. Imagine, for example, a conventional quantitative analysis of evidence on AIDCs with generosity of the welfare state as the dependent variable and left party strength, union strength, industrial corporatism, and sociocultural homogeneity as the independent variables (using the customary interval-scale measures of these variables). Regardless of what exact findings this analysis might produce in the form of a prediction equation, it would be possible to calculate predictions for various kinds of nonexistent cases with the equation that would result from this analysis. For example, the equation would permit calculation of the level of welfare state generosity for countries that combine strong left parties with weak unions and for countries that combine strong left parties with weak corporatism, despite the fact that the researcher lacks evidence on these two kinds of cases. In short, conventional quantitative methods are routinely insensitive to the fact that wide expanses of the multidimensional vector space defined by the independent variables lack cases. In this light, these conventional techniques are comparable to a fuzzy-set analysis that incorporates all possible simplifying assumptions (as in table 10.8), along with assumptions about linearity and additivity, without evaluating their plausibility.

CONCLUSION

The two examples presented in this chapter demonstrate a range of issues in the use of fuzzy-set methods. In addition to illustrating basic techniques for the analysis of causal complexity, they also show that fuzzy sets can be used to address difficult methodological problems that are beyond the scope of conventional quantitative methods. The study of IMF protest shows how to identify necessary conditions, based on the analysis of positive cases, and how to use necessary conditions to constitute the set of relevant negative cases. The analysis of the generosity of welfare states in AIDCs demonstrates (1) how to reconceptualize the problem of multicollinearity as an issue of limited diversity, (2) how to analyze limited diversity and identify simplifying assumptions, and (3) how to use thought experiments to selectively incorporate simplifying assumptions. The two examples offer very strong contrasts with conventional quantitative methods.

ELEVEN

FUZZY SETS AND THE DIALOGUE
BETWEEN IDEAS AND EVIDENCE

INTRODUCTION

After reading an early draft of part 2 of this book, a colleague wrote the following:

> Fuzzy-set methods demand that the analyst have a good command of the relevant theories and good-enough case knowledge to make meaningful judgements about measurements. Sadly, this will rule out these techniques for many scholars, especially those who prefer ready-made measures and methods.

There is a good deal of truth in these remarks. One of the paradoxical aspects of the use of fuzzy sets in social research is the inescapable conclusion that they demand more precision than conventional, "ready-made" measures. For example, it is a simple matter to assess the relative wealth of countries using a ready-made measure such as GNP per capita. This task requires only a reference book with good cross-national statistics. It is much more difficult, however, to specify countries' varying degree of membership in the set of "rich" countries. To specify the concept "rich country" it is necessary to have some knowledge of the world, especially the nature of global inequality. Take another example: It is a simple matter to find out if GNP per capita correlates across countries with a measure of educational development, say, secondary school enrollment as a proportion of the secondary school-age population. It is much more difficult to assess the set-theoretic relationship between fuzzy membership in the set of rich countries and fuzzy membership in the set of countries with well-developed secondary schools. Is being rich necessary for having well-developed secondary schools? Is it sufficient?

The answers to these questions depend in part on the way the relevant fuzzy sets are defined and constituted. Fuzzy sets reflect the theoretical and substantive knowledge and interests of investigators; they
are not "ready-made." Investigators who use fuzzy sets must carefully
define their concepts before they can assess the degree of membership
of cases in the sets corresponding to their concepts. Further, researchers must develop explicit criteria for assessing degree of membership
in sets and for locating full membership, full nonmembership, and the
crossover point. In short, investigators must infuse fuzzy sets with a
substantial amount of theoretical and substantive knowledge. Thus, a
fuzzy set should not be seen as a neutral instrument, comparable to
the way most researchers view continuous variables. Rather, it is the
product of the researcher's effort to interpret evidence in a disciplined
manner.

Fuzzy sets are most useful as tools of discovery. They inject new
sophistication into the interplay between theory and data. Because of
the close correspondence between fuzzy sets and concepts, fuzzy sets
transform and enrich this interplay. Fuzzy sets demand clear concepts.
Thus, researchers must clarify vague concepts and half-formed theoretical notions. Fuzzy sets also demand a well-grounded understanding of
evidence. It is not enough to know that a measure is a rough indicator
of some underlying concept. Instead, the researcher must possess sufficient substantive knowledge to determine the bearing of specific kinds
of empirical evidence on degree of set membership. Thus, in research
that uses fuzzy sets the dialogue between ideas and evidence is much
more demanding of investigators. Fuzzy sets compel researchers to dig
deeper into their theories and into their evidence, compelling them, in
effect, to engage more completely in the discovery process.

My primary goal in this chapter is to reinforce and extend the argument that fuzzy sets are useful as interpretive devices. I demonstrate
this idea in greater depth than in previous chapters. This discussion
emphasizes the analytic flexibility of fuzzy sets, especially the ease with
which they can be constituted and reconstituted to fit the concerns of
investigators. Before addressing their uses as interpretive tools, however, I evaluate the claim that conventional measures and methods offer
a "safe haven." This discussion addresses the likely perception that
fuzzy-set methods permit "too much" investigator input, that they are
not neutral enough. My response takes the form of a general discussion
of the implicit theoretical and substantive knowledge that undergirds
conventional methods—techniques that at first glance might seem
completely neutral, at least compared with fuzzy-set techniques. This

discussion of contrasts also provides the opportunity to summarize of some of the unique strengths of the diversity-oriented approach.

READY-MADE MEASURES AND METHODS: A SAFE HAVEN?

It is easy to champion the analytic flexibility of fuzzy sets, at least in the abstract. In practice, however, many researchers may find this flexibility daunting and seek refuge in ready-made measures and methods. Such tools appear to be both convenient and safe, especially from a career-advancement standpoint. However, researchers—especially social researchers—should avoid seeing any technique as neutral or even as "ready-made." To do so risks overlooking a technique's limitations.

While almost all social scientists would be willing to acknowledge that no method is completely neutral, it is not absurd to believe, as most do, that some methods are more neutral than others. Here, the usual concern is for each method's potential for biased manipulation. Most conventional quantitative methods appear to have a relatively low potential for biased manipulation, and this feature is viewed as one of their great strengths. For example, the use of statistical significance for hypothesis-testing purposes is supported by a large body of work in probability theory spanning decades of scholarship by statisticians. These tests have a conservative bias, favoring alternate or "null" hypotheses over those dear to researchers. While these and other features of conventional quantitative methods are extremely valuable to social researchers, these techniques do exact a price (Loftus 1991). Like many measures and methods that seem ready-made and therefore trustworthy and neutral, they are, in fact, laden with implicit theories and substantive judgements (Cicourel 1964; Sjoberg and Nett 1968). The many contrasts between the fuzzy-set approach and conventional quantitative methods highlight the assumptions and judgements that are embedded in these methods—at least as they are conventionally used. I summarize these embedded features here, bringing together various strands from previous chapters:

1. *The dependence of conventional methods on fixed, preferably "given" populations.* Before researchers using conventional methods can compute a single statistic, much less a correlation between two variables, they must demarcate and fix the boundaries of their sample or population. Once established, such boundaries are rarely questioned or revised. Instead, these boundaries reinforce the embedded assumption of case homogeneity and thus pose a barrier to the recognition

of heterogeneity and diversity. The fuzzy-set approach problematizes population boundaries and permits great heterogeneity, as manifested, for example, in causal complexity. This approach also allows population boundaries to be fuzzy rather than crisp. That is, cases can vary in their degree of membership in the set of cases relevant to a research question, and this varying degree of domain membership can be made an explicit part of the analysis.

2. *The dependence of conventional methods on an "accounting" approach to difference.* From the viewpoint of conventional methods, cases are similar if they have many aspects that are the same and different if they have many aspects that are different. In additive-linear models, similarities and differences are tallied, and cases with mostly similar scores on the independent variables receive mostly the same predicted values on the dependent variable. The embedded assumptions that permit this approach to cases are the following: (1) that all cases included in an analysis are members of the same population (i.e., case homogeneity); (2) that aspects of cases are noninteractive—that is, a case's score on one aspect usually does not modify the meaning or relevance or causal impact of its score on other aspects (i.e., additivity); and (3) that a case can offset its low scores on some variables with high scores on others (i.e., compensation). From a fuzzy-set perspective, however, cases are not always as similar or as comparable as they may seem. Sometimes a single difference between two cases can provide a basis for establishing a difference in kind—a qualitative distinction. The fuzzy-set approach implements its concern for potential differences in kind through its configurational approach to cases. Cases are evaluated in terms of their degree of membership in specific property-space locations, which in turn are conceived as ideal-typic membership profiles. Two cases are considered similar only if they both have strong membership in the same ideal-typic property-space location.

3. *The de facto dependence of conventional methods on simplifying assumptions about kinds of cases not found in a data set.* Limited diversity is the rule, not the exception, in the study of naturally occurring social phenomena. Once researchers identify relevant causal variables, they typically find that many regions of the vector space defined by these variables are void, or virtually void, of cases. When conventional researchers estimate statistical models using data that are limited in their diversity, the additive-linear techniques they typically apply to their data assume, in essence, that if there were cases in the vacant regions of the vector space, they would conform to the patterns

exhibited by cases in the regions that are well populated with cases. Thus, these models incorporate de facto assumptions about kinds of cases that are absent or virtually absent from the researcher's data set. Unfortunately, these assumptions are invisible not only to most researchers but also to the audiences for social research. In the fuzzy-set approach, by contrast, the consideration of limited diversity is an explicit part of the analysis. Not only do researchers identify simplifying assumptions, it is possible as well to evaluate the plausibility of these assumptions and then selectively incorporate those that seem plausible. The process of incorporating simplifying assumptions is explicit and visible. Furthermore, the audiences for social research are free to challenge such assumptions and to construct alternate representations of the same evidence.

4. *The dependence of conventional methods on a correlational understanding of causation, an approach that is insensitive to necessity and sufficiency.* Bivariate correlation, in one way or another, constitutes the backbone of most conventional forms of quantitative analysis. Even a complex multivariate model involving estimates of the net effects of many causal variables on an outcome variable is based, in the end, on a table of bivariate correlations. While very powerful as an analytical tool, the correlational approach to causation is incapable of addressing set-theoretic relationships. Is the outcome a subset of one or more causes (necessity)? Is a cause or causal combination a subset of the outcome (sufficiency)? While it is possible to discern set-theoretic relationships in cross-tabulations of categorical data, few statistical techniques focus on such relationships. The correlational approach to causation equates all prediction errors, whether they constitute violations of necessity or sufficiency, and counts all cases in the ambiguous null-null location, where neither the cause nor the outcome is present, as correct predictions. More telling is the simple fact that the study of set-theoretic relationships is completely outside the scope of techniques that use interval and ratio-scale variables. With these measures, the usual focus is on covariance; set-theoretic relationships, the core of the fuzzy-set approach, are inaccessible. In the correlational view, causes do not delimit possibilities (necessity), nor do they combine in different ways to generate outcomes (sufficiency). Rather, each cause increases or decreases the level or probability of an outcome, net of the effects of other relevant causes.

5. *The dependence of conventional methods on additive, linear models and their consequent inability to unravel causal complexity.* If no single cause is either necessary or sufficient for an outcome (i.e., maximum

causal complexity), then there is little point in examining bivariate relationships or assessing the "net effects" of "independent" variables. To assess causal complexity with conventional multivariate techniques, researchers must use interaction models. Generally, such models work well when (1) the number of cases is very large, (2) the cases are fully diverse (i.e., limited diversity is not present), and (3) the number of independent variables is relatively small. When these conditions are not met, interaction terms tend to be highly collinear, and many different interaction models fit a given data set equally well. In short, when faced with causal complexity, conventional techniques are often confounded. For this reason, researchers are always warned to start with models that assumes perfect additivity (i.e., extreme causal simplicity) and then to add interaction terms (two-way terms first, then three-way terms if several two-way terms pass, and so on) only if the inclusion of interaction terms is strongly supported by both theory and evidence. In general, this is very good advice for users of conventional methods. However, causation is not always as simple as it seems, and it is likely that assuming simplicity merely relegates causal complexity to the error vector of additive models.

6. *The reliance of conventional methods on open-ended "variables" containing unspecified and often unknown quantities of irrelevant variation.* The "variable" is central to conventional social research. The ideal variable is usually portrayed as an interval- or ratio-scale measure, and researchers usually are advised to maximize the variation that each variable exhibits. When variables display a wide range of values (and thus more variation), it is possible to derive better estimates of their effects in multivariate analyses. Generally, the advice to maximize variation is sound. Imagine trying to assess the impact of income on party identification using income values that range from $20,000 to $25,000. While it is generally true that more variation is better than less, it is *not* true that all variation is meaningful. Thus, the assumption that "variation must be maximized" should not be accepted uncritically. The meaningfulness of variation depends on the research question that is being asked and the concepts that are relevant to that question. Consider, for example, the researcher interested in studying the impact of having "too little" income on food consumption. Social scientists know how to conduct a survey asking respondents about their income and how to find out who has more and who has less. That is, they are very good at making relative assessments. But what's *a lot* of income? How much is *too little*?

How many people have *enough?* How many have *far too little?* If the research question concerns the impact of having too little income, then most of the variation in the upper range of income is simply irrelevant. To answer questions that address specific ranges of values (e.g., "too little" or "enough"), it is necessary to go outside the data set and to find out about people—how they live and how they spend their money. This knowledge can be used to develop qualitative anchors that distinguish relevant from irrelevant variation, a central concern of the fuzzy-set approach.

7. *The dependence of conventional methods on mechanistically derived anchors to structure the interpretation of scores.* Most conventional methods of data analysis focus on covariation and correlation—an assessment of the degree to which the values of variables go together. If high values on one variable tend to go with high values on another, and low values with low values, then there is a positive correlation. The definition of "high" versus "low," however, is determined by the means and standard deviations of the relevant variables, which, in turn, are derived mechanistically from the sample in question. For example, a researcher might compute the mean level of income and its standard deviation for a sample of individuals and use these values to define "low" and "high" income levels. Note, however, that the resulting evaluation of income is strictly in terms of *relative* levels within that sample. Note also that these statistics equate very different kinds of income gaps. For example, one single standard deviation unit might separate the well off from the rich, on the one hand, and the destitute from the working poor, on the other. Thus, this "ready-made" measure is only a measure of *relative* income; it is dependent on mechanistically derived anchors, and it treats all variation the same, no matter where in the range of values it occurs. With fuzzy sets, by contrast, "high" and "low" are defined in term of strong and weak membership in sets, using criteria specified by the researcher. These criteria, in turn, are based on the researcher's knowledge. They are not sample specific, nor are they mechanistically derived.

Most of the features of conventional methods just sketched are embedded in these techniques for good reasons. They equip this approach with powerful theory-testing tools. However, theory testing is not the only goal of social science. The very features of the conventional approach that make it useful for testing theories interfere with its use as a tool of discovery, especially when the goal is to study difference and diversity (Richters 1997). The fuzzy-set approach, by contrast, offers tools for conducting a rich, discovery-oriented dialogue between ideas and evidence, tools that challenge conventional conceptions of cases, populations, variables, variation, correlation, and causation.

There is no denying that the dialogue between ideas and evidence in research that uses fuzzy sets is heavily knowledge- and theory-dependent. It is impossible even to construct a useful fuzzy set without a good foundation of knowledge. However, the integration of theoretical and substantive knowledge into fuzzy-set analysis is an explicit feature of the approach. By contrast, the integration of specific understandings of cases, populations, causation, variation, and so on into conventional methods is more implicit than explicit. Furthermore, these embedded understandings are often invisible to both researchers and their audiences. One of the great strengths of the fuzzy-set approach is that the key decisions that structure the analysis must be made explicit by the investigator and are open to evaluation by the audiences for the research. These decisions include, among others: (1) the constitution of the population and specification of each case's degree of domain membership, (2) the conceptualization and definition of the fuzzy sets that structure the analysis, (3) the specification of fuzzy membership scores, along with the qualitative anchors that are used to define breakpoints on continua, (4) the specification of benchmarks and related criteria for the assessment of necessity and sufficiency, (5) the use of theoretical and substantive knowledge to evaluate and interpret the results of these tests, (6) the assessment of the impact of limited diversity on empirical generalizations, and (7) the evaluation of the plausibility of simplifying assumptions and their selective incorporation into generalizations.

INTERPRETIVE ASPECTS AND USES OF FUZZY SETS

Fuzzy-set methods offer researchers a means for integrating theoretical development and empirical analysis. In effect, they provide an interpretive algebra, a language that is half verbal-conceptual and half mathematical-analytical. Consequently, fuzzy sets are as flexible as theoretical concepts. Researchers who are not able to pin down their ideas or their concepts will not be able to pin down their fuzzy sets, either. However, it is possible to exploit the close correspondence between concepts and fuzzy sets to enrich the interaction between theory and data analysis and thus strengthen discovery in social research. As researchers learn more about their cases, they can use this knowledge to refine their specification of fuzzy sets, which, in turn, may provide new interpretive insights about cases and their diversity.

Research that uses fuzzy sets may proceed in a grounded, back-and-forth manner. As this section demonstrates, fuzzy sets often coalesce in the course of an investigation, through a process that parallels "double fitting," a core technique in qualitative inquiry (see Katz 1982; Ragin 1994a). The technique of double fitting comes from the practice of analytic induction (Angell [1936] 1965; Lindesmith 1947; Becker 1953). With this technique researchers use empirical evidence to sharpen and elaborate their theoretical concepts, while at the same time using their theoretical concepts to clarify and delimit their empirical categories. This back-and-forth process is one of progressive refinement, resulting in a mutual clarification of theoretical concepts and empirical categories. In a similar manner, it is often necessary in fuzzy-set analysis for researchers to work back-and-forth between their specification of membership criteria for fuzzy sets, on the one hand, and their empirical analysis of set-theoretic relationships, on the other. In this way, the construction of fuzzy sets becomes a central part of the discovery process.

The potential enhancements to the interaction between theory and data offered by fuzzy sets are many. I discuss three here: (1) the interplay between empirical analysis and the specification of fuzzy membership scores, (2) different ways of combining fuzzy sets to generate "higher-order" constructs, and (3) the interaction between the use of modifiers such as "very," "more or less," and "not" and the assessment of sufficiency and necessity.

The Discovery of Qualitative Anchors

While it is often possible to identify interval- or ratio-scale measures that can be used to gauge membership in fuzzy sets (e.g., using GNP per capita to index membership in the fuzzy set of rich countries), it is not always a simple matter to translate such measures to fuzzy membership scores. The key issue here is the identification of the three qualitative anchors—full membership, full nonmembership, and the crossover point—that structure fuzzy-set membership scores. The problem with conventional interval- and ratio-scale measures is that they reveal only the *relative* positions of cases in a distribution. They rarely indicate how much is "a lot" or how much is "a little."

Qualitative anchors often can be identified through a process of discovery, and a fuzzy set may coalesce in the research process in much the same way that interpretive categories coalesce in the course of qualitative inquiry. Of special value in any effort to identify qualitative anchors is the subset relationship. If theory or substantive knowledge leads the investigator to expect one fuzzy set to be a subset of another (e.g., the expectation that the set of countries with severe IMF protest should be a subset of the countries experiencing IMF pressure), this information can be used to help guide the construction of fuzzy sets.

For illustration, consider the simple example used in chapter 8—the idea that practice shooting baskets ("practicing a lot") is a necessary but not sufficient condition for scoring many point in basketball games ("scoring a lot"). Imagine a researcher trying to document this relationship for twelve-year-old boys playing in a park district league. First, he would collect two important pieces of information about these players: the average number of hours per week each boy practices shooting baskets and the average number of points per game each boy scores. Next, he would transform these two ratio-scale measures into fuzzy sets. But how?

Of course, there are many ways to proceed at this point. One way would be to ask the boys, How much practice is "a lot"? How much is "only a little"? How many points scored in games is "a lot"? How many is "only a little"? Their replies could be used to translate the ratio-scale measures of practicing and scoring to fuzzy-set scores. A more mechanistic approach would be to use conventional distributional criteria. Boys who practice greater than 1.5 standard deviations above the mean hours of practice could be rated as having full membership in the set of boys who practice "a lot," and those who practice 1.5 or more standard deviations below the mean could be scored as having full non-membership in this set. Still another approach would be to base these judgements on the researcher's own in-depth knowledge gained though observation. Still another would be to rely on the coaches' assessments.

No matter what the source of the initial scheme for translating scores on the two ratio-scale measures into fuzzy membership scores (players versus coaches versus ethnography versus distributional criteria), it is important to recognize that the initial scheme should be open to revision—it should be viewed as preliminary. Suppose, for example, that the researcher decided to rely on the coaches' views for the definitions of these two fuzzy sets. Suppose further that the plot of the resulting fuzzy sets following from the coach-based translation scheme resulted in the plot shown in figure 11.1. Note that this plot has the lower-triangular shape characteristic of necessity without sufficiency, but the diagonal is too high. Basically, there is substantial variation in the lower ranges of "scores a lot" that appears to be irrelevant to the set-theoretic

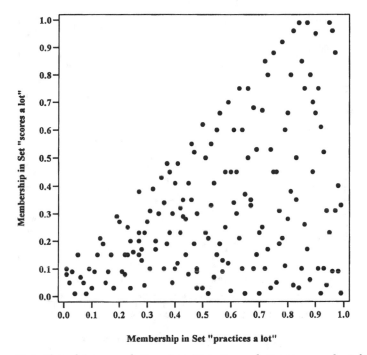

Figure 11.1 Plot of "scores a lot" against "practices a lot" using coaches' definitions.

relationship in question, and there is substantial variation in the upper range of "practices a lot" that also appears to be irrelevant.

From a practical standpoint it is a simple matter to rescale these fuzzy sets so that the values are more consistent with a pattern of necessity (where outcome membership scores are less than or equal to scores in the causal condition). Low values on "scores a lot" can be truncated to .10, and then the fuzzy set rescaled, as follows:

1. recode old "scores a lot": lowest score through .10 equals .10,
2. rescale scores: new "scores a lot" = (old "scores a lot" − .10)/.90.

Likewise, fuzzy scores on "practices a lot" can be transformed to truncate the irrelevant variation in its upper range:

1. recode old "practices a lot": .85 through 1.0 equals .85,
2. rescale scores: new "practices a lot" = (old "practices a lot")/.85.

After these transformations, the plot is much more consistent with an argument of necessity, as shown in figure 11.2. But are these transformations warranted? Can they be justified?

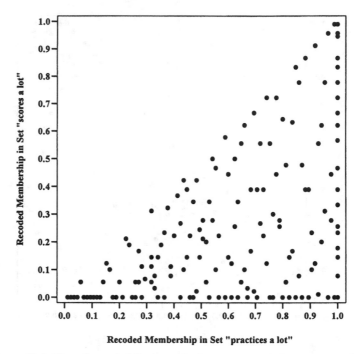

Figure 11.2 Plot of recoded "scores a lot" against recoded "practices a lot."

Suppose, based on observations of league play, the researcher concludes that coaches have several characteristic biases. In order to get the most out of their players, they tend to exaggerate the value of scoring points for players who are not consistent scorers, and they tend to exaggerate the value of additional practice for players who already practice regularly. These specific biases would lead them to pay special attention to the two ranges of set membership that appear less relevant in figure 11.1—the lower ranges of "scores a lot" and the upper ranges of "practices a lot." These biases, if observed, could be used by the investigator to justify the rescaling of the fuzzy membership scores, as just described.

In this example, fuzzy-set analysis of a set-theoretic relationship and in-depth fieldwork go hand in hand. More generally, fuzzy-set analysis and other kinds of empirical analysis can be used to complement and reinforce each other, resulting in a more nuanced understanding of research subjects. Whenever researchers have good reason to anticipate a subset relationship (yielding either a lower-triangular or an upper-triangular plot), they can use this information to help guide the identification of qualitative anchors. In the end, the rescalings that follow from such efforts must be justified empirically—these rescalings must make sense from the perspective of the researcher's accumulated substantive and theoretical knowledge. Ideally, the effort to discover useful qualitative anchors through the examination of subset relationships also should enrich case-oriented knowledge.[1]

The Identification of "Higher-Order" Constructs

The fuzzy-set approach to causal complexity emphasizes the assessment of the sufficiency of all possible combinations of causal conditions. As the number of causal conditions in a property space increases, the number of causal expressions to test expands dramatically. A property space composed of four fuzzy sets generates as many as 80 causal expressions to test; a property space composed of five fuzzy sets generates as many as 242 causal expression to test; and so on. While this expanding analytic volume poses only minor computational issues, it is important to recognize that it may pose significant interpretive problems.

One simple way to address this interpretive challenge is through the use of "higher-order" constructs. The idea of higher-order constructs is not new. In a exchange between Elizabeth Nichols (1986) and Theda Skocpol (1986) the issue surfaced under the guise of Skocpol's use of "macrovariables." The topic crops up often in the literature on comparative methodology, where the formation of higher-order constructs is seen as one way to address the problem of "too many variables and not enough cases" (Berg-Schlosser and De Meur 1997; Collier 1993; Lijphart 1971, 1975) The basic idea behind "higher-order constructs" is that arguments that cite many causal conditions (especially conditions that are jointly necessary or sufficient for an outcome) often can be reformulated by grouping conditions into meaningful sets and then reconceptualizing the resulting sets as higher-order constructs. In effect, researchers move up the ladder of abstraction (Sartori 1970, 1984) as they create concepts encompassing a broader range of empirical conditions.

1. From the perspective of conventional quantitative analysis, especially those forms more concerned with justification than discovery, the rescalings just described are nothing more than an exercise in "overfitting" the data, exploiting the peculiarities of what may be a more or less random pattern. Ultimately, such challenges can be addressed only through further research, which in turn would yield greater knowledge of the research subject and a stronger empirical base for constituting the relevant fuzzy sets.

Using higher-order constructs, an argument that cites, say, ten causal conditions could be reduced to one that cites only a few. This simplification can be achieved by combining sets of causal conditions that tend to go together empirically into a small number of groups and then reconceptualizing each group of conditions at a higher level of abstraction. For example, rather than seeing "autonomous peasant communities" as one of the many necessary conditions for "social revolution," this condition might be viewed instead as a common but not universal ingredient in "agrarian unrest" (a higher-order construct), which in turn would be conceptualized as a necessary condition for social revolution. Viewed in this light, "autonomous peasant communities" is demoted from being a necessary condition for social revolution to being one of the ingredients commonly found in "agrarian unrest." Of course, other causal conditions would be similarly demoted in the formulation of "agrarian unrest," thus streamlining the causal argument while at the same time pitching it at a more abstract level.

There are many ways to construct higher-order constructs. This topic is worthy of a book. Here, I mention only a few starting points. Specifically, I discuss the differences between causal arguments that emphasize the "weakest link" versus those that emphasize either "substitutability" or "compensation."

The fuzzy-set principle of finding the minimum of a case's memberships in the sets that make up a causal expression is basically an argument that embodies a "weakest link" approach to causation. (The full expression of the everyday formulation of this rule is, A chain is only as strong as its weakest link.) For example, if four conditions are necessary for an outcome, then the ceiling for that outcome's occurrence in a given case is set by the case's lowest membership in these four conditions—its weakest link. It is clear that little is gained, mathematically speaking, from grouping causal conditions and then applying the minimum rule within each group of causes and then between the groups. The weakest link still rules the entire expression, no matter how the conditions are grouped. However, there is considerable payoff from grouping causes into sets to form higher-order constructs when alternate principles are invoked within each group of conditions.

One such alternate principle is the "substitutability" rule. This rule, in effect, is the opposite of the "weakest link" rule and emphasizes the strongest link. If one causal condition can be substituted for another, then a case's score in the higher-order construct formed from these two conditions is the maximum of its memberships in the two component conditions. For example, job candidates might be considered "qualified" (the higher-order construct) if they have either "experience" or "training." They need not have both. Using the weakest link rule, by contrast, only job candidates with both experience and training would be considered qualified.

For illustration of the principle of substitutability, consider again the analysis of the conditions for the development of "generous" welfare states presented in chapter 10. Suppose the researcher in this example believed that having either a corporatist industrial system or strong unions could substitute for having a strong left party. In this view, all that matters is having a high membership score in at least one of these three sets. If a country has strong membership in any one of the three, then it has met one of the conditions relevant to the development of a generous welfare state. The higher-order construct in this example might be called "worker power," which could be achieved equivalently though political parties, labor unions, or direct participation in the management of industry. Using fuzzy algebra, the formula for membership in this higher-order construct is simply

$$\text{power} = \text{left} + \text{unions} + \text{corporatist},$$

where "power" stands for membership in the higher-order construct "worker power," "left" stands for membership in "strong left parties," "unions" stands for membership in "strong unions," "corporatist" stands for membership in "corporatist industrial system," and plus signs stand for logical *or* (use of the maximum). To assess degree of membership in "worker power," the researcher would simply take the maximum of each country's memberships in "strong left party," "strong unions," and "corporatist industrial system."[2]

The resulting property space for the causal conditions relevant to generous welfare states now has only two dimensions, as shown in table 11.1. The second, third, and fourth columns show each country's membership in the three substitutable manifestations of "worker power;" the fifth column shows their membership in "worker power"— the maximum of the first three columns; the sixth and seventh columns

2. It is worth noting that the use of the maximum, which is integral to substitutability, results in higher scores, especially when many different causal conditions are combined. Because scores are higher, such constructs are more likely to pass necessity (although this is not the case in the present example). As always, any condition that passes necessity should be subjected to careful scrutiny. This scrutiny is all the more imperative with higher-order constructs formed using the substitutability rule.

Table 11.1
Fuzzy Membership Scores for Analysis of Countries with "generous welfare states," Using Higher-Order Construct "worker power"

COUNTRY	Substitutable Manifestations of "Worker Power"			New Property Space		Outcome
	"STRONG LEFT PARTIES"	"STRONG UNIONS"	"CORPORATIST INDUSTRIAL SYSTEM"	"WORKER POWER"	"SOCIOCULTURAL HOMOGENEITY"	"GENEROUS WELFARE STATE"
(1)	(2)	(3)	(4)	(5)	(6)	(7)
Australia	.25	.40	.17	.40	.25	.26
Austria	.70	.64	.83	.83	.67	.72
Belgium	.54	.84	.83	.84	.29	.79
Canada	.00	.06	.05	.06	.10	.26
Denmark	.85	.81	.83	.85	.86	.86
Finland	.56	.86	.83	.86	.72	.76
France	.12	.11	.33	.33	.31	.57
Germany	.43	.20	.67	.67	.30	.68
Ireland	.11	.63	.67	.67	.84	.67
Italy	.11	.39	.50	.50	.55	.64
Japan	.00	.04	.33	.33	.95	.52
Netherlands	.33	.17	.83	.83	.27	.69
New Zealand	.40	.54	.17	.54	.15	.56
Norway	.95	.53	.83	.95	.95	.95
Sweden	.98	1.00	.95	1.00	.70	.98
Switzerland	.34	.13	.67	.67	.10	.53
United Kingdom	.61	.34	.50	.61	.15	.63
United States	.00	.04	.05	.05	.05	.09

show their memberships in "sociocultural homogeneity" and "generous welfare state," respectively. Columns (5) and (6) now comprise the researcher's property space for the outcome shown in column seven. The solution of this two-dimensional property space is

$$\text{power} \cdot \text{homogeneity} \rightarrow \text{generous},$$

where "power" stands for membership in "worker power," "homogeneity" stands for membership in "sociocultural homogeneity," "generous" stands for membership in "generous welfare state," the symbol → indicates "is sufficient for," and midlevel dots (·) indicate logical and. In other words, the combination of worker power and sociocultural homogeneity is sufficient for generous welfare states.

While not a primary concern here, it is worth noting that the creation of the higher-order construct "worker power" results not only in a very simple property space for generous welfare states, it also results in a property space that is fully diverse. That is, this property space does not exhibit limited diversity. As shown in figure 11.3, there are cases

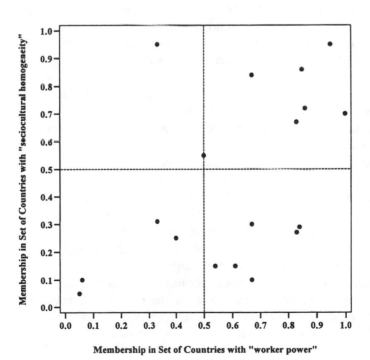

Figure 11.3 Property space showing "worker power" and "sociocultural homogeneity."

in all four regions of this two-dimensional property space (although there is only one case in the high ethnic homogeneity/low worker power quadrant). Thus, creating the higher-order construct "worker power" does more than simply streamline the causal argument. It also ameliorates the problem of limited diversity and results in an empirical generalization that is not dependent on simplifying assumptions (see chapter 10).

Another causal rule than can be invoked as an alternative to the weakest-link rule is "compensation." Consider again the example of job applicants with different levels of training and experience (i.e., different degrees of membership in the fuzzy sets "experienced" and "trained"). The weakest-link rule focuses on each applicant's weakness (i.e., the minimum); substitutability focuses on each applicant's strength (i.e., the maximum). Compensation, by contrast, allows a strength to compensate for a weakness and is accomplished by averaging the relevant scores. Using this rule, an applicant with middle-range training and experience is considered equivalent to an applicant with very good training but no experience and also to one with very good experience but no training. The compensation rule ranks cases with high scores on all conditions highest, and it ranks cases with low scores on all conditions lowest. Lumped in the middle ranks are diverse kinds of cases—those with middle-range scores on all conditions along with cases with different patterns of high and low scores combined.[3]

For illustration, consider the use of this rule in the investigation of causal conditions relevant to the generosity of welfare states. Suppose a researcher is interested in assessing membership in the higher-order construct, "worker solidarity," and believes that this concept has two main components, economic and political. In this view, countries that exhibit worker solidarity in both of these arenas should have the highest membership scores in the higher-order construct, while countries exhibiting solidarity in neither arena should have the lowest scores. Countries that exhibit solidarity in one but not the other arena should be ranked in the middle, as should countries that exhibit only middle-range levels of solidarity in both arenas.

Using the evidence on countries reported in table 11.1, it is a simple matter to compute membership in the set of countries exhibiting worker solidarity: Calculate the average of each country's membership in the set of countries with strong left parties and its membership in

3. The operation of compensation, therefore, is parallel to the operation of linear-additive multivariate models.

the set of countries with strong unions. In general, these two sets of scores are correlated. However, there are some countries with relatively higher membership in "strong left parties" than in "strong unions" (e.g., Norway and the United Kingdom), and there are some countries where the reverse is true (e.g., Ireland and Belgium). Compensation has the greatest impact on these cases. After calculating membership in this higher-order construct (the set of countries exhibiting worker solidarity), the researcher would then include it as a causal condition in the property space for generous welfare states. Using this higher-order construct in place of its two components reduces the four-dimensional property space to three dimensions (worker solidarity, corporatist industrial system, and sociocultural homogeneity) and thus dramatically reduces the number of causal expressions to assess (from 80 to 26).

These examples are offered primarily to demonstrate a few of the ways that researchers can formulate higher-order constructs. It is possible to mix the various rules, nesting and combining them in substantively meaningful ways. Researchers may also use such modifiers as "very" and "more or less" and the mathematical operations associated with these modifiers. For example, a researcher might argue that "worker solidarity" is the average of a country's membership in the set with "very strong left parties" and the set with "very strong unions." Thus, before averaging membership scores, it would be necessary to square them as follows:

$$\text{solidarity} = (\text{left}^2 + \text{unions}^2)/2,$$

where "solidarity" stands for membership in "worker solidarity," "left" stands for membership in "strong left parties," "unions" stands for membership in "strong unions," superscripted 2 indicates concentration (achieved by squaring membership scores), and plus signs indicate numerical addition (not logical *or*). In general, social theory today is too weak to provide strong guidance to the construction of higher-order constructs. However, the close correspondence between fuzzy sets and theoretical concepts that is integral to the fuzzy-set approach may prod social researchers to attempt greater theoretical clarity and specificity.

It is important to point out that using higher-order concepts is not a free ride. There are important costs. Primary among these is the simple fact that higher-order constructs take researchers one step further away from their cases and their evidence. Imagine two researchers: The first has a set of findings based on an analysis of countries' membership scores in "strong left parties," "strong unions," and "corporatist industrial systems." The second has a set of findings based on countries' membership scores in a higher-order construct, "worker power." Both researchers want to use their results to interpret cases—to make sense of patterns and the unfolding of events in each case. The first researcher is in a much better position than the second because his results point to specific kinds of evidence and events, and to the interplay of different aspects of cases (e.g., the interplay of politics and industrial organization). The second researcher lacks this specific guidance and instead must examine a large, amorphous body of evidence, all relevant in some way to the higher-order construct "worker power." While higher-order concepts may help social scientists discern broad, cross-case patterns, they are less helpful when it comes to understanding and interpreting specific cases (Sartori 1970, 1984). A primary emphasis of this work is that the ultimate test of the value of any fuzzy-set analysis is how useful it is for understanding cases.

Use of Modifiers and the Assessment of Causal Complexity

Whether a causal condition is identified as necessary or sufficient interacts directly with how it is scored as a fuzzy set. Shifting membership scores in a causal condition in an upward or downward direction can shift points from one side to the other of the diagonal in the plot of an outcome against a causal condition or a causal combination. This shifting of membership scores is inherent in the use of such modifiers as "very" and "more or less." Membership in a fuzzy set modified by "very," as in "very strong left party," for example, can be approximated by squaring membership scores in the unmodified set, "strong left party." Squaring fuzzy membership scores shifts them in a downward direction. Likewise, the modifier "more or less" can be approximated by taking the square root of membership scores in the unmodified set, shifting them in an upward direction. The use of modifiers can have an important impact on patterns of necessity and sufficiency revealed in plots of causal conditions and outcomes.

Consider the following extreme example: membership in the set of countries with strong left parties is exactly equal to membership in the set of countries with generous welfare states. A researcher viewing this pattern might argue, based on this evidence alone, that having a strong left party is both necessary and sufficient for having a generous welfare state. After all, the causal condition passes both tests. A second researcher, familiar with the relevant cases, doubts that "strong left party" is a necessary condition. This researcher squares membership in strong left parties and argues that the true relationship is one of sufficiency.

Specifically, having "very strong left parties" is sufficient by itself, but not necessary, for having a generous welfare state. After squaring membership in the causal condition, there are now cases with relatively low membership in "very strong left parties" that nevertheless have moderate membership in "generous welfare state." A third researcher has a different view of the relevant case materials and doubts that having strong or very strong left parties is sufficient by itself for developing a generous welfare state. The third researcher takes the square root of membership in "strong left parties" and argues that having "left parties that are at least moderate in strength" is a necessary but not sufficient condition for having a generous welfare state. The third researcher's plot shows that there are some cases with substantial membership in "left parties that are at least moderate in strength" but that have relatively lower membership in "generous welfare states."

Which researcher is correct? Fortunately, empirical data are never this tidy; most plots reveal much more scatter than even the most experienced researchers anticipate. But the issue is still important. Consider a less extreme example: Using data from columns (4) and (7) of table 11.1 it is possible to argue that having an industrial system that is "at least somewhat corporatist" (i.e., the square root of membership in "corporatist industrial system") is necessary for having a very generous welfare state (i.e., squaring membership in "generous welfare state"). In other words, the square root of each case's membership in "corporatist industrial system" is greater than or equal to the square of its membership in "generous welfare state" (see figure 11.4). Is being "at least somewhat corporatist" a necessary condition for having a "very generous welfare state," as suggested by this pattern? Or is being corporatist (unmodified) one of several jointly sufficient conditions for having a generous welfare state (also unmodified), as shown in chapter 10?

Of course, both arguments may be true, and neither may be true. What matters most is whether or not these patterns resonate with substantive and theoretical knowledge. Which pattern is more consistent with what is known about the relevant cases? Does the finding from chapter 10, that corporatism may combine with other conditions to produce generous welfare states, resonate with the available evidence? Does this finding help researchers make sense of cases (i.e., those where corporatism, combined with other relevant conditions, provides the best account of outcome membership levels)? Likewise, does the finding that "at least moderate corporatism" is a necessary condition for the development of a "very generous" welfare state make sense? Does it help researchers understand their cases? For example, does it explain

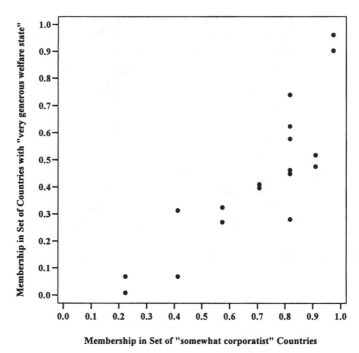

Figure 11.4 Plot of "very generous welfare state" against "somewhat corporatist" industrial system.

why some countries failed to develop "very generous" welfare states? The available evidence may support one or both arguments, or neither. Researchers are always capable of generating multiple representations of social life from the same empirical evidence, no matter which analytic tools they use. The important issues are (1) how well a representation of evidence dovetails with theoretical and substantive knowledge and (2) whether this representation leads to or generates further case-level knowledge or insights.

Another modifier that is central to the dialogue between ideas and evidence in fuzzy-set research is "not" (negation). This modifier can be used to aid the evaluation of necessity and sufficiency. Consider the following example: Table 11.1 shows that each case's membership in "strong left parties" is less than or equal to its membership in "generous welfare state." In short, "strong left parties" is a subset of "generous welfare state," which in turn provides evidence in support of the argument that this causal condition by itself is sufficient for the outcome. The modifier "not" can be applied to both the cause and the outcome, yielding membership in the set of countries with "not strong" (i.e., weak) left parties and membership in the set of "not generous" (i.e., meager) welfare states. As figure 11.5 shows, the plot of these two sets of fuzzy membership scores reveals that having a "weak left party" is a necessary condition for having a "meager welfare state." This result follows logically. After all, if having a strong left party is sufficient by itself for having a generous welfare state, then it is necessary to not have a strong left party to maintain a high level of membership in the set of countries with meager welfare states.

The mathematical and logical equivalence of these two formulations is not the main point here. Rather, the point is that the modifier "not" offers a useful enhancement to the dialogue between ideas and evidence. If a condition can be shown to be sufficient by itself for an outcome, then the researcher can assess not only the plausibility of that relationship, but also the plausibility of the necessity relationship that it implies through negation. Do theory and substantive knowledge support the idea that the cause is sufficient for the outcome? Do they support the idea that the absence of the cause is necessary for the absence

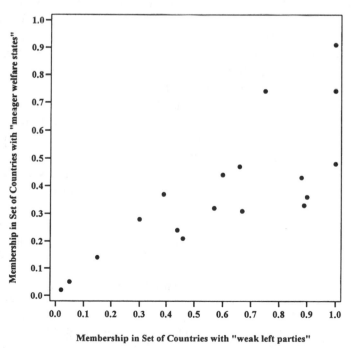

Figure 11.5 Plot of "meager welfare state" against "weak left party."

of the outcome? Is there corroborating empirical evidence that supports either of these arguments?[4]

The analytic flexibility of the fuzzy-set approach demonstrated here derives in large part from the fact that fuzzy sets are infused with knowledge. The greater this infusion, the greater the practical value of fuzzy sets. A central goal of fuzzy-set analysis is to establish a close correspondence between fuzzy membership scores and theoretical concepts. Thus, the use of fuzzy sets obliges researchers to ask penetrating questions about their cases and, at the same time, to clarify their theories and concepts. The very specific demands of fuzzy-set methods compel researchers to specify their concepts in a way that enhances their empirical relevance. Fuzzy sets must be carefully grounded in theory and evidence, and they should, at the same time, help researchers make sense of their cases.

CONCLUSION

The arguments I present in this book are premised on an idea widely shared by social scientists—that it is possible to derive useful empirical generalizations from the examination of multiple instances of social phenomena (i.e., from comparable cases). The central issue I address is how to go about this task in a way that is sensitive to the diversity and heterogeneity of the cases that researchers study. Most conventional approaches to the study of multiple instances are built upon strong homogenizing assumptions: that cases are members of preconstituted, "given" populations; that their main features can be abstracted from their case-specific contexts and treated as freestanding variables; and that causal conditions, understood as independent variables, operate in a relatively uniform, linear-additive manner across all relevant cases. These homogenizing assumptions are rarely warranted. As an alternative, I offer fuzzy-set methods to help researchers identify, comprehend, and systematize the diversity of their cases.

I have argued throughout this work that social research is heavily knowledge- and theory-dependent—that it is interpretive. It is also

---

4. The reverse also holds: If a cause is necessary for an outcome, then its negation is sufficient for the negation of the outcome. For example, membership in the set of countries experiencing IMF pressure is a necessary condition for membership in the set of countries displaying severe IMF protest. It follows that membership in the set of countries not experiencing IMF pressure is sufficient, by itself, for membership in the set of countries not exhibiting severe IMF protest.

self-referential in the sense that social scientists are inescapably a part of the social world they study. Not only does the social world present the problems that social scientists study, it also constructs and shapes how social scientists think about these problems, including the concepts they use to describe and theorize about them. It is impossible for social scientists to talk about social life in a way that frees them from their immersion in it. For these reasons, social scientists are often at odds with the concepts they use. They cannot purge these concepts of their social roots and influences, making them fixed and exact—scientific, without also purging their research of meaning.

Paradoxically, fuzzy sets highlight the imprecision of social scientific concepts and demand that they be sharpened and clarified. The greater the correspondence between the scores indexing membership in a fuzzy set, on the one hand, and the meaning of the concept that parallels the set, on the other, the more useful the fuzzy set. In short, to construct a fuzzy set and assign fuzzy membership scores, researchers must say what their concepts mean, and they must be explicit about membership criteria. It is not enough to have a measure that shows the relative rankings or positions—the minimum requirement of variable-oriented methods. Researchers must go outside of their data sets and anchor their measures and analysis in substantive knowledge.

Social scientists study social life because they want to understand how the world works in all its breadth and depth. Fuzzy-set methods bring researchers closer to achieving both breadth and depth in their attempts to understand social phenomena. This approach frees researchers from homogenizing assumptions and provides them with tools that highlight difference and diversity. It offers a flexible scheme for constituting populations and treats cases as configurations, maximizing potential differences in kind. It assumes maximum complexity in the examination of causal conditions, allowing for the possibility that no single condition may be either necessary or sufficient. Using fuzzy-set methods, researchers can make explicit connections between their measures, their methods, and the social world they study.

REFERENCES

Abbott, Andrew. 1992. "What Do Cases Do? Some Notes on Activity in Sociological Analysis." In *What Is a Case? Exploring the Foundations of Social Inquiry.* Edited by Charles C. Ragin and Howard S. Becker. New York: Cambridge University Press.

Allardt, Erik. 1979. *Implications of the Ethnic Revival in Modern Industrialized Society.* Helsinki: Societas Scientiarium Fennica.

Amenta, Edwin. 1991. "Making the Most of a Case Study: Theories of the Welfare State and the American Experience." *International Journal of Comparative Sociology* 32:172–194.

Amenta, Edwin, and Jane Poulsen. 1994. "Where To Begin: A Survey of Five Approaches to Selecting Independent Variables for Qualitative Comparative Analysis." *Sociological Methods and Research* 23:22–53.

Angell, Robert C. [1936] 1965. *The Family Encounters the Depression.* Gloucester: Peter Smith.

Bailey, Kenneth D. 1994. *Typologies and Taxonomies: An Introduction to Classification Techniques.* Thousand Oaks, Calif.: Sage Publications.

Barton, Allen H. 1955. "The Concept of Property Space in Social Research." In *The Language of Social Research.* Edited by Paul F. Lazarsfeld and Morris Rosenberg. Glencoe: Free Press.

Becker, Howard S. 1953. "Becoming a Marijuana User." *American Journal of Sociology* 59:235–42.

———. 1986. "Telling about Society." In *Doing Things Together.* Evanston: Northwestern University Press.

———. 1998. *Tricks of the Trade: How to Think about Your Research While You're Doing It.* Chicago: University of Chicago Press.

Becker, Howard S., Blanche Geer, Everett C. Hughes, and Anselm L. Strauss. 1961. *Boys in White: Student Culture in Medical School.* Chicago: University of Chicago Press.

Bendix, Reinhard. 1978. *Kings or People: Power and the Mandate to Rule.* Berkeley: University of California Press.

Berg-Schlosser, Dirk, and Gisèle De Meur. 1994. "Conditions of Democracy in

Inter-War Europe: A Boolean Test of Major Hypotheses." *Comparative Politics* 26: 253–280.

———. 1997. "Reduction of Complexity for a Small-*N* Analysis: A Stepwise Multi-Methodological Approach." *Comparative Social Research* 16:133–62.

Bollen, Kenneth. 1993. "Liberal Democracy: Validity and Methods Factors in Cross-National Measures." *American Journal of Political Science* 37:1207–26.

Bollen, Kenneth, B. Entwisle, and A. S. Alderson. 1993. "Macrocomparative Research Methods." *Annual Review of Sociology* 19:321–351.

Bonnell, Victoria. 1980. "The Uses of Theory, Concepts and Comparison in Historical Sociology." *Comparative Studies in Society and History* 22:156–173.

Bradshaw, York, and Michael Wallace. 1991. "Informing Generality and Explaining Uniqueness: The Place of Case Studies in Comparative Research." *International Journal of Comparative Sociology* 32:154–71.

Brinton, Crane. 1965. *The Anatomy of Revolution.* New York: Vintage Books.

Burawoy, Michael. 1979. *Manufacturing Consent: Changes in the Labor Process Under Monopoly Capitalism.* Chicago: University of Chicago Press.

Burawoy, Michael, et al. 1991. *Ethnography Unbound: Power and Resistance in the Modern Metropolis.* Berkeley: University of California Press.

Cameron, David. 1978. "The Expansion of the Public Economy." *American Political Science Review* 72:1243–61

———. 1984. "Social Democracy, Corporatism, Labour Quiescence, and the Representation of Economic Interest in Advanced Capitalist Society." In *Order and Conflict in Contemporary Capitalism.* Edited by John H. Goldthorpe. Oxford: Clarendon Press.

Campbell, Donald T. 1975. "Degrees of Freedom and the Case Study." *Comparative Political Studies* 9:178–193.

Castles, Francis, and Peter Mair. 1984. "Left-Right Political Scales: Some 'Expert' Judgements." *European Journal of Political Research* 12:73–88.

Chatterjee, Samprit, and Bertram Price. 1991. *Regression Analysis by Example.* New York: John Wiley and Sons.

Chirot, Daniel. 1994. *Modern Tyrants: The Power and Prevalence of Evil in Our Age.* New York: Free Press.

Cicourel, Aaron V. 1964. *Method and Measurement in Sociology.* New York: Free Press.

Collier, David. 1993. "The Comparative Method." In *Political Science: The State of the Discipline II.* Edited by A. W. Finifter. Washington: American Political Science Association.

———. 1995. "Translating Quantitative Methods for Qualitative Researchers: The Case of Selection Bias." *American Political Science Review* 89:461–6.

———. 1998. "Comparative Method in the 1990s." *APSA-CP: Newsletter of the Comparative Politics Section of the APSA* 9(1):1–5.

Collier, David, and Steven Levitsky. 1997. "Democracy with Adjectives: Conceptual Innovation in Comparative Research." *World Politics* 49:430–51.

Collier, David, and James Mahoney. 1996. "Insights and Pitfalls: Selection Bias in Qualitative Research." *World Politics* 49:56–91.

Crane, Diana. 1972. *Invisible Colleges.* Chicago: University of Chicago Press.

Cutright, Phillips. 1965. "Political Structure, Economic Development, and National Social Security Programs." *American Journal of Sociology* 70:537–550.

De Meur, Gisèle, and Berg-Schlosser, Dirk. 1994. "Comparing Political Systems: Establishing Similarities and Dissimilarities." *European Journal for Political Research* 26:193–219.

Diesing, Paul. 1971. *Patterns of Discovery in the Social Sciences.* Chicago: Aldine Publishing Co.

Dion, Douglas. 1998. "Evidence and Inference in the Comparative Case Study." *Comparative Politics* 30:127–145.

Dogan, Mattei, and A. Kazancigil, editors. 1994. *Comparing Nations: Concepts, Strategies, Substance.* Oxford: Blackwell.

Dogan, Mattei, and Dominique Pelassy. 1984. *How to Compare Nations.* Chatham, N.J.: Chatham House.

Drass, Kriss, and Charles C. Ragin. 1992. *QCA: Qualitative Comparative Analysis.* Evanston: Institute for Policy Research, Northwestern University.

———. 1999. *QC/FSA: Qualitative Comparative/Fuzzy-Set Analysis.* Evanston: Institute for Policy Research, Northwestern University.

Dubois, Didier, Henri Prade, and Ronald R. Yager, editors. 1993. *Readings in Fuzzy Sets for Intelligent Systems.* San Mateo: Morgan Kaufmann Publishers.

Dumont, Louis. 1970. *Homo Hierarchicus: The Caste System and Its Implications.* Chicago: University of Chicago Press.

Eckstein, Harry. 1975. "Case Study and Theory in Political Science." In *Handbook of Political Science.* Vol. 7, *Strategies of Inquiry.* Edited by Fred I. Greenstein and Nelson W. Polsby. Reading: Addison-Wesley.

Esping-Andersen, Gøsta. 1990. *The Three Worlds of Welfare Capitalism.* Princeton: Princeton University Press.

Feagin, Joe R., Anthony M. Orum, and Gideon Sjoberg, editors. 1991. *A Case for the Case Study.* Chapel Hill: University of North Carolina Press.

Geddes, Barbara. 1990. "How the Cases You Choose Affect the Answers You Get: Selection Bias in Comparative Politics." *Political Analysis* 2:131–52.

George, Alexander. 1979. "Case Studies and Theory Development: The Method of Structured, Focussed Comparison." In *Diplomacy: New Approaches in History, Theory and Policy.* Edited by Paul G. Lauren. New York: Free Press.

Glaser, Barney, and Anselm Strauss. 1967. *The Discovery of Grounded Theory: Strategies for Qualitative Research.* London: Weidenfeld and Nicholson.

Goldhagen, Daniel. 1996. *Hitler's Willing Executioners: Ordinary Germans and the Holocaust.* New York: Knopf.

Goldthorpe, John. 1991. "The Uses of History in Sociology: Refections on Some Recent Tendencies." *British Journal of Sociology* 42:211–230.

———. 1997. "Current Issues in Comparative Macrosociology." *Comparative Social Research* 16:1–26.

Griffin, Larry J., Christopher Botsko, Ana-Maria Wahl, and Larry W. Isaac. 1991. "Theoretical Generality, Case Particularity: Qualitative Comparative Analysis of Trade Union Growth and Decline." In *Issues and Alternatives in Comparative Social Research.* Edited by Charles C. Ragin. Leiden: E. J. Brill.

Griffin, Larry, Christopher Caplinger, Kathryn Lively, Nancy L. Malcom, Darren McDaniel, and Candice Nelsen. 1997. "Comparative-Historical Analysis and Scientific Inference: Disfranchisement in the U.S. South as a Test Case." *Historical Methods* 30:13–27.

Griffin, Larry, and Charles Ragin. 1994. "Some Observations on Formal Methods of Qualitative Analysis." *Sociological Methods and Research* 23:1–12.

Grint, Keith. 1997. *Fuzzy Management: Contemporary Ideas and Practices at Work.* New York: Oxford.

Gubrium, Jaber F., and James A. Holstein. 1990. *What is Family?* Mountain View: Mayfield Publishing Co.

Hays, William Lee. 1981. *Statistics.* 3d edition. New York: Holt, Rinehart and Winston.

Headey, Bruce W. 1970. "Trade Unions and National Wage Policy." *Journal of Politics* 32:407–439.

Hicks, Alexander, Joy Misra, and Nah Ng Tang. 1995. "The Programmatic Emergence of the Social Security State." *American Sociological Review* 60 (3):329–350.

Hobsbawm, Eric. 1981. *Bandits.* New York: Pantheon.

Huber, Evelyne, Charles C. Ragin, and John D. Stephens. 1993. "Social Democracy, Christian Democracy, Constitutional Structure, and the Welfare State." *American Journal of Sociology* 99:711–749.

Janoski, Thomas. 1991. "Synthetic Strategies in Comparative Sociological Research: Methods and Problems of Internal and External Analysis." In *Issues and Alternatives in Comparative Social Research.* Edited by Charles C. Ragin. Leiden: E. J. Brill.

Kaplan, Abraham, and Hermann Schott. 1951. "A Calculus for Empirical Classes." *Methodos* 3:165–190.

Katz, Jack. 1982. *Poor People's Lawyers in Transition.* New Brunswick: Rutgers University Press.

Katzenstein, Peter. 1985. *Small States in World Markets: Industrial Policy in Europe.* Ithaca: Cornell University Press.

King, Gary, Robert O. Keohane, and Sidney Verba. 1994. *Designing Social Inquiry: Scientific Inference in Qualitative Research.* Princeton: Princeton University Press.

Korpi, Walter. 1983. *The Democratic Class Struggle.* London: Routledge and Kegan Paul.

Kosko, Bart. 1993. *Fuzzy Thinking.* New York: Hyperion.

Kvist, Jon. 1999. "Welfare Reform in the Nordic Countries in the 1990s: Using Fuzzy-Set Theory to Assess Conformity to Ideal Types." *Journal of European Social Policy* 9:331–352.

Laitin, David D. 1992. *Language Repertoires and State Construction in Africa.* New York: Cambridge University Press.

Lakoff, George. 1987. *Women, Fire, and Dangerous Things: What Categories Reveal About the Mind.* Englewood Cliffs: Prentice-Hall.

———. 1973. "Hedges: A Study in Meaning Criteria and the Logic of Fuzzy Concepts." *Journal of Philosophical Logic* 2:458–508.

Lazarsfeld, Paul F. 1937. "Some Remarks on Typological Procedures in Social Research." *Zeitschrift Fur Sozialforschung* 6:119–39.

———. 1966. Forward to *Constructive Typology and Social Theory,* by John C. McKinney. New York: Appleton-Century-Crofts.

Lazarsfeld, Paul F., Ann K. Pasanella, and Morris Rosenberg. 1972. *Continuities in the Language of Social Research.* New York: Free Press.

Lazarsfeld, Paul F., and Morris Rosenberg. 1955. *The Language of Social Research.* Glencoe: Free Press.

Leamer, Edward. 1978. *Specification Searches: Ad Hoc Inference with Nonexperimental Data.* New York: Wiley.

Lehmbruch, Gerhard. 1984. "Concertation and the Structure of Corporatist Networks." In *Order and Conflict in Contemporary Capitalism.* Edited by John H. Goldthorpe. Oxford: Clarendon Press.

Leibfried, Stephan, and Paul Pierson, editors. 1995. *European Social Policy: Between Fragmentation and Integration.* Washington, D.C.: Brookings Institute.

Lieberson, Stanley. 1985. *Making It Count: The Improvement of Social Research and Theory.* Berkeley: University of California Press.

———. 1992. "Small N's and Big Conclusions: An Examination of the Reasoning in Comparative Studies based on a Small Number of Cases." In *What Is a Case? Exploring the Foundations of Social Inquiry.* Edited by Charles C. Ragin and Howard S. Becker. New York: Cambridge University Press.

———. 1998. "Causal Analysis and Comparative Research: What Can We Learn from Studies based on a Small Number of Cases?" In *Rational Choice Theory and Large-Scale Data Analysis.* Edited by Hans-Peter Blossfeld and Gerald Prein. Boulder: Westview.

Lijphart, Arend. 1971. "Comparative Politics and the Comparative Method." *American Political Science Review* 65:682–693.

———. 1975. "The Comparable Cases Strategy in Comparative Research." *Comparative Political Studies* 8:157–175.

Lindesmith, Alfred R. 1947. *Opiate Addiction.* Bloomington: Principia Press.

Lipset, Seymour Martin. 1950. *Agrarian Socialism.* Berkeley: University of California Press.

———. 1963. *The First New Nation: The United States in Historical and Comparative Perspective.* New York: Basic Books.

Loftus, Geoffrey R. 1991. "On the Tyranny of Hypothesis Testing in the Social Sciences." *Contemporary Psychology* 36:102–5.

Mackie, J. L. 1974. *The Cement of the Universe: A Study of Causation.* Oxford: Oxford University Press.

———. 1985. *Logic and Knowledge: Selected Papers.* Oxford: Clarendon Press.

McCluskey, E. J. 1956. "Minimization of Boolean Functions." *Bell Systems Technical Journal* 35:1417–44.

McDermott, R. 1985. *Computer-Aided Logic Design.* Indianapolis, Ind.: Howard A. Sams.

McMichael, Philip. 1990. "Incorporating Comparison within a World-Historical Perspective: An Alternative Comparative Method." *American Sociological Review* 55: 385–97.

Mendelson, Elliot. 1970. *Boolean Algebra and Switching Circuits.* New York: McGraw-Hill.

Merton, Robert K., James S. Coleman, and Peter H. Rossi, editors. 1979. *Qualitative and Quantitative Social Research: Papers in Honor of Paul F. Lazarsfeld.* New York: Free Press.

Mill, John Stuart. [1843] 1967. *A System of Logic: Ratiocinative and Inductive.* Toronto: University of Toronto Press.

Moore, Barrington, Jr. 1966. *Social Origins of Dictatorship and Democracy: Lord and Peasant in the Making of the Modern World.* Boston: Beacon.

Myles, Matt, and Stanley Huberman. 1994. *Qualitative Data Analysis.* 2d edition. Newbury Park: Sage Publications.

Nichols, Elizabeth. 1986. "Skocpol on Revolution: Comparative Analysis versus Historical Conjuncture." *Comparative Social Research* 9:163–186.

Nunnally, Jum C. 1967. *Psychometric Theory.* New York: McGraw Hill.

Paige, Jeffrey M. 1975. *Agrarian Revolution: Social Movements and Export Agriculture in the Underdeveloped World.* New York: Free Press.

Phelps, Charles E. *LIMDEP: A Regression Program for Limited-Dependent Variables.* Santa Monica, Calif.: Rand Corporation.

Platt, Jennifer. 1988. "What Can Cases Do?" *Studies in Qualitative Methodology* 1: 1–23.

———. 1992. "Cases of Cases . . . of Cases." In *What Is a Case? Exploring the Foundations of Social Inquiry.* Edited by Charles C. Ragin and Howard S. Becker. New York: Cambridge University Press.

Przeworski, Adam, and Henry Teune. 1970. *The Logic of Comparative Social Inquiry.* New York: Wiley Interscience.

Quadagno, Jill. 1987. "Theories of the Welfare State." *Annual Review of Sociology* 14:109–128.

Quine, W. V. 1952. "The Problem of Simplifying Truth Functions." *American Mathematic Monthly* 59:521–531.

Ragin, Charles C. 1987. *The Comparative Method: Moving beyond Qualitative and Quantitative Strategies.* Berkeley: University of California Press.

———. 1989. "New Directions in Comparative Research." In *Cross-National Research in Sociology.* Edited by Melvin Kohn. Newbury Park: Sage Publications.

———. 1992. "Casing and the Process of Social Research." In *What Is a Case? Exploring the Foundations of Social Inquiry.* Edited by Charles C. Ragin and Howard S. Becker. New York: Cambridge University Press.

———. 1994a. *Constructing Social Research: The Unity and Diversity of Method.* Thousand Oaks, Calif.: Pine Forge Press.

———. 1994b. "A Qualitative Comparative Analysis of Pensions Systems." In *The Comparative Political Economy of the Welfare State.* Edited by Thomas Janoski and Alexander Hicks. New York: Cambridge University Press.

———. 1995. "Using Qualitative Comparative Analysis to Study Configurations." In *Computer-Aided Qualitative Data Analysis.* Edited by Udo Kelle. Newbury Park: Sage Publications.

———. 1997. "Turning the Tables: How Case-Oriented Research Challenges Variable-Oriented Research." *Comparative Social Research* 16:27–42.

———. 1998. "Comparative Methodology, Fuzzy Sets, and the Study of Sufficient Causes." *APSA-CP: Newsletter of the Comparative Politics Section of the APSA* 9(1):18–22.

Ragin, Charles C., Dirk Berg-Schlosser, and Gisèle De Meur. 1996. "Political Methodology: Qualitative Methods." In *New Handbook of Political Science.* Edited by Robert Goodin and Hans-Dieter Klingemann. New York: Oxford University Press.

Richters, John E. 1997. "The Hubble Hypothesis and the Developmentalist's Dilemma." *Development and Psychopathology* 9:193–230.

Robinson, W. S. 1951. "The Logical Structure of Analytic Induction." *American Sociological Review* 16:812–18.

Rokkan, Stein. 1975. "Dimensions of State Formation and Nation-Building: A Possible Paradigm for Research on Variations with Europe." In *The Formation of National States in Western Europe*. Edited by Charles Tilly. Princeton: Princeton University Press.

Ross, Timothy J. 1995. *Fuzzy Logic with Engineering Applications*. New York: McGraw-Hill.

Roth, Charles. 1975. *Fundamentals of Logic Design*. St. Paul: West.

Rothchild, Joseph. 1981. *Ethnopolitics: A Conceptual Framework*. New York: Columbia University Press.

Rueschemeyer, Dietrich. 1991. "Different Methods—Contradictory Results? Research on Development and Democracy." In *Issues and Alternatives in Comparative Social Research*. Edited by Charles C. Ragin. Leiden: E. J. Brill.

Rueschemeyer, Dietrich, Evelyne Huber Stephens, and John D. Stephens. 1992. *Capitalist Development and Democracy*. Chicago: University of Chicago Press.

Rueschemeyer, Dietrich, and John D. Stephens. 1997. "Comparing Historical Sequences: A Powerful Tool for Causal Analysis." *Comparative Social Research* 16:55–83.

Russett, Bruce. 1993. *Grasping the Democratic Peace*. Princeton: Princeton University Press.

Salzinger, Leslie. 1997. "From High Heels to Swathed Bodies: Gendered Meanings under Production in Mexico's Export-Processing Industry." *Feminist Studies* 23: 549–74.

Sartori, Giovanni. 1970. "Concept Misinformation in Comparative Politics." *American Political Science Review* 64:1036–40.

Sartori, Giovanni. 1984. *Social Science Concepts: A Systematic Analysis*. Beverly Hills: Sage.

Shea, Christopher. 1997. "Political Scientists Clash over the Value of Area Studies." *Chronicle of Higher Education*, 10 January: A13.

Sigelman, L., and G. H. Gadbois. 1983. "Contemporary Comparative Politics: An Inventory and Assessment." *Comparative Political Studies* 16:275–305.

Sjoberg, Gideon, and Roger Nett. 1968. *A Methodology for Social Research*. New York: Harper and Row.

Sjoberg, Gideon, Norma Williams, Ted R. Vaughan, and Andrée Sjoberg. 1991. "The Case Approach in Social Research: Basic Methodological Issues." In *A Case for the Case Study*. Edited by Joe R. Feagin, Anthony M. Orum, and Gideon Sjoberg. Chapel Hill: University of North Carolina Press.

Skocpol, Theda. 1979. *States and Social Revolutions: A Comparative Analysis of France, Russia, and China*. New York: Cambridge University Press.

———. 1986. "Analyzing Configurations in History: A Rejoinder to Nichols." *Comparative Social Research* 9:187–194.

———, editor. 1984. "Emerging Agendas and Recurrent Strategies in Historical Sociology." In *Vision and Method in Historical Sociology*. New York: Cambridge University Press.

Skocpol, Theda, and Edwin Amenta. 1986. "States and Social Policies." *Annual Review of Sociology* 12:131–57.

Skocpol, Theda, and Margaret Sommers. 1980. "The Uses of Comparative History in Macrosocial Inquiry." *Comparative Studies in Society and History* 22:174–197.

Smithson, Michael. 1988. "Fuzzy Set Theory and the Social Sciences: The Scope of Applications." *Fuzzy Sets and Systems* 26:1–21.

———. 1989. *Ignorance and Certainty: Emerging Paradigms.* New York: Springer Verlag.

Stake, Robert E. 1995. *The Art of Case Study Research.* Thousand Oaks, Calif.: Sage.

Stephens, John D. 1979. *The Transition from Capitalism to Socialism.* Urbana: University of Illinois Press.

Stephens, John D., and Evelyne Huber. Forthcoming. *Political Choice in Global Markets: Development and Crisis of Advanced Welfare States.*

Stinchcombe, A. L. 1968. *Constructing Social Theories.* New York: Harcourt, Brace, Jovanovitch.

Strauss, Anselm. 1987. *Qualitative Analysis for Social Scientists.* New York: Cambridge University Press.

Tilly, Charles. 1984. *Big Structures, Large Processes, Huge Comparisons.* New York: Russell Sage Foundation.

———. 1986. *The Contentious French.* Cambridge: Harvard University Press.

———. 1997. "Means and Ends of Comparison in Macrosociology." *Comparative Social Research* 16:43–53.

Truzzi, Marcello. 1974. *Verstehen: Subjective Understanding in the Social Sciences.* Reading: Addison Wesley.

Turner, Ralph. 1953. "The Quest for Universals in Sociological Research." *American Sociological Review* 18:604–11.

Vaughan, Diane. 1986. *Uncoupling: Turning Points in Intimate Relationships.* New York: Oxford University Press.

Visser, Jelle. 1989. *European Trade Unions in Figures.* Boston: Kluwer.

Von Wright, Georg Henrik. 1971. *Explanation and Understanding.* Ithaca: Cornell University Press.

Von Eye, Alexander. 1990. *Introduction to Configural Frequency Analysis: The Search for Types and Antitypes in Cross-Classifications.* New York: Cambridge University Press.

Walker, Henry, and Bernard Cohen. 1985. "Scope Conditions: Imperatives for Evaluating Theories." *American Sociological Review* 50:288–301.

Wallerstein, Michael. 1989. "Union Organization in Advanced Industrial Democracies." *American Political Science Review* 83:481–501.

Wallerstein, Immanuel. 1974. *The Modern World-System: Capitalist Agriculture and the Origins of the European World Economy in the Sixteenth Century.* New York: Academic Press.

Walton, John. 1984. *Reluctant Rebels: Comparative Studies of Revolution and Underdevelopment.* New York: Columbia University Press.

———. 1991. *Western Times and Water Wars: State, Culture, and Rebellion in California.* Berkeley: University of California Press.

———. 1992. "Making the Theoretical Case." In *What Is a Case? Exploring the*

Foundations of Social Inquiry. Edited by Charles C. Ragin and Howard S. Becker. New York: Cambridge University Press.

Walton, John, and Charles C. Ragin. 1990. "Global and National Sources of Political Protest: Third World Responses to the Debt Crisis." *American Sociological Review* 55:876–890.

Walton, John, and David Seddon. 1994. *Free Markets and Food Riots: The Politics of Global Adjustment.* Cambridge: Blackwell.

Weber, Max. 1949. *The Methodology of the Social Sciences.* New York: Free Press.

———. 1978. *Economy and Society.* Berkeley: University of California Press.

Western, Bruce. 1997. *Between Class and Market: Postwar Unionization in the Capitalist Democracies.* Princeton: Princeton University Press.

Wickham-Crowley, Timothy. 1991. *Guerrillas and Revolution in Latin America: A Comparative Study of Insurgents and Regimes since 1956.* Princeton: Princeton University Press.

Wieviorka, Michel. 1988. *Sociétés et terrorisme.* Paris: Fayard.

———. 1992. "Case Studies: History or Sociology?" In *What Is a Case? Exploring the Foundations of Social Inquiry.* Edited by Charles C. Ragin and Howard S. Becker. New York: Cambridge University Press.

Wilensky, Harold. 1975. *The Welfare State and Equality.* Berkeley: University of California Press.

Wolf, Eric R. 1969. *Peasant Wars of the Twentieth Century.* New York: Harper and Row.

Yin, Robert K. 1994. *Case Study Research: Design and Methods.* 2d edition. Thousand Oaks, Calif.: Sage Publications.

Zadeh, Lotfi A. 1965. "Fuzzy Sets." *Information Control* 8:338–53.

———. 1972. "A Fuzzy-Set-Theoretic Interpretation of Linguistic Hedges." *Journal of Cybernetics* 2:4–34.

———. 1982. "A Note on Prototype Theory and Fuzzy Sets." *Cognition* 12:291–97.

Zetenyi, Tamas, editor. 1988. *Fuzzy Sets in Psychology.* New York: North-Holland.